PERSUASION
Understanding, Practice, and Analysis

PERSUASION

Understanding, Practice, and Analysis

Second Edition

Herbert W. Simons

Temple University

Random House   *New York*

PERSUASION: Understanding, Practice and Analysis
Second Edition
Herbert W. Simons

987654321

Cover Photo: Paul Silverman
Cover and Text design: Robert Sugar

Library of Congress Cataloging-in-Publication Data
Simons, Herbert W., 1935–
  Persuasion : understanding, practice, and analysis.

  Bibliography: p.
  Includes index.
  1. Persuasion (Rhetoric) I. Title.
PN 187.S5 1986   808   85-25771
ISBN 0-394-35401-X

Manufactured in the United States of America

Acknowledgments

Figure 1.1 (pp. 12–15), from *The Pitch* © 1982 by Hugh Rank. Reprinted with permission.

Figure 3.2 (p. 32), "Two-Factor Model," from W. J. McGuire, "Personality and Susceptibility to Social Influence," in *Handbook of Personality and Social Psychology*, E. F. Borgatta and W. W. Lambert (eds.). Copyright 1968. Reprinted by permission of Rand-McNally Publishing Co.

Excerpt (p. 55), from R. B. Cialdini, *Influence: How and Why People Do Things*, William Morrow & Company, New York (1984). Reprinted by permission.

Figure 4.2 (pp. 66–67), Icek Ajzen, Martin Fishbein, *Understanding Attitudes and Predicting Social Behavior*, © 1980, pp. 8, 66. Reprinted by permission of Prentice-Hall, Inc. Englewood Cliffs, N.J.

Excerpt (pp. 86–87), from p. viii of the "Introduction" by Vivian Gornick from *Gender Advertisements* by Erving Goffman. Copyright © 1976 by Erving Goffman. Introduction copyright © 1979 by Harper & Row, Publishers, Inc. Reprinted by permission of Harper & Row, Publishers, Inc.

Table 5.1 (p. 93), reprinted from C. Jack Orr, "Reporters Confront the President," *The Quarterly Journal of Speech* 66 (1980) by permission of The Speech Communication Association.

Figures 6.1 and 6.2 (pp. 110–111), from P. Watzlawick, J. Weakland, and R. Fisch, *Change: Principles of Problem Formation and Problem Solution*, © 1974. Reprinted by permission of W. W. Norton & Company, Inc.

Poetry (P. 131), from Kenneth Burke, *Collected Poems, 1915–1967*, © 1968 Kenneth Burke, used by permission of the University of California Press.

Excerpts (pp. 162–163), from D. A. Schön, "Generative Metaphor: A Perspective on Problem-Setting in Social Policy," in *Metaphor and Thought*, A. Ortony (ed). Copyright 1979. Reprinted by permission of Cambridge University Press.

Excerpts (p. 187), "Address to the National Organization of Women" in Philadelphia. Reprinted by permission of Michael Caulfield.

Excerpt (pp. 199–208), from Richard M. Nixon, "My Side of the Story," speech delivered as a nationwide broadcast, Los Angeles, CA, September 23, 1952. Reprinted by permission of *Vital Speeches of the Day*, October 15, 1952, pp. 11–15.

Excerpts (pp. 209–210), from Donald T. Regan, "The Reagan Revolution: It Will Not Come Easy," speech delivered at the Young & Rubicam Dinner, New York City, September 21, 1982. Reprinted by permission of *Vital Speeches of the Day*, November 1, 1982. Vol. 49.

Excerpt (pp. 213–215), from Palmer Hoyt, "Civil Rights. The Eyes of the World Are Upon Us," speech delivered to the Arkansas Press Association, Little Rock, January 10, 1958. Reprinted by permission of *Vital Speeches of the Day*.

Excerpt (pp. 280–281), from L. W. Brown, "The Image-makers: Black Rhetoric and White Media," *Black Communication: Dimensions of Research and Instruction*. Speech Communication Asociation, New York (1974). Used with permission.

Excerpt (pp. 282–283), from *Fear of Flying* by Erica Jong. Copyright © 1973 by Erica Mann Jong. Reprinted by permission of Holt, Rinehart and Winston, Publishers.

Excerpt (pp. 294–297), from Edward M. Kennedy, "Statement to the People of Massachusetts," speech delivered in a televised broadcast from the home of Joseph P. Kennedy. Reprinted by permission of *The Washington Post*, July 26, 1969.

Excerpt (p. 317), from Martin Gardner, *Fads and Fallacies*, Dover Publications, Inc., New York, 1957. Reprinted through the permission of the publisher.

Excerpts (pp. 318–319), from Kenneth Burke, *A Grammar of Motives*, © 1969, used by permission of the University of California Press.

Excerpt (p. 455), from J. J. Waller, "Identification of Problem-Drinkers Among Drunken Drivers," *Journal of the American Medical Association* 200 (1967): p. 24. Copyright 1967, American Medical Association. Used with permission.

Excerpt (pp. 323–325), from a student paper. Used with permission of Michael Moughan.

Excerpt (p. 338), from "Soap-powders and Detergents," from *Mythologies* by Roland Barthes. Translation copyright © 1972 by Jonathan Cape Ltd. Reprinted by permission of Hill and Wang, a division of Farrar, Straus and Giroux, Inc.

Except (p. 339), from M. C. Miller, "Massa Come Home," *The New Republic*, p. 29. Reprinted by permission of *The New Republic*, © 1981, The New Republic, Inc.

To Gayle and Michael

Preface

As suggested by the title, this book is designed to help readers understand the process of persuasion, practice persuasion effectively, and analyze the persuasive discourse of others.

The first of these functions is considered primary. Thus, although the book focuses on such practical tasks as speechmaking and campaign planning, its coverage extends to borderline cases of persuasion—an ostensibly scientific report in a psychology journal, a seemingly unintended flicker of an eye at a cocktail party, a psychotherapeutic encounter. Where "how-to-do-it" principles are suggested, they are placed in a research context. Theories are described, studies are cited, and comments are offered about the limitations of research generalizations.

Theorists of persuasion used to label themselves as either behaviorally oriented social scientists or as traditionally oriented humanists. My impression is that there has been considerable movement in the last ten years toward a merger of the two orientations. This book, at any rate, draws ideas, concepts, and methods from both, and tries to show how they might work side by side. It is an amalgam of behavioral theories from social psychology and of Aristotelian and Burkian rhetorical theories; of experimental research findings, but also the fruits of generic scholarship by contemporary humanists.

While the essential purposes and structure of the book remain the same, it has undergone considerable revision. Indeed, the perspective on persuasion, summarized at the conclusion of Part I, and the conception of *co-active* persuasion, introduced at the beginning of Part II, might more properly be called re-VISIONS. As a sign of the times, perhaps, I have included many more samples of mass-mediated persuasion, and of day-to-day image management, and many fewer examples of sixties-style protests. A chapter (16) has been added on analyzing persuasive campaigns (to go with the old chapter on leading them), and there is also a new guide to analyzing persuasion in the guise of objectivity (Chapter 15). Illustrated in several chapters of the book (5, 14, 16) is a framework for practice and analysis, which I call the requirements-problems-strategies (RPS) approach. And there are many more project ideas, sample materials for analysis, and case studies of persuasive practice.

Immodestly, I believe this book can be read with profit by a variety of students—from sophomores taking persuasion as an elective to beginning graduate students. My experience is that students benefit most from a multi-purpose introductory course, and I have adapted the book to fulfill several different learning objectives:

Development of a conceptual framework for understanding the psychological dynamics of persuasion

Awareness of competing theories and perspectives

Sensitivity to persuasion's dimensions and scope

Familiarity with findings from the behavioral and generic research literatures on persuasion

Ability to apply findings from research to practice

Appreciation of the differences between persuasion in conflict and nonconflict situations

Understanding of the role of persuasion in society and culture

Improved skill at preparing persuasive messages

Improved skill at criticaly analyzing persuasive messages

Consciousness of the ethical choices incumbent upon persuaders

Depending on which of these objectives he or she expects to emphasize, the instructor might well wish to supplement this book with others or to modify the reading sequence. For example, you might wish to stress the critical functions of rhetorical study, and thus require students to read Chapters 14 through 16 early in the course. Or you might have a series of performance assignments, and thus move Chapters 7 through 11 ahead in the reading order.

Gayle Simons contributed mightily to the revision of this book and so too, in his own way, did Michael Simons. Dory Segal was an editorial assistant *par excellence;* Dorothy Mewha, Cheryl Jones, and Sharon Smith were typists *extraordinaire.* Aram A. Aghazarian, Marge Demarteliere, Bruce Gronbeck, Ken Mihalik, Allen Scult, Paul Sherrod, and Glenn Shive provided valuable readings; David Birdsell and Carol Winkler were especially helpful in revising Chapters 9 and 10. My thanks also to Nancy Griffin for encouraging me to redraft the book and not simply settle for a cosmetic revision.

Contents

Part Three
Analyzing Persuasion

277

Part One
Understanding Persuasion

"Where shall I begin, please your majesty?" asked the White Rabbit.

"Begin at the beginning," the King said gravely, "and go on till you come to the end: then stop."

Lewis Carroll
Alice's Adventures in Wonderland

Chapter 1
Understanding, Practice, and Analysis

For almost as long as people have practiced persuasion, others have written about it. And for almost that long, it has aroused controversy. The study of persuasion or *rhetoric* is at least as old as the time of the ancient Greeks and Romans, and probably older. One of the first manuscripts in recorded history could be considered a treatise on the subject: It was an Egyptian papyrus that contained advice on how to curry favor with important people (Gray, 1946). Later, when democratic forms of government emerged in Greece, both the practice and study of rhetoric became prominent. Among the noted scholars of early Athens were teachers of persuasion known as sophists. They prepared citizens in the arts of oratory. The ancient Greeks and Romans identified rhetoric with speechmaking in the performance of three vital functions. Citizens in those days argued their own legal cases in the courtroom (*forensic* oratory), presented speeches on ceremonial occasions (*epideictic* oratory), and participated in debates about matters of public policy (*deliberative* oratory). For the Roman citizen, rhetoric was considered an indispensable study, one of the seven liberal arts.

Periodically, the field of persuasion has degenerated and has then had to be regenerated. Systematized by the early Romans, bastardized during the period of Rome's decline, left relatively dormant during the Middle Ages (except as a vehicle for propagating the faith—note the origin of the word "propaganda"), rediscovered during the Renaissance, it has at times been occupied with noble aims and at times been identified with "making the worse appear the better reason." If terms like *rhetoric*, *persuasion*, and *propaganda* have negative connotations, it is partly because practitioners of the art have

3

often been flatterers, deceivers, con artists, and exhibitionists. But if rhetoric is sometimes the tool of the unscrupulous, it is also a tool for making the good appear valuable, the true believable, and the beautiful appreciated. It is for these reasons, perhaps, that the study of persuasion has always attracted sinners and saints alike—on the one hand, Hitler and Goebbels, but on the other hand Aristotle, Plato, Cicero, Quintillian, Augustine, Bacon, Mill, and Emerson.

Practice

This book is designed to improve your competence as a practitioner of persuasion, to sharpen your skills as a critic or analyst, and to enliven your understanding of the subject.

The need for competence at persuading others should be obvious. Although we may object to the terminology, each of us is a human engineer, involved in the tasks of constructing arguments and manufacturing our own images so as to influence others. Like it or not, we cannot *not* function as persuaders, whether on the job or in our personal lives. Virtually all occupations require some degree of the persuasive ability, and the so-called people professions— politics, law, social work, counseling, business management, advertising, sales, public relations, the ministry—might as well be called persuasion professions.

Beyond the personal and professional levels, many of us are interested in working for social and political betterment. We may be seeking population control, or more funds for cancer research, or racial equality, or the election of our favorite candidate. What methods are most appropriate for achieving these ends? If we are seeking donations to the American Cancer Society, should we use fear appeals or sympathy appeals? Should we ask potential donors for more than we expect them to give in the hope of getting what we bargain for, or would that approach cause rejection? This book identifies variables worth considering in framing persuasive messages; it presents general principles of persuasion derived from psychological theory and research; and it suggests other principles that are applicable to particular types of audiences and situations. It also raises ethical questions about the appropriateness of various persuasive strategies.

It does so, moreover, using examples drawn from the vast array of fields and activities encompassed by the term persuasion. Some readers will no doubt object that the examples are too varied, or that their areas of primary interest have not been given sufficient attention. It may indeed be argued that the subject of how to persuade is impossibly broad; that while it may have been feasible for Aristotle to fashion a general set of rhetorical prescriptions for the citizens of ancient Greece, the complexity and diversity of today's world require much more specialized treatments of the subject. Of what use are generalizations about activities as different as mass propaganda and psychotherapy, sermon-giving and attempted seductions, courtroom argument and subliminal advertising? Why should one bother with general prescriptions when there is no shortage of specialized treatments available on these and other topics?

There is no question but that this broad-based text cannot be a substitute for specialized treatments of persuasion, but neither can they serve as a substitute for a general treatment. Psychotherapist Paul Watzlawick (1977, p. xii) provides some sense of the value of a generalized approach to the practice of persuasion when he suggests: "There are two methods of scientific explanation. One is to expound a theory and then show how observable facts bear it out. The other is to present facts from many different contexts to make obvious, in a very practical way, the structure they have in common and the conclusions that follow from them."

In the case of persuasion, it would appear that there are indeed structural principles, and that these become obvious when one has seen how they apply in diverse cases. A colleague in the field, Ann Repplier (1984), provides an example of apparent unity amid diversity in an as yet unpublished review of theory and research on techniques for overcoming resistance to persuasion:

> A review of the literature on the concepts of resistance and persuasion in the areas of consultation, communication, social psychology, sales, psychotherapy, hypnosis and neurolinguistic programming indicates that there is a significant overlap of verbal influence strategies among the various areas despite differences in interpretation of "resistance" and an apparent lack of awareness of research and developments in the other areas. Thus while resistance is defined at one extreme by psychoanalytical therapists as an intrapsychic process resulting from earlier negative experiences and at the other extreme by salespeople as failure to buy, practitioners and researchers in these two areas as well as the others reviewed have identified and developed a number of remarkably similar techniques. The development of so many overlapping communication strategies despite such ostensibly dissimilar perspectives and goals would appear to attest to the cogency and effectiveness of these techniques. (p. 24)

Analysis

Despite the fact that we all practice persuasion, most of us spend more time as consumers of persuasion. We are literally bombarded by these communications from the moment we are awakened to the instant we fall asleep in front of the television set. It has been estimated that young people see 250,000 television commercials on the average by the time they have completed high school (Wolin, 1975). There are over 11,000 newspapers, 20,000 magazines, 4,000 radio stations, and 1,100 television stations in this country. A minute of network advertising time can cost upward of $1,000,000. Our medicine cabinets, to cite one example, are replete with items that were sold to us through commercials: this deodorant because it's guaranteed to work for 24 hours; that toothpaste because it's recommended by the Dental Association; those headache pills because they're twice as fast as brand X; that mouthwash because it tastes like spring. Samuel Becker (1971) has provided an apt account of the communication explosion to which all of us have been subjected:

> This man lives in a veritable pressure cooker of communication; everyone and everything is pushing him. The media are pushing him to buy a car and

cigarettes and to stop smoking; to use deodorants and to wear an auto seat belt
and to vote for the party of his choice and to support our most recent war effort
and to parade against war. His children are pushing him to play with them or to
give them money for the movies or to buy them a car. And his wife is telling him
to mow the lawn and take it easy and fix his tie. And those above him are
pushing him to stop making them work so hard. And all of this pushing is done
through communication. He is pushed by his television set and radios and
newspapers and magazines and billboards and handbills and memoranda and
even the old-fashioned open mouth which is often so uncomfortably close to his
ear. He is attacked not only at the supraliminal levels, but at the barely liminal
and even at the subliminal. He cannot escape this barrage of communication, and
his wife wonders why he is not more communicative in the evening when she
demands, "Talk to me. Why don't you talk to me?" (p. 26)

The analysis of persuasive messages may take place at a variety of levels
and perform a variety of functions. Analysis ranges from microscopic examination of some part of a message (a particularly interesting metaphor in a
speech, for example) to macroscopic examination of patterns common to a
variety of messages (all institutional advertising, for example). Between these
extremes, we may wish to examine a particular message, or an event such as a
job interview involving an exchange of messages, or a campaign or social
movement involving a series of messages over an extended period of time.

One function of analysis bears very directly upon the understanding of
persuasion: the *interpretive* function. As a frequent recipient of persuasive
messages, you will no doubt want to develop skill at identifying hidden meanings
and subtle nuances of meaning in what is said. Not uncommonly, persuasion
is presented in the guise of something else—as entertainment or education or
news, for example. Other messages imply much more than they state explicitly.
And still others are downright deceitful. In all these cases, you will need skill
at interpreting messages.

Beyond taking a careful reading of what is said, you may wish to speculate
on how it was said or on why it was said in this way rather than that, or on
the bases for its effects. What was the speaker trying to accomplish in that
speech? How was the audience brought to such a fever pitch of enthusiasm?
Why did the speaker use such flowery metaphors toward the close of the
speech? These are among the types of questions you might ask about the
motives, methods, and effects of a message.

Rhetorical scholars often take the interpretive analysis of persuasive
messages as a point of departure for theorizing about patterns of persuasion.
The critic may be interested in developing a theory from an analysis of cases,
or in refuting a theory, or in illustrating a theory. Is there, asked Ware and
Linkugel (1973), a predictable pattern in the way public officials respond to
charges of wrongdoing, and, if so, what accounts for that pattern? Why, asked
Goffman (1979), do female models typically touch objects in magazine advertisements, whereas male models grasp them? Do these ads reflect patterns of
behavior actually operative in our culture, or do they reflect advertisers'
perceptions of popular fantasies and expectations? Questions of this kind
transcend particular cases.

A second function of analysis is *evaluative*. Many critics insist that it is not enough to explicate a message, or to speculate on its methods, motives, or effects. " 'Good' criticism," says K. K. Campbell (1972, pp. 21–22) "is evaluative. It makes clear and unmistakable judgments about the quality, worth, and consequences of the discourse." Often an evaluation is implied in interpretive analyses, but there are dangers in not making judgments explicit. Campbell holds that the critic has an obligation to identify and defend the criteria used to evaluate a rhetorical effort, and to show how the criteria apply in a given case. The critic may, for example, hold a politician to campaign promises and ask whether, in the light of the politician's performance in office, they were not "mere rhetoric." Or the critic might evaluate a message in terms of standards of sound evidence and argumentation, as William Buckley (1973) did when he pronounced a speech by then President Richard Nixon on Watergate as "mortally flawed by low analytic cunning." Said Buckley: "Mr. Nixon sought to construct an august scaffolding for himself, whence to preside over the restoration of the public rectitude. He produced a spindle, on which he impaled himself." (pp. 30ff.)

Understanding

The third objective of this book—enlivening your understanding of persuasion—is closely related to the other two. The practice and analysis of persuasion both inform, and are informed by, a thorough understanding of its psychological dynamics and its various *situational contexts*.

The study of persuasion is closely tied to the social sciences. From social psychology, in particular, scholars of persuasion have derived insights about the springboards of audience motivation, about how cognition and emotion interact to influence attitudes, about how persuasive messages are learned and unlearned, and about the relationship between attitudes and behavior. Understanding of this kind is of obvious practical benefit to would-be persuaders and also to analysts of the effects of persuasive messages.

It is also quite helpful to place rhetorical practices within their larger situational context. We get a clearer idea of why politicians say the things they do, for example, by first getting a sense of the cross-pressures they are under because of the position they hold, of role expectations associated with particular types of occasions (presidential inaugurals, Fourth of July celebrations), and of the climate of events surrounding any given occasion. The situational context is like the background and physical setting for the action in a play. Less eye-catching than the action itself, contextual factors nevertheless make the speeches and responses of the actors understandable and may constitute message stimuli in their own right. We may read a Hamlet soliloquy from the printed page, but how much more meaningful it becomes when we know what has happened before, when we are aware of the immediate occasion for his utterance, when we can see him alone in a darkened chamber, when we are made aware of what is impending and what is occurring simultaneously, and when the intricate network of social roles, norms, and relationships is revealed to us.

These same situational factors are at work in real-life settings, and we must learn to "read" them in much the same way we read verbal messages. Is *Pravda*'s call for a resumption of disarmament talks with the West to be taken at face value, or are the Soviets engaging in mere theatrics? When the job interviewer suddenly sits forward in her chair, is she communicating interest in the interviewee's remarks, symptoms of gastric distress, or a desire to end the interview? When the poker player smiles slightly on receiving the last card, is he bluffing, or has he filled an inside straight?

Experienced practitioners often speak of there being a "logic" of situation they can use not only to interpret the actions of others, but also to respond more effectively as persuaders. Indeed, it has been argued that, while there are few "laws" of persuasion like laws in the physical sciences, it is possible to identify situationally based "rules" of what to say and how to say it. Rhetorician Lloyd Bitzer (1968) speaks here of the situational context as "prescribing" a fitting response:

> Rhetorical discourse is called into existence by situation; the situation which the rhetor perceives amounts to an invitation to create and present discourse. The clearest instances of rhetorical speaking and writing are strongly invited—often required. The situation generated by the assassination of President Kennedy was so highly structured and compelling that one could predict with near certainty the types and themes of forthcoming discourse. With the first reports of the assassination, there immediately developed a most urgent need for information; in response, reporters created hundreds of messages. Later, as the situation altered, other exigencies arose: the fantastic events in Dallas had to be explained; it was necessary to eulogize the dead President; the public needed to be assured that the transfer of government to new hands would be orderly . . . (p. 8)

Quite apart from the direct practical benefits it can provide, an understanding of how persuasion functions in society provides insights into our culture that are valuable in their own right. How any given culture conceives of persuasion and distinguishes it from "nonpersuasion" tells us a good deal about that culture's basic values and presuppositions. Our own culture tends to distinguish sharply between persuasion and such generally approved activities as educating, giving information, doing science or mathematics, conveying personal or esthetic feelings, and offering tangible rewards rather than symbolic satisfactions. Whether these distinctions are entirely justified is taken up in Part I of this book.

Finally, the study of persuasion offers important insights into processes of social and cultural change. Human beings are both creators and products of their cultures in a never-ending cycle. In response to situations and events, they engage in persuasive campaigns and movements, which in turn affect public perceptions and values, which lead to new public policies and social customs, which alter situations and events, which lead new groups of people to engage once again in persuasive campaigns and movements. Every institution in our society has its rhetorical legacy. Our economic system, our republican form of government, our commitments to freedom of speech and religion and to equality of opportunity, our conceptions of ourselves as a sovereign people, and even our idea of nationhood can be traced to rhetorical efforts in centuries past (Lucas, 1976; McGee, 1975). Indeed, there is scarcely a cultural truism that was not at one time or another the subject of considerable controversy. And what is considered true today is certain to be questioned in the future as new campaigns and movements take the place of the old. Quite apart from our own roles as practitioners and analysts of persuasion, we might wish to examine the workings of persuasion in society—to examine how society shapes rhetorical choice and how rhetorical choice shapes society. Persuasion is a source of some social problems and a potential vehicle for resolving others, but it is, in any case, a mirror of ourselves—of our passions and foibles and understandings and illusions. You will find, I think, that no subject is more central to a liberal education.

Case Study
The Rhetoric of Advertising

As a way of getting started at the business of understanding, practice, and analysis, compare the two ads for advertising firms on pages 9 and 10.

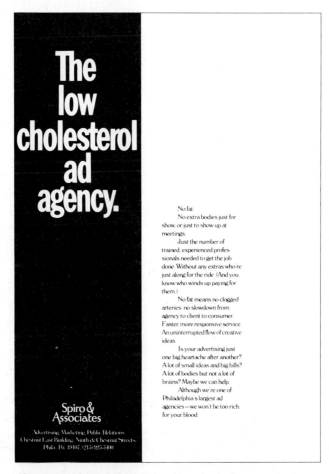

(Courtesy of Spiro & Associates, Incorporated)

SEND US YOUR BEST AD AND WE'LL SEND YOU BACK A BETTER ONE.

No tricks. No gimmicks. What you see is
what you get. Just send us what you think is your
best ad or commercial and within weeks we'll
send you back a better one.*

You see, every advertising agency will tell you
it's great. And some of them are. But to find out
you have to hire them. Or at least endure a
drawn-out formal presentation.

Our way is easier. Neater. You clip the
coupon, we do the rest. No marriage. Not even a
courtship.

We're convinced we're terrific at creating
advertising that sells. If we want to convince you,
the best place to start is with your advertising.

Come to think of it, we've started already.
You're about to respond to this ad aren't you?

*Send us an ad and we'll send you back a tight layout and copy. Send us a radio spot, we'll send you
back a script. Send us a TV spot, we'll send you back a storyboard.

O.K., I'll bite. Here's an ad (or commercial) we think is pretty good. Beat it. I
understand you will call me only for information and/or to set up dates, and
that you will not pitch my business until and unless we ask you to.

NAME _____ TITLE _____

COMPANY _____

ADDRESS _____

CITY _____ STATE _____ ZIP _____

ANESH, VISELTEAR, GUMBINNER INC.
ADVERTISING
711 THIRD AVENUE NEW YORK, N.Y. 10017 (212) 697-8350

*(Courtesy of Anesh, Viseltear, Gumbinner, Inc.
Copy: Ned Viseltear. Art Direction: Jack Anesh.)*

Note how the firms trade on cultural distinctions between persuasion and "non-persuasion" even as they engage in persuasion themselves. Spiro and Associates offers "no fat," "low cholesterol," "no gimmicks," no "drawn-out, formal presentations." These distinctions between the real and the rhetorical are reinforced by the styles of the two ads. Each is spare, unadorned, black and white. And each "speaks" to its readers in a clipped, informal, decidedly conversational tone. From our own reading of these ads, we might begin to discern a recurrent pattern common to comparative advertising-about-advertising, or even to antirhetorical rhetoric-about-rhetoric in general. This enhanced *understanding* of patterns of persuasion might in turn help us better analyze the next such advertisement we come across or do such persuading ourselves.

Having briefly compared the two advertisements, ask yourself at this point how either of them might be made more effective. This is, of course, a tall order: You are now competing with some top-notch rhetorical talents. But at least consider the possibility of employing other copy or other formats. Spiro and Associates advertises itself as "the low cholesterol ad agency." Might it do better as the "no frills" agency? Or might those among its competitors who prefer dining to dieting find a different gustatory image more appealing: "the filet mignon of ad agencies" . . . that "sells the steak, not just the sizzle?"

Trying your own hand at the practice of persuasion should assist you further at interpreting and evaluating either message. Consider the Anesh ad in terms of Figure 1.1 (pages 12–15). Although designed as a guide for analyzing television advertising, it can easily be applied to magazine advertising as well. Note how the Anesh ad draws us by the bold black type at top and the clip-out coupon at bottom. *Confidence-building* begins with the headline of the ad and continues all the way through. In Rank's terms, the ad agency is saying "Trust me!" by offering a deal, not just an appeal. The *need* it appeals to is to get *relief* from agencies that charge for ads its buyers wind up disliking, or that at the very least put clients through long, time-wasting experiences. That need is coupled with the promise of *a good*, a service that is easier, more efficient, and generally superior. Moreover, in sending in their best ad or commercial, customers spend little or no money and make no commitments. Indeed, they get a bargain for their submission to the ad agency in the way of tight layout and copy, script, or storyboard in return.

Completing the pitch is the suggestion for action. No *urgency-stressing* techniques are used, but the company does enjoin readers to respond and makes it easy for them to act *now* by providing the clip-out coupon and, more important, a phone number (few readers are likely to mail back the coupon). Add to that the none too subtle hypnosislike suggestion: "You're about to respond to this ad, aren't you?"

How effective do you expect this ad was at generating new accounts? Having, in Rank's terms, *observed* and *understood*, you are now in a position to render a *judgment*.

My own judgment is positive. Without actual evidence of effects one can only speculate, but my sense is that the ad agency responded to its "logic of situation" by responding to the customer's "logic of situation." Anesh, Viseltear, Gumbinner, Inc., exhibit familiarity with their customers' needs and occasional frustrations. By their offer of a free trial demonstration, they provide a pitch familiar to merchandisers that is also fully appropriate to an ad agency on the make. The demonstration, moreover, engages potential clients as actors rather than passive message recipients, and this, as we will see, is a particularly effective persuasion technique. Some readers of the ad will undoubtedly recognize its "no gimmicks" appeal as a gimmick in its own right, but this should only serve to enhance the attractiveness of the ad maker, for it provides a measure of rhetorical expertise. The ad as a whole functions at two levels (at least): as a pitch for new business, and as a demonstration, via the style of the ad, of the company's skill.

the
30-SECOND SPOT
quiz

* Based on *The Pitch* © 1982 by Hugh Rank.

How to Analyze Ads:
Use this 1-2-3-4-5 sequence of questions, (see next page) to focus on the *"skeleton"* underneath the *"surface variations"* of radio and TV commercials, newspaper and magazine ads.

Recognize that a 30-second-spot TV ad is a **synthesis**, the end product of a complex process in which scores of people (writers, researchers, psychologists, artists, actors, camera crews, etc.) may have spent months putting together the details. TV commercials are often the best *compositions* of our age, skillful combinations of purposeful words and images. Be patient and systematic: **analysis** takes time to sort out all of the things going on at once. **We perceive** these things *simultaneously*, but we must discuss **them** *sequentially*. Use this 1-2-3-4-5 pattern of "the pitch" as a sequence to start your analysis.

Recognize "surface variations": in 30 seconds, a TV spot may have 40 quick–cut scenes of "good times" (happy people, sports, fun, drinking cola); or 1 slow "tracking" scene of an old-fashioned sleighride through the woods, ending at "home" with "Season's Greetings" from an aerospace corporation; or a three-scene drama: a problem suffered by some "friend," a product/solution recommended by a trusted "authority," and a final grateful smile from the relieved sufferer. But, the structure underneath is basically the same.

Recognize our own involvement in a mutual transaction. Persuaders are *benefit-promisers,* but we are *benefit-seekers.* Most ads relate to simple "trade-offs" of mutual benefits: consumers get a pleasure, producers get a profit. However, investigate issues relating to any non–consumer ad; these are paid presentations of only one side of an issue, often involving more than a simple purchase transaction.

Understand that advertising is basically persuasion, not information or education, *and not coercion!* Many important moral and ethical issues (concerning intent and consequences, priorities, individual and social effects, truth and deception, legal and regulatory problems) are related. The more we know about the basic techniques of persuasion, the better able we are not only to cope with the multiple persuaders in our society, but also to consider these ethical issues.

Figure 1.1 The 30-Second Spot Quiz.

1 What ATTENTION–GETTING techniques are used?

Anything unusual? Unexpected? Noticeable? Interesting? Related to:
- ☐ **senses:** motions, colors, lights, sounds, music, visuals (e.g., computer graphics, slow–motion).
- ☐ **emotions:** any associations (*see list below*): sex, scenery, exciting action, fun, family, pets.
- ☐ **thought:** news, lists, displays, claims, advice, questions, stories, demonstrations, contests.
  (*Popular TV* **programs** *function as* attention–getters *to "deliver the audience" to advertisers.*)

2 What CONFIDENCE–BUILDING techniques are used?

- ☐ Do you *recognize, know* (from earlier repetition) the **brand name? company? symbol? package?**
- ☐ Do you *already know, like,* and *trust* the "**presenters**": the endorsers, actors, models?
- ☐ Are these "presenters" **AUTHORITY FIGURES** (expert, wise, protective, caring)? Or, are they **FRIEND FIGURES** (someone you like, like to be, "on your side"; incl. "cute" cartoons)?
- ☐ What key **words** are used? (*Trust, sincere,* etc.) **Nonverbals?** (*smiles, voice tones, sincere look*)
- ☐ In **mail** ads, are computer-written *"personalized"* touches used? On **telephone:** tapes? scripts?

3 What DESIRE–STIMULATING techniques are used?
(Main part of ad)

Consider (a) **"target audience"** as (b) **benefit-seeking;** and persuaders' benefit-promising strategies as focused on (c) **product claims,** or, (d) **"added values"** associated with product.
- ☐ a. **Who is the "target audience"?** Are *you?* (If *not,* as part of an unintended audience, are you *uninterested* or *hostile* toward the ad?)
- ☐ b. **What's the primary motive of that audience's benefit-seeking?** Use chart at right. Most ads are simple acquisition (*lower left*). Often, such motives co-exist, but one may be dominant. Ads which intensify a **problem** (that is, a "bad" already hated or feared; *the opposite, or the absence of,* "goods"), and then offer the product as a **solution**, are here called "**scare-and-sell**" **ads** (*right side*).

To keep a "good" (*protection*)	To get rid of a "bad" (*relief*)
To get a "good" (*acquisition*)	To avoid a "bad" (*prevention*)

☐ c. **What kinds of product claims are emphasized?** (*use these 12 categories*) What key words, images? Any *measurable* claims? Or are they *subjective opinions, generalized* praise words ("puffery")?

SUPERIORITY (*"best"*)	STABILITY (*"classic"*)
QUANTITY (*"most"*)	RELIABILITY (*"solid"*)
EFFICIENCY (*"works"*)	SIMPLICITY (*"easy"*)
BEAUTY (*"lovely"*)	UTILITY (*"practical"*)
SCARCITY (*"rare"*)	RAPIDITY (*"fast"*)
NOVELTY (*"new"*)	SAFETY (*"safe"*)

☐ d. **Are any "added values" implied or suggested?** Are there words or images which associate the product with some "good" already loved or desired by the intended audience? With such common human needs/wants/desires as in these 24 categories:

"Basic" needs:	**"Territory" needs:**
FOOD (*"tasty"*)	NEIGHBORHOOD (*"hometown"*)
ACTIVITY (*"exciting"*)	NATION (*"country"*)
SURROUNDINGS (*"comfort"*)	NATURE (*"earth"*)
SEX (*"alluring"*)	
HEALTH (*"healthy"*)	**Love & belonging needs:**
SECURITY (*"protect"*)	INTIMACY (*"lover"*)
ECONOMY (*"save"*)	FAMILY (*"Mom" "kids"*)
	GROUPS (*"team"*)

☐ d. **"Certitude" needs:**

"Certitude" needs:	**"Growth" needs**
RELIGION (*"right"*)	ESTEEM (*"respected"*)
SCIENCE (*"research"*)	PLAY (*"fun"*)
BEST PEOPLE (*"elite"*)	GENEROSITY (*"gift"*)
MOST PEOPLE (*"popular"*)	CREATIVITY (*"creative"*)
AVERAGE PEOPLE (*"typical"*)	CURIOSITY (*"discover"*)
	COMPLETION (*"success"*)

4   Are there URGENCY-STRESSING techniques used?

(*Not all ads, but always check.*)

☐ If an urgency appeal: What words? (*e.g. Hurry, Rush, Deadline, Sale Ends, Offer Expires, Now.*)

☐ If **no** urgency: is this **"soft sell"** part of a *repetitive, long-term ad campaign* for standard item?

5   What RESPONSE-SEEKING techniques are used?

(*Persuaders always seek some kind of response!*)

☐ *Are there specific triggering* words used? (Buy, Get, Do, Call, Act, Join, Smoke, Drink, Taste, etc.)

☐ Is there a **specific response** sought? (Most ads: to buy something)

☐ If **not**: is it **conditioning** ("public relations" or "image building") to make us **"feel good"** about the company, to get favorable public opinion on *its* side (against any government regulations, taxes)?

Observe. Understand. Judge. (In *that* sequence!) Observe closely what is explicitly said and shown; consider carefully what may be implied, suggested either by verbal or nonverbal means.

Anticipate incoming information. Have some way to sort, some place to store. If you know common patterns, you can pick up cues from bits and fragments, recognize the situation, know the probable options, infer the rest, and even note the omissions. Some persuaders use these techniques (and some observers analyze them) consciously and systematically; others, intuitively and haphazardly.

Categorize, but don't "pigeonhole." Things may be in many categories at the same time. "Clusters" and "mixes" are common. Observers often disagree.

Seek "dominant impressions," but relate them to the whole. You can't analyze *everything.* Focus on what seems (*to you*) the most *noticeable, interesting,* or *significant* elements (e.g. an intense "urgency" appeal, a very strong "authority" figure). By relating these to the whole context of "the pitch," your analysis can be *systematic, yet flexible,* appropriate to the situation.

Translate "indirect" messages. Much communication is *indirect,* through metaphoric language, allusions, rhetorical questions, irony, nonverbals (gestures, facial expressions, tone of voice), etc. Millions of specific concrete ways of communicating something can be grouped in the general abstract categories listed here as "product claims" (3c) and "common needs" (3d). Visuals imply.

Train yourself by first analyzing those ads which explicity use the full sequence of "the pitch," including "urgency-stressing" and a specific "re-sponse-seeking." Always check for this full sequence; when it does not appear, consider what may have been omitted: *assumed* or *implied.* "Soft sell" ads and corporate "image-building" ads are harder to analyze: *less is said, more is implied.*

Practice. Analysis is a skill which can be learned, but needs to be practiced. Take notes. Use print ads. Videotape if possible. Replay in slow motion. No one can "see" or "understand" everything during the actual 30 seconds while watching a TV spot. At best, we pick up a few impressions. Use the pattern of "the pitch" to organize your analysis and aid your memory. Such organization helps to avoid randomness and simple subjectivity.

Are ads worth all this attention? Ads may not be, but *your mind is.* If we can better learn how to analyze things, to recognize patterns, to sort out incoming information, to see the parts, the processes, the structure, the relationships among things so common in our everyday environment, then it's worth the effort.

SUMMARY

From the foregoing case study discussion it should be clear just how closely the tasks of understanding, practice, and analysis are related. In order to become a discriminating consumer of persuasive messages, it is useful to be aware of the techniques others may use to influence you. In order to persuade effectively, it is necessary to anticipate how consumers of messages are likely to respond. And in order to respond discriminatingly or to persuade effectively, it helps to have a general understanding of the psychology of the persuasive process and the role of persuasion in society. Our experiences as persuaders and persuadees may also help us to understand in small ways how persuasion has shaped human choices throughout history, and how persuasion functions in present-day society.

EXERCISES

1. Keep a record of the number of times in the course of a day that you were involved as a persuader, a persuadee, or both. What does this suggest to you about the relative importance of understanding, practice, and analysis?
2. Investigate and compare other books on how to exert influence—books on sales, advertising, political campaigning, editorial writing, health education, public relations, international diplomacy, advocacy in the courtroom, sermon giving, labor-management negotiating. In what respects are their basic principles similar to those of this book? How are they different?
3. Provide an analysis of a television commercial using Rank's 30-second spot quiz as your guide.

Chapter *2*
What Is Persuasion?

What is persuasion? Who practices it? How can it be distinguished from nonpersuasion? Some hints as to how I would answer these questions were provided in Chapter 1, but here I want to identify in greater detail what I believe is central to persuasion and in later chapters to explore persuasion's "boundaries." As you have seen, terms like persuasion, rhetoric and propaganda evoke strong evaluative reactions in many quarters. Moreover, persuaders frequently attempt to persuade us that they are not persuaders. These facts alone should prompt us to attend carefully to questions of scope and definition. But other issues of both a practical and philosophical nature should lead us to exercise prudence in delineating the boundaries of persuasion. Be forewarned that I shall try to do a bit of persuading myself in this book. I will urge upon you a rather broad view of the persuasive domain, one that challenges conventional distinctions between persuasion and its alleged alternatives.

Persuasion and Intent

It must be admitted at the outset that our culture licenses several different conceptions of the term persuasion. Consider these examples:

1. The blizzard *persuaded* me to go indoors.
2. The puppy's sad look *persuaded* me to surrender choice pieces of filet mignon.
3. The full moon *persuaded* us to make rapturous love.
4. Upon seeing the hat on a passerby, I was *persuaded* to buy one just like it.

Each of these examples presents us with an alleged effect, but with no evidence of intent on anyone's part to bring about that effect, or any other. By this extremely broad use of persuasion, any stimulus may persuade. All that is required is that the stimulus affect someone's decisions or actions. Clearly, this view of persuasion is too broad for our purposes. The term should be reserved for deliberate efforts at influencing others.

However, this does not mean that there will always be a one-to-one match between persuasive effects and intentions. Seldom are persuaders fully aware of everything they are saying and doing when communicating a message. And even less often are the effects they intend exactly the effects they achieve. In the process of transmitting intentional messages, they typically communicate a good deal more than they intend. Through inflectional accompaniments to oral messages, for example, they may transmit unconscious feelings. And both intended and unintended messages may produce unintended persuasive effects. Not uncommonly, in fact, persuasive messages *boomerang;* they produce effects opposite to those intended.

In studying persuasion, most scholars focus on the nature and effects of messages that offer evidence of having been designed, at least in part, for the purpose of influencing others. The term persuasion is sometimes used to refer to persuasive *practices,* including those that succeed spectacularly and those that fall flat on their proverbial faces. No matter what the jury's verdict, for example, the attorneys for the plaintiff and the defense are assumed to be engaged in the *practice* of persuasion. At other times, the term persuasion is used to refer to the successful *effects* of persuasive practices. Thus we may say that the victorious attorney persuaded the jury, but the other attorney did not persuade it. So long as the context is made clear, these two uses of persuasion may both be employed without difficulty.

Persuasion and Communication

It should go without saying at this point that persuasion takes place through communication. In the jargon of communication theorists, *communication* always involves a source of the message (A), a receiver or audience (B), a channel or medium through which the message is presented (C), a situational context in which communication takes place (SC), and the message itself (X).

Figures 2.1a–e present diagrams of major patterns of persuasive communication. In the first model, interpersonal communication, each individual performs the roles of persuader and persuadee. Here is the arena for such genres as the attempted seduction and the marital squabble, the job interview, and the bull session between friends. In these situations, the communicator generally cannot prepare a set message and communicate it unaltered. Each individual must pattern planned remarks flexibly, listen carefully and critically, and adjust responses to the messages of the other.

In Figure 2.1b, public communication, the audience is larger, but there is still direct contact between A and B and there is opportunity, albeit somewhat more limited, for A to adjust what she or he says on the basis of feedback from

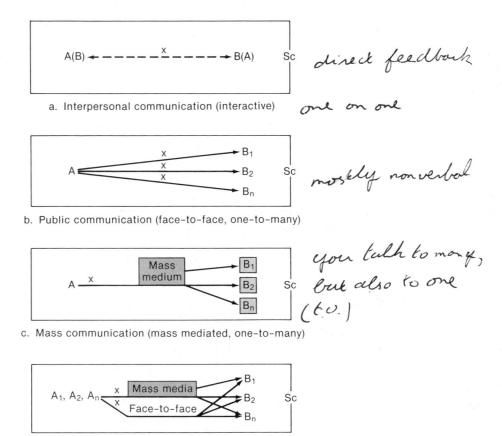

a. Interpersonal communication (interactive)

direct feedback

one on one

b. Public communication (face–to–face, one–to–many)

mostly nonverbal

c. Mass communication (mass mediated, one–to–many)

you talk to many, but also to one (t.v.)

d. Campaigns (same source, multiple messages)

e. From the receiver's perspective (different sources, multiple messages)

Figure 2.1 Five Patterns of Persuasive Communication.

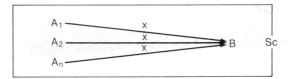

B. Here is the pattern for the typical sermon and lecture, the speech before Congress, and the Fourth of July oration at an outdoor celebration.

The next model, 2.1c, is of a relatively recent phenomenon in human history. Trautmann (1970) has pointed out that not until the middle of the nineteenth century was there mass literacy and the means for dissemination of identical content. Until that time, therefore, there could be no truly mass media persuasion. Public proclamations and pageants, yes, but only for those who could hear or see them. Posters and leaflets, but only for those who could read.

The persuader as disseminator of new ideas. Young Indian couples being taught family planning and welfare. *(Courtesy of United Nations/ILO)*

With the electronic media, it is possible to convey messages more quickly, more vividly, and to much larger numbers of people. Dramatic events in remote corners of the globe and beyond have been brought visually into our living rooms, and other events here at home have been staged for the TV cameras. With the advent of satellite television, persuaders may reach across the globe directly and may reach millions more, indirectly. A major happening like the shooting of Ronald Reagan may be known by two-thirds of the American public within 30 minutes and by over 90 percent of the public within two hours. At the same time, persuaders may be stuck with unintended listeners—or worse still, with overexposed listeners, as in the case of a public that has been hardened to horrors by several years of TV film clips of various wars.

Model 2.1d is an extension of the previous one. A campaign is an organized and sustained effort at influencing others, typically involving multiple message senders (A_1, A_2, A_n), messages transmitted face-to-face as well as through mass communication channels, and a variety of audiences or audience segments. For the political campaigner, the advertiser, and other such mass communicators, B_1, B_2, B_n are typically viewed as undifferentiated demographic entities such as rural Protestants, urban blacks, the 18 to 25 age group; that is why they are represented as blocks. Although it is often convenient to view a speech or brief

An example of mass communications. *(Peter Menzel/Stock, Boston)*

exchange as an independent unit of analysis, such an orientation is of limited value for purposes of analyzing the messages delivered as part of a persuasive campaign. Campaigns are designed to have cumulative impact, each message presenting perhaps just one idea at a time for the purpose of moving audiences one increment at a time.

Model 2.1e is intended as a corrective to a tendency many persuaders have to forget that they are not the only persons attempting to exercise influence on any given subject. Just as it has been easier for students of persuasion to study passive audiences, it is also much easier to study each individual message transmitted to a receiver in isolation from prior and subsequent messages. From a receiver's standpoint, however, the totality of messages received on a given topic during a given period may form a unique and indivisible mosaic. For any one of us, for example, the message unit or composite on the question of whether to purchase a Sony taperecorder may be formed from an advertisement that we saw in a magazine, a few exchanges with friends, an overheard conversation, and a classroom speech on the benefits of taperecorders for improving communication skills. The series of messages that form a composite single message for a receiver is, as Becker (1971, p. 31) puts it, "scattered through time and space, disorganized, has large gaps; he is exposed to parts of it again and again; and there is great variance with the message to which other receivers are exposed."

Persuasion and Judgments

[handwritten: = persuasion shapes your thinking]

Persuasion is a form of influence that predisposes, but does not impose. It alters others' judgments, and not just their behavior. It affects their sense of what is true or false, probable or improbable; their evaluations of people, events, ideas, proposals; their private and public commitments to take this or that action; perhaps even their basic values and ideologies. According to Augustine over 1500 years ago, the fully influenced persuadee:

> . . . likes what you promise, fears what you say is imminent, hates what you censure, embraces what you command, regrets whatever you build up as regrettable, rejoices at whatever you say is cause for rejoicing, sympathizes with those whose wretchedness your words bring before his very eyes, shuns those whom you admonish him to shun . . . and in whatever other ways your high eloquence can affect the minds of your hearers, bringing them not merely to know what should be done, but to do what they know should be done. (Burke, 1969, p. 50)

[handwritten left margin: belief: you can't prove it]

There is no universally accepted set of terms for referring to types of judgments. Of particular importance for our purposes will be the terms attitude, belief, and value. As used here, an *attitude* is an object evaluation, a judgment that a given object is good or bad, desirable or undesirable, something to be approached or avoided. The object may be literally anything: a person, an event, an idea, a proposal for action, an action itself.

The major building blocks of attitudes are *beliefs*, judgments held with varying degrees of certainty that an object possesses a particular attribute. Just as the object may be anything, so the attribute may be anything that could conceivably be linked, whether positively or negatively or neutrally, with the object (Ajzen and Fishbein, 1980). Assume, for example, that the object is Mary Jones, a political candidate. Among the relevant beliefs voters might have with respect to her candidacy are those having to do with such personal attributes as fairness, honesty, and competence, and others having to do with her positions on controversial issues. The subjective probabilities voters attached to these object-attribute linkages would no doubt figure importantly in their attitudes toward Jones as a candidate, and these attitudes would in turn have a good deal to do with their voting behavior.

It should be noted that audience beliefs may be objects of the persuader's attention in their own right. An economist may seek to convince people that a recession is impending, but leave entirely to them the question of whether a recession would be good or bad, as well as the question of what to do about it if it should occur. Note too that beliefs are based on other beliefs. For example, the economist would undoubtedly base the predictions on beliefs that some types of data are particularly good economic indicators of forthcoming recessions, and still other beliefs about the accuracy of the actual data available.

Values are attitudes of a highly general nature to which people adhere rather consistently in their evaluations of the attributes of different objects. If you were to consider buying a car, for example, chances are you would have certain attributes in mind when appraising it: efficiency, beauty, economy, speed, safety, comfort. The relative importance you attach to each of these attributes would probably not change very much from one car examination to another. Other car purchasers might assign different values to these attributes. What a prospective buyer's attitude is toward a given car probably depends on both his or her beliefs about whether the car possesses particular attributes, and the *value* weightings she or he assigns to those attributes. One prospective buyer may believe that the new XL7 Zippo sedan is sexy looking and fuel-efficient and have a highly favorable attitude toward the Zippo for just these reasons. A second prospective buyer may agree that the Zippo possesses these attributes, but view them neutrally or even negatively. A third buyer may value the attributes, but not believe the Zippo possesses them. A fourth buyer may share the beliefs of the third buyer and the values of the second. For this customer, in fact, the perception that the Zippo is not sexy looking may even be a decided plus.

Quite obviously, these variations in beliefs and values have great importance for persuaders. A sales pitch that succeeds with any one of these customers might very well backfire with another. As you will see in Chapter 4, various theories of attitude and attitude change offer competing conceptions of the relationships among attitudes, beliefs, and values, but each in its own way recognizes the importance of these concepts.

Persuasion by Degrees

On any one occasion, a persuader might stop far short of producing wholesale changes from one way of thinking or behaving to another and yet still consider the effort successful. In this connection, Miller (1980) lists under the heading of "being persuaded" three types of outcomes: (1) response shaping, (2) response reinforcing, and (3) response changing:

Response shaping occurs when people acquire new "beliefs" on controversial matters or when they are socialized to learn new attitudes. Shaping may involve, for example, teaching a child to become a Lutheran, a Democrat, a capitalist, or a patriot. And, of course, shaping is not confined to children. Political campaigns may shape voters' attitudes toward previously unknown candidates. Commercial advertising may shape favorable consumer responses to new products and product brands. The key characteristic of shaping is that it leads to the formation of new beliefs and attitudes.

Response reinforcing consists in strengthening currently held convictions and making them more resistant to change. A campaign in behalf of a charity might begin by transforming lip service commitments into strongly felt commitments (*intensification*); then transforming those commitments into donations of time and money (*activation*); then working to maintain strong behavioral support and discouraging backsliding (*deterrence*). All of these are forms of response reinforcing. Says Miller:

The response-reinforcing function underscores the fact that "being persuaded" is seldom, if ever, a one-message proposition; instead, people are constantly in *the process of* being persuaded. If an individual clings to an attitude (and the behaviors associated with it) more strongly after exposure to a communication, then persuasion has occurred as surely as if the individual has shifted from one set of responses to another. Moreover, those beliefs and behaviors most resistant to change are likely to be grounded in a long history of confirming messages, along with other positive reinforcers (p. 19).

harder =

Response changing involves converting others—getting them to switch party preferences, or to become Born Again Christians, or to change cigarette brands, or perhaps to quit smoking. Though Miller does not mention it, I assume he includes *crystallization* under response changing—getting those persons who were uncommitted due to conflicting attitudes on an issue to endorse the persuader's position or proposal. The psychological processes involved in conversions and crystallizations are essentially the same.

That persuasion may involve reinforcing and shaping and not just changing of beliefs and attitudes is reflected in nearly all textbooks on persuasion. Writers typically speak of persuasion as a process of *modifying* or *altering* the judgments of others, not necessarily changing them outright (Scheidel, 1967; Bettinghaus, 1981; Clark, 1984; Brembeck and Howell, 1976; Zimbardo, Ebbesen, and Maslach, 1977; Larson, 1983; Smith, 1982; Reardon, 1981; O'Donnell and Kable, 1982). To Miller's list most writers would add what might be called *response terminating:* Getting a hostile audience to become less hostile *(defusion)*, or perhaps casting so much doubt on their positions that they become ambivalent *(neutralization)*. That persuasion takes place by degrees over a wide span of activities from response terminating to response reinforcing is shown in Figure 2.2. The lines with directional arrows denoting different categories of being persuaded are approximate, but they point up the fact that persuaders typically seek different levels of support, depending upon initial levels of audience commitment. Note that there are two categories of persons who stand initially "on the fence": Those who are uninformed or apathetic, and those who may have so much interest and information that they are unable to make up their minds. These two groups are reached in very different ways.

Defining Persuasion

The preceding discussion of persuasion and intent, persuasion and communication, persuasion and judgments, and persuasion by degrees has barely scratched the surface. What, for example, shall we say of unconscious persuasive messages or of messages in which persuasive intent is passive or secondary? Can a message be designed to persuade and not persuade at the same time?

These and other questions will be saved for subsequent chapters. For now, it is possible to define persuasion both as *a process of communication designed to modify the judgments of others,* and—recalling our earlier discussion—as *success at modifying the judgments of others in intended directions.* Ordinarily I will use the former sense of the term, but there will be times when the latter usage will be employed.

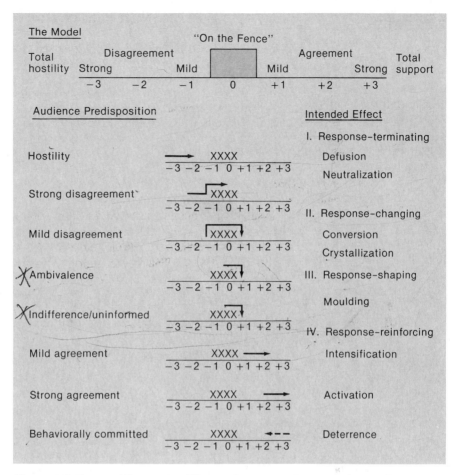

Figure 2.2 Types of Persuasive Effect in Relation to Degrees of Initial Support for a Proposal. Any movement from left to right may be considered at least partially successful persuasion. The broken arrow for *deterrence* means that the effort is directed at preventing backsliding.

SUMMARY

However they define persuasion—whether as process or as effect—most scholars focus their study on messages that offer some evidence of having been designed for the purpose of influencing others. The messages may be mediated efforts at mass persuasion, or one-to-many public communications, or interpersonal exchanges. They may be one-shot efforts or, as is typically the case with mass communications, components of persuasive campaigns.

The purpose of persuasive messages, in any case, is to exercise influence on others by modifying their attitudes, beliefs, and/or value judgments. Attitudes are object evaluations. Beliefs are judgments that the object possesses certain attributes. Values guide the evaluations made of these attributes. The persuader's influence on beliefs, values, or attitudes may be relatively minor: For example, it may consist of no more than reducing another's hostility while still leaving the person opposed to your point of view; or it may involve deterring a committed supporter from backsliding. Success must always be evaluated in relation to where the message recipient stood to begin with.

One final comment concerns the term rhetoric. You have no doubt noticed that it has been used almost as often as the term persuasion and that it is also ambiguous. Most often it is used as a synonym for persuasion, or to refer to a body of principles about persuasion (Aristotle's *Rhetoric*). But the term is also used in our culture to refer to a type of persuasion (speechmaking or essay writing), to particular genres of persuasive practice (the rhetoric of rock music, the rhetoric of social movements, the rhetoric of nineteenth-century feminists), and to polished prose of any kind. As if these many meanings were not troubling enough, there are also the many pejorative senses of rhetoric to contend with. Like persuasion, the meaning intended at any given point should be clear in context, particularly now that you are more aware of rhetoric's many meanings. Be assured that this promise is not an idle boast; it is not "mere rhetoric."

EXERCISES

prejudicive

The following are typical generalizations about persuasion, some of them based on careful research, others based on seat-of-the-pants judgments. Which do you think are true? Which are false? Which are so muddled or so simplistic that they can be answered only with a question mark?

1. "The best way to induce people to stop smoking is to scare them."
2. "It is generally effective to present both sides of an issue and then conclude by indicating why you think the weight of the evidence supports one of those positions."
3. "Because opposites attract, it is generally best when using testimonials in advertisements to present sources as unlike the intended audience as possible."
4. "The more you pay people to argue publicly for a position contrary to their own values, the more likely they are to change their values."
5. "Moderately intelligent people are more likely to be persuaded upon hearing an argument than people of very low or very high intelligence."
6. "The best way to respond to a public attack is to respond with a counterattack that is as strong or stronger."
7. "You are more likely to be perceived as a credible speaker if you look your audience in the eyes throughout your speech."
8. "In a job interview situation, it's best to minimize your past accomplishments."
9. "Emotional appeals are generally more persuasive than logical appeals."
10. "The only rule about how to persuade is that there are no rules."

Note that not all of the generalizations can be true, for if item 10 is correct, the others are not, and if any of the others are valid, then item 10 is not.

There is a good deal to be said for item 10. It could be argued that persuasion is too much an individual thing; that it is too subject to variations in goals, media, contexts, audiences, subject matter; that, while it may be fun to speculate about, it is impossible to generalize about with any degree of reliability. However, item 10 is probably wrong, or at least not very useful. Few persuasion scholars deny that there are limits as to how far we can go in generalizing about persuasion, but they point out that responses to persuasive messages surely are not random either.

Answers to these questions are presented at the end of Chapter 3.

Chapter 3
Generalizing about Persuasion

A key assumption of this book is that it is possible to adduce general principles of persuasion that can be applied with some confidence to a wide variety of cases. Practitioners, message analysts, and even those with a purely academic interest in persuasion all want to impose order upon their subject matter. They want to determine what works and why, to establish benchmarks for evaluation, and to bring their generalizations to bear on particular cases. For those such as advertisers or political campaigners who are engaged professionally in efforts at mass persuasion, generalizing reliably is especially important. At the very least, they want a *technology* of persuasion that will enable them to predict and control the responses of the particular target populations they seek to influence. More ambitiously, and more to the point of this chapter, practitioners seek generalizations that transcend particular campaigns and audiences. Ideally, they would like to be able to draw upon a body of general knowledge about persuasion equivalent in refinement and sophistication to our current knowledge of physics or biology. But there are formidable obstacles to the realization of that goal.

In formulating general principles, rhetoricians since Aristotle have derived insights about how to persuade from observing experienced persuaders at work. Aristotle's own treatise on rhetoric (compiled, it is believed, from lecture notes taken by his students) has stood the test of time remarkably well and has greatly influenced the writing of this text.

As you read this book you should find that many of the principles offered here are consonant with your own experiences as persuaders. All of you have been persuading for a long, long time—since childhood, in fact. Over that period you have acquired a great deal of rhetorical knowledge, much of it tacit rather than explicit. *Tacit* rhetorical knowledge is a bit like the knowledge most of us have of how to speak grammatically or ride a bicycle or maneuver on foot through a crowd of people. These are things we know how to do quite well without having ever consciously articulated the principles underlying their performance. It is true that consciousness of the principles of an art may sometimes interfere with its performance, as when an experienced dancer begins to stumble over a routine step while trying to teach it to a novice. Nevertheless, I believe there is value in making tacit rhetorical knowledge explicit and then internalizing it to the point where it is second nature.

However, we will not have advanced the state of the art very much if we rely exclusively for our principles on informal observations of persuaders at work. Principles need to be tested under controlled conditions, and new ones developed from theories about what works. Moreover, the experiences of persuaders need to be compared systematically, in like situations. Here is where the two major contemporary approaches to generalizing about persuasion come into play: the behavioral approach and the generic approach.

The Behavioral Approach

The behavioral approach is an offshoot of social psychology.[1] It typically involves experimental research on the many communication factors that might contribute to the success or failure of persuasive efforts, as well as psychological theories designed to explain research findings and suggest new hypotheses. The communication factors include variations in source, message, medium, audience, and context—in "who says what to whom, when, where and how." These are known as *independent variables*. Determining their effects on *dependent variables* is the object of research. As McGuire (1978) has put it:

> The independent variables have to do with the communication process; these are the variables we can manipulate in order to see what happens or to test whether a theoretically predicted effect is actually produced. The dependent variables have to do with what happens, with the changes that occur, with persuasion itself; these are the variables that we expect will change when we manipulate the independent variables. Taken together, the independent and dependent variables define what we might call the "communication-persuasion matrix." (p. 243)

The Study of Persuasion

In the typical experiment on persuasion, inferences are drawn about factors promoting persuasive effectiveness from comparisons of groups, known as *treatment groups,* on such communication variables as strength of fear appeal, amount of payment for counterattitudinal advocacy, or degree of speaker

---

[1] The behavioral approach ought not to be confused with a school of thought in psychology known as behaviorism.

trustworthiness. Differences in these independent variables are presumed to exert differential effects on beliefs, attitudes, values, and other such dependent variables. In the well-conducted experiment, *controls* are exercised to ensure that treatment groups are equivalent in all respects except exposure to the independent variable. To ensure initial comparability, the groups are drawn from a common pool of subjects, randomly assigned (such as by lot) to experimental conditions, and perhaps matched on relevant variables. During the course of the experiment, potentially contaminating variables are kept constant or allowed to fluctuate at random. To prevent subjects from reacting unusually, the true purpose of the experiment may be concealed or procedures devised so that subjects are not even aware they are participating in an experiment. Constraints may be placed on experimenters to ensure that their own biases or expectations do not influence the results. Finally, a statistical procedure is used to determine whether the groups differed on the dependent variable beyond what might be expected by chance.

The behavioral approach dates back to World War II, when a large research team headed by Yale professor Carl Hovland began experimenting systematically with different ways of bolstering the morale of U.S. soldiers abroad and U.S. civilians at home. Hovland and his colleagues continued their program of persuasion research at Yale after the war and provided a training ground for subsequent investigators. Because of their great influence, we may appropriately focus on their work in identifying the rudiments of the behavioral approach.

The Yale group conceived of persuasion in theoretical terms as a process of teaching persuadees to learn new attitudes or modify old ones, in much the same way that animals in a learning laboratory are trained to traverse a maze or to modify past maze-crossing habits. The connection between persuasion and learning was emphasized in *Communication and Persuasion* by Hovland, Janis, and Kelley in 1953. "We assume that opinions, like other habits, will tend to persist unless the individual undergoes some new learning experience. Exposure to a persuasive communication which successfully induces the individual to accept a new opinion constitutes a learning experience in which a new verbal habit is acquired" (1953, p. 10).

Typical of the World War II studies by the Yale group was an experiment by Hovland, Lumsdaine, and Sheffield (1949) that compared the effects of one-sided versus two-sided message presentations. Early in 1945, after the Nazis had conceded defeat, the U.S. Army wished to persuade its troops that victory in the European theater did not mean that the war in the Pacific would soon be over. Using this as the topic for an experiment, army psychologists constructed two alternate radio broadcasts for presentation to randomly assigned groups of soldiers. One version offered a one-sided series of arguments; a more balanced but otherwise comparable version added arguments for a more optimistic position. Both messages urged the same pessimistic conclusion and were alike in all other relevant respects. To prevent the soldiers from becoming aware that they were participating in an experiment, the attitude questionnaires were disguised as part of a general survey. Once the data were collected, the group receiving the one-sided approach was compared with the group receiving the two-sided approach to determine which approach was most effective. The researchers found that neither technique enjoyed a clear superiority over the other, although both were influential. What they did discover was a bit more complex. The one-sided approach was most persuasive with predisposed listeners and with those who lacked a high school diploma. The "both-sides" approach had greater success with listeners who were initially undecided or in opposition, those who were better educated, and those who were later exposed to counterarguments.

The Role of Behavioral Theory

Central to the behavioral approach is the development of theory, for without it the research findings would have little meaning or connections. It is useful to visualize a theory as a cylindrical vessel open at both ends and narrow in the middle, as in the diagram below:

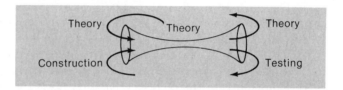

Into the vessel come findings about phenomena, which the theory attempts to summarize and explain. Out of the vessel come deduced hypotheses which, when tested, may add new grist for the theoretical mill. The heart of the theory—the narrow part of the vessel—is a set of assumptions, basic concepts, definitions of those concepts, and explanatory statements or theorems that relate the concepts in a condensed and organized way.

Behavioral theories of persuasion offer psychological explanations for research findings about the communication-persuasion matrix. They include general theories that attempt explanations of a broad range of rhetorical phenomena and miniature theories about such specific phenomena as the nature of source credibility, the effects of fear appeals, and the consequences of counterattitudinal advocacy.

Although we may not be as rigorous or as systematic as the professional social scientist, most of us are persuasion theorists of a sort, and our "theories" probably influence our practice of persuasion as well. Like the social scientist, we have all gathered evidence about persuasion—informally in most cases—that we have then attempted to organize, summarize, and interpret. And like the social scientist, our theories of persuasion are probably rooted in assumptions about human nature.

The Uses of Theory: An Illustration

Whether our theories are useful or not is another matter. Ideally, a theory should be clear, consistent, capable of being tested, and able to yield valid predictions, provocative in that it stimulates new research, and comprehensive as well as elegant, in the sense of explaining a great deal by means of a minimum number of working principles. To illustrate the uses of behavioral theory, let us consider the relationship between intelligence and persuasibility. Who would you predict would be more likely to be persuaded: individuals of relatively high or relatively low intelligence?

When this question is posed to persuasion classes, opinions inevitably divide. Some students hypothesize that the brighter you are, the more likely you are to be persuaded; other predict a negative or inverse relationship between the two variables. These alternative hypotheses are diagrammed in Figure 3.1.

Those maintaining that intelligence and persuasibility are positively correlated typically conceive of persuasion in learning terms as essentially a matter of attention, comprehension, and retention of new information. With this view, those of low intelligence are less likely to be persuaded because they have more difficulty processing the information provided by persuaders and following its logic.

Opponents typically propose an equally plausible "mini-theory," also learning based, which holds that persuasion is a very much more active process, involving decisions by the message recipient as to whether to regard the source as credible and the arguments as valid. With this view, intelligent individuals should be more resistant to persuasive messages, since presumably they have the wherewithal to detect flaws in arguments and the confidence to hold to their own opinions, rather than simply conform to peer or authority pressures.

As is often the case when two competing theories appear plausible, a third that combines their respective insights proves to be the most useful. Just such a two-factor theory was proposed by William McGuire (1968), a disciple of Hovland's and an innovative scholar in his own right. McGuire envisioned the processing of persuasive messages as involving a *reception* stage, which included attention to and comprehension of the message, and a *yielding* stage, which included evaluations of the source and the arguments presented. In the jargon of psychology, reception and yielding were *mediators* of successful persuasion, and both were necessary for it to occur. Additionally, McGuire postulated what

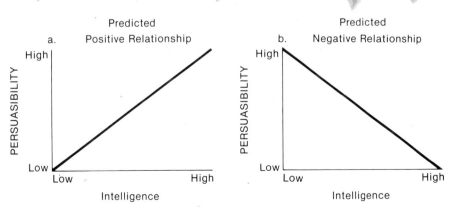

Figure 3.1 Intelligence and Persuasability.

girls doing in a comercial

Poor educated person: works better to happen something to

Well-educated: works to participate — know why reason

he called the *compensatory assumption*. This theorem holds that those character-istics of people which are positively related to reception of a message are negatively related to yielding. As you might suspect at this point, intelligence is one such characteristic. Self-confidence and education operate in similar fashion, whereas anxiety increases yielding, but works against reception. Said McGuire (1968, p. 182): "Nature is deliciously equitable so that any charac-teristic which makes an individual vulnerable to social influence through one of the mediators tends to protect him from influence via the other."

McGuire's two-factor theory led him to the sophisticated hypothesis of a curvilinear relationship between intelligence and persuasibility, as shown in Figure 3.2. He held, in other words, that people of moderate intelligence would be more persuasible, given the compensatory effects of reception and yielding, than persons of high or low intelligence. The hypothesis has received a good degree of research support (Smith, 1982).

McGuire added another wrinkle to his theory which he called the *situational weighting* assumption. This held that the relative importance of reception versus yielding depended on other factors, such as the degree of complexity of the message. A typical television advertisement is probably comprehensible to most people, but its believability may weigh heavily for them. On the other hand, recall that people with relatively little education were won over to the one-sided message presentations in the experiment by Hovland (1953) discussed earlier, but not as readily to the two-sided presentation. McGuire's theory

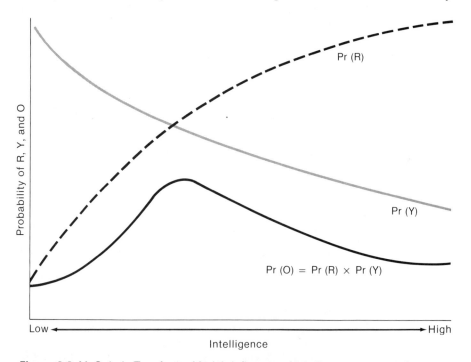

Figure 3.2 McGuire's Two-factor Model. Influence of intelligence on reception Pr(R); of intelligence on yielding Pr(Y); and of both on opinion change Pr(O), where Pr (O) = Pr (R) × Pr (Y). See McGuire (1968).

would account for these findings rather well. The one-sided message should be readily comprehensible to those with relatively little education; the two-sided message, while perhaps posing a reception problem for the less educated, should be understood and found more believable by the better educated.

The Uses of Behavioral Research: An Illustration

The behavioral approach has generated literally thousands of studies and a multitude of theories. For a considerable period of time, more articles on persuasion appeared in journals of social psychology than on any other subject. One theory alone—Festinger's theory of cognitive dissonance—has generated well over three hundred studies. Whatever else might be said about the theories, they have been extremely thought-provoking, each providing a different angle of view and a different metaphoric lens for looking at the subject matter. It is as perspectives that they are featured in subsequent chapters of this text.

Moreover, the behavioral approach has greatly advanced the technology of persuasion. It has suggested new methods of analyzing audiences, selecting messages and appropriate media for mass persuasion, and determining message effects. These methods have been used for such widely divergent purposes as picking jurors, determining product awareness, and planning campaigns for cancer prevention among the elderly (Ajzen and Fishbein, 1980). In the area of political campaigning, well-financed campaign managers are now able within days to craft sophisticated political commercials that are responsive to events of the moment, to anticipate problems by securing in-depth reactions to the commercials from groups of typical citizens, to test the commercials in "bellwether" markets before broadcasting to larger audiences, and to determine on a day-by-day basis what effects the commercials are producing.

But what now of the accumulated research findings? Are not the acid tests of the behavioral approach whether its theories suggest hypotheses that are consistently confirmed by research and whether the research findings themselves add up to general laws? In point of fact, there have been many disappointments, prompting some behaviorists to abandon the quest for laws equivalent to those in physics and biology. But the experiments that have been conducted remain a major source of knowledge.

Both the possibilities and the pitfalls inherent in the behavioral approach are nicely illustrated in the accumulated body of findings on the relative effects of strong versus weak fear appeals. Higbee (1969) examined 35 studies dealing with fear appeals. If anything, his review underscores the fact of differences with which any seeker after generalizations must necessarily contend. The topics included dental hygiene, smoking, tetanus, safe driving, fallout shelters, population growth, mental health, cancer, safety belts, roundworms, grades, tuberculosis, syphillis, viewing an eclipse, army life, and donating blood. The media included printed messages, tape recordings, tapes plus slides, films, and live oral presentations. The receivers have differed in terms of sex, age, cultural and educational background, and personality characteristics. The sources have ranged from those with extremely high credibility to those with extremely low credibility. The messages have differed in terms of strength of fear appeals

One cancer you can give yourself.

Horrible isn't it?

AMERICAN CANCER SOCIETY

Fear appeal used in public service advertisement. *(Courtesy of American Cancer Society)*

(strong, moderate, weak), whether recommendations were given and how specifically, whether reassurances were offered, and whether opportunity was provided to act on the recommendations.

By now the research area must certainly seem complex and perhaps bewildering. To further complicate the picture, let us add that combinations of the variables investigated have interactive effects on attitudes and behavior. Still another factor is that reported descriptions of studies may not be entirely comparable. For example, one researcher's strong fear appeal may be another's weak fear appeal. Finally, the studies often yield contradictory results. There is indeed a temptation to surrender in the face of such confusion, to end all further consideration of the issues with such familiar phrases as "Everything's relative"—"It's all a matter of degree"—"It depends on the situation." Conclusions such as these are perfectly valid, but they are also virtually useless. They are starting points for inquiry, not ending points. What can be done to make better sense of a body of literature such as the research literature on fear appeals? A further look at Higbee's (1969) summary of the literature suggests some useful guidelines.

First, as in most other areas, simplistic, all-or-none, either-or hypotheses are belied by research. Repeatedly in this book I will qualify generalizations with terms like "generally speaking," "more often than not," and so on. The literature on fear appeals suggests that more often than not, strong appeals are more effective than weak appeals, but not always.

Second, expect reversals. For many years it was believed by researchers that strong fear appeals interfered with comprehension of the message and caused defensive avoidance reactions. There is still some evidence for these hypotheses, but recent research tends not to support them, except perhaps with chronically anxious and other disturbed persons.

Third, view the number and variety of studies as an advantage rather than a disadvantage. Generalizations are more reliable when they are based on a great many studies and when each new study varies in some way from what had been done before.

Fourth, and most important, search for contingent generalizations. A *contingent generalization* is one that states the conditions under which a given level of an alleged causal variable (strong fear appeals) is likely to affect a dependent variable (attitude modification) to one degree or another. Although research on persuasion has not yielded very many nontrivial, either-or generalizations, it has unearthed a number of nontrivial contingent generalizations. On the basis of Higbee's review, a number of contingent variables do appear reliably to apply to any number of persons, subjects, and situations. It appears that strong appeals are especially effective when presented by highly credible sources; that the specificity and ease of implementation of recommendations for action increases the effectiveness of fear appeals, regardless of level of fear; and that, in addition to employing strong fear appeals (showing slides of rotted teeth rather than simply describing cavities as harmful), the persuader should also be sure to demonstrate the high likelihood of the unfavorable consequences of inaction (telling children that unless they brush their teeth properly, they are highly likely to get cavities).

From research of this kind, scholars have become better able to understand the dynamics of persuasion and to provide useful advice to persuaders. Still, we cannot apply behavioral research findings the way a cook uses a recipe. You should not only familiarize yourself with the findings, but also attempt to profit from personal experience, and seek other research that may apply more specifically to the particular rhetorical problems you face. It is especially important that you immerse yourself in the details of the situation confronting you, carefully analyzing your own goals, your audience, your subject matter, and the context in which you will be communicating. Behavioral research provides a rough guide to practice, but it is only one means for acquiring rhetorical sophistication—and a limited one at that.

The Generic Approach[2]

In stark contrast to the behavioral approach is the generic approach. Whereas the behavioral researcher attempts under controlled and sometimes artificial conditions to compare the effects of variations in persuasive discourse (e.g., the effects of weak versus strong appeals), the genericist looks at naturally occurring instances of persuasive discourse with a view toward formulating rules for discourse of that type, whether it be a commencement address, a eulogy, a sermon, a jury summation, or a political commercial attacking an opponent. No experiments are run by genericists; indeed, no evidence is necessarily gathered about persuasive effects. Instead, genericists derive generalizations about how to persuade from their own assessments of situational pressures and from evidence of how persuaders in these contexts respond to those pressures. In these respects, their methods are not unlike those used by ordinary people. The generic approach is systematized common sense.

Situational Similarities

A key assumption of the generic approach is that the situations persuaders confront are often quite similar and hence compel and constrain persuaders in similar ways. There are rhetorical requirements for various roles (minister, lawyer, protest leader, parent, student, professor) that derive from the very nature of these roles (Simons, 1970). Being the leader of a protest movement, for example, means having to recruit supporters, to mobilize them for action, to raise funds, to sell to or impose a program of action on outsiders, and to respond to counterpressures from opponents and governmental authorities. Roles such as these largely define rhetorical purposes for the individuals occupying them. And we can often specify roles further for the purpose of pinpointing rhetorical requirements. For example, we may wish to differentiate between the burdens of leading a protest movement seeking to promote radical change from the requirements of leading a moderate protest group seeking reform.

Moreover, particular types of occasions impose their own demands on persuaders. Should a politician be publicly accused of corruption in office, that charge must be refuted or explained away. Should the politician be nominated for high office, he or she is expected to make an acceptance speech. Should the politician lose the nomination, he or she is expected to congratulate the victor and urge supporters not to despair. Should a head of state die in office, the nation's leaders must memorialize him or her appropriately. Bitzer (1968) maintains that events of this kind impel rhetorical responses in much the same way that questions impel answers.

Situations such as these also place limits on what can be said and on how it can be said. There are "thou shalts" and "thou shalt nots" that go with the public memorializing of an American president which, if not inviolable, must

---

[2] This is often referred to as the "genre" approach. There seems to be no satisfactory term to identify the people who do generic scholarship. Often they are referred to as "genre critics" but criticism is only a part of what they do. I have elsewhere coined the term "genre-alist" (Simons, 1978) to designate them, but will use "genericist" here.

ordinarily be honored unless special circumstances permit exceptions. For example, it is permissible, perhaps even mandatory, when memorializing an American president for politicians to make references to God or to the Lord or to the Almighty. But they are generally forbidden by a kind of unwritten contract governing church-state relations to identify publicly with one church or one denomination at the expense of another when calling upon the Almighty for support (Hart, 1977). For various situations there are also predictable rhetorical problems, some of them unique to situations of that type, others much more common. For example, while protest movement leaders share in common with mainstream politicians the problem of having to adapt their messages to widely different audiences, movement leaders tend to have fewer resources at their disposal and less legitimacy.

The point, then, of examining rhetorical situations of a given type is that they tell us a good deal about what is required of persuaders in those situations: about what is obligatory or at least strategically indicated; about what is prohibited and what is permissible; and about characteristic rhetorical problems. The more finely tuned one's comparison—comparing, for example, not just any rhetorical situations for protest movement leaders, but those for leaders with similar organizational roles, in organizations with similar ideologies, confronting similar targets—the more likely one is to generalize reliably about which communication patterns are appropriate for these situations and which are not.

Research on Rhetorical Genres

But of course these assessments of role and occasion are merely speculative; they are "theories," if you will, about types of rhetorical situations. Here is where the study of actual samples of persuasive discourse comes into play. Genericists are fortified in their assessments of situational demands when they discover recurrent patterns of response by persuaders in these situations.

Just what is considered a recurrent pattern of response varies widely from one scholar to another. Some focus on substantive similarities, such as type of argument or form of appeal; others look more closely at stylistic factors, such as similarities in choice of metaphor. Campbell and Jamieson (1978) offer as a somewhat more stringent test of a rhetorical genre that it consist of a recurrent complex of substantive and stylistic features which fit together organically and comprise a unified whole. Concerning the genre of the eulogy, they write that its stylistic features include a shift from present tense to past tense. When a valued member of a community dies, they maintain, "persons must alter their relationship with the deceased and also confront their own mortality." (p. 20) Eulogies are thus "required to reknit the sundered community through rhetorical devices that appeal to the audience to carry on the works, to embody the virtues, or to live as the deceased would have wished." (p. 20)

No one expects, of course, that persuaders will repeat each other verbatim. Genres typically display a dominant pattern reflecting rule requirements and prohibitions, but they also display variations reflecting opportunities to improvise. Although there is no formula for deciding when patterns are sufficiently recurrent to constitute a rhetorical genre, we sense that we have grounds for claiming the existence of a genre when patterns of response become predictable. It is predictable, for example, that the next time a major political figure is charged with violating the oath of office, he or she will admit only what must be admitted, portray himself or herself as a tragic figure who has been victimized by events that were not of his or her own making, remind the audience of the good he or she has done and is likely to do, and cast aspersions on his or her accusers or on others who might profit from his or her fall from grace. These are among the recurrent characteristics of that most studied of all rhetorical genres, the political apologia (Rosenfield, 1968; Ware and Linkugel, 1973).

Although the classification of persuasive discourse goes back at least as far as Aristotle's *Rhetoric*, the systematic comparison of actual samples is relatively recent. Much of what has been labeled generic scholarship has reflected the Greco-Roman heritage in its emphasis upon speechmaking on public affairs. But there is no reason why the same concepts and methods cannot be applied to the full range of rhetorical studies. Indeed, much of the comparative research on such clearly rhetorical objects as magazine advertisements (e.g., Goffman, 1979), ideological tracts (e.g., Rokeach, 1973), and political commercials (Jamieson, 1984) can properly be viewed as generic. I will review some of that research in subsequent chapters.

Generic studies range from those that are relatively anecdotal to those approximating the rigor of the scientific experiment. In his study of the mass media apologia, Rosenfield (1968) looked in great detail at just two cases: the "Checkers" speech of 1952, in which Richard Nixon, running for the vice-presidency, sought to dispel charges that he had improperly used a campaign fund, and an address in 1953 by ex-president Harry S Truman in response to charges that he had allowed a Communist agent to hold high government office. Rosenfield found that both speakers: (1) were quite brief (23 and 30 minutes); (2) employed similar forensic strategies (motives were defended and factual accusations were either denied or justified in terms of higher values); (3) presented counteraccusations in the form of invective and innuendo about the moral qualities of their accusers; (4) offered documented support for claims in only the middle sections of their speeches; (5) disclosed new items of information; (6) but introduced no new arguments beyond those offered in public statements during the previous weeks.

An example of generic scholarship on the scientific end of the continuum is Clark's (1977) study. Clark compared 15 sermons against samplings of campaign orations and other speeches on matters of public concern. Three sections of each speech were fed into a computer for purposes of comparing such things as type of claim, nature of support materials, and stylistic choices. Clark found that among the rhetorical attributes more prevalent in sermons were (1) a sense of certainty, (2) subordination of the speaker to a higher authority, (3) abstractness, (4) "presentism" (dealing with the here and now), and (5) coherent arrangement of materials.

Unlike the companion term *genus* in biology, which stands taxonomically between *class* and *species*, rhetorical genres may be identified at any level of abstraction. As regards the division of speechmaking into forensic, deliberative, and ceremonial, one could classify speechmaking itself as a rhetorical genre, compared, say, with essay writing. Or one could divide each of the three types into subtypes. In his treatise on rhetoric, Aristotle distinguished between lines of argument appropriate to the accuser in the law tribunal and those appropriate to the accused. In the category of defensive forensic rhetoric, one might also place the political apologia. Similarly, alongside the accusatory rhetoric of the courtroom prosecutor, one might place political campaign advertisements that attack opponents. And one need not stop at this level of specificity. For example, Rosenfield (1968) speaks of the mass media apologia as opposed to apologias delivered in face-to-face settings. And the genre of the apologia might be further divided by type of mass medium, or by nature of the accusation, or by defenses under conditions of actual guilt or innocence.

The Generic and Behavioral Approaches Compared

Let us pause at this point to compare the generic and behavioral approaches. Although each is aimed at providing generalizations about how to persuade and explanations for those generalizations, they are really very different. The behavioralist typically does experiments; the genericist studies messages. The behavioralist isolates message variables for purposes of research; the genericist sees how they fit together to make patterns. The genericist looks for similarities in rhetorical patterns among persuaders with similar roles in similar situations. The behavioralist looks for differences in message variables that make a difference in terms of effects on audiences. In a sense, the behavioralist picks up where the genericist leaves off. Whereas the genericist is primarily interested in the actions of persuaders, the behavioralist is primarily interested in the reactions of persuadees.

Finally the genericist is *rules-oriented*, the behavioralist *law-oriented*. Much has been made by communication theorists of the differences between rules and laws, and two recent textbooks on persuasion have featured "rules" perspectives (Reardon, 1981; Smith, 1982). These terms, unfortunately, have not been used with great consistency, so it is important that their usage here be clarified.

"Rules" are guides to persuasive action that persuaders are free to disregard, albeit at some risk. To know the rules is to be aware of what is prohibited, what is permissible, and what is mandated in a given rhetorical situation. It is to know how to adapt to the situation. Experienced persuaders develop largely tacit knowledge of the rules; genericists try to make that knowledge explicit, based on observations of recurrent patterns, in somewhat the same way that linguists attempt to make grammatical rules explicit.

Whereas, according to genericists, rules are what persuaders are guided by, laws are what behavioralists assume make the responses of audiences predictable. Rules emerge from the interactions of people in particular cultures, subcultures, or even small groups; while laws are cross-cultural and largely unchanging, like the law of gravity. Laws of persuasion, if there are any, presumably reflect behavioral regularities that are biologically determined, like a dog's conditioned salivation to the sound of a bell which had been paired with food. Rules can be violated, but laws cannot; they are the essence of what is human about human nature.

Combining the Generic and Behavioral Approaches

The generic and behavioral approaches are, in many respects, complementary. Genericists tell us about the demands of situation and about the collective wisdom of persuaders in situations; behaviorists tell us about audience characteristics and provide us with some indication as to whether the rhetorical strategies of persuaders are actually effective.

A combination of generic and behavioral methods is almost always helpful in planning campaigns. At its workshops for congressional aspirants, the Republican National Committee covers a number of topics, each of which might be considered a rhetorical genre. They include the formal declaration of candidacy, preparing the set speech to partisans, fundraising, generating free publicity, debating opponents, manipulating expectations and interpretations of opinion poll outcomes, press conferences, leaf-leting, and outdoor rallies.

On each of these topics the experts bring to bear the collective wisdom of those who have campaigned for Congress before. On the subject of televised press conferences, for example, the candidates are offered such rules as the following:

1. Talk mainly to the cameras, not to the questioners.
2. Respond briefly to the stickiest questions, contrary to your own natural inclination to dwell at greatest length on these questions.
3. In recognition of the fact that TV news items are typically no longer than 45 seconds in running time, help the stations covering you do their job of editing by preparing a well-rehearsed statement of exactly that length which gives auditors exactly what you want them to hear.

In addition to offering prescriptions based on past practice, the workshop leaders present evidence of actual message effects. For example, there is behavioral research evidence that while political commercials lambasting one's opponent tend to increase name recognition, they also cast the attacker in a negative light and tend to arouse sympathy for the opponent (Jamieson, 1984). This generalization, based largely on evidence from polls taken before and after these commercials have been shown, has helped confirm the judgment of experienced campaigners that attack commercials ought to be used only as a last resort by little-known candidates engaged in uphill electoral battles.

Another example of how the generic and behavioral approaches might be combined was provided by Atkinson (1984) in his study of techniques for eliciting prolonged and intense applause at political rallies. Reliable applause-getters included calls for appreciation displays, "us-them" comparisons, elegantly worded antitheses, and three-part lists (e.g., "Life, liberty, and the pursuit of happiness"). These, he noted, were accompanied by appropriate gestures and inflections. For example, when identifying the first and second parts of a three-part list, the rally speakers would end each phrase or sentence with a rising inflection to suggest that there was more to come, then lower their pitch and increase their volume as they uttered the third and final point.

Atkinson defends his preoccupation with applause-getters at political rallies on several grounds. First, rallies tend to be noisy affairs, with many stimuli competing for the listener's eyes and ears. Frequent and sustained applause provides evidence that the audience is giving close and favorable attention to the speech. Second, such applause is socially contagious, and as it prompts even normally reticent audience members to clap hands, it leads others who are present, including representatives of the media, to conclude that the speech was well received and to form favorable judgments themselves. Third, the media tend to highlight items in the speech that received the greatest applause.

Compare the political rally speech with the television speech, particularly one delivered without benefit of a live audience. Even when a television audience "eavesdrops" on a live presentation, argues Atkinson, the speaker had best adopt a more conversational style, as Ronald Reagan did in delivering what Alistair Cooke described as "the first conversational inaugural" in American history. Said Atkinson:

> For those skilled in the traditional techniques of spellbinding oratory, the advent of mass television coverage is a very mixed blessing. . . . Practices which are visible, audible, and impressive to those sitting in the back row of an auditorium or debating chamber are likely to seem grossly exaggerated, unnatural, and even oppressive when viewed on a small screen from a distance of a few feet. A booming voice, poetic phrases, finely coordinated intonational cadences, and expressive non-verbal actions are unlikely to impress when witnessed at close quarters.

Elsewhere I have argued (Simons, 1978; Simons and Aghazarian, 1986) that the generic approach nicely complements the psychologically oriented behavioral approach by providing a "sociology of rhetorical choice." The generic approach has been particularly useful in rhetorical criticism, for it imposes some semblance of order on a field which, according to political scientist Steven Wasby (1971), had been too long preoccupied with "the idiosyncratic in discourse." The identification of rhetorical regularities provides a departure point for the study of individual messages and invites comparison and contrast between them. It makes somewhat more explicable the choices of individual persuaders and provides benchmarks for evaluating their message output as consistent or inconsistent with the rules for a given genre. The generic approach also provides guidance to persuaders. It suggests in broad outline what rules their experienced predecessors have followed and presumably what rules they ought to follow in responding to similar situational pressures.

As with the behavioral approach, however, the generic approach has limitations. First, in the process of identifying significant similarities, genericists may gloss over significant differences. There is a temptation among genericists to see uniformity where there is only similarity and only similarity where there is difference as well. The most rigorous generic scholarship (e.g., Hart, 1986) generally discovers a range of acceptable strategic options, and not just a single homogeneous pattern. The generic approach can contribute only in broad outline to practice or analysis. Even assuming that the situation you are in (or are analyzing) is unusually constraining, the mix of factors comprising it will nevertheless be unique and will require a unique response. Third, the mere fact of recurrence is not in itself proof that a generic pattern is required or even appropriate in a given type of rhetorical situation. In conflict situations, for example, contending parties frequently scream and shout obscenities when trying to win adherence to their positions, but this does not mean that screaming and cursing are necessarily appropriate. Critics of the generic approach maintain that it chases its proverbial tail in extracting rules about how to persuade from observations of persuaders at work. They are surely correct in suggesting that one ought to have independent bases for deciding that a given pattern is appropriate. Here theoretical explanations for patterns based on independent assessments of situational demands can provide further grounds for using them as prescriptive guides.

SUMMARY

As illustrated by the pioneering experiments of Hovland et al. (1953) on the influence of one-sided messages, behavioral research has added considerably to our understanding by suggesting nontrivial, contingent generalizations. The accumulated findings from repeated studies of a given independent variable tend to be particularly reliable, but they need to be interpreted critically and applied judiciously. Persuaders may also use behavioral methods in applied research on how best to secure *their* ends with *their* audiences. It is possible, for example, to test-market political campaign advertisements in bellwether cities before airing them nationwide.

Moreover, research findings, like those on message sidedness and fear appeals, can become grist for the development of interesting new theories. McGuire's two-factor theory, with its compensatory assumption and its situational weighting assumption, provides vivid illustration of how theory can help order and explain what we already know about a phenomenon while suggesting interesting new hypotheses which, when tested, are confirmed by research.

The generic approach also involves a search for generalizations about how to persuade, but it relies on naturalistic study of how experienced communicators have responded to similar situational pressures. There are virtually no limits on the ways persuasive discourse may be classified generically, and, indeed, this book will offer commentary on a wide variety of generic types, from patterns of textbook rhetoric to patterns of response to situations in which a prospective employer sits across from you at lunch with a piece of fish perched precariously on his chin. In most cases, I will be assuming that the past experiences of presumably competent others can serve as a reliable guide to future practice and analysis, but we need also at times to violate generic rules. On this point, I am reminded of the enthusiasm with which the public relations staff of a large oil company talked about their new boss. "Our old boss," one said, "would ask us if what we proposed had been tried elsewhere in the industry. If it hadn't he'd tell us not to act on it. Our new boss does just the opposite. His rule is that we can only be better than the others if we're different from the others."

EXERCISE

Ask 10 respondents to characterize oranges and grapefruits by requiring each of them to decide which citrus fruit is (a) sunnier, (b) younger, (c) faster, (d) friendlier, (e) warmer (as opposed to cooler), (f) more intimate, (g) more intellectual, and (h) more like the respondent. If this is done as a class exercise, pool the findings and summarize proportions of O (for orange) and G (for grapefruit) ratings per each adjective. Try to account for the findings. Also, speculate on how, as an advertiser of either oranges or grapefruits, you might make use of the findings. (*Note:* this exercise is discussed at length in Chapter 4.)

Answers to True-False Exercise from Chapter 2

1. *False*. On the whole, fear appeals are probably not as effective as guilt appeals ("Think of your children the next time you smoke"). However, moderate to strong fear appeals are probably better at getting people to stop smoking than mild fear appeals.
2. *?*. The success of a both-sides approach generally depends on whether the audience is reasonably educated, is initially undecided or in disagreement, or is likely to be exposed to counterarguments. Also note that the statement speaks of offering a conclusion only after the two sides have been presented. This approach tends to work well with reasonably intelligent auditors; those who are less intelligent may lose interest or miss your point entirely. The approach is sometimes risked with sharply critical or hostile audiences.
3. *False*. As we will show in Chapter 7, testimonials should ordinarily feature persons perceived as "superrepresentatives" of their audiences.
4. *False*. Dissonance theory (discussed in Chapter 4) predicts that the least payment necessary to induce counterattitudinal advocacy produces self-persuasion, and its hypotheses on this matter have been confirmed more often than a contending approach called incentive theory.
5. *True*. For reasons suggested in this chapter.
6. *False*. Especially if your opponent is a prominent opinion leader like a news columnist. But this is a rule for the apologia that has been successfully broken many times.
7. *False*. The hooker is in the words "throughout your speech." It suggests a mechanical eye-gaze pattern that is likely to be a turnoff. Dropping your gaze at times is likely to seem more natural.
8. *False*. Just the opposite, generally.
9. *?*. The problem is in distinguishing the two. Both are needed.
10. *False*.

RECOMMENDED ADVANCED READINGS*

A. Behavioral Approach

1. Ajzen, I., and Fishbein, M. (1980). *Understanding Attitudes and Predicting Social Behavior*. A lucid presentation of their widely used approach to theory, measurement, and research. Includes examples of applications to family planning, health, consumer behavior, and politics.
2. Cialdini, R. B. (1984). *Influence: How and Why People Do Things*. A highly readable treatment of major techniques of influencing others. Based on a combination of behavioral research and anecdotal reports by experienced practitioners.
3. Eagly, A. H., and Himmelfarb, S., eds. (1974). *Readings in Attitude Change*. A large and impressive collection of research studies and theoretical syntheses.
4. Gergen, J. K. (1982). *Toward Transformation in Social Knowledge*. The best critique I've seen of the behavioral approach. Gergen is a major social psychologist who has come to embrace a rhetorical perspective on the nature and functions of social science.
5. Miller, G. R., Burgoon, M., and Burgoon, J. K. (1984). *The Functions of Human Communication in Changing Attitudes and Gaining Compliance*. Reviews and commentaries on the behavioral research literature by three of the best "behavioralists" in the field.
6. Pentony, P. (1981). *Models of Influence on Psychotherapy*. An ingenious application of cybernetic and general systems theories to the subject of social influence, with particular reference to psychotherapy. Includes a powerful critique of more traditional theories of influence in social psychology.
7. Petty, R. E., and Cacioppo, J. T. (1981). *Attitudes and Persuasion: Classic and Contemporary Approaches*. See in particular their own very interesting theory and research.
8. Roloff, M. E., and Miller, G. R., eds. (1980). *Persuasion: New Directions in Theory and Research*. An anthology of original essays on a wide range of subjects, from power in the family to persuasion in jury trials.
9. Smith, M. J. (1982). *Persuasion and Human Action*. A comprehensive synthesis of behavioral theory and research, filtered through Smith's rules-oriented, information-processing perspective.
10. Zimbardo, P. G., Ebbesen, E. B., and Maslach, C. (1977). *Influencing Attitudes and Changing Behavior*. A bit weathered by age, but still a useful and highly readable text on the subject.

B. Generic Approach

1. Atkinson, M. (1984). *Our Masters' Voices: The Language and Body Language of Politics*. Microanalytic studies of speechmaking yielding generalizations about applause-getters and why they are so important in politics.
2. Bailey, F. G. (1983). *The Tactical Uses of Passion: An Essay on Power, Reason, and Reality*. An exploration of unconscious and semi-conscious codes underlying displays of emotion in rhetorical situations. Focused on image management.
3. Black, E. (1965). *Rhetorical Criticism: A Study in Method*. A pioneering effort at bringing "genre-alizations" to bear upon criticism of speechmaking.
4. Burke, K. (1966). *Language as Symbolic Action*. The first several essays in this book are about as good an entree as any into the ideas of this difficult but richly rewarding

*See Reference section for full citations.

writer. Burke is not a genre theorist per se, but his writings have greatly influenced the contemporary development of that approach.

5. Campbell, K. K., and Jamieson, K. H., eds. (1978). *Form and Genre: Shaping Rhetorical Action.* A major collection of original essays, including a lead essay by the editors that has been highly influential.

6. Goffman, E. (1981). *Forms of Talk.* All Goffman's books cited in the Reference section are useful. In *Forms of Talk,* see in particular his "lecture-on-the-lecture."

7. Hart, R. (1984). *Verbal Style and the Presidency: A Computer-Based Analysis.* An excellent demonstration of what can be done in the way of generic scholarship with a computerized dictionary *and* a probing intellect.

8. Jamieson, K. H. (1984). *Packaging the Presidency.* A comprehensive historical treatment of a major rhetorical genre, the political pitch.

9. Medhurst, M. J., and Benson, T. W. (1984). *Rhetorical Studies in a Media Age.* Critical case studies of mass media "rhetorics" and an excellent bibliography.

10. Simons, H. W., and Aghazarian, A. A., eds. (1986). *Politically Speaking: Forms and Genres of Political Discourse.* A collection of original essays, including a more developed treatment of the rules-oriented perspective presented in this chapter.

Chapter 4
Behavioral Theories of Attitude Change

In the study of persuasion there is no question more central than that of how to induce changes in attitudes. Attitudes, you will recall, are directly tied to beliefs and values and are also directly related to how we act. They are thus of great theoretical interest. Influencing behavior by changing attitudes, rather than relying exclusively on bribes or threats, also has obvious practical value in that it generally is less expensive and longer lasting, and is by most accounts more ethical. But changing attitudes is also apt to be difficult—far more difficult in most cases than strengthening existing attitudes. The study of attitude change provides a useful introduction to behavioral theories of persuasion. And the basic principles to be gleaned from these theories provide a framework for the co-active approach to persuasion prescribed in Part II.

Whether in sales, politics, or psychotherapy, there are essentially two routes to attitude change. The first is to alter the belief or value premises on which the attitude is based through various communication inputs. This has been by far the dominant focus of behavioral theories of persuasion and will be the focus of this chapter. The second is to place individuals in situations where, as a result of changes in behavior, they are likely on their own to question the premises on which their attitudes were based, and thus to engage in what is sometimes called self-persuasion (Cialdini, 1984; Smith, 1982). We will focus on Festinger's accounts of this phenomenon later in the chapter.

Attitudes as Conditioned Responses

The acquisition and modification of attitudes may be viewed as forms of learning. Virtually all theorists share McGuire's (1968) view, noted in Chapter

3, that persuasive messages must be learned in the sense of being attended to and comprehended before they are favorably evaluated. And while not all agree with McGuire's theorem that those characteristics of people which are positively related to reception of a message are negatively related to yielding, the notion of a decoding or reception stage during which the message is initially processed enjoys widespread support. Disagreements arise, however, over how messages are evaluated—over how "yielding" occurs.

Among the learning theories that are applicable to persuasion, several hold that attitudinal responses may be classically conditioned (Staats and Staats, 1963). Just as a caged rat in a laboratory may learn to avoid some stimuli and approach others, so may a human being learn that Communist China is "bad" and Nationalist China is "good." And just as rats may modify their behavior as a result of the experimenter's "messages," so many humans modify their attitudinal responses toward the two Chinas on the basis of persuasive communications. The key to the conditioning of both rats and humans, say the conditioning theorists, is *linkage* or *conjunction*—pairing the previously neutral stimulus with stimuli known to evoke favorable or unfavorable reactions. As regards The People's Republic of China, whereas our government used to cast the Communist government in a negative light, it later began linking it rather consistently with admired qualities. Conditioning theorists have developed principles governing the acquisition of responses to new stimuli, their transfer to new situations, their extinction, and so on. Theoretically, at least, these same principles should be applicable to persuasion.

What kinds of linkages or associations can the persuader exploit in seeking to promote an idea or image? The exercise on oranges and grapefruit at the conclusion of Chapter 3 suggests some possibilities. In your survey, you probably found that oranges were more often judged sunnier, faster, friendlier, and more intimate than grapefruit, while grapefruit was regarded as older and more intellectual. No doubt part of the reason for these associations is advertising itself. We have been bombarded with advertisements linking Florida oranges with the sun—to the point where little children now tend to color it orange rather than yellow. Here the product is linked to its surroundings.

The orange-sun-Florida connection helps to explain perceptions of the orange as sunnier than the grapefruit, although in point of fact grapefruit is also grown under the Florida sun. But these ads also play on earlier associations. If we regard oranges as younger, it is perhaps because children prefer them to grapefruit for their sweetness. If we regard grapefruit as the more intelligent citrus fruit, it is perhaps because we have been culturally conditioned to see age and intellect as going together.

Because associations trigger other associations, the sequencing of adjective pairs becomes important. For example, grapefruit is more often shared than oranges, yet respondents are more likely to regard oranges as more intimate. Perhaps this would not be the case had they not first listed them as friendlier. But what of the "warm-cool" dimension? If your respondents are like those studied by motivation researcher Ernest Dichter (1960), chances are that they divided on this variable, giving nearly the same number of "cooler" ratings to

Orange vs. Grapefruit theories: oranges are associated with happiness, youth, etc.
(Courtesy of the Food Service Department, Foote, Cone & Belding/San Francisco. Creative Director: Rich Vitaliano. Art Director: Linda Laing. Writer: Joel Fugazzotto.)

oranges as to grapefruit. This, it turns out, is an extremely ambiguous dimension; warm and cool each evoke both positive and negative associations in our culture. The findings on this variable serve as a warning of sorts to take care in the selection of images with which to link a product or proposal, lest they evoke unanticipated and unwanted associations.

While humans with complex conditioning histories are no doubt more difficult to "train" than naive rats, the central claim of classical conditioning theories remains that all of us are likely to approach some objects and avoid others not on the basis of their innate qualities, but as a result of nonlogical, tangentially relevant associations, and perhaps even arbitrary or accidental ones.

An interesting case with which to compare classical conditioning theories of persuasion against other theories is the phenomenon of *prestige suggestion*. This is alleged to occur when a prestige source such as a sports hero is favorably linked to a product or proposal. According to classical conditioning theory, attitude modification resulting from prestige suggestions can occur automatically, without critical or even conscious thought. Pavlov's dog, you will remember, was classically conditioned to salivate at the sound of a bell after the bell was linked to the presence of meat powder. In the same way, a listener might be conditioned by way of a product endorsement to respond more favorably to the product. The already favorable source can be seen as akin to the meat powder, the more neutral product akin to the bell.

Readers familiar with conditioning theories might wish, for comparison's sake, to contrast the classical conditioning model, applied to prestige suggestions, with the *operant* or *instrumental* conditioning model presented by B. F. Skinner. In the latter case, the persuadee might first be asked his or her opinion of the advertised product. If the response was favorable, it could be strengthened by *positive reinforcers* such as "good" or a friendly nod of the head by the prestige source. If it was unfavorable, the source could scowl or withdraw affection (forms of punishment), apply irritants or other aversive stimuli to the persuadee until the persuadee reversed his or her position (known as *negative reinforcement*), or reinforce successive approximations of the ultimately desired response until the response itself was forthcoming *(shaping)*. The paradigm suggests the importance of engaging persuadees in dialogue rather than simply communicating at listeners, as in the typical platform speech. It also underscores the importance of offering persuadees incentives, either in the form of direct rewards or escape from punishment. Here is an example of a conversation at a supermarket in which a salesperson combines these techniques:

SALESPERSON   (S):   Sir, how would you like to try a sample of our newest imported cheese? It's called Saga Blue.

CUSTOMER   (C):   Well, I'm not sure. I'm not much of a cheese eater.

S: *(Noncommittally)* Oh? How's that?

C: Well, you see I do like some cheese, but—

S: Mhm! *(Enthusiastically)*

C: But I don't like the presliced stuff and I don't enjoy slicing it myself either.

S: (*Laughing*) Great! This is a spread. Do you like blue cheese dressing on your salad?

C: Yes, I do.

S: (*Nods vigorously*) Well Saga Blue combines blue cheese and brie. It's delicious!

C: Sounds good, but—

S: Here, try some on this cracker. It won't cost you a penny.

C: Ummm, good! I'll take a small slice.

S: Half a pound okay?

C: Well, all right.

Both classical and Skinnerian conditioning theories tend deliberately to make as few inferences as possible about what goes on inside the person or other organism on being presented with a stimulus. They are in this sense S-R (stimului-response) theories as opposed to S-O-R (stimulus-organism-response) theories (Smith, 1982). Whereas S-R theories attempt to predict behavior strictly from a knowledge of observable stimuli and responses, S-O-R theorists find it necessary to hypothesize the existence of "mediating" forces within the organism, directly linkable to external stimuli and responses, which help to predict behavior. S-R conditioning theories are relatively simple, but that is also a limitation. If S-R accounts seem unsatisfactory, it may be because they say nothing about the internal state of the receiver at the time he or she is persuaded. What prompts the receiver to listen to the commercial in the first place? Why does he or she want the product at all, let alone the brand being advertised? And how did some stimuli come to serve as reinforcers, but not others? What, in short, are the motivational bases for the message recipient's behavior?

One alternative for conditioning theorists has been to posit some internal state of motivation, directly linkable to stimulus and response, that must be triggered in order for persuasion to take place (see Hovland, Janis, and Kelley, 1953). The motivational state is generally described as painful or unpleasant; it "drives" the organism to seek relief from the discomfort. Biological drives such as hunger and thirst are said to be primary and quite powerful. Others, such as curiosity, social approval, and acquisition, are believed by some learning theorists to be secondary or acquired drives, learned by association with primary drives. Why might viewers want a given product, such as tea or ginger ale? Because their thirst drive has been activated? Why might they want Lipton's or Canada Dry in particular? Perhaps because they are driven to seek the approval of the source who has been linked to the brand name.

Unfortunately for the conditioning theorists, the notion of persuadees as driven has come under sharp attack. Research on what White (1959) calls *competence motivation* suggests that people and even some lower-order animals are as often motivated by desire or interest as by need or pain. According to White, competence motives include desires to explore, to be active, to master problems, and to satisfy curiosities. Human beings and other animals evidently engage in competence-increasing activities not simply to gain food or shelter or to reduce anxiety or pain, but often in spite of these needs. White's impressive summary of research includes evidence of apes that try to solve complex problems simply to be able to look out of a window; of rats that choose the longer of two otherwise equivalent paths to food; of children who, within limits, prefer novelty to familiarity; and of animals that endure electric shock simply to be able to explore a new environment. The point of White's evidence, so far as this discussion is concerned, is not that associations or reinforcements or even drives are unimportant in persuasion, but that accounts of attitude change that rely on them alone are surely inadequate. In a typical public speaking situation, for example, the speaker has little opportunity to reward or punish directly. What he or she *is* able to do is influence the audience's expectations of the benefits likely to be accrued from acting on his or her recommendations.

But this depends upon cognitive processes that tend to be ignored or minimized by conditioning theorists. Most critics of S-R conditioning theories as well as of the trigger-action S-O-R drive theories would probably endorse the following assumptions by Bandura (1977) about the relation between cognition and motivation in decision-making: (1) Humans reciprocally act on and are acted upon by their environments. They are neither "driven by inner forces nor buffeted helplessly by environmental influences." (2) By dint of our symbol-using capacities, we are capable of insights that are not under the control of external rewards and punishments. In particular, we can foresee the probable consequences of different actions and alter our behavior accordingly. (3) We are capable of self-regulative influences. We can reward ourselves or withhold rewards from ourselves, depending upon whether we have reached our goals.

Attitudes as Perceptual Categories

Whereas conditioning theorists tend to focus on internal inputs and outputs, other theorists are primarily concerned with the world of inner experience, the way the world looks to the individual doing the perceiving. To cognitively oriented theorists such as Smith (1982) and Reardon (1981), decoding is a highly active and selective process, based as much on values and expectations as on environmental inputs. Even the listener seated in a large auditorium is viewed as an active message processor, forever seeking to give meaning to his or her experience.

From this vantage point, moreover, decoding is not entirely separable from evaluation; the distinction is at best a useful oversimplication. In the work of Watzlawick, Weakland, and Fisch (1974) and of Schön (1979) (discussed in Chapter 9), the distinction collapses entirely. How we expose ourselves to messages, how we attend to them, perceive them, and remember them has a great deal to do with how we evaluate them. Attitudes are not so much behavioral responses as they are evaluatively laden frames of reference that may predispose us toward behavioral responses. Persuasion is viewed as a way of reordering these perceptual categories for the message recipients—for example, by suggesting other ways of labeling their experiences than those they have been accustomed to.

Far from picturing prestige suggestion as an automatic conditioning process, cognitively oriented theorists such as Soloman Asch (1952) have held that some linkages between prestige sources and the positions they advance are not at all persuasive; moreover, those that do have an impact are persuasive precisely because they lead receivers to restructure their perceptions of the attitude object. Thomas Jefferson's plea for "revolution every twenty years" would have quite another meaning to a receiver if the utterance were attributed to Karl Marx.

In his comments on prestige suggestion, Asch has anticipated the flavor of two related variants of perception theory: attribution theory (Kelley, 1971) and self-perception theory (Bem, 1965). *Attribution* theory is concerned with how an observer assigns causation to the actions of another. According to the attribution theorists, all of us function as amateur psychologists when confronted with this routine task. On the basis of whatever limited information we have at our disposal, we attempt to make reasonable inferences about the intentions, motivations, and abilities of others, and we use these inferences to evaluate them and to decide on actions based on what they have said or done.

Chief among the questions we ask ourselves is whether the other's actions are internally or externally caused. In the case of a message by a prestige source, for example (or a message about a prestige source by an experimenter), we are more likely to discount the message as untrustworthy if we perceive it to be dictated by such external factors as social pressure, status or power deprivation, or opportunity for personal gain (Smith, 1982).

The important lesson of attribution theory, for our purposes, is that knowledge of how audiences typically assign causation or motivation to others can help us to persuade them. Attribution theory instructs us, for example, to employ ingratiation techniques sparingly, so that we do not give the impression of pleasing others for the sake of personal gain (Jones, Gergen, and Jones, 1963).

Whereas attribution theory is concerned with explaining the behavior of others, *self-perception* theory is concerned with how we explain our own behavior, and with how these self-perceptions influence our subsequent decisions and actions. Bem (1965) maintains that the same attributional processes used to interpret the behaviors of others are also used to interpret our own behavior.

Particularly in situations perceived to be relatively free of external constraints, we examine our behavior to "discover" our attitudes. (Did I say that? I must have meant it! Did I do that? I guess I must be that kind of person.)

Once having decided what kinds of people we are, we use this information to guide subsequent decisions and actions. Suppose, for example, that you are coaxed into giving a small donation to a charity that has only your lukewarm support. Chances are, according to self-perception theory, that you will come to think more highly of the charity, but not until *after* you have made the donation. By then you will have inferred your attitude from your behavior. And you might even be susceptible to the more general interpretation that you are a charitable type of person, and hence become predisposed to give to other charities as well.

Just such a label evidently proved quite successful in a New Haven, Connecticut, study where, according to Cialdini (1984), housewives gave much more money to a canvasser for the Multiple Sclerosis Association after hearing that they were considered "charitable people." Encouraging people to make behavioral commitments to a cause—getting them to write down their ideas and not just think them, for example—is a principle much used by professional persuaders. Cialdini (1984) reports that the enormously successful Amway Corporation spurs its sales personnel on to greater accomplishment by encouraging them to set individual sales goals and then commit themselves to these goals in writing. Similarly, high-pressure door-to-door sales representatives often encourage their customers to complete the sales agreement in their own writing as a way of discouraging them from backing out of the contracts once the deal has been agreed to. Cialdini reported on another research finding, that horse bettors were much more confident of their horse's chances of winning after they had placed their bets than before betting. While there are many possible explanations for these findings (including those provided by dissonance theorists), there seems to be no doubt at this point that we often infer our beliefs, values, and attitudes from a retrospective look at what we have said or done. The observation is an important one, since common sense tells us that the reverse process is by far the more typical one—deciding what to say or do on the basis of our attitudes. Self-perception theorists have provided impressive evidence that we are frequently unaware of why we have acted until we have, and then we lean on external cues to infer inner states (Smith, 1982).

Reason versus Unreason in Persuasion

From the theories examined thus far in this chapter, it would be possible to conclude that persuasion is not a terribly rational process. Our discussion of classical conditioning theories underscored the importance of linkages in persuasion, but not necessarily rational connections. Rather, we saw how attitudes toward oranges and grapefruit might be formed from accidental, arbitrary, logically irrelevant associations. Not much more rational is the picture of persuasion painted by Skinnerian conditioning theorists, with their emphasis on humans as highly malleable animals whose attitudes can be shaped in a manner akin to rats in a psychological laboratory. In the discussion of self-perception theory, we saw how attitudes may be inferred from behaviors through processes more akin to rationalization than to reason.

There are yet other "irrationalist" accounts of persuasion, some of them emphasizing unconscious, often *subliminal* (below the level of awareness), processes (see Key, 1974; Dichter, 1960), others stressing the importance of emotion or blind faith (see Bailey, 1983; Fish, 1973). And yet others characterize persuasion as involving "click-whirr" responses akin to triggered "fixed-form" responses in lower-order animals (Cialdini, 1984; Conway and Siegelman, 1978). Cialdini, for example, likens the power of persuasive techniques such as prestige suggestion to the power newborn turkey chicks have of eliciting preprogrammed responses from their mothers. So automatic is the mother's response that when a stuffed replica of its mortal enemy, the polecat, is fitted out with a small taperecorder playing the "cheep-cheep" sound of turkey chicks, the mother turkey will gather the polecat under her rather than attack it.

Cialdini says that humans too have preprogrammed tapes, and although they usually work for us, "the trigger features that activate them can be used to dupe us into playing them at the wrong times" (p. 18). One of these triggers, says Cialdini, is the giving of reasons—not necessarily *good* reasons, just *any* reasons. A dramatic example that he cites in support of his claim involved an experiment by psychologist Ellen Langer comparing ways of requesting permission to skip ahead of people waiting in line to use a library copying machine. In one version of the experiment, the request took the form: "Excuse me, I have five pages. May I use the Xerox machine?" To this request, in the second version of the experiment, was added a reason: "because I'm in a rush." Not surprisingly, compliance to the request-plus-reason jumped from 60 percent to 94 percent. More impressive are results of a third experimental variation in which all Langer added to the request were the words: "because I have to make some copies." The results matched the success rate of "because I'm in a rush." Nearly everyone complied, even though no real reason, no new information, was added to justify the request. Said Cialdini:

> Just as the "cheep-cheep" sound of turkey chicks triggered an automatic mothering response from maternal turkeys, even when it emanated from a stuffed polecat, so the word "because" triggered an automatic compliance response from Langer's subjects, even when they were given no subsequent reason to comply. Click, whirr!

Attitudes as Products of Beliefs and Values

A good deal more will be said about reason versus unreason before we are through, but enough has already been said to suggest that not all human decisions and actions are rationally based. Still, this does not mean that all of our responses are of the "click-whirr" variety either. We have seen that conditioning theories could not contend very well with perceptual and cognitive processes or with the whys and wherefores of human motivation. Even Cialdini acknowledges that we do not always run our lives on automatic pilot; that we are able to say "No!" to persuaders. We are indeed capable of being enlightened about techniques of persuasion and, in consequence, to become more critical, more discriminating message consumers (Gergen, 1982). Moreover, there is evidence to suggest that we do indeed operate reasonably in bringing beliefs and values to bear upon attitudes, and this brings us directly to the next theory to be reviewed.

Recall that in Chapter 2, I characterized an *attitude* toward a given object (e.g., a new car, a political candidate, a proposed policy) as a combination of an individual's *beliefs* about whether the object possesses certain attributes (e.g., speed, comfort, fuel economy, etc., for a car), and the *value weightings* the person assigns to those attributes.

This notion of attitudes as a combination of cognitive and evaluative components is Fishbein and Ajzen's (Fishbein and Ajzen, 1975; Ajzen and Fishbein, 1980), and it is one of many features that has commended their *theory of reasoned action* to political consultants, market researchers, and others engaged in the business of mass persuasion. With considerable justification, the authors argue that indications of each component are helpful in measures of attitude and in preparation for persuasion. They fault experiments and survey researchers who so often rely on one alone (Fishbein and Ajzen, 1975, Chap. 3).

Suppose, for example, that you had sought to determine attitudes toward grapefruit from evidence that people believed them to be sour, large, old, and dull-colored. On this basis, you might conclude that people look more favorably on the sweet, small, youthful, bright-colored orange. That is probably the case for most people. But surely there is a grapefruit market of people who believe the citrus fruit possesses these attributes, and who are also not at all unhappy that it does. In formulating an ad campaign, in any event, it would help to know people's attribute evaluations and not just their beliefs.

Suppose, on the other hand, that you attempted to measure evaluations of grapfruit directly—for example, by asking people to rate them on a bipolar scale from likable to unlikable. Fishbein and Ajzen argue that traits such as likability have evaluative implications in reference to some concepts but not others, and are thus not always valid indicators of attitudes toward objects. They add that, in any case, the use of evaluative measures alone does not tell persuaders very much about where to direct their attacks. With knowledge of the beliefs supporting an attitude, the relative "true-false" probabilities assigned to those beliefs, and the value weightings assigned to the perceived attributes of an object, persuaders have a formidable array of information indeed. In seeking to change an attitude, they can suggest new beliefs ("Grapefruit is the thinking person's citrus fruit.") or suggest reasons to modify belief probability estimates ("Grapefruit only looks old; it is young on the inside.") or alter attribute evaluations ("Large is more; more is better."). Before pushing ahead, however, they must know which beliefs are relevant to the change target's attitude, and especially which beliefs directly support that attitude. All too often, say the theorists, persuaders focus on beliefs *they* think are important while ignoring the audience's most salient beliefs.

Attitude Change as Unbalancing and Rebalancing

The assumption that we seek a psychologically consistent view of the world, first articulated by perception theorists, serves as the major premise for a number of *balance* theories, some referred to by that name (Heider, 1958; Cartwright and Harary, 1956), others referred to variously as *consistency* theories (Abelson and Rosenberg, 1958), or *dissonance* theories (Festinger, 1957; Brehm and Cohen, 1962). Like S-R learning theorists, some balance theorists (Osgood and Tannenbaum, 1955) maintain that reactions to communications are automatic and predictable. For most balance theorists, in fact, the need for psychological consistency is a basic drive, although Festinger and others would not agree that the drive is automatic or that the response to a message is entirely predictable.

All balance theories hold at least three premises in common: (1) That psychological imbalance (i.e., dissonance, incongruity, etc.) is unpleasant or uncomfortable; (2) that we are therefore driven to reduce or eliminate the imbalance; and (3) that one way we can "rebalance," or at least reduce imbalance, is by modifying our attitudes in the directions intended by a communicator.

Intuitively, we can grasp the concepts of balance and imbalance through examples from our own experience. For the most part, our inner world is balanced or consistent. If we are registered as Democrats, we generally vote for Democratic candidates. If we call ourselves conservative, we generally support programs that reflect a conservative position. If we have recently purchased a new Ford, we generally do not tell our friends that it is better to buy a Chevrolet. If we respect another person's judgments, it is generally because those judgments correspond with ours.

In some respects, however, we are likely to experience psychological inconsistencies. Some imbalances are qualitative, while others are a matter of degree. An esteemed friend may hate a movie that we loved, or like it but not nearly as much as we did. We may despise city life and find ourselves living in the city, or we simply prefer the country to the city and still find ourselves living in the city.

Broadly speaking, we may identify three types of discrepancy, each serving as a different source of psychological imbalance.

1. *Source-proposition discrepancies* are of the kind generated by prestige suggestions, or by the pressures exerted on a deviant group member by other members of the group, or by knowledge that a cognition we hold is discrepant from even so vague a reference group as "the academic community."

2. *Attitude component discrepancies* are inconsistencies between any two attitudes and/or the beliefs and values that bear upon them. If we regard ourselves as liberals, it is cognitively consonant to promote the reelection of an incumbent governor on grounds that he has run a liberal administration. Should we become convinced, however, that our beliefs about his past record are ill-founded or that we err in valuing liberal administrations, a state of cognitive dissonance would probably now exist.

3. *Behavior-attitude discrepancies* are typified by the worker who hates his boss but whose job requires that he be nice to him. Or by the individual who purchases one product but still recalls many advantages of a competing product. Or by the individual who knows that she smokes and also that smoking is bad for her health.

Thus far, I have stressed similarities among balance theories. Now let us examine two quite different formulations, Osgood and Tannenbaum's congruity theory and Festinger's dissonance theory.

Congruity Theory

Congruity theory takes source-proposition discrepancies as its special province. Let us imagine that a highly admired source such as Bill Cosby tells us that he likes Jello. Like the S-R conditioning theorists, Osgood and Tannenbaum would treat this as a relatively predictable instance of prestige suggestion. Unlike most S-R theorists, however, they would foresee changes in our evaluations of Cosby as well as the proposition he advocated.

The congruity model is not confined to cases of prestige suggestion. It is designed to handle all cases, in fact, in which a source (S) and a concept (C) are linked positively (p) or negatively (n) by an evaluative assertion. A unique feature of their theory is its attempt to quantify the predicted effects of incongruity.

The first step in quantifying predictions is to determine whether an assertion is positive (e.g., S likes C) or negative (e.g., S is opposed to C) and to assess receiver evaluations of S and C. To secure these evaluations, Osgood and Tannenbaum utilize a series of scales similar to the one represented below:

Bill Cosby   Bad -3 -2 -1 -0 $+1$ $+2$ $+3$ Good

Suppose we initially regard Bill Cosby as a $+2$ and Jello as a -1. The theory predicts that, having heard Cosby applaud the dessert, we would experience incongruity. It further specifies that our evaluations of both will move to a balanced or congruous position, but not in equal amounts.[1]

There are, of course, many possible combinations of evaluative assertions linking a source and a concept. In order to provide a sense of the predictions

---

[1] Technically speaking, the movement toward congruity of S and C will be in inverse relation to their respective degrees of polarity. What this means is that Cosby, a $+2$ (the ultimate in polarization is 3, whether $+$ or $-$), will move less toward the middle than Jello, a -1. By means of the following formula, the theory predicts that Cosby (S) will go down in value, but we will have become converts to Jello (C); specifically, that S and C will balance at a $+1$ position.

$$\text{Formula: change for C} = \frac{/S/}{/C/ + /S/} P \qquad \text{change for S} = \frac{/C/}{/C/ + /S/} P$$

Where /S/ and /C/ = the absolute degree of polarization of the evaluator's attitude toward S and C, respectively (in this case /S/ = 2 and /C/ = -1); and where P = the algebraic difference in evaluations of S and C for positive statements and, for negative statements, the amount of change necessary for the evaluator's attitude toward the source to be equidistant from zero. (In this case P = 3. Had Cosby said that he hated Jello, P would have equaled 1, S would have moved ⅓ to $+1.67$, and C would have moved ⅔ to -1.67.)

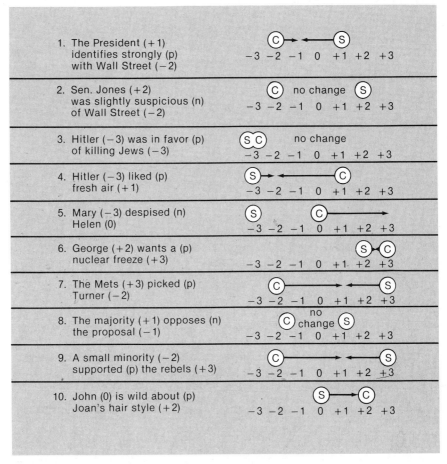

Figure 4.1 Some predictions of congruity between source (S) and concept (C) for a hypothetical receiver reacting to a series of hypothetical assertions.

made by the theory, Figure 4.1 presents illustrations of predicted congruity outcomes for a hypothetical receiver reacting to a series of hypothetical assertions.[2]

We can find much to criticize in the congruity theory. In looking at examples, it is not always possible to identify who the source is or what the

---

[2] The predictions are not identical to those which Osgood and Tannenbaum would make since the theorists have added two correction factors to their model that are somewhat beyond this discussion. These correction factors include a "correction for incredulity" (when an assertion is so incongruous that it is not believable) and an "assertion constant" (an empirically derived correction of $\times \pm .17$ that is subtracted from the amount that the source moves in the original formula and added to the amount that the concept moves). Basically, the predictions are as I have given them. Note that some relationships between psychological elements are balanced from the start. Note, too, that the theory allows for imbalances of degree and not just of kind. Note, finally, that for positive statements, balance occurs at the same point for S and C whereas, for negative statements, balance occurs at points equidistant from zero.

concept is or whether an assertion is positive, negative, or neutral. When the president of the United States toasts the Russian ambassador at a formal dinner, is either the source or the concept the man, his office, or the country he represents? Is the toast a neutral assertion because of its formality, or is it a genuinely positive assertion? Still other problems stem from the fact that the theory makes no provision for differences in the intensity of a positive or negative assertion. Independent of whether Cosby loved Jello or merely liked it, the same prediction would be made by the theory. Another problem is that the theory offers only three ways of balancing psychological elements: by reevaluating the source, the concept, or both. We will see that there are probably many other ways. Finally, some examples make the theory appear ludicrous. Take the assertion "Horses like to eat oats." I might personally rate horses as $+2$ and oats as -2, but my belief that horses like oats causes me no special fits of discomfort, certainly no automatic urge to eat oats for dinner. The problem here is that the theory makes no provision for differences in the relevance of an assertion to a receiver.

Despite the many valid criticisms that can be leveled at the theory, the general directions of change it predicts (as opposed to its specific quantified predictions) have been confirmed by research. Another virtue of the theory is its relative clarity. Moreover, some predictions are not at all obvious, as when it is estimated that a person we admire moderately (a $+2$) can pull a hero of ours (a $+3$) down simply by saying something positive about him.

Cognitive Dissonance Theory

In sharp contrast to the congruity model is Festinger's (1957, 1964) theory of cognitive dissonance. Whereas Osgood and Tannenbaum offer specific, quantified predictions, Festinger's theory is only loosely predictive. Whereas in Osgood and Tannenbaum's theory, rebalancing is automatic, in Festinger's theory it is not. In general, the congruity model has more in common with mechanistic, S-R learning theories, whereas Festinger's approach has more in common with the cognitive S-O-R theories.

According to Festinger, any two cognitions or clusters of cognitions (the term *cognition* is used loosely to include any item of organized experience) may be mutually dissonant, mutually consonant, or mutually irrelevant. More realistically, as Kiesler, Collins, and Miller (1969) have observed, there are not just two cognitions in most cases, but two clusters of cognitions. We associate many factors with smoking (lighting of matches, movement of arms, ingestion of nicotine, etc.) and many other factors with health (keeping trim, physically relaxed, free from disease, etc.). Some smoking factors are irrelevant to some health factors, some are compatible, and some are incompatible. What Festinger really means by a dissonant relationship in this case is that the elements we consider most important in the cluster of factors that make up smoking are fundamentally incompatible with the aspects of health that we value most. Put another way, the drive to reduce dissonance increases in relative proportion to the number and importance of dissonant versus consonant relations between clusters of cognitions.

This same principle can also be understood at a higher level of abstraction to explain how it is that, in general, we feel comfortable or uncomfortable with our smoking habit. The knowledge that we smoke is not only linked to the perception that it is fundamentally harmful to our health, but also to perceptions that smoking is a costly habit, that it relieves boredom, that it is enjoyable after meals, and so on. Again, these relations may be fundamentally consonant, dissonant, or irrelevant, and again our general "dissonance index" with respect to smoking is proportionate to the number and importance of dissonant to consonant relations between elements.

Festinger emphasizes that attitude modifications do not automatically follow experiences of cognitive dissonance. Pressures to reduce dissonance are increased as the number and/or importance of dissonant cognitive elements increase. All of us manage to live with some dissonance, however. Moreover, attitude shifts are only one means of relieving dissonance; reduction may occur through various forms of psychological fight or flight. In the case (once again) of a prestige source urging a position discrepant from our own, we may (1) derogate the source; (2) decide that our disagreement is not very important, or rationalize in some other way; (3) seek social support or supportive evidence for our own viewpoint; (4) misperceive the source's position; (5) compartmentalize (ignore or forget that the cognitions are discrepant); (6) attempt to convince the source (if available) of his or her error; (7) modify our own attitudes.

Festinger's theory has been criticized on the grounds that its basic terms (cognitions, dissonance, etc.) are vaguely defined. Critics have also charged that the theory is imprecise with respect to predicting dissonance-reducing outcomes. Because there are so many outcomes, it is difficult to know which of them will be employed by an individual in a given case.

Problems of this kind present something of a dilemma for persuasion theorists in general. On the one hand, explanations that seem to do justice to persuasion's complexity invariably require terms which are difficult to operationalize. On the other hand, those terms that seem capable of being indexed behaviorally never seem to add up to a picture of the persuasive process. Festinger has opted for a richly provocative theory, but one that is loosely predictive and that calls upon us to exercise intuitive judgments about the meanings and applications of his basic concepts. At this stage of scholarship in the field, Festinger would seem to have made an intelligent decision. In particular, dissonance theory acknowledges the possibility that individuals will at times choose to live with their dissonance rather than attempt to reduce it. In this respect, the theory is consistent with evidence that Robert White (1959) has accumulated on competence motivation. Clearly we are not static entities; sometimes we seek self-protection, but we may tolerate dissonance and other forms of psychological pain when they accompany opportunities for growth and development. Dissonance theory also includes a large number of dissonance-reducing alternatives, even if this impairs its predictiveness. The theory serves as a reminder that persuaders must do more than "unbalance" cognitions by creating dissonance; they must also "rebalance" them by directing the receiver in specified ways and by closing off alternative methods of reducing dissonance. Except in rare circumstances, for example, a prestige source cannot simply attach his name to a proposal that is repugnant to receivers. He must show them it has elements that are consonant with their cognitions, that it satisfies cherished values, that it has social support from others whom they hold in high esteem, and that it meets objections which they or others might raise.

Fishbein and Ajzen on the Attitude-Behavior Inconsistency Problem

Let us turn to Fishbein and Ajzen's (1975) theory once again, this time to look at the relationship between attitudes and overt action. Unlike the conditioning theorists, Fishbein and Ajzen assume that people are on the whole rational in the way they go about making decisions. So rational are most people, assume the theorists, that if we have enough information about their beliefs and values, we can predict not only their attitudes, but also their behavior.

Relationship Between Attitudes and Overt Behavior

A capacity to account for the relationship between attitudes and overt behaviors has been a litmus test of sorts for behavioral theories of persuasion. If an attitude is a predisposition toward something, presumably individuals should act toward that something in ways consistent with their attitudes. Compared to relatively unprejudiced persons, those who score high on measures of prejudice toward blacks should also be found to be more discriminatory toward blacks. Workers who assign relatively high ratings to their jobs should also perform more effectively on their jobs. Students who express disapproval of cheating should also be less likely to cheat when given the opportunity. And if any of these persons should modify their attitudes, their behavior should presumably be modified as well. So, at least, psychologists have thought. The presumption of attitude-behavior consistency has, in fact, been a cornerstone of persuasion theory over the centuries.

The problem Fishbein and Ajzen and other psychologists have had to confront is that the attitude-behavior hypotheses has not been confirmed by research, or at least not to the same degree that psychologists had anticipated. On the basis of a review of 15 studies, Vroom (1964) found that job attitudes and job performance were only slightly and insignificantly correlated. Wicker (1969) summarized research on the relationship between attitudes and a large variety of behaviors: civil rights participation, cheating, labor union attendance, petition-signing, voting in student elections, providing public accommodations to minority group members, and many others. He concluded that, on the whole, attitudes were only slightly related to actions, if they were related at all. Although there have been comparatively few studies on the relationship between changes in attitude and changes in behavior, the studies that have been reported have revealed similar findings (Festinger, 1964; Greenwald, 1965, 1966).

To be sure, not all studies have found insignificant correlations between attitudes and behavior or between attitude change and behavior change. In most circumstances, for example, election surveys are extremely accurate predictors of how people actually vote. Changes in attitudes toward candidates are similarly reflected at the polls. It is a safe bet that persons who join groups like the Women's Christian Temperance Union are not adamant enthusiasts of drinking parties; that Foreign Legionnaires are rarely pacifists, and so on. Still, the preponderance of evidence has failed to confirm expectations.

What are we to make of the findings that attitudes and behaviors are often poorly correlated? Before we see how Fishbein and Ajzen handle the problem, let us consider for a moment how we might address it. Since all we can measure directly are publicly observable behaviors (attitudes are always inferred and can never be measured directly), should we abandon the notion of attitude entirely and content ourselves with talking about only that which we can observe? The approach is tempting, but intuitively we know that there is such a thing as a private attitude and that it is not always the same thing as what we say in public. If we abandoned the notion of attitude, how would we ever distinguish between voluntary changes in behavior (those produced by persuasion) and involuntary changes in behavior (those produced by pure coercion)?

Perhaps we should retain the notion of attitude, but abandon the expectation that attitudes are in some way related to behavior. This approach is also tempting, but it once again violates our intuitive knowledge that the two variables are related in some way. Is there a third alternative?

Fishbein and Ajzen are among a number of theorists (Rokeach, 1968; Keisler, Collins and Miller, 1969; Burhans, 1971) who have proposed a third alternative, one that underscores the importance of the situational context. All of them agree that attitude-behavior discrepancies can be understood or explained away without either abandoning the notion of attitude entirely or concluding that attitudes and behavior are related. There are some differences in their positions, but I shall focus on their similarities.

First, as Fishbein and Ajzen have emphasized, researchers have often done a poor job of measuring attitudes. Since an attitude is a relatively enduring and consistent predisposition, we should not be content with a single measure of an attitude (the typical procedure in research on attitudes), but should utilize instead a procedure in which we measure the attitude across time and in a variety of situational contexts. Suppose, for example, that a prospective juror asked to be excused from a murder trial on grounds that, as a pacifist, he was so opposed to capital punishment that he could not render an impartial verdict. Since many people attempt to avoid jury service in extended trials, the judge would have had grounds for suspicion. But should the individual have been a known Quaker and should he have volunteered for alternative service, the examiner might have reasonably inferred that pacifism was a genuinely held attitude in that case.

Second, any given behavioral act seems to be a product of not one but several attitudes. Whether we sign a petition to save the California redwoods, for example, may be determined not only by our attitude toward the redwoods, but also by our attitude toward the act of signing petitions and toward the person who solicits our signature. When researchers or practitioners fail to find strong relationships between attitudes and behavior, it is frequently because they have not adequately or comprehensively assessed all the relevant attitudes.

Third, when measures of attitude and measures of behavior are not correlated, it is often because the situational contexts are different. Concomitantly, attitudes measured in typical testing situations are not the same attitudes as those in real-life situations. In two early studies of the relationship between prejudice and discrimination, for example (LaPiere, 1934; Kutner, Wilkins, and Yarrow, 1952), managers of restaurants and hotels were first asked in the abstract whether they would serve "a Chinese couple" or "a Negro." Many refused. When these same subjects were confronted with a real Chinese couple or a real Negro, they served them. The discrepancy may be explained, however, when it is recognized that stereotypical attitudes toward a given group and attitudes toward specific members of that group are not necessarily the same, especially when, as in both studies, the latter were well-dressed, polite, charming, and so on.

A fourth point, related to the third, is that factors in the situational context may constrain individuals from acting on their attitudes. We may be convinced of the proposition that our boss should be tarred and feathered, but be realistically loath to act on it. In the protective atmosphere of the classroom it may be easy to agree with a student who decries reports of onlookers standing around helplessly while innocent persons are being attacked; it is another thing, however, to go to a stranger's defense, especially when there is imminent danger to self.

In these cases, the constraints on behavior involved the possibility of economic or physical punishment, but other, less tangible, situational pressures may be equally constraining. As indicated in Chapter 1, all of us conform in one degree or another to various cultural, subcultural, institutional and group norms of "appropriate" behavior. Sometimes we obey these norms because we have internalized them; at other times, because disobedience carries with it the threat of direct punishment. We obey at other times, however, out of a fear of censure, embarrassment, loss of face, or out of a positive sense of identification or attraction toward groups with which we are affiliated. When pressures such as these have been found to be present in psychological experiments on persuasion, some critics have viewed them as artifacts that confound and distort the results. In a sense they do, but as Fishbein and Ajzen have observed, all real-life situations carry such "demand characteristics," at least to some degree.

Let us picture a woman who has been asked to donate to the Red Cross by a neighbor in the apartment building. Weighing on the decision about whether to give and how much to give will be such factors as the prospective donor's attitude toward charities, toward the idea of being solicited, and toward the Red Cross in particular. In a relatively free-choice situation these attitude factors would be decisive, but it is quite conceivable that in this situation the woman might also be saying to herself: "I'd better give or he'll think I'm cheap and spread the word around the building. . . . Maybe I'd better give a dollar since that's what the others are probably giving. . . . Since I have a baby coming, I'd better not give more than a dollar. . . ." More than likely, these situational pressures would cause an otherwise reluctant woman to want to give, at least her "fair share." The situational context would not only influence her behavior, but would also influence her attitude toward the object.

There are undoubtedly a number of additional factors that help us to understand why changes in attitudes are not always accompanied by changes in behavior. One often-neglected factor militating against behavior change is inertia, especially when people are asked to give up old habits. Another reason behavior does not always change is that people do not always know *how* to act in the face of their new attitudes unless they are given explicit directions. What does it mean in behavioral terms, for example, to become a religious mystic? Finally, new attitudinal commitments may be sufficiently satisfying in themselves so that action becomes psychologically unnecessary. The conviction that we have come to see the spiritual light of day, for example, may be just the excuse we need to maintain our old behaviors.

But all things considered, the concept of attitude is still quite useful. As Kelman (1974, p. 112) has put it: "The low correlations between attitude and action found by many of the studies in this genre, though pointing to the limitations of the attitude concept, do not demonstrate its invalidity." On the contrary, he implies, the studies merely point up the many things persuaders must consider when they seek to analyze a receiver's current attitudes, and the many things they can do when they seek to modify those attitudes. Consistent with the previous discussion, he argues that attempts should be made to discover both the motivational and the situational determinants of present attitudes.

Recall now that Fishbein and Ajzen attempt to predict behaviors precisely. As a first step in wrestling with the attitude-behavior problem, they distinguish between attitudes toward objects (A_O) and attitudes toward behaviors (A_B). The former is an evaluation of an object (e.g., Zippo sedans) in the abstract. The latter is an evaluation of a specific act (e.g., buying a Zippo sedan in the next six months). It is the latter, Fishbein and Ajzen maintain, which is more predictive of how an individual will act. Rather than measuring attitudes toward birth control pills in general terms, they suggest asking women about the consequences they anticipate of their using birth control pills. These perceptions they call *behavioral beliefs* (Ajzen and Fishbein, 1980).

Suppose that on being asked the advantages and disadvantages of using birth control pills, a woman names the five behavioral beliefs listed in Table 4.1. To determine the value weightings of these consequences, she might be asked to evaluate each on a 7-point, good-bad scale, as follows:

Causes me to gain weight

Good	$(+3)$	$(+2)$	$(+1)$	(0)	(-1)	(-2)	(-3)	Bad
extremely	quite	slightly	neither/nor		slightly	quite	extremely	

TABLE 4.1   A WOMAN'S BELIEFS ABOUT USING BIRTH CONTROL PILLS

My Using Birth Control Pills	Outcome Evaluations	Belief Strength	Product
1. Causes me to gain weight.	-2	$+3$	-6
2. Is convenient.	$+1$	$+3$	$+3$
3. Enables me to regulate the size of my family.	$+2$	$+2$	$+4$
4. Gives me guilt feelings.	-1	$+2$	-2
5. Regulates my menstrual cycle.	$+3$	$+1$	$+3$
Total			$+2$

Adapted from Ajzen and Fishbein (1980), with permission.

Column 1 of Table 4.1 shows the hypothetical results. The respondent in this case felt that the weight gain was quite bad, but regulating the size of her family was quite good. The next step is to determine how certain the person is of these consequences. One possibility is to use a question such as the following:

> How certain are you that using birth control pills will cause you to gain weight?
>
> _____ not at all certain (0)
>
> _____ slightly certain $(+1)$
>
> _____ quite certain $(+2)$
>
> _____ extremely certain $(+3)$

In column 2 of Table 4.1 the results of questions such as this one are provided. According to Fishbein and Ajzen's theory, a person's A_B can be predicted by multiplying her evaluation of each of the behavior consequences by the strength of her belief that performing the behavior will lead to that consequence, and then summing the products for the total set of beliefs. These calculations are illustrated in column 3. It can be seen that the woman's attitude toward using birth control pills is predicted to be quite positive $(+2)$. Presumably, users of birth control pills should have more positive A_B scores than nonusers. And, in fact, say the theorists, this turns out to be the case. Their research provides numerous examples of tests of this kind.

While A_B is a better predictor of behavior than A_O, it is not always sufficient. Fishbein and Ajzen argue that the best predictor of behavior is *intentions,* and that they are a joint product of attitudes toward behaviors and subjective norms (SN). Just as A_B has a cognitive and an evaluative component, so SN is said to be a combination of the person's beliefs that specific individuals or groups believe the behavior in question should be performed, and the person's evaluation of how desirous he or she is of complying with those norms. Together these factors should provide a rather accurate indication of how an individual will act in a given situation.

Fishbein and Ajzen's theory, summarized in Figure 4.2, provides a clear and convincing account of how attitudes and behaviors are related, *and it suggests as well a useful approach to measurement and prediction of attitudes and behaviors from evidence of their cognitive and evaluational components.* Some critics have complained that evidence of these predictors is generally inaccessible to persuaders, but Fishbein and Ajzen reply that it can usually be secured through direct questioning.

The theory of reasoned action underscores the importance not just of any situational norms, but of norms *as perceived and evaluated by the audience.* Quite obviously, these constitute potential targets of change by persuaders. And there are other implications for persuaders that derive from the discussion of the relationship between attitudes and behaviors. Rather than simply attempting to modify attitudes in the abstract, persuaders can help to make a modified attitude *salient* to a situational context. They can provide specific instructions on *how* to act. They can help message recipients *interpret* the context, including the context of their own past actions, so that it appears conducive to favorable action. They can lead the receivers to view the recommended action as *expected* or even *inevitable.* Finally, they can *alter* the context itself so that different situational pressures or more intensified situational pressures are brought to bear on receivers.

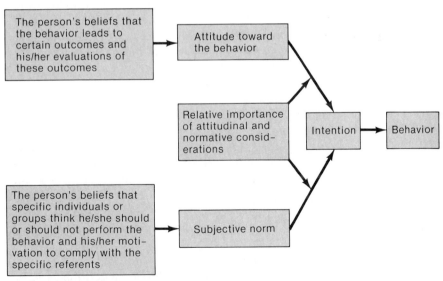

Note: Arrows indicate the direction of influence.

Adapted from Ajzen and Fishbein (1980), with permission.

Figure 4.2 Factors Determining a Person's Behavior.

From Actions to Attitudes: Festinger's Forced Compliance Hypothesis

Thus far, we have focused on communication-induced attitude change and on how changes in attitudes may influence behavior. We turn now to the second route to attitude change identified at the outset of this chapter, the path from actions to attitudes. For this purpose, let us return to Festinger's theory.

The focus of Festinger's dissonance theory and subsequent research has been on behavior-attitude discrepancies. It is in this important area that the theory has made its most distinctive contribution through tests of its *forced compliance* hypothesis. More and more, persuasion theorists have come to recognize that our attitudes and beliefs are as often the *result* of our actions as the reverse. Recall Bem's claim that we characteristically attribute motives to ourselves from evidence of how we have behaved. Recall too Skinner's emphasis on learning through reinforcement. Petty and Cacioppo (1979) found that merely asking people to think about an issue can bring about self-generated attitude shifts. Their recent book (Petty and Cacioppo, 1981) reports other such findings. It is well known that active participation, through role-playing or actual practice, is often more productive of belief or attitude change than passive attention to a speech or essay. Says theorist Herbert Kelman (1974, p. 316): "Attitude and action are linked in a continuing reciprocal process, each generating the other in an endless chain. Action is the ground on which attitudes are formed, tested, modified, and abandoned." The consequences of action, he adds, "bring to the fore challenging insights, role expectations, social supports, or direct experiences, which are the stuff out of which attitudes emerge" (p. 314).

Festinger's forced compliance hypothesis focuses on situations in which the persuader actually creates behavior-attitude discrepancies for persuadees by pressuring them to engage in various counterattitudinal activities. (The term *forced compliance* is somewhat of a misnomer, since in most of the research conducted by Festinger and his colleagues, subjects were induced to comply rather than forced or coerced.) According to Festinger, two things must happen before attitudes will be modified following forced compliance. First, individuals must be *pressured enough so that they will comply, but not so much that they will feel as though they have had no choice.* The pressure, then, must be subtle, mild, or indirect. If it is too forceful, it may produce grudging compliance, but it will probably intensify negative attitudes. Second, individuals must be *prevented from reducing in other ways the dissonance they experience.* If they can claim that they acted because they had to, or if they can find other rationalizations for performance of their discrepant acts, then they need not modify their attitudes. The general proposition advanced by Festinger is that the less justification provided to receivers for complying with counterattitudinal requests, the greater the likelihood that they will modify their attitudes. Let us consider a number of offshoots of this general proposition.

Role-Playing and Degrees of Choice, Effort, and Justification

That changes in behavior can lead to changes in attitudes is well known. Not uncommonly, for example, workers promoted to supervisory positions begin to look down on their former mates, where before they were antimanagement. While self-persuasion of this sort is not surprising, experimenters have been able to produce attitude shifts in more transient role-playing situations. In several experiments involving pressure to role-play, subjects have been asked to defend positions they did not privately support—for example, to write essays favoring higher tuition. In general, the results of these studies have supported Festinger's predictions. Subjects who acceded to the experimenter's pressure to comply were more likely to modify their attitudes under conditions where they felt they had a choice in the matter, or where they could not rationalize away their discrepant behavior on the grounds that compliance was effortless or justified by the circumstances.

Boring Tasks and Severity of Threat

Several forced compliance experiments have involved getting subjects to perform extremely boring tasks. In one well-known study (Brehm, 1962), fraternity pledges were "asked" by a fraternity brother to copy random numbers for 3 hours. They were threatened with paddling (low threat) or a tribunal with possible expulsion (high threat) if they did not comply. Although the threat of paddling was regarded as less likely to be carried out than the tribunal, Brehm's findings still provide general support for Festinger's theory. As reported to a supposed third party (an Interfraternity Council), compliant pledges threatened with paddling experienced less dissatisfaction with the boring task than pledges in the high-threat condition of the experiment. Presumably, those in the high-threat condition did not need to modify their attitudes toward the task. They could hate doing it and still do it on the ground that they had little choice.

As might be expected, the very opposite of the generalization about severity of threat applies to situations in which the activity in question is something we initially regard as pleasant or valuable. The evidence suggests that, other things being equal, paying a high price for something that was valued in the first place increases our attraction for that object. In one experiment, Aronson and Mills (1959) applied varying degrees of punishment as conditions for entrance into an ongoing discussion forum. Unknown to the subjects, the actual discussion to which they were later exposed was prearranged to be extremely boring. Still, the subjects given severe initiations rated it highly; more highly, at least, than given those mild initiations. Presumably, the experience of a severe initiation was dissonant with the experience of unanticipated boredom. Rather than admit to themselves that they had been bored, the subjects modified their attitudes toward the discussion and persisted in their desire to join the group. There are other possible interpretations of these findings, but the dissonance explanation cannot be ruled out. Further confirmation has been provided by Gerard and Mathewson (1966).

Forced Compliance and Disliked Communicators

One of the real surprises predicted and evidenced by dissonance theorists is that *disliked communicators are more apt to secure attitude change following forced compliance than highly attractive communicators.* Ordinarily, of course, we are swayed more by attractive than by unattractive sources. But what happens in the special case where we are pressured into doing something that we would not otherwise be inclined to do? Dissonance theory argues that when the source of pressure is attractive, we can rationalize away the discrepancy between our attitudes and behaviors by saying to ourselves that we performed the noxious task as a favor to the source. But when the source is unattractive, that potential rebalancing alternative is foreclosed. Hence, we have little choice but to modify our attitudes.

This principle has been well supported by research (Smith, 1961; Zimbardo et al., 1965; Powell, 1965). In the Zimbardo study, as in the Smith study, pressure was placed on subjects to perform the noxious task of sampling fried Japanese grasshoppers. As in many other "forced compliance" studies, the "force" exerted upon subjects to comply stemmed not from explicit threats by the communicators, but rather from their role or position as authority figures conducting scientific research. Although the subjects were "strongly urged" to eat the unusual food, it was also made quite clear that they could refuse, and many in fact did just that.

One sample used in the study consisted of ROTC students who were told by either an attractive or an unattractive ROTC officer that the experiment was concerned with physiological and intellectual reactions to food deprivation. The attractiveness variable was manipulated quite cleverly by the experimenters by having the officer interact with an assistant. In the "attractive" role condition, the officer gave politely phrased requests to the assistant, called him by his first name, responded to a "mistake" by the assistant with equanimity, and in general was considerate and pleasant. The negative condition required that the officer be perceived as unpleasant, a person one would not want to know, work with, or work for. This perception was largely induced by the officer's quite formal interaction with the assistant. At one point the assistant mistakenly brought in the "wrong" experimental food (a tray of eels in aspic instead of grasshoppers). The officer, who was in the process of talking to the subjects in his most pleasant manner, suddenly blew up and said, "Oh, dammit, can't you remember the schedule? That food is for the next group. . . . Let's get with it and hurry up about it!" As the assistant left, obviously embarrassed, the officer shrugged his shoulders disgustedly, *then reversed his role behavior in front of the subjects* and proceeded again in the same tone as previously (Zimbardo and Ebbeson, 1969, p. 74).

The results of the Zimbardo et al. study are quite revealing. About half the subjects in both experimental groups refused to participate, and *their* attitudes toward fried Japanese grasshoppers became less favorable. Of those who did participate, the attractiveness of the communicator made a considerable difference. By a wide margin (as much as 50 percent), subjects who ate the grasshoppers for the negatively valued communicator increased their ratings of the food more than those who complied for the positively valued communicator.

There are, it seems to me, at least three important lessons for persuaders which are illustrated by the Zimbardo study. First, the study attests to the *extraordinary power of legitimate authority* as a vehicle for getting people to perform noxious tasks. Second, the study illustrates how pressure to comply is *apt to produce backlash effects among those who refuse to bend*. Finally, the study's main finding—that disliked communicators created more attitude-change following compliance—underscores *the importance of closing off other possible dissonance-reducing alternatives* for the receiver once attitude-behavior discrepancies have been created.

Taken together, the literature on Festinger's mini-theory of forced compliance provides us with insights into some of the less obvious ways in which attitudes may be modified. The basic principle, once again, is that under certain conditions, it is possible to change attitudes by first bringing pressure on people to change their behaviors. That principle has a number of applications. Contrary to the notion, for example, that attitudes cannot be legislated, we can see that new laws or executive decrees may indeed lead to attitude modification by creating attitude-behavior discrepancies. We can see too why those in authority frequently take potentially unpopular actions first and then seek confirmation of their policies afterward. Once policies are put into practice, the easier dissonance-reducing alternative for those affected is to modify their attitudes. Another potentially powerful weapon, as we have seen, is counterattitudinal role-playing. In conflict situations, this device is often employed by those in positions of institutional authority. One way to blunt opposition, for example, is to give potential partisans important positions of responsibility within the system. Partisans are not simply "bought off"; they are also placed in a role in which the need to publicly defend official positions may lead them to modify their own attitudes.

The finding that we value attitude objects all the more if we have had to pay dearly for them also has direct application to conflict situations. Machiavelli observed long ago that those in power could reduce domestic discontent by going to war. We should not be surprised to learn that wounded veterans often identify more with a war effort than soldiers who escape unscathed. Antiwar sentiments are dissonant with the price they have paid, while prowar sentiments provide justification for their wounds. Seizing on this same principle, leaders of militant movements have deliberately placed their followers in situations where they would be subjected to repressive actions by "the enemy."

SUMMARY

Pooling Theoretical Insights

I suggested in Chapter 3 that the behavioral theories of persuasions could most profitably be viewed as complementary perspectives, rather than as rival visions. Each of the theories of attitude change reviewed here has made important

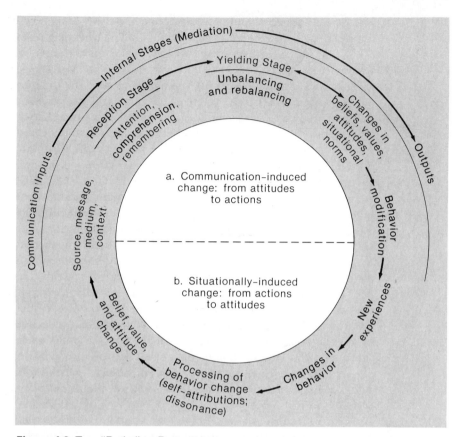

Figure 4.3 Two "Paths" to Persuasion.

contributions. The S-R conditioning theories have advanced our understanding of the role of reinforcements and associations in persuasion, including arbitrary, nonlogical linkages. While we might like to think that our attitudes and actions are always rationally based, they are surely not.

Yet reason does have a role in persuasion, along with such other internal factors as attention, comprehension, and motivation. Albeit with admittedly fuzzy concepts like "frame of reference," cognitively oriented perception theorists have led us into the inner world of the message recipient and have shown us how attributional processes may affect persuasion.

From Fishbein and Ajzen we see underscored the importance of "moving toward" persuadees—building on their beliefs and values in moving them to action, and building especially on beliefs and values associated with attitudes toward action and situational norms. From Festinger and the other balance theorists, we see the importance of challenging belief and value premises— creating intrapersonal discrepancies by unbalancing cognitions, then working to rebalance them. Whereas most theories of persuasion are primarily focused on communication-induced attitude change and resulting actions, Festinger's theory is especially helpful in understanding the alternative path to attitude change, placing individuals in situations leading to "self-persuasion."

Figure 4.3 illustrates the two alternative routes to attitude change and incorporates other highlighted ideas as well, including McGuire's two-factor distinction. The model is designed as a composite—a way of making connections among variables and among theories about those variables. In using the model, ask yourself how one set of factors is likely to affect the others or be caused by others. For example, what are the effects of a given set of communication inputs on decoding and evaluation? How do perceptual frames shape comprehension of incoming messages? How might the messages "reframe" perceptions? What is the interplay in a given situation between attitudes and behavior? How does each shape the other?

A Summary of Basic Psychological Principles

I. Persuasion is a learning process.
  A. Attitudes, beliefs, and values are learned and can therefore be unlearned.
    1. Learning may take place through conditioning or through more complex information-processing activities.
    2. Learning of a desired attitudinal response is facilitated when the response is rewarded or when the persuadee believes that it will be rewarded.
  B. Before a message is favorably evaluated, it must first be decoded.
  C. Information is generally necessary to produce persuasion, but seldom sufficient.
II. Persuasion is a perceptual process.
  A. The human being is a meaning-seeking animal who monitors incoming stimuli.
  B. Restructuring people's perceptions is itself a form of persuasion.
  C. Among people's most important perceptions are their attributions of causation.
    1. People tend to discount the trustworthiness of persuaders when they attribute their messages to external causes.
    2. People tend to infer their attitudes, beliefs, and values from their own actions when they have reason to believe that their actions are not attributable to external causes.
    3. Perceiving oneself to have been subjected to powerful persuasive forces is often sufficient to produce persuasion, whether this perception is illusory or not.
III. Persuasion is an adaptive process.
  A. Persuasive messages must be geared to levels of audience receptivity.
    1. Message recipients include those who are hostile, in disagreement, "on the fence" (including those who are apathetic, uninformed, or ambivalent), or already in agreement and perhaps committed to favorable action.

    2. Concomitantly, persuaders may seek to *defuse* hostility, *neutralize* or *convert* those in disagreement, *shape* "on the fence" attitudes to their liking, and *reinforce* already favorable responses.

  B. Beliefs and values constitute the cognitive and affective components of attitudes, respectively.

    1. An attitude toward an object is a combination of probabilities assigned to relevant beliefs about the object, as well as value weightings of perceived attributes of the object.

    2. To alter attitudes toward objects, one may prompt message recipients to alter their beliefs, or belief probabilities or value weightings.

IV. Persuasion is an unbalancing and rebalancing process.

  A. People strive to maintain psychological balance (consistency).

    1. Psychological elements (cognitions, evaluations of source and advocated proposition) may be mutually balanced, imbalanced, or irrelevant to each other.

    2. Inconsistencies between psychological elements may be logical or psychological.

    3. Imbalances are of three kinds:

      (a) Behavior-attitude discrepancies

      (b) Source-proposition discrepancies

      (c) Attitude component discrepancies

    4. Imbalances may be of kind or of degree.

  B. Psychological imbalance is unpleasant or uncomfortable to the individual.

  C. The drive to reduce imbalance is not automatic. Individuals can tolerate low levels of imbalance and *must* if they are to grow and develop.

  D. The drive to reduce imbalance increases in relative proportion to the number and importance of unbalanced (versus balanced) relations between clusters of psychological elements.

  E. Imbalances may be reduced or rebalanced in several ways, only one of which is attitude modification.

    1. Rebalancing may occur through *changes* of psychological elements (including intended attitude changes as well as "boomerang" effects).

    2. Rebalancing may occur through various forms of *psychological fight* (seeking new information or social support, for example).

    3. Rebalancing may occur through various forms of *psychological flight* (compartmentalization and rationalization, for example).

  F. The persuader must not only create imbalance; he or she must also *close off* undesired forms of rebalancing.

V. In formulating judgments about how to act, message recipients are generally rational information processors.

  A. Intentions to act in a particular way closely parallel actual behaviors.

  B. Intentions to act in a particular way are a joint function of attitudes toward the behavior and situational norms.

       1. Attitudes toward behaviors are influenced by beliefs about the consequences of acting in a particular way and evaluations of those consequences.

       2. Situational norms are influenced by perceptions about what significant others would have us to, as well as motivation to conform to their opinions.

VI. Attitudes may be modified through processes of self-persuasion.

    A. Merely being asked to think about an issue may lead to self-persuasion.

    B. Situations calling for active participants (e.g., role-playing) are at least as likely to lead to attitude modification as those requiring only passive message reception.

       1. Direct reinforcements of actual behavior tend to be more powerful than projected reinforcements of anticipated behaviors.

       2. Engaging in counterattitudinal actions under conditions of perceived choice is likely to be dissonance-producing, and may thus lead to attitude change.

EXERCISE

Find out more about one of the theories discussed in this book. Write a paper that adds information about the theory, as well as an evaluation of your own (recall the criteria for evaluation suggested in Chapter 3). Or consult *Psychological Abstracts* to determine what applications have been made of the theory by researchers or practitioners of persuasion. How, for example, has Fishbein and Ajzen's theory been utilized by market researchers?

Chapter *5*
Persuasion and Image Management

Thus far, the examples I have presented have been of the sort that virtually all readers would label as persuasive practices. Campaign speeches, editorials, sermons, television advertisements, legal briefs, are sometimes referred to as *paradigm cases;* they are persuasive practices that virtually announce themselves as such. Cases such as these involve no complex admixture of motives, no masking of persuasive intent, no questions about whether they are attempts at persuasion or some other form of influence. Typically it is clear from their contexts what sorts of practices they are, and what they are designed to accomplish. For example, editorials are featured in an Editorial or Op-Ed section of the newspaper; sermons are usually given in places of worship by persons designated to present them. If persuasive intent is not apparent from the context, it is made manifest by what is said and by how it is said. Paradigmatic persuaders rely, at least in part, on linguistic or paralinguistic (languagelike) messages. And these messages are clearly promotive of a point of view or a proposed action of some sort, or both. For example, the editorial writer might blast the mayor's desegregation plan. The minister might decry American materialism. The advertiser might urge us to purchase a particular product. The campaigner might plead for our votes. Other examples of paradigm cases include sales presentations, recruitment efforts, charity solicitations, polemical pamphlets, panhandling, peaceful protest demonstrations, appeals for extensions of time on term papers, reasoned refusals of time extensions, flirtatious smiles and winks at pickup bars, parental advice on whom to marry. *Generally speaking, when I use the term persuasion, and especially when I offer advice or bring research to bear on how to practice persuasion, it will be paradigm cases that I have in mind.* At the same time, it would be a serious mistake to treat paradigm cases as the whole of persuasion. Focusing exclusively on paradigm cases would greatly simplify the task of this book, but we would miss out on nonobvious persuasive influences, including some that are quite powerful.

How far, then, should we go in extending the scope of persuasion beyond paradigm cases? If we view paradigm cases as the *core* of persuasion's domain, what constitutes its *periphery?* Answering these questions will require that we look more carefully at alleged alternatives to persuasion, such as coercion and information-giving, so as to assess the merits of conventionally drawn distinctions between persuasion and nonpersuasion. In general, conventional distinctions tend to be overdrawn. Rather than assuming that a given act must either be classified as "persuasion" or "nonpersuasion," we should recognize that the same communicative act may spring from multiple motives, operate at multiple levels, and have multiple effects. Indeed, as I argue next, communication always operates on at least two levels.

Substantive Messages and Image Projections

Human beings are self-reflexive animals. They don't just provide information about substantive issues; they label it and classify their labels. They comment upon it and comment upon their comments. Moreover, through the manner and style of their presentations, they express feelings about their message content that in turn provides additional information about what they are like as people, how they view their audiences, how they view their audiences viewing them, and so on.

Watzlawick, Beavin, and Jackson (1967) speak in this connection of messages as having a *content* level and a *relationship* level. Every utterance about substantive matters, they argue, is also an interpersonal encounter that invariably projects an image of ourselves. And these image projections, in turn, "comment" upon the substantive message. In Watzlawick et al.'s terms, messages at the relationship level *metacommunicate:* They communicate about communication. For example, a simple "please" at the end of a sentence may transform an order into a request. A twinkle of the eyes may transform a serious request into apparent kidding. Both the twinkling eyes and the "please" are image projections—statements at the relationship or image level.

Note that Watzlawick et al. are saying that we cannot *not* project an image of ourselves as we communicate about substantive matters. We can see this most vividly when we *try* to not present an image to others—when we try to be natural, to avoid artifice, to express our thoughts or feelings directly. What we often wind up communicating is the *image* of not appearing to project an image—one of the many paradoxes of communication we will have to confront.

The distinction between substantive messages and image projections appears to be extremely important for the study of persuasion. It suggests that, quite apart from whether we are functioning as persuaders at the content level, we may still be persuading at the relationship level. At the content level, the sportscaster who brings you the latest scores may be doing little more than reciting a series of facts. At the relationship level, however, she may, by the manner of her presentation, help to reinforce or undermine your identification with the station as one that shares your interests and concerns. Indeed, a large part of the job evaluation of the sportscaster may consist of an assessment of how convincingly she promotes the impression that her own happiness depends on the fate of the home team. In long-term relationships between friends or relatives, image projections are often more important rhetorically than what gets said at the content level.

Whereas substantive messages are carried largely by verbal means, messages at the relationship level are transmitted mostly by nonverbal means. Whether accurately or inaccurately, message recipients have been known to interpret all manner of nonverbal stimuli as messages, from clearly intentional winks to innocent-appearing blinks. Nonverbal stimuli are used to form perceptions of a speaker's personal attractiveness, self-concept, liking for the other, sexual interest, truthfulness or deceit, and behavioral intentions (Leathers, 1976).

Just how much of our lives is occupied with concerns about the images we project is a matter of some debate. The issue is a sensitive one, particularly for those who pride themselves on their individuality, or who regard manipulation of any kind as intrinsically immoral (Johannesen, 1971). Nevertheless, it would appear that sensitivity to how others perceive us develops early in life and leads to rhetorical sophistication at image management (Reardon, 1981). From the recognition that we communicate images of ourselves whether we want to or not come attempts at *doing* something about how we are perceived—at *promoting* an image and not just *projecting* one. While we may applaud the spirit of those critical of efforts at image management, it would appear naive to assume that we can do without façades entirely.

Yet this does not mean that most people care only about how others see them. Rather, our efforts at impression management may be paired with or balanced against other concerns, including some that we ordinarily view as exclusively nonrhetorical. Recall the earlier point that the same act may be multimotivated. We may wear blue jeans, for example, because they are comfortable, relatively inexpensive, because we like the way they look, *and* because wearing them may please or impress valued others. Similarly, we may attempt to inform or entertain or please others esthetically *and* seek to impress them.

Sometimes our motivations are so complex that we ourselves have great difficulty deciding which ones are primary. A former student commented in a paper that she had "banished" makeup from her face because she did not like having to be careful of the finished product, unable to laugh, cry, or touch for fear of marring the surface. She added that she had grown ashamed of her need to fix and angered by the feeling that something always needed repair. But upon further reflection, it occurred to her that another motive might have been operative.

> Dipping a bit further into my psyche, I also find that by wearing make-up I was announcing that I had done the best I could—this is it, folks; I'm not going to get any better. But without make-up, I can protect the flaws of my naked face

with the belief that if I really wanted to spend the time, I could be a ravishing beauty. I am somewhat like the second-grade child who refuses to risk his self-esteem by trying to read; he is secure as to the results of not-trying, but an attempt to read opens the way to *real* failure.

Among textbook writers (Clark, 1984; Miller, 1980), there is general recognition that impression management is a part of persuasion, but it tends to be assigned secondary importance or recognized as significant only as an adjunct to the promotion of positions on issues or proposals for action. The ancient Greek rhetoricians recognized the importance of what they called *ethos*, the character and personality of the speaker as perceived by the audience, but they viewed it as instrumental to more substantive goals. Contemporary rhetoricians also advise speakers on how they can enhance their images by the manner in which they deal with substantive issues, but they tend to have particular ends in mind, like getting a political candidate elected. In point of fact, much of the "imaging" we do is not designed for any particular or immediate purpose. It is more like putting money in the bank and trading on it when we need it. We literally bank on our images. Moreover, as we will see, image management is a matter of considerable concern even to those engaged in coercion or other activities sometimes assumed to be clear-cut alternatives to persuasion.

Persuasion and the "Real Thing"

From the recognition that we cannot not communicate it is but a short step to the realization that it may be impossible in some contexts *not* to function as persuaders. Consider, for example, the "no-frills" box of tissues that sits on my table. Ordinarily, boxes of tissues, like most supermarket packages, announce themselves as instances of attempted persuasion. They are attractively adorned and delicately scented. They display a brand name made famous by expensive advertising.

Not so this generic box. It presents a surface image of "the real" as opposed to the rhetorical. Indeed, there is something so starkly "unrhetorical" about the package that one gets the impression of extra effort expended to distance the product from its brand name competitors by making it seem "antirhetorical." *No* name, not just the absence of a brand name, appears on the box. The lettering announcing its contents is plain black on white. We are told with rather unnecessary exactitude that its 200 2-ply tissues are 8.25 inches by 9.71 inches in size. My impression is that the packagers, while providing a reduction in price, are also trying to persuade us that the box is in some sense "virtuous" for being nonrhetorical. They would be hard pressed, in any case, *not* to present a persuasive message of any kind within a supermarket context.

Deception about Persuasive Intent

No-frills packages are by no means the only things made to seem nonrhetorical. Persuaders often go to great lengths to persuade us that they are not persuaders. Erving Goffman (1974) provides the example of the professional actor who completes a commercial pitch and, with the cameras still on him, turns in obvious relief from his task, now to take real pleasure in consuming the product he has been advertising. Says Goffman, this is but an example of the way in which TV and radio commercials are coming

> to exploit framing devices to give an appearance of naturalness that (it is hoped) will override the reserve auditors have developed. Thus, use is currently being made of children's voices, presumably because these seem unschooled; street noises, and other effects to give the impression of interviews with unpaid respondents; false starts, filled pauses, byplays, and overlapping speech to simulate actual conversation; and following Welles, the interception of a firm's jingle commercials to give news of its new product, alternating occasionally with interception by a public interest spot, thus presumably keeping the faith of the auditor alive. (p. 475)

As a general rule, whatever yardsticks we employ to distinguish persuasion from nonpersuasion others may exploit to deceive us about persuasive intent or at least to make their messages appear more authentic or more objective. Is seeming unrehearsed a sign of the nonpersuader? The makers of campaign commercials for Ronald Reagan in 1980 deliberately staged scenes that would have an unstaged look, and they encouraged Reagan himself to seem as little like an actor (or former actor) as possible. Is looking away from the job interviewer a sign of the nonpersuader (or at least the not very skilled persuader)? By a kind of perverse logic, some persuaders deliberately look away from job interviewers (or other VIPs) to create the appearance of being nonpersuaders. Similarly, "yes men" learn to disagree with their bosses enough to negate the impression of being panderers while still playing up to them. Is one-sided argument evidence of promotional intent? Skilled persuaders learn the techniques of "partial impartiality," including the use of a "both sides" approach in which at least tacit recognition is given to the merits of the opposing view.

In the category of deception about persuasive intent is deception about deception. This takes us beyond the relational level of communication to meta-meta levels (communications *about* relational communication and beyond). Most deceptive messages carry with them the implicit metacommunication: "This is not a deceptive message."[1] To carry conviction, these deceptive metacommunications may require deceptive meta-metacommunications in their support. (Note here that all deception is persuasion, though not all persuasion is deception.)

In situations where actors are suspected of concealing or distorting information, observers attend to the expressions they exude, rather than to their apparently deliberate messages. Here the semantic content of a verbal message counts for less than its style, and winks count for less than blinks. On detecting

---

[1] There are times when deceivers will acknowledge to observers that they are being untruthful, while concealing the actual truth. This can be a blatant power move in a relationship—a deliberate show of indifference about the other's feelings. Or, paradoxically, it can be the result of a tacit agreement between two people to deceive openly about matters, such as marital infidelities, that are too sensitive to be discussed truthfully. In this latter case, a show of deceptiveness may be intended and interpreted as a sign of regard for the other.

a furtive glance, an embarrassed hesitation, a guilty look, the observer will not be able to determine *what* it is that is being concealed, but may be able to determine that *something* is being concealed.

However, this only gives rise to *expression games* (Goffman, 1969), contests over the control, and detection of control, of expressive behaviors. For example, deceivers may deliberately emit signs of guilt or embarrassment over relatively minor concealments in the hope that observers will not investigate their more serious evasions. Apparently, much behavior that is regularly assumed to be uncontrollable is, in fact, controllable. Psychiatric and physical symptoms ranging from headaches to paralysis of limbs may be consciously or unconsciously faked or used rhetorically as "loss of control" tactics in conflict situations (Haley, 1976).

As Goffman observes in this essay on the subject, expression games can get extremely complicated, particularly in military conflicts. Rival nations may go to great lengths to stage deceptions or to conceal their detection from those who staged them. During World War II, for example, the British arranged for the Germans to discover false secrets on the corpse of a high-ranking but fictitious military officer. Dummy airfields were constructed to camouflage real air war preparations and to invite the Germans to expend effort and ammunition on false targets. Phials of chemicals were dropped behind enemy lines with instructions to German troops on how to foil their medical officers by creating the impression that they had succumbed to major diseases. When German spies were detected, they were allowed to remain in the field and generally fed innocuous or false information. Sometimes they were fed true and important information, however, as a way of persuading them and their superiors that they had not been detected.

To deceive others about manipulative intent, it is often effective to be in the dark about one's own motives. Rather than instructing resistance workers to con the Germans about Allied invasion plans, the British gave them false information, instructed them to keep it secret, and assumed that, as a matter of course, some would be captured by the Germans and would reveal the false information very credibly under torture.

More commonly, we deceive ourselves about our manipulative designs upon others, and this in turn helps us to appear sincere to them while sparing us conscious feelings of guilt or shame. Beware, says Peter Berger (1963), of the person who is consistently sincere; that person is probably suffering from a good dose of self-deception. In general, says Berger, we deceive ourselves far more than we deceive others. This may range from relatively harmless rationalizations for manipulative stratagems (e.g., the parent who denies any selfish motives in persuading a child to go to bed) to the development of real physical symptoms.

Image Depictions in Art and Entertainment

To the maxim that we cannot *not* communicate images of ourselves must be added a corollary principle, that we cannot *not* communicate images of others as well. Our principal concern here is with the daily molding and reinforcing and occasional altering of group stereotypes that occurs on a massive scale through our art and entertainment media.

There is an onus in our culture against bending "high Art" to "low Rhetoric," the assumption being that dramatists, poets, composers, and the like cannot fulfill their "proper" mission of esthetic expression and at the same time concern themselves with whether their work is being favorably perceived or with the uses to which it is being put. A parallel distinction is often made between rhetoric and entertainment. Like artists, it is said, entertainers should perform *consummatory* functions. Their job is to please or amuse us as an end in itself—unlike persuaders, who may use artistic or entertaining expressions *instrumentally*, as a way of achieving attitude or behavior modification.

Although these distinctions are not without value, they obscure the actual pervasive effects of art and entertainment in our culture on attitudes and behaviors. Historically, a great deal of what we call art, even "great" art, has served rhetorically to undermine prevailing values. Witness, for example, the satiric plays of Aristophanes, the tradition of protest theater in Europe and America, the underground poetry that still flourishes in the Soviet Union, the passionate antiwar message of Picasso's "Guernica."

More often than not, art and entertainment serve to reinforce dominant cultural values and stereotypes, rather than to overturn them. The Greeks staged the Olympic Games to affirm communal values and insisted that drama serve the state. Today's college football spectacle provides a clear example of similar reinforcement through entertainment. The game is not complete without the singing of the national anthem, the patriotic half-time show, and the all-American cheerleaders invoking the gods to bless dear old U.

The celebration of communal values is often performed in our culture through such mundane vehicles as sitcoms, soap operas, and comic strips. No doubt the creators of these entertainment vehicles are often indifferent to the rhetorical implications of their work, so long as they continue to be popular. But they are enormously influential nonetheless—all the more so because they are not thought of as instruments of persuasion and hence are not as likely to arouse our defenses (Medhurst and Benson, 1984).

Whereas in other societies popular art and entertainment are required to serve the state, in our own society it is often the profit motive that impels the mass media to support popularly held values and, in so doing, to intensify them. Over time, such values as effort and optimism, individuality and achievement, efficiency and progress become well nigh unchallengeable as one after another soap opera or situation comedy lends implicit support to them. It may be objected that soaps deal far more explicitly with controversial themes than in the torpid days of *Life Can Be Beautiful* and *Our Gal, Sunday* on radio. Life is not nearly as beautiful on today's "soaps," as one character after another experiences nervous breakdowns, tumors, unwanted pregnancies, cancers, divorce, rape, and even incest.

But what Marjorie Perloff observed in *The New Republic* over a decade ago (May 10, 1975) remains largely the case today. With remarkable sameness, she said:

> [T]hey portray sophisticated, Waspish protagonists who reside in attractive sub-
> urban towns within safe distance from the Big City, and who live out their days
> snaring handsome men from each other, or performing miraculous operations
> between affairs or sipping lunchtime cocktails at French restaurants, or sneaking
> idyllic weekends at Far Away Places. (p. 11)

As the media alter the images of others that they project, the new images
are no less subject to homogenization and rigidification than the old. The so-
called emancipated woman that we so often see in the movies today is no less
a media product than the variety of female gender types that populated the
movie screens during the thirties and forties when, as Annette Kuhn (1978)
observed, they tended almost uniformly to be narcissistic objects of domestic
identification or of sexual, voyeuristic delight. Increasingly, observed Erving
Goffman (1979), our media images and our culture's images are becoming
indistinguishable.

Gender Displays in Advertising

While we are on the subject of image depictions in the mass media, consider
the role of gender displays in advertising. A casual inspection might reveal
nothing sexist in the vodka ad on page 85, but consider the many ways in
which the woman is subordinated to the man. He is the czar, she is perhaps
his czarina. He drinks, she does not. He is in the center, she is off to the side.
He stands, she sits on the floor. He poses for the camera, she is a mere adjunct.
He holds part of the head of the large adult dog, she gently nurtures the little
ones. The ad as a whole links Wolfschmidt's to wealth and aristocracy, and
perhaps points nostalgically to an era before the Communists took over; it is a
clear example of prestige suggestion. And the dominant figure, as in nearly all
liquor advertisements, is a powerful male, one who displays sexual potency as
well.

Lest the Wolfschmidt ad be construed as an exception, I would urge you
to examine other ads for alcoholic products, and indeed product ads generally.
Vivian Gornick, in her introduction to Goffman's (1979) *Gender Advertising*,
points to a number of nonverbal patterns of male dominance:

> (1) Overwhelmingly a woman is taller than a man only when the man is her
> social inferior; (2) a woman's hands are seen just barely touching, holding or
> caressing—never grasping, manipulating, or shaping; (3) when a photograph of
> men and women illustrates an instruction of some sort the man is always
> instructing the woman—even if the men and women are actually children (that
> is, a male child will be instructing a female child!); (4) when an advertisement
> requires someone to sit or lie on a bed or a floor that someone is almost always a
> child or a woman, hardly ever a man; (5) when the head or eye of a man is
> averted it is only in relation to a social, political, or intellectual superior, but
> when the eye or head of a woman is averted it is always in relation to whatever
> man is pictured with her; (6) women are repeatedly shown mentally drifting from
> the scene while in close physical touch with a male, their faces lost and dreamy,
> "as though his aliveness to the surroundings and his readiness to cope were

(Courtesy of The House of Seagram)

enough for both of them''; (7) concomitantly, women, much more than men, are pictured at the kind of psychological loss or remove from a social situation that leaves one unoriented for action (e.g., something terrible has happened and a woman is shown with her hands over her mouth and her eyes helpless with horror). (p. 8)

Interestingly, the distilled spirits manufacturers find it necessary to undermine in the message on page 86 the very connection between booze and sexual potency which they labor so hard to create in ads for particular products.

Persuasion, Inducements, Coercion

Once it is recognized that communication may be multimotivated and multileveled, a great many apparent controversies turn out to hinge on false

"You dropped an olive down Norma Gray's blouse last night."

It's amazing how just one drink too many can turn a normally charming, witty, intelligent person into a loud, ridiculous, boring nincompoop.

Drinking is supposed to be a social pleasure. And it's no pleasure when you indulge in it to the point where you become unpleasant to be around.

That's why we, the people who make and sell distilled spirits, urge you to use our products with common sense. If you choose to drink, drink responsibly.

Be the life of the party. Not the laugh of it.

IT'S PEOPLE WHO GIVE DRINKING A BAD NAME.

Distilled Spirits Council of the U.S. (DISCUS)
1300 Pennsylvania Building, Washington, D.C. 20004

Compare this ad with ads for particular brand names. Do they also warn against drinking to feel powerful, or do they promote that very image? Is there a discrepancy and, if so, how would you explain it? *(Courtesy of the Distilled Spirits Council of the U.S.)*

dichotomies. Let us here examine distinctions between persuasion and inducements and persuasion and coercion.

As a form of influence, persuasion is frequently distinguished from the power of the carrot and the stick; from such positive inducements to action as the promise of money or job security, and from such negative incentives as threats of bodily harm (Simons, 1974). These distinctions are freighted with value connotations.

Although persuasion is conceded to be a weak sister in comparison to its relatives within the influence family—note such expressions as "talk is cheap," "talk rather than substance," and "mere rhetoric"—it is also heralded as the most ethical. Understandably, therefore, people avoid the coercive label, take pains to deny that they are bribing others when offering them inducements, and represent themselves as persuaders—if possible as "rational persuaders." In textbooks on persuasion, coercion, especially, tends to be sharply contrasted with persuasion and regarded as intrinsically evil. Under the headings of persuasion and coercion, respectively, "moderate" protesters have been distinguished from "militant" protesters, "nice" bosses from "authoritarian" bosses, and the "mouths of diplomats" from the "mouths of guns."

It should be clear at this point that words like "persuasion," "coercion," and "inducement" are hardly neutral terms in our society. How they are defined and how they are linked to particular persons or groups has real consequences. Textbooks on persuasion tend to reflect dominant societal values by the examples they provide, and these examples tend in turn to influence popular conceptions of the meanings of these terms. The sharp contrast between persuasion and coercion, offered in many textbooks on persuasion, constitutes a "rhetoric about rhetoric" that is in need of correction.

That persuasion alters judgments, not just behaviors—that it allows for choice or the perception of choice—has been the traditional basis for distinguishing persuasion from coercion and from material inducements (Gamson, 1968; Kelman, 1961; Smith, 1982; Miller, 1980; Tedeschi, Schlenker, and Bonoma, 1973). Coercion and inducements are said to lead to changes in overt behaviors without corresponding internal changes—the former as a result of punishments or the threat of punishments, the latter as a result of tangible rewards or the promise of same. Persuaders, by contrast, are said to secure agreement and not just compliance. And while they may identify the benefits or harms from the adoption or nonadoption of a proposal, they do not claim to be the agents of those consequences. Should a chemical company warn its employees about the dangers of inhaling certain chemical particles as a way of getting them to wear air masks, that would be persuasion. Should the company combine these fear appeals with the assurance that wearing air masks will filter out harmful chemicals, that would still be persuasion. But should the company offer bonuses to workers who wear the masks, that would be an inducement; and should it threaten to fire employees who do not comply with its air mask regulations, or actually fire a few as a way of setting an example, that (it is argued) would be coercion.

To illustrate this point further, consider the following nursery school situation. Janie covets a toy truck that Robert has been sitting on. Here are some of her options, under the headings of persuasion, inducements, and coercion:

Persuasion	*Inducements*	*Coercion*
1. Aren't you tired of being on this truck?	1. If you let me on that truck, I'll play with you.	1. If you stay on that truck, I'll stop being your friend.
2. That doll over there is fun. Why don't you play with it?	2. I'll stop annoying you if you let me play with that truck.	2. Get off the truck or I'll tell Mrs. S.

Not all scholars distinguish sharply between persuasion and inducement or between persuasion and coercion. In fact, a few of them view *all* efforts at gaining-compliance as forms of persuasion (Cody, McLaughlin, and Schneider, 1981). Everyone acknowledges that persuaders provide persuadees with some degree of choice over how to think or act. But how much choice? Forcibly injecting a prisoner with a truth serum to get him to talk may not be persuasion, but inducements and coercive threats are not so restrictive. Indeed, rewards and promises of reward are not typically restrictive of choice at all.

Those scholars who set persuasion apart from inducements and coercion presuppose by their distinctions a view of persuasion as confined to efforts at promoting attitude change toward proposals for action. But it makes more sense in this context to speak of such efforts at attitude change as "pure persuasion," while recognizing that persuasion also performs other functions, including a *belief modification* function with respect to inducements and coercion.

Recall the earlier observation that communication is simultaneously substantive and image-projecting. Every attempt at coercing or inducing compliance, beyond conveying substantively a threat or promise of reward, also involves a display of the influence agent's *willingness* and *capacity* to go through with the threat or promise. The robber who offers his victim a choice between "your money and your life" must somehow convince the person that there is not some third, more attractive alternative available. Likewise, the negotiator who pledges amnesty to hijackers if they release their hostages unharmed must make her promises credible. Hence, these threateners and promisers attempt to look and act their parts. Their efforts to convince others that they mean business are surely not persuasion in the paradigmatic sense, but they are instances of persuasion nonetheless—aimed at modifying beliefs rather than attitudes.

Threats and promises are particularly important components of the rhetoric of social conflict. Indeed, to ignore these messages would be to leave the study of persuasion in social conflicts extremely impoverished. A *social conflict* is a clash over incompatible interests. A familiar example is a wage dispute between management and labor. In typical wage negotiations, persuasion and the power to reward and punish go hand in hand. Each side amasses power resources (e.g., a union strike fund, a labor replacement pool) to better prepare the other to "listen to reason." Appeals to reason and to common interests are buttressed with talk and gestures designed to establish the credibility of promises and threats. In the gamelike atmosphere of the bargaining table, considerable use is made of such rhetorical ploys as bluffing, issuing vague rather than explicit promises or threats, packaging meager inducements attractively, ignoring counterthreats, and acting as though one lacks the authority to bargain further.

These same ploys and counterplays are exhibited in virtually all ongoing relationships, although not always so manifestly. To escape the onus of appearing to bribe or threaten another, influence agents frequently frame offers or threats as persuasive appeals and only hint at their roles as agents of those consequences. Mother to child, speaking in a slightly menacing tone: "Darling, I think you should eat more green vegetables. Mind you, I'm not telling you what to do." Implication: Eat those green vegetables or else. Boss to employee, speaking in a parental tone: "Ours is a company that values initiative. I'd therefore like to see you volunteer for more overtime." Implication: Work late or else.

Most of life's situations require of people that they simultaneously compete and cooperate with each other. In these *mixed-motive* conflicts, persuasion and the power of rewards and punishments go hand in hand. The desire to please the other in the interests of maintaining a harmonious relationship must be balanced against the desire to secure one's own interests at the expense of the other. Between good friends, as between spouses, there is always the possibility that people will employ pseudocooperative appeals for self-serving purposes or shift abruptly from displays of cooperation to combative postures. In these situations, actions tend to have multiple meanings reflecting multiple motives. A denial of affection may be a form of punishment *and* a plea for attention and emotional support. A conspicuously generous act may be an expression of commitment to a relationship *and* a message obligating the marriage partner to reciprocate in kind.

Although we might wish that persuasion were "pure"—that it were not used deceptively or intermixed with coercion or inducements—the requirements of mixed-motive relationships dictate otherwise. Thus Kenneth Burke (1969) sets as the task of his own treatise on rhetoric that it "lead us through the Scramble, the Wrangle of the marketplace, the flurries and flare-ups of the Human Barnyard, the Give and Take, the War of Nerves, the War . . ." (p. 23). And he instructs us to expect in these situations that talk (including deceptive talk) and "action-as-language" (including actual rewards and punishments) will work hand in hand.

By way of summary, I have argued, contrary to the conventional view, that persuasion, coercion, and inducements are not mutually exclusive. There is "pure" persuasion, free of threats and promises, but there is also a rhetoric of power—persuasion in the peripheral sense—that serves, when effective, to make threats and promises credible. "Pure" persuasion is persuasion in the paradigmatic sense, designed by use of arguments and appeals to secure attitude change as a precondition for behavior change. Seldom in social conflict situations is persuasion entirely pure. Much of the persuasion that takes place in conflicts is persuasion *about* power, made credible by imagistic displays.

Image Management and the RPS Approach

One way of capturing the pull and tug of conflicting pressures on persuaders is through an analytic framework known as the *requirements-problems-strategies* (*RPS*) approach. First developed as a way of understanding the often anomalous rhetoric of those who lead protest movements (Simons, 1970), the RPS approach has since been applied analytically to a wide variety of cases and also used to provide guidance to persuaders (Simons, 1982). The basic assumptions of RPS are given below.

Requirements

Rhetorical choices are largely role-related. What we say to others generally reflects the demands of the situation and the pressures on us with respect to them. Less so are our rhetorical choices influenced by purely personal considerations. Because the situations we are in are not entirely unique—because others have been in similar roles before us—our rhetoric is in some respects predictable. This, you will recall, is consistent with *genre* theory, as discussed in the previous chapter.

The notion of rhetorical requirements is easily illustrated with respect to work-related activities in groups or organizations. Much of the time we are expected to speak for or in the name of a collectivity—as movement leaders, representatives of a congressional district, advertisers, PR experts, corporation lawyers, salespersons and the like—and, in one or another of these capacities, to identify closely with the goals of the collectivity. But even when we are not assigned any official role as spokesperson for the collectivity, its imprint shows in what we say and do. If you were analyzing my everyday rhetoric as an academic professional, you might do well to consider how the university that employs me, the field I am in, and the academic department with which I am affiliated affect the performance of my roles as teacher, adviser, writer, committee member, and so on.

As a professional person, for example, I enjoy a privileged status relative to other occupations, but only so long as the audiences of my life are convinced that members of my profession, and I in particular, possess the information, the knowhow, and the commitment necessary to provide society with services that it values and could not otherwise obtain. These are characteristics, I should emphasize, that inhere in the very idea of being a professional, as that concept is generally used in our culture. Hence, all professionals are rhetorically required to exhibit these qualities, although *how* they manifest them seems to vary somewhat from one profession to another. For physicians, for example, this includes conspicuously displaying diplomas and certificates on office walls— activities that would bring great laughter in an academic setting.

Problems

Our role requirements tend to conflict, one with another. And this, of course, creates rhetorical problems. Not only do we play multiple roles, we also confront multiple and conflicting pressures in the same role. For example, there may be cross-pressures upon us to appear at once dependent and independent, flexible and consistent, conforming and individualistic, cooperative and competitive. Just as our role requirements are predictable, so are the rhetorical problems stemming from conflicting requirements. And this is the great virtue of the RPS approach. Having a clear sense of the cross-pressures persuaders confront makes their rhetorical choices more comprehensible and provides a basis for assessing their message strategies.

Thus, as indicated in Chapter 3, we can fairly well predict the rhetorical problems protest leaders are apt to confront and how they are likely to differ from the problems confronting mainstream politicians. Moreover, we need not stop at so broad a level of comparison. It is possible, for example, to predict the problems of militant protest leaders as opposed to moderate protest leaders, and of protestors promoting violent civil disobedience versus those promoting nonviolent means of achieving their objectives. We may indeed extend our assessments of competing pressures to particular time periods, to moments in a campaign, and to specific types of audiences and occasions. These are precisely the sorts of considerations that will occupy us as we look more closely at the rhetoric of protest in Chapter 13.

Strategies

The rhetorical strategies we humans devise generally reflect *tradeoffs* among conflicting requirements; seldom are we able to reconcile them completely. And the strategies we implement almost always create new rhetorical problems in the process of reducing or resolving old ones. In ongoing situations, rhetorical problems never cease; they merely change.

Uses of the RPS Framework

These, then, are the basic assumptions of RPS, and they are entirely compatible with the argument of this chapter, with its emphasis on the simultaneous playing out of substantive and image management functions. Indeed, while I have thus far stressed the complementarity of these functions, the fact is that they are often incompatible, thus leading to rhetorical problems. Orr (1980) speaks in this connection of the need to sustain "counterpoised definitions of the situation" and of the immense difficulties many of us have in doing so. How, for example, in the face of pressure from a boss to achieve immediate results, does a sales representative build an image of trustworthiness that gets customers returning time after time for reorders? How in running a political campaign does the politician play it straight with constituents when she knows that on polarizing issues like abortion she is bound to alienate significant segments of the electorate? How would you get community leaders to oppose the building of an asphalt plant that you recognize is in the interests of the larger community, but that happens to be upwind from your home? How would you foster an image of honesty when you recognize that your interests and theirs are actually opposed? How, by the same token, would you convince outsiders that the community organization you lead is strong and united when you know that in fact it is weak and fragmented?

The RPS approach is a useful framework for examining image-management efforts associated with particular roles and situations. In utilizing the framework, the persuader or message analyst moves from the general to the specific, from characteristics of the genre or genres most relevant to the case at hand to characteristics of the case itself. In planning or studying extended attempts at persuasion, it may be necessary to conduct one assessment of requirements, problems, and strategies for the campaign as a whole, and other assessments for particular moments in the campaign.

A full-scale analysis of problems includes those stemming from predictable conflicting rhetorical requirements and other problems that may be unique to the situation. Having identified requirements and problems, one moves next to an assessment of strategies. This involves a comparison of what was said (or is planned) against alternative plans. Strategies are evaluated in terms of their capacity to ameliorate the problem and thus help to fulfill requirements.

In Ch 14 we look at an extended illustration of the RPS approach, focusing on former President Jimmy Carter's 1980 nomination acceptance speech and the image-management problems he encountered. For now, here are two brief illustrations of RPS as applied to problems of image management.

Case A. Presidential Press Conference

The role: White House reporter.

The occasion: A presidential press conference.

The essential problem: How to confront the president with criticism while at the same time honoring the predominant definition of the situation as a presidential proceeding demanding an appropriate style of decorum.

In this, C. Jack Orr's (1980) own study of a "counterpoised situation," 145 actual press conference questions that had previously been identified as "confrontational" were content analyzed with a view toward determining how White House reporters during the Kennedy, Johnson, and Nixon administrations balanced their conflicting requirements. Orr's analysis of the situation made clear the essential conflict. On the one hand, reporters believe they have a right and a responsibility to quiz the president, to gather "real" news as they define it, and to hold the administration to account. At the same time, they recognize that the press conference is predominantly a presidential event. As Orr notes: "It is the President who decides when a press conference will be called, where it will meet, and what ground rules shall prevail. And it is the President who decides which reporters will be recognized to ask questions, how long a conference will last, and whether the proceedings will be televised (p. 18). He adds that an abrasive questioning style may injure the reporter's long-term relationship with the president, and may even cause the reporter to be transferred or fired. Clearly, as Orr puts it, "a presidential proceeding should be accompanied by a unique sense of deference and decorum" (p. 19). In addressing the chief executive, reporters routinely employ the official title rather than referring to the president's personal identity. That is, the president is recognized as "Mr. President," or "Sir," but not as "Mr. Kennedy" or "President Johnson."

In seeking to identify preferred strategies of confrontative questioning, Orr broke down each question into elements and variations on those elements, as shown in Table 5.1. The reason that no variations are identified for the opening acknowledgment is that it was almost always deferential.

TABLE 5.1 ELEMENTS, VARIATIONS, AND PREFERRED STYLES OF CONFRONTATION

Elements	Variations	Examples
Acknowledging the president		"Mr. President, sir . . ."
Presenting the critic	As external source	"Senator Smith says . . ."
	As reporter	(I believe)
Defining the presidential target	Ambiguously	". . . the administration . . ."
	Clearly	". . . you . . ."
Conveying criticism	Explicitly	". . . failed to deliver the inflation policy you promised to the American people last January."
	Implicitly	". . . indicated in January that an inflation policy would be forthcoming to the American people but nothing has appeared in eight months."
Posing the question	As a free response question	"Would you care to comment on this, please?"
	As a restricted response question	
	Confirmatory	"Do you see this as a failure?" or "Is it fair to say the administration has (you have) failed to deliver on the promise?"
	Explanatory	"Why?"

Preferred Styles of Confrontation

1. External source, explicit criticism, free response question: "Mr. President, sir, Senator Smith says you have failed to deliver the inflation policy you promised to the American people last January. Would you care to comment on this, please?"

2. Reporter as source, implicit criticism, confirmatory, or explanatory question: "Mr. President, sir, you indicated in January that an inflation policy would be forthcoming to the American people, but nothing has happened in eight months. Is it fair to say that you have failed to deliver on the promise?" (or "Why?")

The basic strategic rule derived from Orr's study of confrontative press conference questions was that questions must be structured so as to exhibit a balance between confrontation and deference, but the playing out of this rule allowed for a variety of patterns. Thus, for example, if a reporter elected to present the president with an explicit criticism, he might balance it with a free response question derived from conversations with an external source:

> Mr. President, I apologize for this question before I ask it. The only reason I do is because I think you should have an opportunity to answer it. But I was in Richmond shortly after your reelection, at a public meeting, and a state senator, who was a Negro, got up and asked me, when is Mr. Nixon going to stop kicking the blacks around? And I thought you might like to respond to that. (p. 29)

The two dominant patterns identified by Orr are also found in Table 5.1. As Orr concluded: "When the literal content of reporters' words explicitly confront the President with criticism, reporters present themselves and question the President in a style consistent with deference to a Chief of State; but when their words are literally informative and only implicitly critical, reporters assume a style of self-presentation and questioning consistent with an interpellative assembly" (p. 31). Here, quite clearly, are tradeoffs between conflicting rhetorical requirements.

Case B: The Wog on the Chin

Let us examine another conflict between substantive and relational goals, this one discussed by Russell Baker in the *New York Times Magazine* (August 30, 1981).

Assume that you are at lunch with a rather pompous, easily irritable individual who happens also to be a prospective employer looking you over for a much-needed job. Assume further that, unknown to him, the employer has a tiny piece of food on his chin which you are finding so distracting that you are unable to respond effectively to his questions. Assume finally that the piece of food, called a "wog" by Baker, is of the type that rarely falls off of its own accord: a piece of fish, perhaps, or a snippet of oily lettuce leaf—as opposed, say, to a nice, crisp bread crumb.

Although you may never have had the experience of dining opposite a prospective employer with a wog on his chin, chances are that you have been in similar situations—enough so that you can assess rhetorical problems arising from competing pressures in this situation (e.g., need to impress employer; need to protect his ego; need to get the wog removed) and formulate an appropriate pattern of response accordingly. Thus you might rule out such strategies as reaching across the table and swiping at the employer's chin with a napkin or pointing at the man's chin while laughing uproariously. Nor are you on sufficiently intimate terms to venture a direct statement: "I'm afraid you've got a fish wog on your chin."

Rather than calling direct attention to the wog, Baker suggests a body language maneuver that relies on the "monkey-see, monkey-do" principle: Looking the employer hard in the eye, bring your hand directly to a point on your face that matches the wog's location on your victim's face, and rub gently, back and forth. The prospective employer will very likely imitate your gestures without even noticing it, and rub away the wog in the process.

Field Experiments on Image Management: Two Case Studies

Image management has been the subject of a good deal of experimental research, much of it dealing with the effects of nonverbal stimuli, such as the body language signals recommended by Baker (for sample reviews, see Leathers, 1976; and Knapp, 1978). Investigators have sought to determine which factors contribute to image perceptions and how important they are in the total mix of factors. The importance of nonverbal cues was underscored in a study by Mehrabian (1971). He found that when subjects of an experiment were confronted with discrepant cues about a person, liking for the person was influenced only 7 percent by verbal cues, while vocal and facial cues influenced liking 38 and 55 percent, respectively.

A catalogue of nonverbal behaviors would surely include vocal pauses and inflections, head and body movements, punctuality, touch, and physical proximity. These and other such behaviors lend themselves to student field studies.

In one such study, Carol Mickey took advantage of her nonstudent role as head waitress at a busy downtown crèperie to enlist her subordinates in a study of the effects of nonverbal closeness on the amount of tips they would receive from their predominantly male customers. Over the course of several weeks, Mickey's team alternated between their normal, businesslike way of approaching customers and a more intimate style that included increased eye contact (the waitresses looked at the customers as they ordered, then wrote the orders down on their pads), greater physical proximity (the waitresses would rub shoulders with their customers as they pointed out menu specials), and greater indivi-duation (the waitresses wore name tags on their uniforms). The increases in tips were quite startling—as much as 20 to 30 percent—but there is another lesson to be drawn from this experiment, one that underscores the point made earlier about conflicting role demands. While Mickey and her team enjoyed the money, they could not sustain the requisite levels of closeness. Some reported feeling guilty at having been dishonest with their customers and themselves. Others simply found it too difficult to maintain the level of intimacy called for in the experimental regimen.

The importance of facial and gestural cues was borne home in another study by a former student. Saul Fox used his extensive knowledge of the research literature on nonverbal communication, as well as his extensive hitchhiking in 40 states, to devise an experiment by which to test his hypothesis that there are more effective ways of hitchhiking than those traditionally employed. Fox asked friends to hitchhike back and forth on the same thoroughfare and to alternate randomly between method A, the traditional method, and method B, the "scientific" approach. Here were the major characteristics of his method B.

1. H (the hitchhiker) stands at 45° angle to road, rather than 90° angle. H is now in psychological path of motorist and cannot as easily be dismissed as an irrelevant object.
2. Rather than the traditional rigidly extended arm, clenched fist, and protruding thumb, H extends arm loosely and presents raised hand and open palm (as when getting attention in a classroom) toward oncoming traffic. This relaxed, friendly posture begs recognition and bespeaks desire for familiarity. Moreover, it acts as a larger "flag" than the closed fist and calls attention to his facial area, where the greatest amount of persuasion occurs.
3. H seeks eye contact with motorist and attempts to maintain its duration beyond the conventional "glance" period by emitting an eyebrow flash at the moment contact is made. If eyes lock into each other for more than a brief instant, motorist becomes psychologically responsible for making some type of response to H. Raised eyebrows serve as an additional "asking"

cue and may even put the question of a ride on a level beyond that of simply asking for one by communication of a presumption of assent to a previously asked question. In other words, it may signify, "Is it true that you are willing to give me a ride?"

Method B proved significantly more effective. Whereas H had a 27 percent chance of getting a ride within 10 minutes using the traditional method, he (or she) got a ride within 10 minutes 52 percent of the time using the scientific approach.

SUMMARY

Communication is multileveled. It involves not just substantive messages, but also messages at a relational level that project images of self and other as they "comment" upon the substantive message. Relational messages are often communicated unintentionally, through manner and style of presentation. Indeed, whenever we communicate about substantive matters, we invariably project images of ourselves as well. From the recognition that we cannot *not project* images of ourselves comes the realization that we might just as well actively *promote* selected images of ourselves—hence the subject of image management.

Image management is a vast and complex subject that we shall take up again in Chapter 7. The focus here has been on the nature and scope of "imaging," and on its relation to substantive messages. Among the principles offered in this chapter are the following:

1. The relationship between image and substance is interactive and reciprocal: A credible image *(ethos)* helps make one's ideas more credible, and vice versa.
2. Acts may be multimotivated, and they may perform different functions at different levels. The same act may entertain, inform, or genuinely express feelings at one level (usually the content level), while being simultaneously rhetorical at another level.
3. Although clear distinctions can be made between persuasion and coercion, and between persuasion and inducements at the content level, these distinctions are blurred at the relational level; even threats and promises need to be made credible. Seldom in conflict situations is persuasion entirely "pure."
4. Deceptions are inherently rhetorical, and they generally carry with them the implicit metacommunication: "This is not a deceptive message." In expression games, deceivers may go to great lengths (at meta-meta and meta-meta-meta levels) to convince us that their messages can be taken at face value. In so doing, they exploit conventional distinctions between "the real" and "the rhetorical."
5. In some contexts, it is impossible *not* to function as a persuader. Even "no-frills" packages in a supermarket are rhetorical.

6. Among the major persuasive influences in our culture are messages labeled as something other than persuasion—such as art or entertainment. Popular art and entertainment tend to reinforce mass values and stereotypes in the process of merely reflecting them.

Image management may be enhanced by application of the requirements-problems-strategies (RPS) approach. Rhetorical requirements may be gleaned from knowledge of occupational and organizational role expectations and of expectations and obligations associated with particular tasks and occasions. Rhetorical problems stem from incompatible role requirements and from other constraints on goal accomplishment. The rhetorical strategies we employ to cope with problems generally reflect tradeoffs among conflicting requirements—for example, between the obligation incumbent upon White House reporters to extract information at press conferences from presidents reluctant to provide it, while at the same time displaying an appropriate style of decorum. Occasionally, as in the wog-on-the-chin example, one may hit upon a *strategy* that fulfills all requirements simultaneously.

EXERCISES

1. Do a research study of image management in interpersonal relations. For example:
   a. Ingratiation techniques used by job applicants and status maintenance techniques used by employers
   b. Impression management techniques used at cocktail parties or in dating situations
   c. Techniques used by job supervisors to handle employee complaints or rule infractions
   d. Methods used by toddlers to wrest privileges or avoid punishments from parents
   e. Techniques used to deal with a distracting "chin wog"

   For the last of these examples, here are some sample suggestions:

1) *Library research*. Consult a number of etiquette books to see how, if at all, the problems of wogs has been addressed. Etiquette books are frequently a useful guide to cultural rules.
2) *Surveys*. Present a number of people (preferably strangers) with the problem posed earlier. See how they would respond; then ask them what they think of Russell Baker's solution. Assess their knowledge (tacit or explicit) of how to handle this situation.
3) *Experiments*. A number of ideas suggest themselves. One possibility is to place others in the situation of having to cope with your wog. You might experiment with wog-wearing with friends versus strangers, people of high versus low status, and so on. You might also control for who is doing the wog-wearing by having a number of different wog-wearers in your study, and by having them alternate between wearing and not wearing wogs.

   Another possibility is to assess the effects of different ways of calling attention to a stranger's wogs. For example, you might compare the effects of a verbal stare versus the Baker method of placing your hand on your own chin in hope of a sympathetic response. Or you might compare various verbal means of calling attention to the wog and then survey experimental subjects for their attitudes toward your wog-removal effects.

2. **"Oh, Did I Wake You?": Case Study in the RPS Approach.** You are fast asleep when the telephone rings. You pick up the phone near your bed, murmur "Hello" or something to that effect, and then collapse back on to your pillow with the phone dangling somewhere near your left ear. The caller says in a slightly surprised manner: "Oh, did I wake you?" How would you respond? How predictable are our responses in these situations?

Note that the key crosspressures here are the need to save one's own face versus the need to save the caller's face; the need to realize the short-range substantive goal of getting back to sleep versus the long-range goal of preserving one's good reputation; and the value of honesty versus the temptation to stretch the truth a bit in the interests of face-saving.

Typically we need more information in cases such as these before we can decide which responses might be most appropriate: Is the caller a friend, an acquaintance, or a stranger? Someone we like or dislike? Is our status relationship to the caller "one-up," "one-down," or about equal? Is this the first time the caller has awakened us, or is this a repeated occurrence? Could most callers be reasonably expected to assume we would be awake at this hour, or is this an ungodly time of day to be calling?

Below is a list of response alternatives that might be used, depending on the circumstances. Compare the circumstances under which you would be likely to choose each with the choices of other members of your class.

a. No.

b. Thanks for waking me; I must have slept through my alarm.

c. I was just getting up.

d. I couldn't sleep last night because the Smiths next door were having a party. . . .

e. It's my day off.

f. I've got a bad cold.

g. Well, sort of.

h. I was almost awake.

i. I was thinking of getting up.

j. Let's just say that submarines don't have screen doors.

k. It's possible, John, but I may have only been dreaming I was asleep.

l. I was, John, but it's always good to hear from you.

m. Yes, dammit!

Chapter 6
Persuasion and Objectivity: A Rhetorical Perspective

News articles. Newscasts. Scientific reports. Textbooks. Courtroom testimony. Medical histories. Psychiatric diagnoses. Historical narratives. Film documentaries. Classroom lectures. Accounting statements. Messages classified in these ways make serious claims on our psyches. Each claims to provide "truth" or "knowledge" of some sort. And there are numerous other messages which, while perhaps more obviously biased or partisan in nature, nevertheless purport to provide objective "fact," "information," "logic," and the like.

Later in this book (Chapter 15), we will be concerned with how to recognize persuasion in the guise of objectivity—and with how to analyze and assess it. But the first question we need to ask is whether it is possible to be entirely free of rhetorical elements in human communication. Is there a language of persuasion as opposed, say, to a language of instruction or information-giving? The question has important moral implications.

> If we would speak of things as they are, we must allow that all the art of rhetoric, besides order and clearness; all the artificial and figurative application of words eloquence hath invented, are for nothing else but to insinuate wrong ideas, move the passions, and thereby mislead the judgment; and so indeed are perfect cheats: and therefore, however laudable or allowable oratory may render them in harangues and popular addresses, they are certainly, in all discourses that pretend to inform or instruct, wholly to be avoided; and where truth and knowledge are concerned, cannot but be thought a great fault, either of the language or person that makes use of them. . . . It is evident how much men love to deceive and be deceived, since rhetoric, that powerful instrument of error and deceit, has its established professors, is publicly taught, and has always been had in great reputation.

In this famous passage from his *Essay on Human Understanding*, philosopher John Locke was suggesting that while rhetoric may have its place in partisan appeals to popular assemblies, it is both possible and desirable to avoid it entirely in discourses that purport "to inform and instruct . . . and where truth and knowledge are concerned." This same distinction between the rights and obligations of partisan persuaders and those of persons expected to tell us what the world is "really like" is put even more strongly by sociologist Andrew Weigert (1970).

Morality, says Weigert, is chiefly a matter of truthful identity management—of communicators presenting themselves as they really are. Those, like the stereotypical used-car salesman, who use every rhetorical technique on their customers, are not immoral for doing so, for they announce themselves as partisan persuaders and thus do not create false expectations on the part of their audiences. Those in the allegedly nonpartisan group, on the other hand, announce themselves as "carriers of 'unbiased' truth buttressed by evidence of the stated condition of reality." And they impose a corresponding obligation on their audiences to believe and accept them for what they announce themselves to be. Thus, for example, "if a sociologist practices rhetoric, but identifies himself (to self and/or others) as a scientist, he renders his rhetoric immoral, the immoral rhetoric of identity deception" (p. 111).

Persuasion and Message Classification

One of the difficulties we confront in this chapter is that communicators may persuade not only by the manner in which they "picture" the external world, but also by the way they "frame" their messages as being of a certain type. For example, Locke would undoubtedly have characterized his own philosophical discourse as being of the sort concerned with "truth and knowledge," rather than rhetorical partisanship. But Locke readily employs rhetorical devices even in his characterization of the "artificial and figurative" use of words as "perfect cheats," and in his depiction of rhetoric itself as "that powerful instrument of error and deceit." By Weigert's definition, is Locke here guilty of an "immoral rhetoric of identity deception"?

Within our own contemporary culture there is, apparently, a good deal of persuasion about persuasion. Whereas persuasion tends to be a positive term in relation to coercion or force, it is typically a negative term in relation to its allegedly more objective alternatives. Along with such roughly synonymous terms as "rhetoric," "propaganda," and "indoctrination," its usage tends to reflect political and cultural values.

Thus, for example, the conventional wisdom holds that our nation exports documentary films abroad, while our enemies distribute propaganda films. Our schools are said to educate or acculturate, but schoolteachers do not claim to persuade or indoctrinate. Employers orient or train but never brainwash employees. Scientists and philosophers describe, explain, reason, or prove, but they never employ rhetoric or persuasive appeals. When persuasion, propaganda, and rhetoric are used in references to scientists, newscasters, and so on, they are almost always terms of derision, ways of indicating the language user's belief that the scientists, journalists, or other professionals have pretended to be what they are not—that they have somehow violated principles held in high esteem by their professions. In these contexts, the terms have come to mean "deception" or "impurity," something that the language user wishes to expose. No wonder that the words "persuasion," "propaganda," and "rhetoric" are often preceded by such adjectives as "mere," "just," and "only"; worse yet, by such expletives as "malicious," "devious," and "dishonest." In popular discourse, we might say: "I wish my teacher would stick to the facts and stop trying to persuade us." Or, "His rhetoric stood in the way of his art." Or, "The argument that males are inherently stronger than females isn't scientific, it's male chauvinist propaganda."

Understandably, therefore, communicators of all stripes attempt to distance themselves from the "persuasion" label if they believe they can get away with it. Many reporters, educators, and scientists deny that they practice persuasion; even some paradigmatic persuaders such as advertisers, political campaigners, trial lawyers purport to allow "the facts to speak for themselves." At the very least, persuaders may adapt some of the trappings of objectivity to a clearly promotional effort. An Anacin commercial features what appears to be a scientific diagram of the pain reliever working its way more quickly through the digestive system than competing tablets. A shareholder's report masks a corporation's low profit potential by surrounding the relevant data in a sea of largely irrelevant and unreadable statistics. A salesperson seeks to mystify a customer by using technical-sounding terms.

Here, quite clearly, are examples of persuasion in the guise of objectivity. But it is not always so clear that a communicator is merely employing the trappings of the objective scientist or reporter in an effort to enhance persuasive effectiveness. By what "objective" grounds, after all, may we distinguish the appearance of objectivity from the "genuine article"? Suppose, for example, that a similar visual comparison of painkillers had been prepared by a scientist for publication in a reputable pharmaceutical journal. Should we then believe the diagram was factual and therefore nonrhetorical? How, in general, might we distinguish persuasion from "pure" description or "pure" logic? Is the very idea of objectivity a myth that any thinking person must reject? But if so, on what rational grounds could we possibly accept (or reject) any idea, including the idea that objectivity is a myth?

An Essay on Persuasion and Objectivity

As you can see, questions about the relationship between persuasion and objectivity quickly lead to paradox and puzzlement. There have been a number of attempts to distinguish persuasion from objective news reporting, education, scientific writing, and so on, but none is entirely satisfactory.

One view circumscribes the study of persuasion to controversial matters, those matters over which there might legitimately be doubt or disagreement, good or bad feelings. Messages on matters that are entirely noncontroversial are presumed to be outside the realm of persuasion on the grounds that they are capable of objective description. On these grounds, for example, Miller (1980) maintains that teaching a child how to tie his or her shoes is not persuasion. Having observed that persuasive messages tend to be opinionated, even impassioned, a few scholars go so far as to characterize persuasion as influence by nonlogical, or even irrational, means. However, as Burke (1969) has observed: "Many of the opinions upon which persuasion relies are outside the test of truth in the strictly scientific, yes-no sense." But, even assuming the validity of these distinctions, we can readily see that there might be some intense arguments over how to apply them. What is and what isn't controversial? By what criteria should we decide that an argument is nonlogical or unreasonable?

If persuaders are not necessarily *illogical* or *irrational*, can we at least grant that their arguments are *extra*-logical? Is this not a basis for distinguishing the argument-making of persuaders from objective conclusion-drawing? According to this view, prototypical persuaders such as salespeople and politicians offer facts and reasons to their audiences, but acceptance of their arguments by audiences always rests on something *more than*, or *other than*, the evidence or logical arguments they present. By contrast, the scientist and the philosopher are said to offer "proofs" that are free of extra-factual and extra-logical factors. Whereas persuasion begins from premises that are acceptable to a particular audience (whether true or not), logical proof begins from premises that are indubitably and universally true. Whereas the persuader's arguments are value-laden, the scientist's or philosopher's are value-free. Whereas the persuader is partial, the scientist and philosopher may be presumed to be impartial.

Campbell (1982) addresses the relationship between persuaders, scientists, and philosophers from a slightly different perspective. Persuaders, says Campbell may draw upon the contributions of philosophers and scientists when marshaling arguments on the value-laden issues they typically confront. Philosophers may point out contradictions in our thinking and spell out the logical implications of a position. Likewise, scientists can provide data about such factual questions as the ages at which women become pregnant, the storage of nuclear wastes, the rates of commission of capital crimes. But, says Campbell, "when we have looked at the data and examined the logic of the conclusions drawn by them, we still must make decisions that go beyond the facts and make commitments that go beyond logic" (p. 4). Campbell adds: "While rhetoric, like science and philosophy, is concerned with justification, i.e., with logical processes for drawing conclusions from facts and premises, not all of the reasons used by rhetors will make sense to logicians and scientists. Some rhetorical reasons will be grounded in facts and logic, but many others will be grounded in religious beliefs, history, or cultural values, in associations and metaphors, in hunger, resentments or dreams" (p. 5).

Let us grant that the discourse of ordinary persuaders is extra-factual and extra-logical. It is in these respects not objective. But the question I would ask is whether scientists or philosophers are as different from ordinary rhetors as Campbell seems to suggest. Scientific and philosophical discourse may not be extra-factual and extra-logical in quite the same way that advertising copy is, but it is nevertheless the case that scientists and philosophers must adapt to their respective audiences, selecting appeals and arguments that are most likely to win assent. There is abundant evidence, for example, that the believability of scientific claims may be influenced by the reputations of scientists, or by the prestige of the journals in which their work appears, or by the number of eminent authorities they cite in support of their claims, or by the manner in which they display their data (Simons, 1980). Let none of us profess shock at this, for as Albert Einstein once remarked: "If an angel of God were to descend and drive from the Temple of Science all those . . . motivated by display and profit, I fear the Temple would be nearly emptied." And, while we need not condemn all scientists for practicing an "immoral rhetoric of identity deception," I think we can agree with Weigert (1970) that many scientists quite consciously attend to the informal norms of their disciplines concerning how to get published, impress superiors, earn tenure and promotion, secure foundation grants, and so on—sometimes at considerable sacrifice of competent performance. The seedier side of academe's "publish or perish" ritual is reflected in such rules of the game as the following, which tend to be passed on informally from one generation of scholars to the next:

1. Dignify your assemblage of ideas by labeling it a "theory." No one knows what a theory is exactly, but everyone agrees it's a good thing.
2. Frame your "theory" in ambiguous enough language that you can always explain away potentially disconfirming research findings.
3. Create the impression that your research hypotheses follow directly from your theory. Make abundant use of such words as "thus," "hence," and "therefore."
4. Selectively review research literature in support of your theory and research hypotheses. If you can find only one source that agrees with you, say "at least one expert agrees."
5. Stretch out the reporting of your research findings. With some skillful writing, one piece of research can be made into two or three research articles.

The Status, Ethics, and Scope of Persuasion: A Rhetorical Perspective

It could be maintained that these claims do not apply to all scientific discourse, or at least to "good" scientific discourse, but there is another class of arguments that cannot so easily be dismissed. Here it is argued that science (and scientific discourse) cannot be what it has been familiarly depicted as being; that "good" science relies on extra-factual and extra-logical considerations. Koch (1964) has asserted, for example, that "the scientific process is in principle, and at all stages, underdetermined by rule" (p. 21). Perelman (1971) has argued that persuasive elements are "unavoidable in every philosophical argument, in every discussion which is not restricted to mere calculation or seeks to justify its elaboration or its application, and in every consideration of the principles of any discipline whatever, even in the programming of a computer" (p. 119).

Others (Kaplan, 1964; Bridgeman, 1959; Polyani, 1958) have insisted that the first premises of scientific theories are unprovable; that "good" theories suggest hypotheses that are not logically deducible from their premises; that theories gain acceptance by being intuitively or at least subjectively satisfying; that the rules of induction are imprecise; that the ultimate test of "objectivity" in the sciences is subjective agreement among scientists at a particular time, and in a particular culture.

How, in the light of these comments, shall we evaluate the contributions of a giant such as Einstein? Thomas Kuhn (1970) has argued that men like Einstein have ushered in scientific revolutions. In every such revolution, says Kuhn, the scientist is not simply extra-factual or extra-logical. By his or her contribution, the scientist transforms what other scientists mean by fact and logic; the scientist makes them think in a fundamentally new way. According to Kuhn, the scientific revolutionary induces "conversion." He or she employs "techniques of persuasion . . . in a situation in which there can be no proof . . ." (p. 151). If we are to believe Thomas Kuhn, was Einstein a persuader?

Hallmarks of a Rhetorical Perspective

Rather than distinguishing sharply between the discourse of scientists or philosophers and that of ordinary rhetors, I would propose the adoption of a *rhetorical perspective* on all discourse. Such a perspective carries with it a built-in skepticism toward any and all claims to objectivity, impartiality, pure logic, and so on. It also has implications for persuasive practice.

Critics operating from a rhetorical perspective practice what Nietzsche called "the art of mistrust." Their job is to examine discourse, including scientific discourse, with a view toward highlighting its extra-factual, extra-logical dimensions. The hallmarks of the rhetorical perspective may be summarized as follows.

1. "Truths" of all kinds, whether articulated as scientific facts or as philosophical logic, are themselves reflective of one or more perspectives. As regards "facts," Poincaré (1929) put the matter thus: "For a fact is not a thing or event, it is a statement about a thing or event, and it is impossible, or nearly so, to make a statement without implying some theory of events— what is 'important' for instance. Thus every statement of fact is an abstraction. It refers to some aspect only of events."
2. "Truths," if they are to be certified as such, must, in Campbell's (1982) words, "be carried by people to people." In the carrying they will take on the character of the language or other vehicle of expression used to communicate them. As critic Northrop Frye (1957) has maintained: "Anything which makes a functional use of words will always be involved in all of the technical problems of words, including rhetorical problems. The only road from grammar to logic, then, runs through the intermediary territory of rhetoric" (p. 331).
3. The way "truths" are expressed reflects the interests, the values, and the

frames of reference of language-users, including their interests in adapting their ideas to others to gain their understanding and assent.

4. Just as substantive "truths" are adapted to others, so are communicators' explanations for their statements and actions. Part of what it means to engage effectively in image management is to present accounts of rhetorical aims and motives that others will find believable and acceptable. This leads to an ever-present consciousness of the relevant audiences of our lives, an anticipation of what "they" might think.

5. Theories, philosophies, ideologies are never true or false, but more or less useful, and this applies as well to the ideal of objectivity. Objectivity may indeed be a useful ideal in some contexts, but it is never achievable in any absolute sense.

Does adoption of a rhetorical perspective necessarily demean science or other such ostensibly objective enterprises? Only if one begins with an oversimplified and overinflated view of science. Sociologist Joseph Gusfield (1976) put the matter well when he suggested:

> To be relevant or significant, data must not only be selected, they have to be typified and interpreted. In doing this, language and thought are themselves the vehicles through which such relevance is cast. They lead us to conclusions and thus to new perspectives. It is not that Science is reduced to Rhetoric and thus rendered corrupt and useless. It is rather that the rhetorical component seems to be unavoidable if the work is to have a theoretical or a policy relevance. Thus an analysis of scientific work *should* also include its rhetorical as well as its empirical component. (p. 31)

It may indeed be maintained that rhetorical analysis of scientific discourse is an essential part of the scientific process. John Stuart Mill observed long ago that the best test of truth was its capacity to survive in a competitive marketplace of ideas. Toward that end, he urged that all competing views be given the fullest and most capable expression, that they be subject to revision in light of new ideas, and that audiences be critical but open to views which challenged their own. Mill intended his essay as a defense of democratic government, but it can also be seen as a more accurate depiction of the scientific enterprise. Their pretensions aside, scientists can lay claim to employing Mill's procedure for arriving at truth. They are distinguished not so much by their particular brand of logic as by their willingness to engage in honest and open dialogue with other scientists.

The Rhetoric of Reporting

But surely, it will be argued, there must be some criteria that can help us to differentiate, say, the self-serving propagandist from the objective reporter. Is it not at least possible to report objectively on relatively simple and uncontroversial matters and thus not always function in the role of persuader?

Most contemporary rhetoricians would admit to possible differences in degrees of objectivity, but they would nevertheless insist that the various standards that have been proposed as markers of objectivity are not all consistent or fully realizable in practice. The following observations provided further support for a rhetorical perspective on the role of the reporter.

What We Call "Facts" Are Constructions. They Don't Exist "Out There." The story goes that three umpires disagreed about the task of calling balls and strikes. The first one said, "I calls them as they is." The second one said, "I calls them as I sees them." The third and cleverest umpire said, "They ain't nothin' 'till I calls them."

The Language Used to Report Any Given Fact Is Necessarily Selective. Even a simple request for the time may be greeted legitimately by a host of responses, each placing a different "face" on things: "Around five o'clock." "Four fifty-nine." "Time to stop work." "It's late." "Martini time."

It Is Never Possible to Say Everything about an Object; The Number of Facts That Can Be Cited Is Limitless. Try exhausting what you can say about something relatively simple, like a piece of chalk. At first you will undoubtedly comment on its more obvious qualities: white, brittle, smooth, round, cylindrical. But that will hardly exhaust matters. What of its taste, its smell, the things it can and cannot be used for, and so on?

Since It Is Never Possible to Say Everything about an Object, Every Report of "the Facts" Is Necessarily a Selection of Some Facts, Not Others. As suggested earlier, language usage always deflects attention from some things in the process of *reflecting* other things; it always emphasizes *and* deemphasizes.

Evenhanded Reports Are Not Necessarily Accurate Reports. These two criteria of objectivity often rub against each other (Hackett, 1984). Suppose, for example, that the subject of a given newscast is deception in political campaigning and that the newscaster is reporting on a particularly deceptive campaigner. Based on the rule that as many good things as bad should be said about candidates, the reporter would distort the truth of this candidate's exceptional deceptiveness.

In Some Situations There Is No Neutral Middle Ground. During the 1980 presidential contest, Jimmy Carter rejected an invitation by the League of Women Voters to join candidates Reagan and Anderson in a three-way debate. In their news coverage of the debate, the networks were then faced with the question of whether to give equal time to Carter's nonparticipation. How Carter responded to the debate was, in one sense, big news. However, coverage of the Carter response would have left the networks vulnerable to the charge that they had taken the spotlight away from the true participants in the drama.

Consensus Opinion Is Not Necessarily Accurate Opinion. A Harvard professor, well known for his expertise on the subject of intelligence testing, recently complained in the *Atlantic Monthly* that he could "count on the fingers of one hand" all the journalists he had met who were committed to "telling the truth about my field as well as they can discover it" (Herrnstein, 1982, p. 73). He noted, for example, that of 15 reviews dealing with intelligence testing which appeared in the *New York Times* from 1975 to 1981, not one was sympathetic to IQ testing or to those who promoted it. All but two of the books reviewed were opposed to testing and were praised for their position. Only one of the books written by psychometricians (experts on testing) was reviewed during this period, and it was panned. Moreover, the *Times* published not a single review by a trained psychometrician. Apparently, he says, reporters have an anti-IQ test bias because the test data rub against their egalitarian belief systems.

Reporters Are Bound to Reflect Institutional Interests in Rendering Descriptions. The news media in general and the networks in particular have been roundly criticized for pandering to public tastes by playing up the spectacular, the fast-moving, the superficial (Hackett, 1984). It may well be, as Mankiewicz and Swerdlow (1978) have argued, that the need to make a profit in an inherently entertainment medium literally compels the commercial networks to play up the dramatic.

Reporters and Others Whose Business It Is to Disseminate Information Are Not Saved from the Problems of Objectivity by Restricting Their Coverage to Innocuous Details. Historians have largely abandoned efforts to restrict textbook coverage of events to names, dates, and places; they recognize that facts must be interpreted if they are to have any meaning. Similarly, some news media analysts now speak of the "fairness" test rather than the test of objectivity as the basic criterion by which news reports should be judged (Friendly, 1971). They maintain that if the news is to have meaning and significance, it must be "dramatized," "interpreted," "placed in perspective"— in other words, it must contain rhetorical elements. Such a position necessarily raises many more questions than it answers. Basically, what is "fair" reporting? When does dramatic coverage become yellow journalism? Are "fair" interpretations of the facts always "balanced" interpretations, or are there times when only "extreme" judgments "follow" from the facts (Hackett, 1984)? These are difficult questions about the rhetoric of news reporting, but they are infinitely more realistic than those which presuppose the possibility of reporting on controversial matters objectively.

Implications of a Rhetorical Perspective for Persuaders

Let us shift our attention at this point to the implications of a rhetorical perspective for "ordinary" persuaders—for salespersons, advertisers, politicians, and the like, and also for ourselves. If not even scientists or journalists or historians can be expected to communicate objectively, are we absolved of any responsibility to evidence our claims or to reason logically in communicating with others?

There are, it seems, two major implications for persuaders from what we have been discussing, the first in the form of a danger, the second in the form of an opportunity. The danger is that we might interpret the critique of objectivist assumptions as license for an "anything goes" philosophy of rhetorical practice. Challenges to "objectivism" notwithstanding, there remain sufficient grounds for holding persuaders to account—grounds of *reasonableness*, if not those of empirical "proof" or "pure" logic. And while it is perhaps more difficult to specify what counts as reasonableness in persuasive discourse than to recite the tenets of objectivism, it is possible to provide general rules of thumb and examples that most of us can agree upon. This I will attempt to do in Chapters 9 and 10.

The "upside" of a rhetorical perspective for persuaders is that it invites greater use of the imagination in thinking about problems and their solutions, and in the exploitation of what Kenneth Burke (1969) has called "the resources of ambiguity" in language. One need not abandon notions of evidence and argument to recognize that what we experience as problems has at least partly to do with how we label them; correspondingly, creative problem-solving can often come about by *reframing* the problem, and thus seeing it from another perspective. A major part of what persuasion is about consists in giving people new ways of coding reality and thereby, in effect, altering their perceptions of reality itself. But the fulfillment of this important function of persuasion is impeded by an objectivist perspective.

In the standard, objectivist view, language is, or ought to be, a mirror of reality. A parallel image is that of language as a windowpane that enables us to see the world without interference or distortion of any kind (Rorty, 1979; Gusfield, 1976). In this view, reality exists independent of the language used to characterize it. People and places, problems and their causes, all exist "out there," and their existence is objectively demonstrable. The job of the problem analyst, then, is to characterize problems and their causes accurately and unambiguously. This requires that language be used "correctly"; that the language user "discover" the "right meanings" of the words to be employed and then "tell it like it is."

From a rhetorical perspective, language is in some respects *constitutive* of reality, rather than merely reflective of it (see Gregg, 1984; McGee, 1975; Scott, 1976). *Who* we are as individuals and as people, *how* we understand ourselves to be joined together in time and space, *what* we consider to be problems or nonproblems, all depend on the language we select to "create," as it were, the worlds we inhabit. For example, different cultures regard infant mortality very differently, and conceptions of what it meant to say one was an Englishman or an American changed quite radically as a result of the rhetoric of anticolonialists preceding the American Revolution (Lucas, 1976).

In hewing to a rhetorical perspective, we need not reject objectivism altogether. The objectivist view reminds us of the need to define our terms carefully and to show evidence for our more controversial claims. It also serves as a corrective to those who would see all realities as solely a matter of linguistic constructions and all constructions as equally appropriate. Although it may be true, for example, that cultures vary greatly in their attitudes toward "the problem" of infant mortality, the death of infants is not in itself solely a matter of linguistic construction.

But there is not always one best way to define a term or to describe a thing. In their insistence on the "out-thereness" of problems and solutions, objectivists are often unable or unwilling to see things from a variety of perspectives, still less to communicate them to others. They would have us *play* by linguistic rules, but not *with* the rules. And they would eliminate ambiguity, rather than exploiting its rhetorical potential. For these reasons, they often seem stuck in existing frames of thought, unable to capitalize on possibilities for reframing.

The concept of *reframing* has been receiving a great deal of attention in recent years—from psychotherapists (Watzlawick, Weakland, and Fisch, 1974; Pentony, 1981), sociologists (Goffman, 1974, 1981), and even design engineers (Schön, 1979). Earlier in this chapter I offered examples of message classifications as frames (films as "documentaries" versus "propaganda"), and in Chapter 4 we saw how substantive messages may be reframed by relational messages (e.g., how saying "please" could turn an order into a request). Watzlawick et al. have attempted to give the term a more precise definition. To reframe, say the authors, "means to change the conceptual and/or emotional setting or viewpoint in relation to which a situation is experienced and to place it in another frame which fits the facts of the same concrete situation equally well or even better, and thereby changes its entire meaning" (p. 95).

A classic example of reframing that they provide is the familiar story of Tom Sawyer and the whitewashed fence. On being ridiculed by a friend for having to whitewash a large board fence when all the other boys he knows are on holiday from work, Tom looked at the boy and said:

> "What do you call work?"
> "Why, ain't *that* work?"
> Tom resumed his whitewashing, and answered carelessly:
> "Well, maybe it is, and maybe it ain't. All I know, is, it suits Tom Sawyer."
> "Oh come, now, you don't mean to let on that you *like* it?"
> The brush continued to move.
> "Like it? Well, I don't see why I oughtn't to like it. Does a boy get a chance to whitewash a fence every day?"
> *That put the thing in a new light.* Ben stopped nibbling his apple. Tom swept his brush daintily back and forth—stepped back to note the effect—added a touch here and there—criticized the effect again—Ben watching every move and getting more and more interested, more and more absorbed.
> Presently he said:
> "Say, Tom, let *me* whitewash a little."

In the Tom Sawyer story, the whitewashing of the fence is placed in another category and thus recontextualized, but there are other paradoxical strategies that serve primarily as disarming techniques. The authors tell the story of the police officer whose issuance of a citation for a minor traffic violation had drawn a large and hostile crowd: By the time he had given the offender his ticket, the mood of the crowd was ugly and the sergeant was not certain he would be able to get back to the relative safety of his patrol car. It then occurred to him to announce in a loud voice: "You have just witnessed the issuance of a traffic ticket by a member of your Oakland Police Department."

Here is a third example, this one involving another crowd dispersal technique: During one of the many nineteenth-century riots in Paris, the commander of an army detachment received orders to clear a city square by firing at the *canaille* (rabble). He commanded his soldiers to take up firing positions, their rifles leveled at the crowd, and as a ghastly silence descended he drew his sword and shouted at the top of his lungs: "Mesdames, m'sieurs, I have orders to fire at the *canaille*. But as I see a great number of honest, respectable citizens before me, I request that they leave so that I can safely shoot the *canaille*." The square was empty in a few minutes.

The notions of reframing, of exploiting ambiguity, and of playing with the rules are particularly well illustrated by Watzlawick, Weakland, and Fisch (1974) by reference to the nine-dot problem (Figure 6.1). To solve this problem, you must connect the nine dots shown in the figure by four straight lines without lifting your pencil from the paper. On being initially confronted with this problem, it is almost always assumed that the dots comprise a square and that the lines must be drawn within the confines of the square. This self-imposed rule dooms all attempts to solve the problem. It is only by questioning our assumption, recognizing that the ambiguity of the task allows us greater freedom than we initially assumed, and finally, as a consequence, entertaining other rules—stepping outside the frames of our own making—that we can deal with this and other problems effectively (see Figure 6.2).

Watzlawick et al. emphasize that it is not simply the perspective we have on particular issues that impedes solutions to problems, but our more general tendency to regard any and all categories as fixed and proper:

> Once an object is categorized as the member of a given class, it is extremely difficult to see it as belonging also to another class. This class membership of an object is called its "reality;" thus anybody who sees it as the member of another class must be mad or bad. Moreover, from this simplistic assumption there follows another, equally simplistic one, namely that to stick to this view of reality is not only sane, but also "honest," "authentic," and what not. "I cannot play games" is the usual retort of people who are playing the game of not playing a game, when confronted with the possibility of seeing an alternative class membership (p. 99).

Figure 6.1 The Nine-dot Problem.

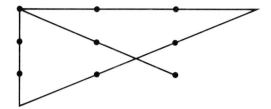

Figure 6.2 Solution to the Nine-Dot Problem.

Another way to make this point is to distinguish between *first-order perspectives* (i.e., views of *particular* "realities," experiences, messages, relationships, and the like) and *metaperspectives* (ways of thinking *about* reality, experience, language, relationships, and the like). John and Mary are having an argument about an unanswered phone: "For God's sakes, Mary, why didn't you answer it?"

"It wasn't my turn, John. Besides, you were nearer to the phone."

"Don't give me that. I answered the phone three times in a row this morning. Besides, I'm watching the game."

"You think that's important, don't you. Well I'll have you know I was cooking *your* dinner."

From the looks of things, John and Mary have very different perspectives on the same event:

Mary	*John*
Whoever is nearer to the phone should answer it.	Whoever is least busy should answer the phone.
You were nearer to the phone.	I was very busy (watching the game).
You should have answered it.	You should have answered it.

Conceivably, one of them could have convinced the other to shift perspectives, and on this basis to conclude that the other was "right." For example, John might have found it difficult to dispute Mary's contention that she was doing something very important—cooking *his* dinner. Chances are, however, that John would have remained unpersuaded, and might well have regarded the "his dinner" argument as an obvious ploy. He might even have become further enraged at what he took to be her air of smug superiority in the matter. As so often happens, what begins as a minor dispute at the content or substantive level becomes a major blowup at the relational level.

While John and Mary's first-order perspectives in the case of the unanswered phone are superficially quite different, there are a number of basic similarities in their *metaperspectives*. Note the following objectivist assumptions in their approach to the conflict:

1. There is a "substance" to this dispute—an unanswered phone. That is what it is *about*.
2. The substance of the dispute exists "out there," independent of the language used to characterize it.

3. There is a *correct way* of characterizing it.
4. Someone is to *blame* in this case.
5. Exactly *who* is to blame can be assessed *objectively*, in much the same way one might attempt to determine why a toaster isn't working. To identify who is to blame is to identify the *cause* of the problem.

When once John and Mary can get past their objectivist assumptions, they are free to deal with this and many other struggles for control in their relationship more imaginatively. There remains the paradoxical problem, however, that an "objective" analysis of their shared metaperspectives might only exacerbate the problem, while the "ultimate" solution may be to reframe not just the immediate problem, but the "metaproblem." Watzlawick et al. (1974) observe that presenting novel ways of dealing with immediate problems has a way of feeding back on our metaperspectives and is often the most effective way of altering them. Thus, for example, they might urge John and Mary to cease answering the phone for a week, no matter how urgent they think the incoming calls might be (thus disturbing the rule pattern in the relationship), or they might urge them to perform a detailed, "objective" analysis of the rules governing their phone-answering activities (always requiring greater specificity than they provide), thus bringing the very idea of objectivist analysis into question for them and freeing them to entertain other possibilities.

The Resources of Ambiguity in Language

A persistent argument of this chapter has been that things are not just a matter of black and white, particularly where language is concerned. I can think of no better way to illustrate how the same idea can be expressed in myriad ways than by bringing some of the resources of ambiguity in language to bear upon the concepts of "black" and "white" themselves:

Continuity/Discontinuity. Black and white may be seen as polar opposites or as degrees on a continuum. We can also see each as unitary or picture shades of each, as in off-white, milk-white, ivory. The shades of black and white can become a common substance, gray, and through that commonness, become *identified*, one with another. And we can identify black and white as parts of the same noncolor system, as when we speak of a black and white versus a color TV. Since there is no "objective" way to determine where black or white begins and ends, we may make these determinations somewhat arbitrarily. We may decide, for example, that anything not "purely white" is black. Meta-phorically speaking, we may also have black gang up with gray against white.

Selection/Differentiation. We can use a shade or quality of black or of white to *represent* either of these colors. Each such selection *reflects* some ideas while *deflecting* attention from others. There is a world of difference, for example, between representing black as onyx or ebony versus representing it as pitch or coal. Rather than selecting any single representative of black or white, we can offer a large list of colorations—including, for example, pitch, coal, onyx, *and* ivory in our list for black. Differentiations have a way of undoing stereotypes.

Associations. Words like "black" and "white" are rich in associative meanings. And the words they are associated with are also rich in their associative meanings. Thus, as in the above example, black has positive associations to onyx and negative associations to pitch, and each of these associated terms is linked to others: onyx to rubies, sapphires, and so on; pitch to coal, peat, coke, and so on. *Metaphors, similes,* and *analogies* linking one word to another evoke complex clusters of associations. For example, when we hear "black as pitch," we get not only an image of a very black blackness, but also of some of the oily, unpleasant qualities of pitch.

Sound-Sense. Among our associations are those to a word's homonyms (words that sound like it), including words that rhyme with it. Thus, for white we have "light," and this term's relationship to white is reinforced by its *semantic* associations. Note that light is opposed to dark, and black is the darkest of dark. And note further that white and light rhyme with and are also linked semantically with "bright" and "sight," and that these terms have multiple meanings which evoke images of lustrousness, intelligence, seeing, understanding. Here is how Shakespeare exploited the resources of ambiguity in words associated with black and white: "For I have sworn thee fair, and thought thee bright, who art as black as hell, as dark as night" (Sonnet 147, 13–14).

Emphasis/Deemphasis. Color, or particular colorations, can be played up or played down. We can be color-conscious or color-blind. Paradoxically, one defense against racism is to play up color differences (as in the shift during the sixties from brown to black), while another is to play them down.

The Real and the Rhetorical

This concludes our consideration of definitional issues. We have seen that our culture tends to restrict the term persuasion to *paradigm* cases (e.g., political campaign speeches, advertisements, sermons), and "persuasion," "rhetoric," and other allied words are often used as though they referred to "enemy territory." Sharp distinctions are commonly drawn between persuasion and expression, art, entertainment, inducements, description, logic, and coercion. These distinctions tell us a lot about cultural attitudes toward persuasion. For all but the last distinction, persuasion is often treated as a "devil" word, a reflection of the language user's belief that someone—an educator, newscaster, poet, scientist—has appeared to be what he or she is not; that the individual has violated a "purity principle" associated with his or her craft or culturally assigned role. Educators, artists, scientists, and the like are understandably loath to label themselves as persuaders. Not uncommonly, the term figures in "persuasion about persuasion," as in Locke's critique of rhetoric.

The chief objection to persuasion over the ages and the chief basis for distinguishing it from nonpersuasion has been that it deals in *appearances*. Although the Greeks were aware that rhetoric could serve to make the good *appear* good, the true *appear* true, and the beautiful *appear* beautiful, they were nevertheless rightfully concerned, as Plato put it, that the persuader might make "the worse appear the better reason." Similar cries are of course echoed in our own day. Associated with persuasion are adornment and artifice, pandering and ingratiation, myth and illusion. Persuaders are said to "sell the sizzle and not the steak." They give us "only" rhetoric, "just" rhetoric, "mere" rhetoric, "nothing but" rhetoric. Worse yet, they may traffic in evasions, deceptions, and outright lies. Depending on one's choice of metaphor, they put a "face" on things or a "mask" around the face.

Juxtaposed against persuasion as the creation of appearances are various conceptions of "the real." In one way of thinking, "the real" consists in being *purely expressive*. Purely expressive individuals are said to be authentic, natural, spontaneous. They communicate directly and honestly, without artifice or manipulation. They impart themselves as they "really are." In another way of thinking, "the real" consists in being *purely descriptive* or *purely logical*. By this way of thinking, language can serve as a windowpane upon the world. Presumably it is possible to describe and draw logical inferences objectively, without bias, selection, or personal judgments. Purely objective communicators are said to tell us what the world is "really like." They offer us "the truth, the whole truth, and nothing but the truth." They "let the facts speak for themselves" and apply "laws of logic" in "letting the facts add up." By implication, persuaders are *extra-factual and extra-logical*. They rely on something more than, or other than, pure description or pure logic. Persuaders render value judgments or interpretations, and they are subjective and one-sided.

In a third way of thinking, "the real" consists in the power of the carrot and the stick. It is said in our culture that "money talks," that "power (to reward or punish) is the name of the game," that "sticks or stones may break my bones but names will never harm me." Persuaders are said to offer symbolic or psychological satisfactions in place of "real" rewards or "real" punishments. While they may identify the benefits or harms from adoption of a proposal, they do not claim to be the agents of those consequences. On these grounds, persuasion is differentiated from material inducements and constraints or coercion.

I have tried to show in the last two chapters that traditional distinctions between persuasion and nonpersuasion tend to be grossly overdrawn—that they seriously underrepresent its scope, reflect erroneous assumptions about persuasion's alleged alternatives, and unjustifiably undermine the status of persuasion. At the same time, I hope I have not given the impression that everything a person says or does is persuasion, or that there are essentially no differences between what such prototypical persuaders as advertisers and politicians do and the persuasion typically practiced by poets, scientists, or others of their ilk. What we ordinarily call persuasion (whether as act or effect) typically involves human communications designed to influence others by modifying their judgments, not just their behavior. By these definitional criteria, a great deal of what people say and do ought not to be classified as persuasion—or at least not exclusively as persuasion. No doubt some artists neither consciously nor unconsciously seek to persuade. An infant's birth cry is surely pure expression, not persuasion. There are also acts of force (e.g., the injection of "truth serums") that alter behaviors without first modifying beliefs or attitudes. Most important, a great many acts and artifacts are rhetorical in only a *peripheral* sense. They may involve a mix of rhetorical and nonrhetorical motives, as in a decision to wear makeup. They may be rhetorical at the image-management or relational level and essentially nonrhetorical at the substantive level, as in the case of a sportscaster's report of the day's baseball scores. Or they may fail to be nonrhetorical only because of the nature and limits of human observation, thought, and language, rather than because of any intent on the communicator's part to move or impress others. The rhetoric of scientists like Einstein is surely a far cry from the paradigmatic rhetoric of commercial advertisers.

With the concept of peripheral cases in hand, we may construct a conceptual "map" of persuasion that better reflects the "territory" than the map represented by the conventional wisdom. Note that the areas covered in the map in Figure 6.3 are not intended to be precise. Given the very rhetorical perspective proposed here, for example, you might well complain that the map does not go far enough; you may insist, for example, that there is no information-giving that is *not* rhetorical. The point of the map is to underscore, once again, the rhetorical dimension in most human activities and the need for attention to those outlying areas within the boundaries of persuasion that are here called *peripheral cases*.

SUMMARY

This chapter has presented a rhetorical perspective on the relationship between persuasion and objectivity. There are those, like Locke, who would use rhetorical devices even as they claim the high road of objectivity in distancing themselves from the label "rhetoric." But objectivity in reporting, textbook writing, and so on, is an unattainable ideal; even good scientific discourse is extra-factual and extra-logical. Indeed, from a rhetorical perspective, "truths" of all kinds are themselves reflective of one or another perspective, and their expression reflects inevitably the interests and values of language-users. Rhetorical components are particularly likely to be manifest whenever communicators move from fact to opinion, inference, or interpretation—for example, when scientists impart to their research a theoretical or policy relevance.

A rhetorical perspective should sensitize us to the way communicators exploit the "resources of ambiguity" in language, and it might well lead us to be more imaginitive in our thinking about problems and their solutions. This does not mean, however, that we are free to bend argument and evidence to our will. Barring possibilities for complete objectivity, persuaders should still adhere to standards of reasonableness.

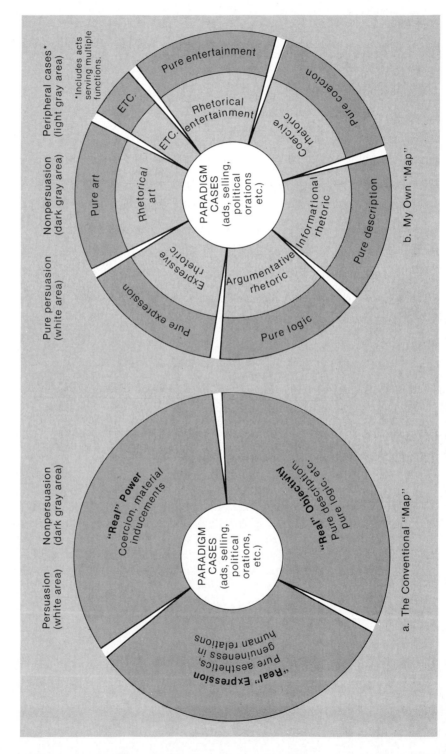

Figure 6.3 Two conceptual "maps" of persuasion's domain (a) the conventional "map" (b) my own "map".

EXERCISE

If we can generalize from Weigert's article on scientific sociology, each of the professions in our society should have similar self-justifying rhetorics that mask ideologies with the pretense of objectivity. For any of the professions (e.g., law, social work, medicine, political science, etc.), see if you can identify the following genres:

a. A rhetoric of special expertise (claims to valid theories and methodologies; insistence on specialized jargon)

b. A rhetoric of social passage (justification for professional training programs, licensing, etc.)

c. A rhetoric of public service (boasts about how the profession serves the public interest)

d. A rhetoric of self-regulation (insistence that the profession is regulating itself and corresponding denials that anyone else could possibly have the expertise to regulate it)

e. A rhetoric of affiliation (characterizations of the profession as akin to higher-status professions and different from lower-status professions)

f. A rhetoric of the rhetoric of "outsiders" (ridicule of heretics, traitors, debunkers, simplifiers, and other "cranks" as "pseudoprofessionals")

*P*art Two
Practicing Persuasion:
The Co-active Approach

*P*oliticians have a deep contempt for the art of conveying thought. Quite a few make speeches over a lifetime without ever learning to make, write or even read a speech. Lecture-circuit impresarios are worse; all feel that nothing so impresses an audience (and justifies their fee) as a suffocating recital of the commonplace, combined with a deeply condescending manner. Social scientists, although perhaps improving, have their special instinct for fraternal obscurity. But there is no doubt that business executives are the worst of all. Theirs is the egregiously optimistic belief that people will believe anything, however improbable, if it is said with emphasis and solemnity by the head of a big company. With the ultimate promotion comes the right to proclaim truth.

John Kenneth Galbraith

Chapter 7
The Co-Active Approach To Persuasion

Why can't the Arabs and Jews solve their problems like good Christians?

Former State Department official

Why can't the coal miners think like coal mine operators?

Coal mine operator

Why can't a woman be more like a man?

H. Higgins in *My Fair Lady*

Persuasion begins from the perception of differences—differences between where we stand on a given issue and where others stand, or differences between their overt actions and how we as persuaders would have them act. Even attempts at reinforcing existing beliefs may involve perceived differences of a sort. For example, a political campaign manager may perceive a gap between the current level of activity by campaign volunteers and the amount needed to win at the polls and may attempt to reinforce their commitments to the cause.

Persuasion may thus be conceived of as a process of *bridging* differences—reducing *psychological distances*—so as to secure preferred outcomes. How we may best bridge the psychological divide is the subject of this part of the text. The overall approach to persuasion featured here is called *co-active persuasion*. This is an umbrella term for a variety of more specific strategies and tactics that have in common moving toward persuadees psychologically in the hope that they will be moved, in turn, toward acceptance of the persuader's position or proposal for action. Just what form co-active persuasion will take will depend on the situation: on whether, for example, it involves mass, public, or interpersonal communication; if interpersonal, on whether persons A and B are locked in a conflict of interests or merely have a difference of opinion; if the former, whether the object of their talk is to convince each other or to persuade some third party such as the voters in a political contest or the jurors in a trial.

Still, it can be said in a general way that co-active persuasion is *receiver-oriented;* that it reaches out to persuadees both physically and psychologically; that it emphasizes similarities between persuader and persuadee at the same

A good example of co-active persuasion in a situation where threats of punishment are more generally employed. By these three signs the owner of the parking space entreats rather than demands; he or she metacommunicates pleasantness and equality rather than power. I would not park in this spot. *(Photo courtesy of Miles Orvell)*

time that it promotes images of source credibility; that it works toward understanding of the message through references to shared meanings and experiences; and that it addresses controversial matters by appeals to premises the audience can accept. Let us look more carefully at these components of the co-active approach.

Components of the Co-Active Approach

Receiver Orientation

Co-active persuasion is receiver-oriented rather than source-oriented; it adheres to the maxim that persuasion takes place on the message recipient's terms. Just how important this is was illustrated for me some time ago when I ran into an example of the Peter Principle, the rule of organizations that sooner or later all employees are promoted beyond their level of competence. My acquaintance had been a top-notch engineer, but now he was sales manager for the computer division of a large electronics firm and he was doing miserably.

"I can't understand why my company isn't selling computers as effectively as IBM," he said. "We have the best computers in the world. What's more, I've written out a sales spiel for my people that's dynamite. All they have to do is memorize it and say it smoothly. Our products should do the rest."

I asked my friend how IBM achieved its success. "Oh well, you see they use a different type of salesperson than we do. Our sales staff are all former engineers; what we care about is our products and our people know them inside and out. IBM hires these 'personality types' who sit down with the customers and get real chatty with them. The fact is, they spend more time listening to the customers yak about their problems than on selling their products. It's a waste of time to me, but I have to admit that it works."

What the sales manager failed to realize, of course, is that by "wasting time" listening to the customer's problems, IBM's salespeople were accomplishing a great deal. Besides showing interest in the customer as a human being— a factor of no small consequence in itself—they were learning at first hand how to tailor their messages to achieve their intended effects. IBM's approach might be characterized as receiver-oriented. The approach contrasts quite favorably with the source-oriented approach of IBM's competitor. Here are the essential differences between the two approaches.

Source-Oriented	Receiver-Oriented
Assumes that all receivers are alike	Assumes that all receivers are unique, or, at the very least, that some differences make a difference
Decides for the receivers what they need, want, know, value, etc.	Learns from the receivers if possible, what they need, want, know, value, etc.
Selects specific persuasive goals for any one occasion on the basis of his or her own timetable	Selects specific persuasive goals for any occasion on the basis of the receivers' readiness to be persuaded
Communicates at the receivers by means of a "canned" presentation	Communicates with the receivers by adapting the message on the basis of a mutual interchange if at all possible
Promotes solutions on the basis of their supposed intrinsic merits	Promotes solutions on the basis of their capacity to resolve or reduce the receivers' special problems

Reaching Out

The co-active persuader reaches out to the persuadee both physically and pyschologically. This involves much more than just initiating interaction, though in many conflict situations that may be a very difficult thing to do.

All other things being equal, the co-active persuader opts for "warm" message forms over the more impersonal forms. For example, the co-active business manager tends to prefer discussions with subordinates over lectures, face-to-face interactions over communication by telephone, oral communication of any kind over such written forms as the bulletin board announcement or the interoffice memo. Likewise, the co-active persuader tends to prefer close physical settings over more distant ones. Better to lecture in a room with too few chairs than too many. Better to air disagreements over a drink or a meal than in an atmosphere that announces itself as "strictly business." Better to be seated at a table adjacent or perpendicular to the other than in a position directly across from the other.

Reaching out is also reflected in patterns of oral delivery of the message. Between erring in the directions of too much formality or too little, the co-active persuader will usually opt for the latter. For example, he or she may deliberately breach the rules for a platform speech by stepping out from behind the lecture to address them directly, perhaps interrupting the formal presentation by engaging members of the audience in conversation.

Combining Similarity and Credibility

The co-active persuader moves toward the audience psychologically by establishing relational bonds. Verbally and nonverbally, the co-active persuader expresses caring and concern for the audience as people, respect for their feelings and ideas, and perhaps affection as well. Moreover, the co-active persuader attempts to promote an image of herself or himself with which the audience can identify. Especially important in this regard are evidences of membership group similarities. The persuader may move toward the persuadee by emphasizing similarities in background, experience, and group affiliations; also by displaying evidences of commonality through dialect, dress, mannerisms, and the like.

The signs of commonality not only enhance the persuader's attractiveness to the audience, they also serve indirectly as expressions of shared beliefs, values, and attitudes. It is little wonder, therefore, that advertisers often feature "plain folks" in testimonials. On television, for example, the advocate of a brand name detergent is often the neighbor next door, apron and all. Former governor of Louisiana Huey Long is supposed to have launched his fabulous political career during the Depression of the thirties by use of the *plain folks* device. In the film *All the King's Men*, there is a scene of a local carnival where Huey Long (given the name Willie Stark in the movie) stands before a group of downtrodden farmers and says:

> You're all a bunch of hicks. That's right.
> Hicks! You's hicks and I'm a hick and us
> hicks are gonna run the state legislature.

Evidences of interpersonal similarity are clearly essential, but so too is it important on most occasions for persuaders to appear *different* in ways that make them seem more expert, better informed, and more reliable. The relationship between similarity, credibility, and attitude change is complicated but very important. In general, it can be said that the relationship depends on type of issue and type of similarity. The "ideal" communicator is often one who seems both similar enough and different enough to appear overall as a "superrepresentative" of the audience.

Shared Experiences

Co-active persuasion honors the principle that meanings are in people rather than ideas. It aims at effecting understanding through appeals to shared meanings and shared ideas.

People selectively expose themselves to messages and they sometimes are prone, when exposed, to hear what they want to hear, and see what they want to see. But even when they are predisposed to decode messages accurately, there are apt to be many problems. Numerous examples can be provided of persuasive efforts that failed because of problems in translation or other problems in bridging linguistic divides. A notorious example was the campaign to market a style of Chevrolet in South America that had been selling very well in North America. It was called the Nova. Unfortunately, Nova in Spanish means "no go."

Language has its pitfalls, of course, even among those who share a common tongue. How does one convey the pain of a toothache or a feeling of rapturous love, or describe any other internal state? How does one define terms like "freedom" and "justice," words that not only have widely varying usage in our culture, but are loaded with surplus emotional meanings? How does one disentangle the many meanings for "simple" words like "is," "may," "ought," "must"?

The co-active persuader takes pains to indicate how he or she understands potentially troublesome concepts, but does not insist that these are the only definitions or interpretations. In anticipation of confusion or misunderstandings, the persuader generally attempts to place key ideas within shared fields of experience. The notion of shared fields is depicted by Schramm (1960) using a simple communication model (Figure 7.1). Think of the circles in this figure as the accumulated experience of the two individuals trying to communicate.

> The source can encode, and the destination (i.e., the receiver) can decode, only in terms of the experience each has had. If we have never learned any Russian, we can neither code nor decode in that language. If an African tribesman has never seen or heard of an airplane, he can only decode the sight of a plane in terms of whatever experience he has had. The plane may seem to him to be a bird, and the aviator a god borne on wings. If there has been no common experience—then communication is impossible. If the experiences of source and destination have been strikingly unlike too, then it is going to be very difficult to get an intended meaning across from one to the other. (p. 6)

The source, then, tries to encode in such a way as to make it easy for the receiver to comprehend the message—to relate it to parts of experience which are much like those of the receiver. Young, Becker, and Pike (1970) provide this illustration:

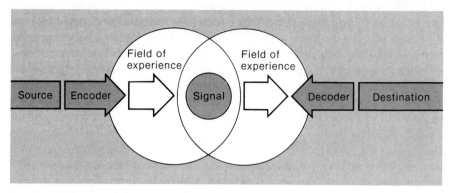

Figure 7.1 Schramm's Field's of Experience Model.

Suppose someone wants to explain the distinction between nuclear and marginal focus. He begins by telling his audience that nuclear focus is centered attention and marginal focus is marginal awareness. If the audience replies that the distinction is not clear, he then explains that he has in mind the phenomenon discussed by Michael Polanyi in Chapter 4 of *Personal Knowledge*. They protest that they have not read this book; he tries again. "When we drive a nail with a hammer," he says, "we are aware of both hammer and nail, but aware of them in different ways. Our attention is centered on the effect of the hammer on the nail, but we are also aware of the hammer in our hand, of the sensations in our hand that help us guide our blows. The point of contact between hammer and nail is the center of attention, but we have a marginal awareness of the other related events that are occurring simultaneously." Finally they understand. (pp. 172–173)

Building on Acceptable Premises

The distinctive character of co-active persuasion is nowhere more manifest than in interpersonal conflicts or where there are sharp differences of opinion between people. Picture a persuader, A, and a persuadee, B, who differ over issue X. The issue for A and B may be whether X exists, whether X causes Y, whether X is desirable or ethical or useful, how to get X (assuming they both value it), who should get X, or how to divide X.

In the face of these differences, a number of options are available. One approach is that of the *dogmatist*. Operating from what he or she perceives as greater knowledge or wisdom on the matter, A may elect to *tell* B what is best for him or her. Parents do that, and sometimes teachers as well, not always with great success. A close cousin to the dogmatist is the *objectivist*, whom we met before. A may attempt to "demonstrate" by the cold light of logic why his or her way of thinking is the only way. For the thoroughgoing objectivist, reason is, and ought to be, the sole arbiter of disputes, and everyone ought to reason as the objectivist does. A third way is that of the *expressivist*, who merely asserts his or her feelings on the matter at hand, offering no reasons, no appeals, no support for the views of any kind. If B remains unconvinced of the merits of A's views, that's okay. If B shifts position, so much the better, but A does nothing to bring that shift about. Expressivism stems from a deep-seated antipathy toward persuasion. To the expressivist, all persuasion is immoral manipulation.

Should B remain unmoved by such declarations of truth, cold logic, or personal feelings, A may be tempted to move against B by vilifying, ridiculing, threatening, or perhaps by pressuring him or her into activities that run counter to B's attitudes but that, once undertaken, might lead B to reassess and perhaps modify those attitudes. These *combative* modes of influence may sometimes be appropriate, but they also involve great risks. Often they prompt message recipients to become increasingly antagonistic or perhaps to withdraw from further discussion.

The co-active persuader tends to prefer the carrot to the stick and attempts, where possible, to rely exclusively on talk to ameliorate or resolve differences. But it is not talk of a merely uncalculated, expressive nature. Co-active persuaders reason with their audiences. They offer arguments in support of their more controversial claims and evidence in support of their arguments. In these respects, the methods of the co-active persuader are not unlike those of the objectivist. However, the co-active persuader is less concerned with showing that he or she is right—with *winning arguments*—than with *winning belief*. This requires arguments that begin from general premises the audience can accept.

A *premise* is a hook on which to hang an argument. Depending on the context of the discussion, it may be a definition, a value assumption, or a general observation. Get people to grant the premise, and they are halfway to granting the conclusion as well. Hence the importance of appealing to *accepted* premises and, if necessary, of making a case for the reasonableness of a premise. Thus, for example, you may oppose recognition of the new Slobovian regime on the grounds that it is ruthlessly tyrannical. But someone may be able to convince you that our government and most other governments typically extend formal recognition to regimes that violate the rights of their citizens. Once you grant the premise that recognition does not necessarily mean moral approval, the persuader is then in a much better position to convince you that we should recognize the Slobovian regime:

> (*Major premise*) To recognize a government isn't necessarily to signal approval of it, but rather to acknowledge that it exercises control over its people.
> (*Minor premise*) The new Slobovian regime surely is in control of its people.
> (*Conclusion*) Therefore, the United States should recognize it.

In building from acceptable premises, persuaders generally build on premises that they themselves accept, and they make a point of emphasizing their points of agreement. In addition to providing hooks on which to hang arguments, these *common ground* appeals serve to make the persuader appear more trustworthy and more attractive. Typically, the co-active persuader moves from agreement to disagreement on highly sensitive controversial issues, or at least delays direct confrontation until agreed-upon issues have been identified. Two variants of this bridge-building process are the *yes-yes* technique and the *yes-but* technique (Minnick, 1957). In both cases, little or no hint of any disagreement with the audience is expressed until after a whole string of assertions is communicated about which agreement is sure. The object is to establish a habit of assent, to get receivers nodding "Yes," "That's right," "You said it," either aloud or to themselves. Once this is done, the audience will presumably be receptive to more controversial assertions.

Using the *yes-yes* approach, the persuader lays the groundwork for his or her case by identifying a number of acceptable principles or criteria in terms of which the case will later be supported. Thus, the vacuum cleaner salesman might say:

> If you're like most of the people I meet, you also want a vacuum that really cleans, one that picks up the ashes and the threads and the crumbs that hide in the corners. I'd guess too that in these days of galloping inflation you don't feel like getting stuck with big bills. . . . Well, okay, I know just what you mean. . . . Here's our new kind of vacuum cleaner, and it fits your specifications exactly.

Using the *yes-but* approach, persuaders begin by noting those arguments of the opposition with which they can agree, and then, having shown how fair-minded they are, they offer a series of "buts" that constitute the heart of their case. A credibility gap example might go something as follows. It would be partly appropriate for a hostile or critical audience:

> Look, I'm one of these people who'll tell you that our government has got to tell all; that it's got to conduct diplomacy in a fish bowl; that it's got to give away secrets that are vital to national security; that it's got to make its widest contingency plans public. These are valid reasons for keeping things under covers, BUT. . . .

Although co-active persuasion generally builds on areas of agreement between persuader and persuadee, it need not do so to be successful. What counts from a purely practical standpoint is that the persuadee find the arguments attractive, not that the persuader be enamored of them. Though it might enhance the agnostic's credibility were he or she to share friends' religious convictions, the agnostic need not be a believer to convince them of the disadvantages to believers of mandating prayer in schools. The agnostic can simply make the case from their perspective, pointing out, for example, the many occasions in history when religious groups have benefitted from separation of church and state. Similarly, the college professor may not care whether students get As or Cs in their courses; he or she may even decry their obsession with grades and be concerned only with whether they learn what he or she has to teach them. But knowing that grades are a major concern of most students, the professor may nevertheless appeal to their desire for good grades as a way of inducing them to keep up with the readings in the course. In these, as in other examples, co-active persuaders may move toward the message recipient to the point of offering reasons for belief or action that are not their own and that they even find personally distasteful, but that they expect the receiver will find compelling.

How ethical is reasoning from the perspective of the other? Is it dishonest to advance reasons for belief or action that one does not personally find appealing? Reason-giving of this sort is surely one reason that mere mention of the word "persuasion" often elicits negative feelings. The persuader may take a coldly calculating approach to the task, much like the Roman poet Ovid in his playful advice to would-be Casanovas:

> On deceiving in the name of friendship; feigning just enough drunkenness to be winsome; on astute use of praise and promises; inducement value of belief in the gods; deceiving deceivers; the utility of tears; the need to guard against the risk that entreaties may merely feed the woman's vanity; inducement value of pallor, which is the proper color of love; advisability of shift in methods, as she who resisted the well-bred may yield to the crude; ways to subdue by yielding; the controlled use of compliments; become a habit with her; enjoy others too, but in stealth, and deny if you are found out; give each of her faults the name of the good quality most like it. (quoted in Burke, 1969, p. 160)

While reasoning from the perspective of the other can be ethically objectionable, this depends on how it is done. The key question is whether the persuader is honest about his or her own feelings in respect to those reasons. So long as the persuader makes clear that he or she is looking at matters from the audience's frame of reference and that the arguments being advanced are not necessarily arguments the persuader finds appealing, he or she is on safe moral ground. The persuader might say: "Okay, I've told you my reasons for the plan I have proposed, but they don't have to be your reasons. Let's look at matters in terms of your interests in the matter. How can you stand to benefit?" This is the essence of taking the perspective of the other.

One final point before we turn to a review of behavioral research on co-active persuasion and credibility, and that concerns the use of co-active persuasion in adversarial proceedings, such as when two presidential candidates are locked in a television debate, or when attorneys for the prosecution and the defense are squared off in a jury trial. Co-active persuasion is essentially "friendly" persuasion, but it is not without its weaponry. Indeed, it may be highly combative toward the adversary even as it appeals co-actively to the target audience. Ronald Reagan communicated co-actively to his overhearing television audience, for example, when, in response to questioning by Carter about the accuracy of his factual claims, he would say, "There you go again!" Similarly, Walter Mondale was communicating co-actively to his audience when, in the first of the 1984 presidential debates, he reminded Reagan of his use of the phrase in 1980, and declared that Reagan had distorted matters then and continued to do so in 1984. The acceptable premise that both Reagan and Mondale were appealing to was fairness in the use of argument and evidence.

Similarity, Credibility, and Attitude Change: A Review of Behavioral Research

In my initial comments on the relationship between similarity and credibility, I suggested that one should limit expressions of commonality with audiences, and should also—at least some of the time—exhibit and emphasize certain differences. *Credibility*, it turns out, is a complex notion consisting, essentially, of (1) *respect variables* (e.g., perceived intelligence, knowledge of subject); (2) *trust variables* (e.g., perceived objectivity, fairness); and (3) *attraction variables* (e.g., perceived warmth, dynamism, interest in audience). The same image-management devices that produce positive effects with respect to one dimension of credibility may produce negative effects with respect to another. As any business manager will tell you, for example, being respected and being liked do not necessarily go together.

Some time ago I helped prepare a thoroughgoing review of the behavioral research literature on the relationship between similarity, credibility, and attitude change (Simons, Moyer, and Berkowitz, 1970). Here I should like to summarize the results of that review and supplement it with references to more recent findings on these and related variables.

Types of Similarity

Persuaders may link themselves with their audiences in numerous ways. Recall that one component of the co-active approach to persuasion is emphasis on membership group similarities, such as commonalties in religious affiliation, place of birth, schools attended, ethnic background. A second broad class of similarities consists of shared beliefs, values, and attitudes. These may be labeled collectively as *dispositional* similarities, and they are the basis for *common ground* appeals.

Similarities of both the membership group and the dispositional variety may be articulated or merely hinted at. Surprising though it may seem, for example, we may hint at our attitudes on all manner of social and political issues by displays of food preferences. In one study reported by the Associated Press (*Philadelphia Evening Bulletin*, November 8, 1981), Edward Sadalla and Jeffrey Burroughs grouped several hundred survey respondents into five categories—vegetarian, gourmet, health food, fast food and synthetic food—according to their expressed preferences for specific foods. The researchers found that health food lovers were almost uniformly pro-solar and antinuclear, while gourmets tended to be atheistic liberals who live alone, enjoy glamour sports and fast living, and indulge in more drug use. Vegetarians tended to be noncompetitive and preferred intellectual challenges and crafts. They also claimed to be weight-conscious, used "recreational" drugs, and saw themselves as sexy. Health food enthusiasts tested as noncompetitive, intellectual, mechanically inclined, hypochondriacal, antinuclear and, by their own definition, "weird" and individualistic.

Similarities (or dissimilarities) may also be classified as logically relevant to the issue in question or logically irrelevant. When a door-to-door vacuum cleaner salesman says he admires his customer's garden, this logically *irrelevant* similarity serves primarily to enhance his image. When the same salesperson says that he shares the customer's annoyance at vacuum cleaners that are forever getting clogged up, he is doing more than enhancing his image; he is using the assertion as a first premise on which logically derivable conclusions may be anchored. In the same way, another persuader may use the premise that "All of us want truth from our government" as the basis for a reasoned condemnation of the government's credibility gap. These, of course, are examples of common ground appeals.

Appeals to membership group similarities and dispositional similarities are forms of *identification*. Kenneth Burke (1969) observes: "You persuade a man only insofar as you can talk his language by speech, gesture, tonality, order, image, attitude, *identifying* your ways with his. True, the rhetorician may have to change an audience's opinion in one respect; but he can succeed only insofar as he yields to that audience's opinions in other respects" (pp 55–56). Burke characterizes identification as a symbolic "joining together" which deflects attention from human differences. In being identified with B, A is "substantially one" with a person other than himself. Yet at the same time he remains unique, an individual locus of motives. Thus he is both joined and separate, at once a distinct substance and consubstantial with another.

> Identification is affirmed with earnestness precisely because there is division. Identification is compensatory to division. If men were not apart from one another, there would be no need for the rhetorician to proclaim their unity (p. 22).

Somewhat cynically, Burke observes that it is always possible to identify with one's audience. This is expressed in a poem of his entitled "He was a sincere, etc."

He Was a Sincere, Etc.

He was a sincere but friendly Presbyterian—and so

If he was talking to a Presbyterian,
He was for Presbyterianism.

If he was talking to a Lutheran,
He was for Protestantism.

If he was talking to a Catholic,
He was for Christianity.

If he was talking to a Jew,
He was for God.

If he was talking to a theosophist,
He was for religion.

If he was talking to an agnostic,
He was for scientific caution.

If he was talking to an atheist,
He was for mankind.

And if he was talking to a socialist, communist, labor leader, missiles expert, or businessman,
He was for
     PROGRESS.

Relevant and Irrelevant Similarities

There seems little doubt that *relevant* dispositional similarities are potent forces in persuasion. They seem to be effective primarily because they serve as shared premises in reasoning. If this assumption is valid, we should find that dispositional similarities have less effect on attitudes when they are logically *irrelevant* to the position being advocated.

Berscheid's two-part experiment (1966) was concerned with irrelevant as well as relevant dispositional similarities and dissimilarities. Presuming that the relationship between similarity-dissimilarity and attitude change was mediated by degree of attraction to the source, she attempted to control for attraction by having a communicator depict himself as similar to the subject on one issue and dissimilar on another. In one experiment, a confederate either expressed agreement with the subject on an underlying value issue relevant to the object of judgment and disagreement on an irrelevant issue, or the reverse. The communicator then attempted to influence the subject on one of the two issues. Relevant similarity was found to contribute to attitude change; irrelevant similarity did not. In the other experiment, a "relevant-dissimilar" communicator and an "irrelevant-dissimilar" communicator took the same position as the subject on the object of judgment. Under the former condition, the subjects *shifted away* from the position expressed by the communicator; in the latter condition, shifts were not significant.

The Similarity-Attraction Relationship

There seems no question but that we tend to like and want to be with persons who are dispositionally similar, although the evidence on membership group similarities is less clear-cut. In over 30 studies, Byrne and his associates (1971) have found that attraction of a subject to a bogus stranger increases as the proportion of the stranger's reported attitudinal similarities to the subject increases. *In general, we tend to gravitate toward dispositionally similar others, to assume that similar others like us, to exaggerate the degree to which beliefs, values, and attitudes are shared, and as a result of these interacting and complementary factors, to solidify our attraction to them.* Other things being equal, attraction does in turn seem to contribute to attitude change.

Several studies have compared the relative effects of dispositional versus membership group similarities on attraction. For example, are whites generally more attracted to a dispositionally dissimilar white person or to a dispositionally similar black person? It would appear from reviewing an admittedly ambiguous body of research findings on the "race versus belief" controversy that for white subjects who are low in prejudice, race does not affect attraction; for white subjects who are high in prejudice, race exerts a greater effect than attitudinal similarity except where the degree of similarity is complete or virtually complete.

Increasing Respect and Trust toward a Source

While attraction is one ingredient in a receiver's attitude toward a source, respect and trust are, from all accounts, more significant determinants of attitude change than attraction. Kelman (1961) has suggested that we are likely to *conform* with the recommendations of attractive sources so long as we remain attracted to them. We are more likely to *internalize* the arguments of competent and trustworthy sources, however, and internalization involves a deeper level of attitudinal commitment than conformity.

In general, there seems to be a weak but positive relationship between attitudinal similarity and the factors of respect and trust and a still less dependable relationship between membership group similarities and these same factors. Utilizing such indices of respect and trust as ratings of a stranger's intelligence, his or her knowledge of current events, and his or her morality, Byrne and his co-workers have not found attitudinal similarity to be related to respect and trust with anywhere near the consistency that they obtained for the similarity-attraction relationship.

Although no measures were taken of respect or trust, Brock's (1965) field experiment strongly suggests that these factors may be affected by similarity of experience, and that in some cases, at least, perceptions of shared experience may cause receivers to be persuaded. In Brock's study, paint store clerks were purported to have had experiences in the use of a product similar or dissimilar to the experience anticipated by a customer. After the customer had signaled a decision to purchase, the clerk either recommended a higher- or a lower-priced product of the same type, based on that personal experience. Although the study would have been more impressive had each of the clerks been required to employ both strategies alternately, all other potentially confounding factors seemed adequately controlled. Regardless of price, the clerk whose experience was similar produced significantly greater shifts in purchasing decisions.

Several researchers have directly investigated the relationship between membership group similarities and the factors of respect and trust, and in these studies, the common ground doctrine has fared weakly at best. In one study (Lambert et al., 1960), French and English Canadians concurred in judging the readers of a passage in English as more intelligent and more dependable than the same communicators reading the passage in French. In another study (Anisfeld et al., 1962), Jewish and gentile subjects were led to believe, on the basis of dialectical cues, that the same passage was being read to them by either a Jewish or a gentile speaker. The subjects then rated the speakers on such traits as dependability, leadership, intelligence, and so on. Gentile subjects tended to give higher ratings to the speaker they assumed was a member of their own group, while the overall ratings by Jewish subjects tended to present a balanced profile, reflecting neither higher nor lower ingroup estimates. In one phase of still another study, Haiman (1949) compared ratings of a graduate versus an undergraduate student speaker on such dimensions of respect and trust as sincerity, fairness, and competence. Differences tended to favor the dissimilar, but presumably more prestigious, graduate student speaker.

Common Ground and Source Credibility: Some Grounds for Questioning or Limiting the Common Ground Principle

So widely accepted is the principle that communicators should emphasize interpersonal similarities that exceptions to it may be of greater interest than the principle itself. Despite its widespread acceptance, it is by no means obvious that emphasis on these similarities will necessarily work to the advantage of the communicator. A distinguished professor of economics, speaking to a lay audience on the subject of international trade, might do well to stress differences between himself or herself and the audience. With the same audience and subject, a lay speaker who admitted sharing the audience's lack of expertise might well be graded high on candor, but not believed. This is but one example of an exception to the common ground principle. Now that we have made a case for establishing common ground, let us use the *yes-but* technique to qualify and limit the generality of the doctrine. Yes, dispositional similarities increase attraction and have some effect on respect and trust. Yes, they serve as first premise when they are logically relevant, and this is important. Yes, it's true, similarity of experience does facilitate decoding and may increase credibility. Yes, membership group similarities often increase attraction. BUT. . . .

The Source as a Superrepresentative

A careful reading of the case for establishing common ground should suggest some reasons for qualifying the principle, at least as applied to membership group similarities. Recall that a dissimilar graduate student speaker was regarded as more competent and trustworthy than a similar undergraduate and that French Canadians evinced greater respect and trust toward an English Canadian speaker. Many other studies support the generalization that some perceived differences work to the advantage of the persuader. Boncheck (1967) found that a professional clinician influenced the sexual identification ratings of students to a greater degree than another student. Haiman (1949) reported that a speech attributed to the surgeon general of the United States on socialized medicine exerted significantly greater influence on students than one given by a sophomore or by the secretary general of the Communist Party. Differences between the latter two sources were not significant. Paulson (1954) found that, for male auditors, a dissimilar but more prestigious source was more persuasive. A similar finding was obtained by Aronson, Turner, and Carlsmith (1963), using T. S. Eliot as the dissimilar source.

What is the explanation for these discrepant findings? Note that effective nonmembers of a group tended to be different in the direction of greater competence, expertise, fairness, honesty, and so on; they all evinced greater respect and trust. Put this together now with the general rule that respect and trust are more significant determinants of attitude change than attraction. The inescapable conclusion is that while similarities may lead to attraction, the relationship between membership group similarity and image of the source is strongest for those source components least significantly related to attitude change. Put another way, it would appear that sponsorship by similar sources or emphasis on membership group similarities may not always have persuasive value, and in certain cases may even be disadvantageous. The persuader might do well to stress differences in the direction of greater status, expertise, objectivity, and so on.

Does this mean that organizations seeking to effect persuasion should necessarily employ highly competent, trustworthy sources, no matter how distant they may appear to the receiver? Does it mean that individual persuaders should always work to create psychological distance? Studies in which peers or slightly older children were found to be more convincing than adults (Berenda, 1950; Duncker, 1938) would seem to suggest that the "uncommon ground" principle can also be taken too far. Commenting on these studies, Hovland et al. (1953) speculated on the possibility that the term "expert" should be "broadened to include persons who have found adequate solutions to the problem an individual faces, even though in other respects, they may be no more experienced than he and very much like him" (p. 50). Their judgment is strongly supported by research on opinion leaders.

These shapers of mass opinion have consistently been found to share dispositional and membership group similarities with the persons they influence. According to Katz (1957), they are "in a certain sense the most conformist members of their groups—upholding whatever norms and values are central to their groups" (p. 73). Frequently they share membership in the same primary groups with those they persuade. Similarities of age, occupation, and socioeconomic status have also been noted. Consistent with the experimental findings we have reviewed, the differences tend in the direction of greater credibility. Klapper (1960) has aptly described the opinion leader "as a kind of superrepresentative of his own group" (p. 34). Whether on matters of widespread interest or on issues of concern only to a specialized group, opinion leaders are generally more competent than their peers, more interested, better informed, more gregarious, and have access to wider sources of information (Lazarsfeld and Menzel, 1963). Generally of the same class as those they influence on public affairs issues, they nevertheless tend to belong to higher levels of that class (Katz, 1957). People may be influenced by their elders, by persons of higher economic status, or by members of ethnic groups culturally stereotyped as more prestigious, but the reverse is seldom true (Katz, 1957).

What emerges from this review is that persuaders should be similar to the audience, yes, but they should also be different in ways that increase their credibility. By what they say and do, they should appear as superrepresentatives of the persons they are attempting to persuade.

Matching Persuaders to Issues

Related to the principle that persuaders should be superrepresentatives of the audience they seek to influence is the principle that attractive communicators tend to be more effective on issues of value or taste; dissimilar but more expert sources tend to be more effective on questions of belief. If, for example, you were looking around for a new brand of coffee, chances are that you would be more influenced by the judgments of friends than by experts. But you would ordinarily trust experts on medical matters, on the question of where to invest your money, or other such technical matters.

There is, indeed, evidence that audiences process messages from attractive and expert sources very differently. In one experiment (Norman, 1976), on the question of how much sleep per night was needed, a young, physically attractive male undergraduate was compared with a 43-year-old male professor of physiological psychology. The two sources proved to be equally effective at getting audiences to agree with them. However, the effect of the message content was quite different. The expert source was significantly more influential when his message contained arguments than when it did not. In contrast, the presentation of arguments had no effect on agreement with the attractive source.

Self-Rejecting Audiences

The similarity principle assumes that message recipients will entertain a reasonably high estimate of themselves and of the groups with which they are affiliated. This is not always a valid assumption. Rightly or wrongly, many receivers are likely to be self-rejecting, if not as a general predisposition, at least as applied to specific topics and to relative differences between themselves and other groups. This may be why French Canadians rated English Canadians as more intelligent and more dependable. In the absence of cultural consensus or an objective basis for choosing between members and nonmembers, ingroup identification would probably lead members to regard other members as more credible, but in this case a long history of second-class status had been internalized and confirmed by the French Canadians. An abundance of evidence suggests that other groups also tend to be self-rejecting. Bettleheim (1943) has vividly described the plight of some inmates in German concentration camps who, having been stripped of their egos, began to identify strongly with the norms and behaviors of their brutal guards. In this and in other cases, self-rejection may lead not only to greater trust and respect for outgroups, but to greater attraction as well. McGuire (1969) has assembled evidence from a variety of studies: of anti-Semitism among Jews; of greater hostility toward immigrants expressed by new than by old Americans; of the adoption of white stereotypes regarding blacks by black college students.

Flattery

Contrary to the old saw that "flattery will get you nowhere," there is fairly reliable evidence that it works quite well, especially when the recipient of the flattery believes it has been sincerely offered (Smith, 1982). The clever "yes man" will occasionally take issue with the boss as a way of reinforcing the impression of sincerity, but be careful to agree on matters of greatest importance to his superior. Expressed liking for one's audience turns out to be a highly reliable predictor of attitude change (Smith, 1982; Miller, Burgoon, and Burgoon, 1984). Likewise, the use of ingratiation techniques in employment interviews correlates highly with success at getting hired.

Interestingly, the flatterer often denies that ingratiation has taken place. In experiments in which subjects were specifically urged to play up to a stranger, they were later unwilling to admit that they had taken any steps to enhance their attractiveness. They seemed to have convinced themselves that the strangers liked them for no other reason than their inherent likableness (Colman, 1980).

Two theories of flattery offer inconsistent hypotheses on the effects of flattery on self-rejecting persons. One theory, the *need satisfaction* view, holds that flattery helps satisfy people's needs to see themselves favorably. According to this view, it is always reassuring to be told one is likable; it satisfies a basic need to be liked and evokes liking in turn for the flatterer. The second theory, the *cognitive consistency* view (discussed in Chapter 4), predicts that people with low self-esteem will reject flattery because it is inconsistent with their view of themselves.

At a test of these hypotheses, Colman (1980) compared research subjects judged previously to be either very high or very low in self-esteem in terms of their reactions to flattering or neutral evaluations of their character by a psychologist who had interviewed them. The results provided clear support for the cognitive-consistency theory. The high self-esteem subjects generally ended up with a much more favorable impression of the evaluator when he flattered them than when he offered neutral comments. Subjects who had a low opinion of themselves preferred the neutral evaluator to the flatterer—that is, the flattery backfired when it was used on these subjects. The results suggest that flattery succeeds in eliciting liking from the recipient only when it confirms the latter's self-image. People who have low opinions of themselves are not merely impervious to flattery—they react against it by disapproving of the flatterer.

The status of the flatterer seems to make a considerable difference. In a subsequent experiment, Colman and his colleagues introduced the evaluator to the undergraduate subjects as either a high-status person (a graduate student) or a low-status person (a high school dropout). Here flattery was individually tailored to each subject's self-image, which had been previously assessed by means of a paper-and-pencil test. High-status evaluators were judged much more attractive when they flattered, and it made little difference whether the flattery seemed valid or phony. Low-status flatterers were disliked most when their flattery seemed insincere, but their apparently valid flattery backfired as well.

Physical Attractiveness

Another highly reliable predictor of success at persuasion is physical attractiveness (Smith, 1980). Evidently, judgments of physical attractiveness influence perceptions of talent, fluency, kindness, honesty, and intelligence (Cialdini, 1984). In the 1974 Canadian federal elections, according to Cialdini, voters went for physically attractive candidates two and a half times more often than unattractive candidates. Moreover, only 14 percent allowed in a follow-up survey that they might have been influenced by the candidates' looks.

A charitable explanation for these findings is that intelligence, talent, fluency, and the like are indeed unequally distributed in our culture, with good-looking people possessing a larger share of them. The possibility exists that they are socialized differently from less attractive persons. There is indeed some evidence, according to Smith (1982), that physically attractive persons have greater confidence in themselves, expect more of themselves, and are more skilled socially, all as a result of different patterns of socialization. One study reported by Smith found that physically attractive people had higher scholastic aptitude test scores and higher grade-point averages; also, that they were faster and more fluent speakers—factors previously found to be associated with persuasiveness.

SUMMARY

Co-active persuasion is a method of *bridging* differences, of moving toward persuadees psychologically in the hope that they will be moved in turn to accept the persuader's position or proposal. It consists, essentially, of five components:

1. Being receiver-oriented rather than source-oriented—communicating on the message recipient's terms.
2. Reaching out—opting for warm message forms over more impersonal ones, speaking conversationally rather than formally, preferring closer physical settings over more distant ones.
3. Combining expressions of interpersonal similarity with manifestations of expertise, knowledge of subject, trustworthiness, and the like—responding to the persuadee's desire to be addressed by a credible source, not just a likable source.
4. Building on shared experiences.
5. Using the yes-yes, yes-but, and other such techniques in building from shared premises, and also, if necessary, offering reasons for belief or action that are not the persuader's but that the persuadee is likely to find compelling.

Research findings on the relationship between similarity, credibility, and attitude change lead to conclusions such as the following:

1. Relevant dispositional similarities are potent forces in persuasion. They enhance all three components of credibility—attractiveness, trustworthiness, and competence.
2. Membership group similarities increase attraction, but not necessarily respect and trust.
3. Sources should ideally be matched to issues: peers to matters of taste or value; experts to factual questions.
4. Opinion leaders tend to be "superrepresentatives" of those they influence.
5. The similarity-attraction relationship is not found with self-rejecting audiences.

EXERCISE

As a way of appreciating further what co-active persuasion entails, try composing two different versions of a letter to someone with whom you disagree on a matter of concern to both of you. Version 1 should exhibit the style of the objectivist. In this form of the letter, you should state your position, provide the best reasons you can find to support that position, and undermine your opponent's arguments. Prove that you are "right."

Version 2 should exhibit a co-active style. Rather than lecturing at your reader, reason with him or her. Try organizing your letter as follows:

1. State the issue under consideration.
2. State the reader's position as clearly and as fairly as you can. Show that you understand the opposing position.
3. Indicate areas of agreement, including contexts in which the reader could be "right."
4. Identify areas of doubt or disagreement, while at the same time affirming your respect for the other.
5. Suggest consideration of your ideas. Promote them in terms of premises the reader is likely to find attractive. Perhaps point up ways in which your respective ideas are complementary, each supplying what the other lacks.

Chapter *8*
Audience Analysis and Adaptation

There is a tendency in our culture to assume that some persons—advertisers, propagandists, Philadelphia lawyers—have magical powers of persuasion, while the rest of us wallow in the mud of our own impotence. The truth is that professionals and amateurs are much alike in their capacity to influence others. What, then, are the differences? First, we frequently do not know what we want from our audiences on any one occasion. Second, even when we do know what we want, we often expect the impossible. We assume that we can change fundamental attitudes in unconducive social contexts through a single transaction. Then we complain that we have not succeeded.

Often we have a sense of our own convictions, some idea about the audience's convictions, but little sense of what we can expect from the audience in the way of specific covert or overt responses following the reception of our message. Broadly speaking, are we seeking hostility reduction, conversion, or intensification? Are we attempting to mold attitudes, to change them, to arouse them, or to create indecision? And within those broad goal categories, what specific goals are we seeking to accomplish?

Assume for a moment you will be addressing a student audience that is mildly sympathetic to your position in favor of welfare reform, and that you are seeking, in a general way, to intensify their attitudes. Beginning speakers are often content with such vague goal statements, but there is considerable value in specifying them further. Let us note that the following, more specific, statements of purpose would lead to quite different approaches to the audience:

> Arousing the audience's anger at welfare officials to the point where they are willing to stage a demonstration at the local welfare office

Providing a better intellectual appreciation of the nationwide scope of the problem

Instilling an intense emotional sense of what it is like to be totally dependent upon welfare

Crystallizing favorable attitudes around a specific plan of action

Goals such as these should not be nailed down before you have made a careful assessment of audience predispositions. It would be foolhardy, for example, to make a plea for donations to a cause your audience initially opposes. It would be equally foolish to ask people for a small donation when they are ready to provide a big one.

Suppose you have lost a good friend as a result of a drunk driving incident and that you are genuinely committed to doing something about the problem in your community. The opportunity has arisen to discuss the matter with your classmates. What should you do?

One alternative might be to aim at getting the audience more concerned about the problem, and letting matters go at that. But on this topic and with this audience you can probably aim for something more. Should you try to get classmates promoting the cause to others, and perhaps not just talking about it but doing something about it, like launching a citizen education campaign or donating support to lobbying efforts in behalf of stiff penalties for drunk driving in your state or local community? If it is legislative change you want, do you wish to promote mandatory prison sentences for drunk driving, or stiffer fines, or license suspensions, or mandatory counseling, or some combination? Or are you more concerned about preventing accidents as a result of drunk driving, perhaps by increasing the drinking age in your state? And if it is stiffer penalties that you are concerned about, do you want to list for your audience the details of how such sentencing would work—for example, five years for vehicular homicide, six months for second offense, and so on? Or do you want to leave the recommendation more general, trusting that whatever legislation is passed will help to alleviate the problem?

The point, of course, is not that any one of these goals is necessarily better or worse; only that these and others need to be thought about before you settle on a plan of action. What goals you select will surely be influenced by your personal beliefs and values, but considerations of audience and situation may also be relevant. For example, you would probably have much clearer sailing with a college audience if you pushed for stiff penalties for drunk driving than for an increase in the drinking age. On the other hand, the drinking age question may be the better issue for your audience precisely because it does affect them directly.

Despite contrary evidence from psychological research on persuasion, it is probably unwise to expect sweeping changes in attitudes or behavior on any one occasion. The typical psychological experiment utilizes uninvolving issues, captive audiences, and classroom settings that frequently place the subject under unusual pressure to comply with the position advocated in the message.

The experimental research evidence of sweeping changes wrought by persuasive messages has not been confirmed by research on mass communications in more naturalistic settings (Hovland, 1959). There are remarkably fewer instances, in fact, in which a single message, by itself, has produced wholesale conversions of mass audiences. When claims of this kind are made, they are usually exaggerated. More often than not, seemingly spectacular successes at persuasion serve *triggering* or *catalytic* functions; the message initiates or crystallizes concern about an issue, but depends on other causal forces to facilitate its effects.

Targeting

Targeting Goals

In mass communication situations particularly, it is essential to differentiate among audience segments. A television editorial about public transportation subsidies will be heard by people who drive to work every day and resent the noisy, aggressive buses that block streets, by people who depend on buses and trains for their mobility, by pedestrians who fear increased traffic, by taxpayers who see public transportation as a drain on their budgets, by environmentalists who predict dire consequences as a result of carbon monoxide levels in the air we breathe, and undoubtedly by many other competing interest groups. How do you communicate a message that will be acceptable to even two of these segments?

Even in public communication situations, you may well find yourself with a *mixed audience:* some persons strongly in support of your position, others as strongly opposed; some highly knowledgeable, others completely in the dark. Generally speaking, you should settle on a single specific purpose for any one audience or audience segment. Even with a very heterogeneous audience, you may speak on a single, abstract theme, hoping that a pleasing demeanor or ambiguous appeals to cultural truisms will carry the day. Or you may virtually ignore some segments of the audience—admittedly, at the risk of offending them—in the hope of appealing to other segments. In some cases, persuaders may aim at only a small minority of their listeners, as when a representative of the Marine Corps attempts to recruit college students. In other cases, they may aim their messages at the majority (still ignoring some), as when a presidential candidate attempts to forge a winning constituency.

Let us suppose you are requested to give a short speech to a group of students about proposed changes in the state welfare system. You wish to spark the interest of these students sufficiently so that they will contact their legislators about the proposed law, asking that they vote against it. You find out what you can about the group, and conclude that some of them may not feel very favorably about welfare recipients, but on the whole they are either neutral or slightly in favor of maintaining a humane welfare system in the state. In light of this audience analysis, you might modify your goal statement as follows:

> I intend to arouse the interest of the audience about the proposed change in our welfare laws, and to encourage those most sympathetic to urge their elected

A word to smokers
(about nonsmokers and anti-smokers)

In the expressive jargon of jazz, a lot of folks are "into" segregation these days—for smokers.

If you've ridden any planes lately, you've found yourself banished to the back of them, last to be served, last to leave.

Here on the ground there's a sudden sprouting of "No Smoking" signs. And if, by mistake, you happen to light up in the wrong place, you get a sharp reminder, annoyed frown or cold shoulder.

When that happens, it's easy to get the feeling you're being picked on, and made to feel like a social outcast.

But there's another side to this.

In Seattle some time ago, two restaurants tried segregation —an area for nonsmokers.

After a month, one had served 9,389 meals in the smoking side, and only 21 in the nonsmoker side. In the other, of 17,421 customers, only 23 asked to be segregated from the smokers.

The point is that most non-smokers think smokers are O.K. and they like to be around us—when the choice is left up to them.

So take heart.

That doesn't mean that the tiny minority of *anti*-smokers are going to go away. They won't. Some of them have very sensible reasons for objecting. Smoke bothers them. And a discourteous smoker bothers them as much as he bothers us smokers. And then there are people, perfectly rational about everything else, who turn kind of paranoid when a smoker approaches.

We don't know what to do about these anti-smokers any more than you do—except to treat them all with the courtesy and kindness we deserve from them.

It works with our friends, the nonsmokers; it may also work with the anti-smokers.

THE TOBACCO INSTITUTE
1776 K St. N.W., Washington, D.C. 20006

Freedom of choice is the best choice.

A word to nonsmokers
(about smokers)

A great jazz musician once said of his art, "If you don't understand it, I can't explain it."

That's the way it is with smoking.

If you've never smoked, it just *looks* puzzling—the whole ritual of lighting, puffing. What's the point?

There's really no way to explain it.

We've all heard from the people who think the 60 million American smokers ought to be, like you, nonsmokers. But even those people know there's *some-thing* going on that smokers like.

Maybe that's the key to the whole tobacco thing from the beginning. It's a small ritual that welcomes strangers, provides companionship in solitude, fills "empty" time, marks the significance of certain occasions and expresses personal style.

For *some* people. And by personal choice, not for you. That's the way it ought to be. Whether your preference is carrot juice or bottled water, beach buggies or foreign cars, tobacco smoking or chewing gum or none of the above. Personal style.

What we're saying is that, like jazz or chamber music, some people like it and some don't.

And most of you nonsmokers understand that. It would be a dull world if everybody liked the same things.

The trouble is that some people (*anti*-smokers, as distinguished from *non*smokers) don't like those who march to the sound of the different drummer, and want to harass smokers and, if possible, to separate them from your company in just about everything.

And the further trouble is that even the tolerant *non*smokers, and that's most of you, are honestly annoyed by the occasional sniff of tobacco smoke that's a little too pervasive.

It annoys us smokers equally.

But it would be a shame if we allowed a tiny handful of intolerant anti-smokers, and a small group of discourteous smokers, to break up the enjoyable harmony we find in each other's personal style.

Maybe if we ignore them both, they'll go away and leave the rest of us to go on playing together.

THE TOBACCO INSTITUTE
1776 K St. N.W., Washington, D.C. 20006

Freedom of choice is the best choice.

Warning: The Surgeon General Has Determined That Cigarette Smoking Is Dangerous to Your Health.

Warning: The Surgeon General Has Determined That Cigarette Smoking Is Dangerous to Your Health.

Good examples of targeting. Compare these ads with the messages for "those who don't . . . and do" by the Reynolds Tobacco Company. *(Courtesy of The Tobacco Institute)*

representatives to vote against it. With those who are openly opposed to my position, I hope to defuse or neutralize their hostility by providing them with specific information about how current laws affect welfare recipients and what harmful results will come about from the proposed changes.

The point of targeting, of course, is that it should affect what you say to whom. Health researchers learned, for example, that different groups of women

A message from those who don't to those who do.

We're uncomfortable.

To us, the smoke from your cigarettes can be anything from a minor nuisance to a real annoyance.

We're frustrated.

Even though we've chosen not to smoke, we're exposed to second-hand smoke anyway.

We feel a little powerless.

Because you can invade our privacy without even trying. Often without noticing.

And sometimes when we speak up and let you know how we feel, you react as though *we* were the bad guys.

We're not fanatics. We're not out to deprive you of something you enjoy. We don't want to be your enemies.

We just wish you'd be more considerate and responsible about how, when, and where you smoke.

We know you've got rights and feelings. We just want you to respect our rights and feelings, as well.

A message from those who do to those who don't.

We're on the spot.

Smoking is something we consider to be a very personal choice, yet it's become a very public issue.

We're confused.

Smoking is something that gives us enjoyment, but it gives you offense.

We feel singled out.

We're doing something perfectly legal, yet we're often segregated, discriminated against, even legislated against.

Total strangers feel free to abuse us verbally in public without warning.

We're not criminals. We don't mean to bother or offend you. And we don't like confrontations with you.

We're just doing something we enjoy, and trying to understand your concerns.

We know you've got rights and feelings. We just want you to respect our rights and feelings, as well.

Brought to you in the interest of common courtesy by

R.J. Reynolds Tobacco Company

Compare this ad with the ads by the Tobacco Institute. Together, these ads are part of a campaign by the American Tobacco Industry, How effective do you think the campaign is? *(Courtesy of R.J. Reynolds Tobacco Company)*

were not getting free Pap tests for cervical cancer for very different reasons: some because they didn't know about them, others because they knew about them but were afraid to come in. Correspondingly, it was discovered that different groups were influenced by different types of appeals. The more affluent college-educated women were moved to action by utilitarian appeals. Those who were poorer and less well educated were influenced more by opinion leaders in their communities.

A balance must often be struck in determining how to adapt to a mixed audience. Some speakers end up taking no real position at all because they do not want to offend anyone. A lecture on handgun control couples a plea to reduce the availability of handguns with the observation that "guns don't kill people, people kill people." The audience is left to wonder which is to be regulated, the gun or the person? Without clearer direction from the speaker, no decisive action by the audience can be expected. The speaker may not have alienated any part of the audience, but he or she has accomplished little or no change.

Ideally, of course, persuaders should consider all audience members in framing a specific purpose, and they may well have different purposes in mind for different segments of the audience. Such may have been the case when Stewart Udall, former secretary of the interior and a prominent conservationist, presented a rather unusual testimonial on television in behalf of a Sears product. That it was unusual for a major political figure to endorse a commercial product was acknowledged by Udall himself, but he pointed out that the product was also unique. It was, he said, a new nonphosphate detergent which, unlike other detergents then in use, did not pollute rivers and streams. Udall emphasized, moreover, that his earnings from performance of the testimonial had been donated to a worthy charity.

Ironically, the substitute ingredients used in nonphosphate detergents have since been found to have polluting effects also, but disregarding this parenthetical tidbit of information, let us ask what goals Udall hoped to accomplish by doing the advertisement. It seems a reasonable estimate that he had different goals in mind for different audience segments. Among those who were already conservation-minded, Udall undoubtedly sought to change buying patterns and to spark a word-of-mouth campaign in which others could be led to purchase nonphosphate detergents as well. Among those who were indifferent or uninformed about conservation issues or about phosphates in particular, Udall probably hoped to provide the beginnings of an education and to stimulate further thought. Udall's protestations notwithstanding, he might also have attempted to enhance his own image in the public eye. Finally, Udall may have given special thought to a small but highly influential audience segment, the manufacturers of other detergents. By promoting a nonphosphate, the conservationist probably sought to pressure these manufacturers into following Sears' example.

Targeting Appeal Strategies

The Unique Selling Proposition (USP). Related to goal-setting is deciding what appeals to use. Advertisers speak in this connection of providing for each product a *unique selling proposition (USP).*

Selection of USPs can be guided by behavioral research. Knowing that strong fear appeals accompanied by reassurances and concrete recommendations tend in general to be more effective than weak fear appeals at inducing compliance with health and safety recommendations, you might choose the former in your antismoking message. Knowing that guilt appeals tend to be more effective than fear appeals in antismoking messages to expectant mothers or parents of young children, you might opt for a guilt appeal in a speech delivered to a local Parent-Teacher Association.

Still, the generalizations provided by research on one set of audiences are no substitute for careful analysis of your own target audience. Finding the right appeal consists, once again, of taking the perspective of the other and possibly building on shared premises. Here are examples of how Watzlawick, Weakland, and Fisch (1974) attempt to overcome resistance by clients to suggestions that they display symptoms they are anxious to conceal:

> To the engineer or computer man we may explain the reason for this behavior prescription in terms of a change from negative to positive feedback mechanisms. To a client associating his problem with low self-esteem, we may concede that he is evidently in need of self-punishment and that this is an excellent way of fulfilling this need. To somebody involved in Eastern thought we may recall the seeming absurdity of Zen *koans*. With the patient who comes and signals, "Here I am—now *you* take care of me," we shall probably take an authoritarian stand and give him no explanation whatsoever ("Doctor's orders!"). With somebody who seems a poor prospect for any form of cooperation, we shall have to preface the prescription itself with the remark that there exists a simple but somewhat odd way out of his problem, but that we are almost certain that he's not the kind of person who can utilize this solution (p. 126).

In formulating USPs, recall Ajzen and Fishbein's advice. Make sure the appeal you offer is believable *and* consistent with the target audience's dominant values. In the 1960s a brewery known as Gablinger's produced the first light beer and advertised it as a dieting device. Beer drinkers, however, turned out not to be terribly impressed with dieting appeals. Though they believed that Gablinger's had half the calories of regular beer, they kept on drinking Budweiser. A decade later, light beer was introduced by other breweries with a new appeal. The message was not that you consume fewer calories, but that because of the beer's lightness you can consume more of it. That appeal was consistent with the beer drinkers' values.

The problem of belief arose with another set of advertisements. In the 1950s Phillip Morris launched a campaign in which it boasted that its cigarettes wouldn't cause "sandpaper throat." Until then most smokers had not known what to attribute their sore throats to. When they found out, many chose to quit smoking. Few believed they would benefit if they switched to Phillip Morris products. Soon after, a lozenge company cashed in on the idea, promising to relieve sandpaper throat. That appeal was convincing.

Multistage Strategies. Careful consideration may have to be given to power-related factors with respect to the topic you are addressing. Is it open to mass action? Does it require judicial or legislative action? Can general attitude changes bring about the reforms you seek? An understanding of the various institutions and power structures involved with the issue may be essential to goal setting and accomplishment. Reform of the criminal justice system may be important to the lives of thousands of inmates, tens of thousands of their family members, and ultimately to the entire populace of the country, but the moving force behind such reform probably must come from the legal community and the legislators. Conversely, a safe neighborhood cannot be gotten from lawyers or mayors, but from the commitment of the residents who live and work there.

The audience that lacks power to impose sanctions or provide rewards may nevertheless have indirect influence; you may thus influence those in power through a multistage approach. Children are learning in school about our environment, the energy shortage, atomic power, and many other controversial issues, and they are taking newly acquired attitudes home to parents and families. In my home, lights in unoccupied rooms are routinely turned off by my son, with an admonition against wasting electricity. Children cannot influence public policy, but they certainly can influence their parents.

Directing Thought and Action

Among the paramount issues for persuaders are when to state a position, how far to go in directing thought or action on any one occasion, whether it is better to ask for much more than you know you can get at a first meeting with your audience or simply to get a "foot in the door." These and related issues have been the subject of a good deal of behavioral research. As is so often the case, the answers depend on the type of audience one is addressing.

Explicit versus Implicit Conclusion-Drawing

Your audience should generally have a clear notion of *what* it is you will be discussing and *why*. Persuaders run a risk if they leave their position implied or if they conceal it until the very end of the message (Smith, 1982). Leaving the position implicit has the theoretical advantage of preventing defenses from being raised. In addition, there is evidence from clinical settings that receivers are more effectively persuaded when, through nondirective therapeutic methods, they are compelled to state the repugnant conclusion for themselves (Pentony, 1981).

Generally speaking, then, you should make your position explicit in the introduction to your speech or essay. Should your position be highly unpopular, it might be advisable to avoid disclosing it until the very end. Or you might state part of the position at the outset, perhaps speaking in very general terms, and provide the remainder later. If there are several alternatives being considered, should you discuss the proposal you favor first or last?

The research findings on order effects are inconsistent and confusing

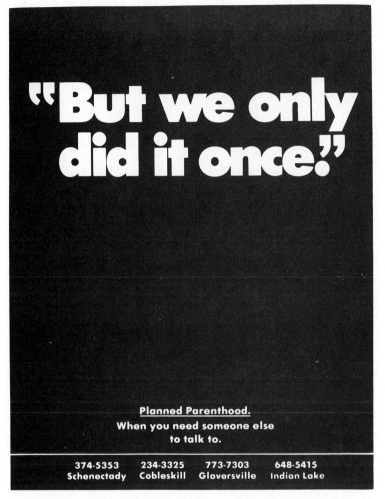

Directing action. Note also how this ad invites participation in its implicit reasoning process. *(Courtesy of Planned Parenthood of Schenectady and Affiliated Counties)*

(Smith, 1982). As a general rule, you should begin with the proposal you favor, then deal with the alternatives, then provide a summary statement of why your solution is best. With a hostile audience, however, it is often a good idea to withhold consideration of your proposal until the others have been shown to be deficient in some way. Then you may gain a fairer hearing for your ideas. In these circumstances, you may even use what is called the *method of residues*. Name the alternatives. Indicate in what ways A, B, and C are deficient. Then suggest that since the other possibilities do not work, D (your solution) must be a pretty good one after all.

Should you be urging your audience to action of some kind, it is extremely important that you tell people how to act. Just after he had finished his now famous "Checkers" speech in 1952, Richard Nixon broke down and cried. He had delivered a masterful defense against charges of political corruption, providing evidence and arguments that could turn near-certain political defeat into a moment of personal glory. Yet the speech called for telegrams of support and Nixon, poor fellow, had neglected, in the conclusion of his speech, to tell viewers where the telegrams should be sent.

Fortunately for Nixon, the telegrams went everywhere, and in sufficient abundance to insure his political future. Other persuaders are not as fortunate, however. Often it is necessary to provide quite explicit instructions for action in the conclusion of a message—in the case of a radio advertisement, for example, by providing a telephone number or an address and repeating it several times.

Magnitude of Discrepancy Controversy

Explicitly or implicitly, the persuader always communicates a position that is more or less *discrepant* from the position initially endorsed by the audience. Perhaps he or she is an advocate of a 6 percent sales tax addressing those who believe only a 3 percent tax is needed, or a fundraiser for a charity whose audience is sympathetic to the cause but not as committed to it. In any case, the persuader must "guesstimate" when the discrepancy between the proposition and the attitude of the audience will be too great to gain acceptance. Should the tax advocate suggest the need for an 8 percent sales tax in order to get the audience to compromise on a 6 percent tax, or would it be better to ask for only 4 percent the first time around in the hope of getting at least some attitude shift? Let us note once again that the question of what to ask for is somewhat different from the question raised earlier of what to expect to achieve.

Persuasion theorists have taken conflicting positions on the issue we have just raised. Festinger (1957), Anderson and Hovland (1957), and others have argued that if we ask for the moon, we are at least likely to get a sizable chunk of it; Sherif, Sherif and Nebergall (1965) have held that in asking for the moon, we may only get a piece of green cheese. The controversy has sparked considerable research and the results are not entirely consistent. Confounding the issue are other variables; the communicator's credibility, the audience's degree of ego-involvement, and the communicator's chances of getting a fair hearing from the audience on subsequent occasions.

Although the findings from research in naturalistic settings suggest the need to exercise some caution, the experimental research literature generally supports the conclusion that up to extremely large magnitudes of discrepancy, the more persuaders ask for initially, the more they are likely to get (Karlins and Abelson, 1970; McGuire, 1969). Persuaders are not likely to get *as much* shift of position as they ask for (see, for example, Bochner and Insko, 1966), but, particularly if they are perceived as highly credible, greater attitude change will occur than if a less extreme position is espoused. On the other hand, several investigators (Freedman, 1964; Greenwald, 1964; Miller, 1964) have provided support for the hypothesis preferred by Sherif et al. (1965) that positions perceived as extreme will be rejected with possible boomerang effects. Rejection of extreme positions is especially likely when receivers are highly committed to the correctness of their initial positions.

By way of summarizing this complex issue, we might say that persuaders should ask for more than they expect to get, but also attempt, where possible, to avoid arousing defensive reactions. Issues can be made to seem important without threatening egos. Under these circumstances, and particularly if the source is respected, more extreme positions can then be stated with some degree of safety.

Foot-in-the-Door versus Door-in-the-Face

A variant of the magnitude of discrepancy controversy concerns how much to ask for from another in the form of donations to a charity, budgetary increases, and the like. At a university confronting a serious budgetary crisis, a department chair seeks funding from the dean for a costly new program. Recognizing that she will be turned down flat if she asks for it directly, she first makes a series of requests for bits and pieces of the desired innovation. The object is to establish precedents and thereby create a favorable context for later submission of the proposal for the costly new program. This is the foot-in-the-door technique.

Another department chairman approaches a similar task in a very different way. Instead of asking for less than he really wants, he asks for considerably more, knowing full well that he will be refused. His strategy is to frame what he really wants as a compromise between what he has asked for and what the dean was initially willing to give. This is the *door-in-the-face* approach.

Clearly both approaches have advantages and disadvantages. In one study, potential donors to a charity were asked to contribute what previously had been established was a reasonable amount, or they were first asked to give more than that amount and, on a subsequent occasion, asked to conform to the norm (Schwarzwald, Raz, and Zoibel, 1979). Overall, two requests produced more donors than one. Making two requests was most effective if the second was moderately greater than the first. If the first request was in an unreasonable range, fewer people contributed on the second round. Those who *did* contribute contributed less than when the request was at the upper limit of reasonability. Apparently the door-in-the-face approach can breed resentment at being abused and manipulated if the initial request is too high, but it can work quite well (at least in a charity situation) if kept within bounds (Burgoon and Bettinghaus, 1980).

A particularly striking example of the foot-in-the-door technique is reported by Cialdini (1984). A researcher posing as a volunteer went door to door in California residential neighborhoods asking homeowners if they would allow public service billboards to be installed on their front lawns. Typically the refusal rate for this kind of request was over 80 percent, since as the residents could plainly see from a demonstration photo, the billboards would occupy considerable space on their lawns and obscure their views. Yet 76 percent acceded to the request under one condition of the field experiment. These people had two weeks earlier agreed to display a little three-inch-square sign saying BE A GOOD DRIVER. Because they had innocently complied with this trivial request, they became remarkably receptive to a later request that was massive in size.

Dealing with Counterarguments

In the discussion of rebalancing mechanisms in Chapter 4, I suggested that persuaders must not only unbalance cognitions to change attitudes, they must also *close off* undesired forms of rebalancing if they are to rebalance cognitions in intended directions. This is particularly true of the various forms of psychological *fight:* rationalization, differentiation, derogation of the source, search for social support or supportive information, and minimization of the importance of a dissonant relationship.

Let us note that each of these mechanisms may be conceptualized as ways of finding *counterarguments* to maintain or reestablish one's initial attitudes. In some cases, as with minimizing, differentiating, and rationalizing, receivers formulate their own counterarguments. In other cases, they set out to secure counterarguments from other sources of opinion or information.

Let us suppose that the logic of your case has been compelling enough to cause doubts in the receivers' minds about the wisdom of their own positions. Chances are that unless you can anticipate and deal with their counterarguments or with those to which they will become exposed, significant attitude change will not take place, or it will not persist. This can be accomplished in part by associating your proposition with sources to whom the receiver normally turns for social support, by displaying your own expertise and trustworthiness, and by underscoring the importance of the issues. Even more significantly, it requires the use of the "both sides" approach, discussed in Chapter 3.

Anticipating and minimizing counterarguments is essential with opposed, critical audiences, but for other reasons it may be important with uncritical, sympathetic audiences, especially in dealing with unchallenged cultural truisms. McGuire (1969) has likened such cultural truisms to being in a germ-free environment. In both cases, there is no apparent "danger," but paradoxically, for that reason, the organism is extremely vulnerable should germs (i.e., counterarguments) suddenly appear. Extending the analogy, receivers should be more resistant to counterarguments if they are immunized or innoculated against them. By getting a small dose of the "poisonous elements," they should become better motivated to stay on guard and they should develop the intellectual wherewithal to combat them when they occur.

McGuire has tested this important theory in a number of experiments involving several variations of experimental conditions. In general, it can be said that resistance to counterarguments is greatest when (1) the receivers not only hear arguments that support a truism, but also refutations of counterarguments; (2) the receivers are not simply handed supportive arguments or refutations of counterarguments, but must also construct their own refutations of novel counterarguments that they were not warned to anticipate.

Ordinarily, it is probably ineffective to mention counterarguments that the receivers themselves would not have anticipated and would not be likely to receive from others. Should such arguments be mentioned, they should also be refuted. But where persuaders seek to reinforce attitudes that enjoy a "monopoly propaganda" position in our culture, it is probably a good idea to unsettle the receivers and to help them cope with potential counterarguments.

General Rules for Particular Types of Audiences

We have observed repeatedly that what works with one type of audience may fail miserably with another. The following are some rules of thumb for particular audience types, some of them already discussed, others to be discussed in subsequent chapters.

Hostile Audience or Those Who Strongly Disagree with You

1. Work hard to build rapport, establish good will, attraction.
2. Use a yes-yes or yes-but approach. Build from areas of agreement to areas of disagreement.
3. Establish acceptance of principles before advocating specific proposals.
4. If possible, establish credibility and "unbalance" audience on one occasion; delay specifics of a plan until the next occasion.
5. Use sources, evidence, and so on that audience can accept.
6. Disarm the audience with humor.
7. Use method of residues when discussing alternative solutions.

Critical, Discriminating Audiences; Conflicted Audiences

1. Use a lot of evidence. Understate, don't overstate. Document controversial evidence.
2. Show consistency with your positions on other issues.
3. Reveal first premises. Reason logically *with* audiences to conclusions.
4. Use the both-sides approach. Patiently and tactfully minimize audience objections.
5. Use fair definitions.
6. Maintain attention and interest, even as you deal with evidence.

Sympathetic Audiences; Reinforcing Attitudes

1. Use extended factual illustrations.
2. Use colorful, intense language.
3. Use evidence to dramatize rather than prove.
4. Ask for specific behavioral commitments. Secure public commitments.
5. Overstate, don't understate.

Uninformed, Less Educated or Apathetic Audiences—Molding Attitudes

1. Work especially on decoding. Get attention, comprehension.
2. Introduce only a little information at one time. Repeat with variations.

3. Appear to inform rather than persuade. Stress your expertise.
4. Use a one-sided approach.
5. Don't *tell* audience why they should know and care; make them want to know and care.
6. Use successful role models.

Activating Audiences

1. For action desired, indicate who, what, when, where, how.
2. Secure public commitments. Encourage immediate action; stress urgency and opportunity.
3. Encourage active participation by audience.
4. Where time permits, encourage audience to role-play the position you advocate or to summarize its main arguments.
5. Have successful others model the action you desire. Create bandwagon effects.
6. Remind audience that they have had decisional freedom *after* they have made public commitments.
7. Encourage audience to practice refuting others who may later offer counterarguments.
8. Arrange possibilities for future contacts with audience.

Learning about Audiences

In order to move toward audiences psychologically, one must first have a fairly good idea of their relevant interests, beliefs, values, and the like. Finding this out, however, may involve great effort and great expense. Substantial portions of the product advertising dollar go toward determining who attends to what messages, over what media, when, how, and why. Jury selection has become a highly sophisticated undertaking, relying in some cases on computerized data banks to inform attorneys of the probable sympathies of persons with given sets of demographic characteristics. Millions are spent by political campaign organizations on weekly, sometimes daily, political polling, on in-depth interviewing of selected voters, and on test-marketing of sample campaign materials.

While few of us are in a position to expend such resources, we can perform more modest audience analyses consonant with our more limited rhetorical objectives. Before running a campaign for campus office, for example, it might be helpful to poll a number of students at random to determine what they are looking for in an elected student official, and what campus issues they are most concerned about. A follow-up survey might test reactions to the plan developed for the campaign, or it might be used to assess the success of efforts already underway.

Among the items of information most readily available to persuaders are data about demographic makeup. From knowledge of such factors as age, sex, race, ethnic background, level of education, and socioeconomic status, one may derive inferences about relevant audience beliefs, values, attitudes, interests, and the like. For example, city dwellers should be more supportive of federal

Analyze this audience. What would it have been like to be this woman addressing this group on this particular occasion? *(Paul Conklin)*

funds for mass transportation than rural people, whereas the latter should have a much greater interest in federal farm subsidies.

But while these inferences would seem to follow as night follows day, others may prove unreliable and perhaps downright misleading. The question persists, therefore, as to the reliability of estimates based on demographics as well as of other available information. From research on person perception, it would appear that certain combined characteristics of the predictor, the object of analysis, and the context influence the accuracy of predictions.

1. Reliability is increased when the predictor has knowledge of both the person being judged and the context. By superimposing the same photograph of one of his actors on pictures of three different settings, Eisenstein, the great Russian film director, was able to evoke enthusiastic admiration of the actor's capacity to communicate joy, anger, or suffering, depending on the context in which the receiver saw it. A grimace may obviously mean one thing for someone at a funeral; another for someone in a track meet. Similarly, knowledge of context may be insufficient. Although we may reliably infer a stranger's feelings from knowledge that his best friend has just died, reliability is increased if the object of judgment is someone we know. "Taken separately," Tagiuri concludes (1969), "either the person or the situation allows nonrandom, but indeterminate, judgments. Jointly they yield highly determinate judgments" (p. 421).

2. Judgments about groups are more accurate, generally, than judgments about specific individuals. In estimating average group characteristics, there is a kind of "law of sufficient mistakes" operating, a tendency to make compensating errors. Value-laden judgments about groups are subject to great error, however, especially when predictions are based on unrepresentative samples.

3. The reliability of our perceptions about people increases with added knowledge of an individual's group characteristics. Knowledge that Jones (or a group of Joneses) is from New York City tells us something about him, but not enough to gear a persuasive message to him on most subjects. Knowledge that he is 70 years old, that he is widowed, that he lives in a nursing home, tells us a great deal more. Of course, each bit of knowledge is drawn from a stereotype. Still, and this is vital for purposes of persuasion, although any one datum may provide an unreliable basis for predicting attitudes, values, or beliefs, the composite tends to form a highly reliable whole.

4. Some predictors are characteristically more accurate than others. No one knows quite how it is that accurate assessments of another are made— whether it is a process of inference and analogy, or empathy, or directly perceiving qualities of another that are innately knowable, or some combination. It does appear, however, that characteristics of the "good judge" include broad personal experience, self-insight, social skill, and detachment; furthermore, some persons are distinctly adept at sizing up strangers, while others display unusual sensitivity only toward persons familiar to them. One somewhat surprising characteristic of "good judges" is that they tend to be "average" or "conventional" in other ways. The reason for their reliable judgments is that, like most persons, they tend to assume that others are like themselves. Unconventional people tend to make mistakes when they act on this premise; conventional persons do not. That people tend to assume others to be similar to themselves was borne out by a study I conducted (Simons, 1966). I found that predictors used themselves as standards for deriving estimates of the "open-mindedness" of others, independent of whether the yardstick led to accurate or inaccurate predictions.

5. Accurate predictions may be made not only of others' feelings, but also of their judgments about our judgments about their judgments, and so on, in an endless chain. Schelling (1960) has pointed out that such capacities are essential to well-managed interpersonal conflicts. That accurate predictions of this kind can be made is supported by several informal classroom experiments conducted by Schelling that readers might well wish to try themselves. In each "study," two persons who are perfect strangers must make the same independent prediction if each is to "win." For example, they must guess "heads" or "tails," or they must think of the same playing card from a list of thirteen or the same monetary figure from a list of six, given no other information. Schelling's students did far better than would be predicted by chance. Note that here too, the predictor draws on inferences from perceptions of demographic characteristics of other group affiliations.

This research has important implications for persuaders. It seems to suggest that accurate audience analysis is possible; that it should focus on characteristics of both the receiver and the social context; that social sensitivity can be improved with experience and self-insight; and that persuaders may utilize known group characteristics to draw inferences about attitudes, beliefs, or values, provided that they use enough of them in combination, and provided that they check out their own value-laden stereotypes.

It stands to reason, of course, that you need not rely on stereotypical knowledge if you have access to more direct data. In preparation for a speech to the local Rotary, for example, you would no doubt profit from an examination of printed materials describing Rotary International as well as other material about the local organization. A visit to a Rotary luncheon in advance of your presentation might give you a better idea of the group's rules and routines, including such important details as how speakers are typically introduced, how attentive they tend to be to their postluncheon guest speakers, what length of speech is considered appropriate, and who might be expected to ask questions following the speech.

Still other information can be gleaned from conversations with typical audience members or official representatives of the group. One of the most difficult speeches I ever gave was a panel presentation in 1968 to a general session of the Republican Women of Pennsylvania on the subject of American involvement in Vietnam. In preparation for that speech, I talked at length with the woman who had invited me and would later introduce me. In many respects the conversation confirmed what I already suspected: that the group would be strongly opposed to my dovish stance on Vietnam. It became apparent from our conversation that under no circumstances would the audience accept my moral arguments; all, or nearly all, saw American participation in the war as just and necessary; they regarded "peaceniks" like myself as the immoral ones. Nor, it turned out, could I find common ground with my audience on the matter of American losses in Vietnam. Most considered these losses to be regrettable but acceptable. I learned from my informant that few in the audience had sons in Vietnam. Most who might have seen service there had gotten college deferments. Yet I learned also from the conversation that the women were much concerned about the chances of their party in the upcoming state and national elections. They were particularly anxious to see Richard Nixon, the likely Republican nominee, elected president.

Sensing that I had little common ground with the audience, I was also able to effect some degree of psychological convergence with them by pointing up the practical advantages to Republicans of a dovish political platform, one that might help to steal the Democrats' thunder. The information I had gained had enabled me to take the perspective of the audience and, on this issue at least, to move toward them effectively.

SUMMARY

In keeping with the first principle of co-active persuasion, that persuaders should be receiver-oriented rather than source-oriented, this chapter has offered research-based advice on how to analyze and adapt to audiences, how to deal with the problems of selecting realistic goals and appeal strategies for mixed and multiple audiences, and the need, in any case, of having clearly defined goals and strategies.

There is also the need to direct the audience's thought and action. Evidence from available research suggests the following principles.

1. The persuader's position should generally be made clear early in a speech or essay, or at least hinted at in the introduction, with details provided later on.
2. You should generally provide audiences with explicit details on how to act when you are calling upon them to take some overt action such as sending a telegram or ordering by phone.
3. Positions extremely discrepant from those held initially by the audience can be asserted with reasonable safety and effectiveness, provided that the source is respected, and that they are stated in such a way as not to arouse defensive reactions.
4. It is generally prudent in asking for charity donations, budgetary donations, and the like to use the foot-in-the-door approach, but there are apparently upper limits of acceptability below which the persuader may chance using the door-in-the-face approach.
5. To induce support for a cultural truism and corresponding resistance to counterarguments, it is generally better to refute the counterarguments rather than merely recite arguments for the truism, and it is also better to encourage people to formulate their own counterarguments than to have them learn your reasons for adhering to the truism.

Finally, note that accurate audience analysis is possible. In analyzing *your* audience, derive inferences from known group characteristics. Better still, speak with some of them; find out about them directly.

EXERCISE

Constructing a Plan of Attack

Let us go back over the issues raised in this chapter in a somewhat different way. Presented here is a list of questions for consideration in preparing an essay or detailed speech outline. In preparation for one of your assignments, try addressing these questions—or at least those that seem most relevant—in writing. Pay particular attention to the question about obstacles and strategies.

I. *Goal-Setting*
  A. What are your immediate goals?
    1. Are you seeking to change what people think? What they say to others? How they behave or act?
    2. How specific does the change need to be? Are you promoting a general principle? A specific plan? A range of alternatives?
    3. Specify as clearly as possible the response(s) you are seeking from your audience.

    B. What contributions do you intend this persuasive message to make toward a larger cause to which you are committed? Is the one-shot message part of a campaign or movement? How long does the desired change need to last?

    C. What image-management goals are you seeking to achieve in addition to your substantive goals? In this situation, which is more important: winning acceptance of your substantive proposition, or achieving more favorable images of you, your group or organization?

    D. For these goals to be achieved, *who* needs to be changed? The entire audience? Those "on the fence"? Those most opposed? Key opinion leaders? In terms of the typology of intended effects introduced in Chapter 2, what responses are you seeking: Defusion? Neutralization? Conversion? Molding? Crystallization? Intensification? In terms of the above, do you have different goals for different audience segments? If so, specify.

II. *Audience and Situation*

    A. *Background.* What background information is most relevant to an understanding of your topic? Briefly indicate such things as past history, current status of the controversy, impending events.

    B. *Knowledge.* What does your audience know about your topic? Will new information make a difference?

    C. *Interest.* How much does your audience care about the topic? Are they concerned or apathetic?

    D. *Persuasibility.* How critical is your audience? Are they easily persuaded or highly resistant to persuasion?

    E. *Source credibility.* What are the audience's attitudes toward you as a persuader? Do they consider you competent? Trustworthy? Attractive? Friendly? Dynamic?

    F. *Attitude toward position advocated.* On a continuum from strongly agree to strongly disagree (or favorable-opposed), where does most of your audience stand on the position(s) you are advocating?

    G. *Relevant beliefs.* What beliefs support audience attitudes? How confidently are they held? Which ones can be changed by persuasion? Are there other beliefs that can be made salient to your audience?

    H. *Relevant values.* What values do most audience members attach to attributes in belief statements? (Recall the discussion of the Fishbein/Ajzen theory in Chapter 4) How strong are those values? Can any be strengthened or weakened in line with your goals?

    I. *Normative influences.* What persons or groups (e.g., opinion leaders, family members) are likely to be most influential on this topic for your audience?

    J. *Normative pressures.* How much pressure is there on the audience to conform to one or another group?

III. *Major Obstacles to Goal Accomplishment*

    From the foregoing analysis of topic, goals, audience, and situation, it should be possible to identify the major problems you are likely to have to contend with. Typical problems, as you have seen, include audience ignorance or lack of information; complexity of the topic, leading to possible confusion or misunderstanding; audience apathy or disinterest (frequently accompanied by lack of information); negative or skeptical attitudes toward the persuader (e.g., lack of trust or respect; perhaps overt hostility); disagreement over definitional issues; differences in values; doubts or disagreements about questions of fact (e.g., trustworthiness of evidence to be presented); ego-defensiveness leading to message distortion, selective forgetting, denial, and so on; inattention; inertia, fear of ostracism or other reprisals by valued others; audience diversity (multiple audiences or a mixed; heterogeneous audience); lack of control (audience not in a position to act on the recommendations to be presented); time or space limitations; environmental constraints (e.g., noisy air conditioner). Make clear the three or four biggest problems you face and, in the next section, how you intend to handle them.

Strategy

How can you best adapt your ideas and information to the audience? What appeals should you use? What benefits should you promise? How can you best present yourself as a person? How can you structure your arguments and appeals for maximum psychological impact? Think in particular about the obstacles you have identified. For each problem, indicate what you plan to do to minimize their effects.

Chapter 9
Thinking about Issues

Before you promote ideas to others, you should ask yourself whether the position you are about to endorse is one you truly believe. You should consider also whether you have sufficient grounds for your belief. Once you become satisfied that an argument is sound, advocacy becomes a much easier process.

The roles of inquiry and advocacy are not entirely compatible. Inquiry requires openness; advocacy requires closure. The inquirer is forever attuned to new possibilities; the advocate is mindful of the need for commitment. Clearly a middle ground must be found between endless inquiry and premature commitment.

Where should you begin? In doing research on your topic, you should initially read for ideas and basic information. What are the basic issues or points of contention on the controversy you are addressing? Are there any areas of agreement among opposing factions? What are the basic facts in the matter that all would concede? What assumptions does each side bring to bear on the issues? What arguments and evidence do they offer in support of their views?

While you are about it, check your own basic assumptions. Have you been treating assumptions as facts, or ignoring counterarguments, or perhaps trusting too much in the opinions of others without thinking things through yourself? The process of inquiry may lead you to abandon your initially held convictions or it may strengthen them. It should lead in either case to a more sophisticated sense of the issues and to a position reflecting the topic's complexities.

Thinking about Policy Questions

People argue about what to believe, and about questions of value, but most often they bring their beliefs and values to bear on discussions of policy issues. Recall the discussion of the rhetorical perspective in Chapter 6, and in particular, the challenges it poses to objectivist ways of thinking about problems and their solutions. Although what might be called the "standard" objectivist model— that solutions should be addressed to the causes of empirically demonstrable problems—still reigns supreme and has influenced many prescriptions about policy advocacy presented in this book, rhetorical perspectives on inquiry have helped make thinking about problems and their solutions more innovative, more flexible, more imaginative.

Three assumptions of the objectivist model seem to have particularly stifled productive policy analysis: (1) That problems are largely a matter of objective fact, much less a matter of how the facts are labeled or classified; (2) that proposals for new policies are justified only if they meet a demonstrated need; and (3) that it is always better to get at the causes of problems, rather than at their symptoms or effects. In the following three sections, I will review alternative perspectives for each of these objectivist assumptions.

Problem-Setting versus Problem-Solving

Recall the discussion of reframing in Chapter 6. Often, as with the nine-dot problem, we fix on the task of problem-solving before we have given sufficient thought to how we have framed the problem. An especially provocative application of the concept of reframing problems has been provided by Schön and his colleagues (Schön, 1979; Schön and Argyris, 1978). Schön coined the term *generative metaphor* to refer to verbal frames that lead us to see one thing *as* another. Schön holds that generative metaphors serve to structure perceptions, and new generative metaphors may stimulate thought and discovery. He provides a vivid example of reframing by generative metaphor that concerns the mundane subject of paintbrush design.

> The Making of Generative Metaphor: A Technological Example
> Some years ago, a group of product-development researchers was considering how to improve the performance of a new paintbrush made with synthetic bristles. Compared to the old natural-bristle brush, the new one delivered paint to a surface in a discontinuous "gloppy" way. The researchers had tried a number of different improvements. They had noticed, for example, that natural bristles had split ends, whereas the synthetic bristles did not, and they tried (without significant improvement resulting) to split the ends of the synthetic bristles. They experimented with bristles of different diameters. Nothing seemed to help.
> Then someone observed, "You know, a paintbrush is a kind of pump!" He pointed out that when a paintbrush is pressed against a surface, paint is forced through the *spaces between bristles* onto the surface. The paint is made to flow through the *"channels"* formed by the bristles when the channels are deformed

by the bending of the brush. He noted that painters will sometimes *vibrate* a brush when applying it to a surface, so as to facilitate the flow of paint.

The researchers tried out the natural and synthetic bristle brushes, thinking of them as pumps. They noticed that the natural brush formed a *gradual curve* when it was pressed against a surface whereas the synthetic brush formed a shape more nearly an angle. They speculated that this difference might account for the "gloppy" performance of the bristle brush. How then might they make the bending shape of the synthetic brush into a gentle curve?

This line of thought led them to a variety of inventions. Perhaps fibers could be varied so as to create greater density in that zone. Perhaps fibers could be bonded together in that zone. Some of these inventions were reduced to practice and did, indeed, produce a smoother flow of paint. (p. 257)

Paintbrush-as-pump is an example of what I mean by a generative metaphor.

Schön maintains that generative metaphors have a particularly important role to play in policy analysis. Focusing on these metaphors forces the realization that problems are open to a number of possible interpretations. Depending on how the problem is framed, or *set* in Schön's terms, different solutions will emerge. The framing of the problem, rather than the solution, then, becomes the most important aspect of policy analysis. As Schön puts it:

Problem settings are mediated, I believe, by the "*stories*" people tell about troublesome situations—stories in which they describe what is wrong and what needs fixing. When we examine the problem-setting stories told by the analysts and practitioners of social policy, it becomes apparent that *the framing of problems often depends upon metaphors underlying the stories which generate problem setting and then set the directions of problem solving.* One of the most pervasive stories about social services, for example, diagnoses the problem of "*fragmentation*" and prescribes "*coordination*" as the remedy. But services seen as fragmented might be seen, alternatively, as autonomous. Fragmented services become problematic when they are seen as the shattering of a prior integration. The services are seen something like a vase that was once whole and now is broken.

Under the spell of metaphor, it appears obvious that fragmentation is bad and coordination, good. *But this sense of obviousness depends very much on the metaphor remaining tacit.* Once we have constructed the metaphor which generates the problem-setting story, we can ask, for example, whether the services appropriate to the present situation are just those which used to be integrated, and whether there may not be benefits as well as costs associated with the lack of integration. In short, we can spell out the metaphor, elaborate the assumptions which flow from it, and examine their appropriateness in the present situation. (p. 255)

Schön dramatically illustrates the organizing functions of generative metaphor in the very different ways city housing experts talked about lower-class neighborhoods in the 1960s versus the 1950s. During the fifties the metaphors of blight and renewal were dominant. So-called blighted areas were treated as though they possessed a dread disease. This led the experts to conclude that only a wholesale solution to the problem was workable; otherwise the blight or cancer would remain and grow. The entire area needed to be razed and redesigned so that a balanced, integrated plan could be developed, one that would reverse the cycle of decay and prevent the birth of new slums.

By the sixties, as dissatisfaction with massive urban renewal projects mounted, the same neighborhoods that had previously been described as "blighted" were now labeled "natural communities." The new metaphor prompted researchers to discover new features of the environment and to draw new analogies. Now it was recognized, for example, that at least some neighborhoods were highly stable and that they served as a fulcrum for friendships and social support. Now some experts were even likening the slums to communities frequently observed in folk cultures. Each story constructs its view of social reality through a complementary process of *naming* and *framing*. Things are selected for attention and named in such a way as to fit the frame constructed for the situation.

From Schön's own stories, it is clear that problems do not simply exist "out there." As you think about your speech or essay topic, ask yourself: What shared premises, what collective understandings have guided policy thinking in this area in the past? Have these assumptions been useful in problem-solving, or have they stultified thinking? What new metaphors might be useful in problem-setting? Are there stories I can tell that can make the new frame appealing—that can help message recipients make the leap from data to recommendations seem plausible, even natural?

Need-Plan versus Comparative Advantages

Whether making decisions about our personal lives or appraising social or political systems, we generally assume the desirability of existing policies or systems unless a need for a change has been demonstrated. Car owners generally do not change their cars unless they perceive something is wrong with the old car. Physicians generally do not operate unless the patient has a defective respiratory system, circulatory system, or other system. In the same way, most of us would not endorse basic changes in welfare laws unless we believed there was something seriously wrong with those laws. Existing policies and systems are presumed "innocent" until proved "guilty."

Correspondingly, we assume that the solution does not go beyond what is needed. Rather than buying a new car when the old one gets a flat tire, we are more likely to repair the flat tire. Rather than operating, physicians may prescribe medication to heal a minor respiratory problem. Rather than getting rid of welfare policies on the grounds that they are inefficiently administered, we are likely to prefer keeping the policies but correcting the inefficiencies. On the other hand, a proposed policy should not, if possible, fall short of the need. If our old car is wrecked beyond repair, we feel compelled to get a new one. If medication will not suffice, the physician may decide to operate. If inefficient administration is inherent in the present welfare law, we may feel obliged to support a new law.

The assumption that policies should always be addressed to problems is most often associated with philosopher John Dewey (1910). In his book *How We Think*, Dewey proposed a five-step sequence for reflective thinking.

1. Perceiving a felt difficulty or recognizing that a problem exists
2. Analyzing the problem, including attempts at definition
3. Exploring possible solutions and evaluating them
4. Selecting the best solution
5. Discovering how to implement the selected course of action

The first two steps involve the discovery and analysis of a real problem, described by Dewey as a *felt need* for change of some sort. The problem should be one that is widespread and that has truly harmful consequences. As a former debate coach of mine used to put it: "Don't ever let your opposition win on the 'So What?' question. If it's a question of national policy, show them that the problem exists from Maine to Hawaii, Alaska to Florida. And prove to them that it's not just some abstract, academic problem. Show them the pain, the suffering, the deprivation."

My debate coach's advice was basically sound. But rather than always conceiving of proposals in essentially negative terms, as something we must be *driven* to by a felt need, it is sometimes advisable to approach them as ways of bringing about a desirable end state. This is the essence of what is sometimes called the *comparative advantages* approach (Riecke and Sillars, 1975). Bypassing considerations of need, it focuses attention on advantages versus disadvantages of alternative proposals. Suppose, for example, that you and your friends are trying to decide how best to spend a Saturday evening together: going to a basketball game, having a party, going to the movies. None of these alternatives is "needed" exactly, but each may be justified in terms of its relative benefits.

Similarly, the thinking goes, why wait for serious problems to develop before taking action in business matters or questions of public policy? The stock you own may be doing fine, but another might do better. A government agency might be quite efficient, but streamlining its operations might increase efficiency. One need not always be preoccupied with considerations of need.

Getting at Effects versus Getting at Causes

The generally held view is that solutions are best which get at causes of problems and not just their effects. The problem-cause-solution approach works off a medical metaphor: Treat only the symptoms and the real problem will persist and perhaps get worse, often revealing itself in new symptoms. In this view, antipoverty measures such as the food stamp program are like aspirins for pneumonia; they do nothing to erase the underlying problem.

Some theorists, known as cyberneticists, argue otherwise. Cyberneticists posit that actions aimed at effects may not only be more practical (i.e., "do-able," achievable), but also more sweeping and long-lasting. Usually, they maintain, it is fruitless to try to eliminate causes: They are obscure or they are hopelessly intertwined or there are simply too many of them. Moreover, getting at a bad effect need not be a mere palliative. Hunger, unemployment, lack of education, and so on are parts of a system. Change one part of the system, and you will probably change other parts as well. With enough food in their bellies, poor people may be more prone to look for jobs and better prepared to succeed once they are hired. These are among the *cybernetic* (feedback) effects that can occur by getting at symptoms.

A particularly impressive case for shifting from the standard problem-cause-solution sequence has been proposed by Watzlawick, Weakland, and Fisch (1974). In their experience as psychotherapists, it is not the initial difficulties people experience that get them into real trouble; rather, it is the solutions they devise to remove these difficulties. Fearing that he might be lost for words if he dares to present a classroom speech from notes, a student commits the entire speech to memory, but then goes blank at the time of the presentation and is thus truly lost for words. Concerned that his wife has been behaving flirtatiously at parties, a husband reacts with jealous rage, thus virtually guaranteeing that his wife will seek solace in the arms of other men. Here, once again, are cybernetic processes—effects looping back on their causes, but this time in negative ways. To deal with problems, Watzlawick et al. recommend a four-step procedure:

1. A clear definition of the problem in concrete terms
2. An investigation of the solutions attempted so far
3. A clear definition of the concrete change to be achieved
4. The formulation and implementation of a plan to produce this change

The first step involves distinguishing real problems from pseudoproblems. In the pseudoproblem category are the frustrations, petty annoyances, and other such difficulties all of us experience and most of us learn to cope with or else live with without making things worse. In a work plant, for example, some amount of hostile gossip is bound to travel through the grapevine. Lowering one's expectations of being able to solve the problem is probably the best way for management to handle this difficulty. Similarly, the police often find it expedient not to go after petty gamblers, marijuana users, and the like, because the effort expended on so-called victimless crimes may prevent them from coping effectively with more serious problems.

The second step involves charting prior attempts at handling (or mishandling) the problem. In a great many cases, say the authors, the mishandling of difficulties reaches the point where all concerned are locked in a "game without end." Operating from the premise that *they* are fine but that their spouses need help, husbands and wives work harder at "reforming" their respective mates, not realizing it is the premise itself that needs changing. No doubt the most spectacular example of a game without end in the international arena is the nuclear arms buildup between the United States and the USSR. Once again, each side sees its buildup of arms as a response to the other's escalation.

The third step in Watzlawick et al.'s model emphasizes specificity. What is the purpose of the plan? What is it designed to accomplish? All too often the goals of long-term health or education efforts are left vague and meaningless. For example, "The students should gradually come to achieve realistic self-insights" might be the goal of a high school sex education program. Stated this way, it is not possible to ascertain when success has been achieved. Goal statements such as these contribute more to the problem, say the authors, than to its resolution.

Finally, the model provides a plan of action. Generally speaking, the plans Watzlawick et al. propose to their patients are concrete, narrowly defined, and immediately do-able. Similarly, we may expect of policy-makers that their proposals be practical, feasible, do-able, and not just workable in some abstract theoretical sense.

Overview

By way of summary of the foregoing section, consider the following in thinking about problems and their solutions:

I. Why alter the present way of doing things?
   A. Can it be demonstrated that there is widespread harm—such as real and pervasive suffering—resulting from the present way of doing things?
   B. Have past efforts to solve the problem helped make it worse?
   C. Has the way the problem has been framed contributed to the problem? Would a reframing contribute to its solution?
II. What exactly is being proposed, and why?
   A. Is the plan workable?
      1. Will it help eliminate the causes of the problem?
      2. Will it help reduce the effects of the problem and perhaps have favorable feedback effects as well?
   B. Is the plan practical? Can it be put into effect?
   C. How does the plan compare with other alternatives?
      1. If there is no demonstrable need for change, can it at least be shown that adoption of the plan would be relatively advantageous over keeping things the way they are?
      2. Does the plan proposed offer greater benefits and fewer costs than other proposals for change?

Thinking about Value Questions

Recall that in Chapter 2, I defined a *value* as a generalized attitude that is adhered to rather consistently in judging particular attitude objects. Among our values are those derived from our biological or genetic inheritance (e.g., survival, safety, sleep), from cultural and subcultural influences (e.g., in our culture, progress, success, bigness, freedom of opportunity, etc.), from identification with the norms of the groups with which we are affiliated (e.g., a particular work group's definition of a "fair day's work"), and uniquely personal, idiosyncratic values (e.g., a given individual's food tastes).

Some rhetoricians have compiled lists of values that can be incorporated into premises used in arguments. Here, in no special order, is one such list:

cleanliness	domesticity	devotion
pleasure	activity	status
rest	sex	independence
health	reproduction	dependence
protection	conformity	property
belonging	acquisition	gregariousness
cooperation	exploration	sympathy
conflict	ambition	
mothering	curiosity	
power	creating	

The trouble with such lists is that they provide no index of which values might be most important at any one time to a particular audience. Controversies frequently arise over questions of taste, morality, justice, propriety, importance. And they are not easily resolved because we generally cannot agree on what we mean when we use terms such as these, let alone on how each ought to be weighted (assigned a relative value) in the overall scheme of things. Not uncommonly, we treat values as things in much the same way we treat problems as things, but this only serves to postpone the task of making reasoned value commitments, and possibly defending them to others.

Rokeach (1973) has distinguished between *instrumental values* (means to an end, such as rest and cooperation) and *terminal values* (ends in themselves, such as self-fulfillment and happiness). He argues further that the total number of values a person possesses is relatively small, and that all people everywhere possess the same values to different degrees. He adds, however, that values are organized into value systems very differently in different cultures, and that there is similar diversity in the *expression* of values. In one African culture, obesity in women is considered a mark of great beauty. Among some peoples, the deflowering of a virgin is felt to be so repugnant that it is performed by a hireling as menial labor. In sharp contrast to our own culture, many Eastern peoples wear white at funerals and smile to express grief.

To get a clearer sense of our own culture's values, it also helps to look at ourselves as though we were an alien people. Using the jargon of the professional anthropologist, Horace Miner (1956) has provided a remarkably incisive description of the toilet habits of the Nacirema people, a culture that might seem strangely familiar to ours (try spelling Nacirema backwards).

According to Miner, the Nacirema are preoccupied with health, and hence have one or more "shrines" in their homes in which they engage in private rituals and ceremonies designed to ward off debility and disease. The shrine contains, among other things, a "charm-box," built into the wall, which houses various "magical potions." These are prescribed by "medicine men" and purchased from "herbalists." For every real or imagined malady, the medicine man prescribes a different potion, "in an ancient and secretive language." The

Nacirema are horrified and at the same time fascinated with the mouth. "Were it not for the rituals of the mouth, they believe that their teeth would fall out, their gums bleed, their jaws shrink, their friends desert them, and their lovers reject them" (p. 504). Yet the "mouth-rite" involves a rather grotesque practice: "It was reported to me that the ritual consists of inserting a small bundle of hog hairs into the mouth, along with certain magical powders, and then moving the bundle in a highly formalized series of gestures" (p. 504).

Value conflicts arise frequently in rhetorical interactions. Quite commonly they are raised by audiences, so persuaders had better be prepared to defend their value choices. At other times, the conflicts are raised by persuaders themselves. Cognizant of the potential conflict in audience members' minds, persuaders may choose to directly confront the opposing value claims. How might a persuader defend one value as more important than another?

Resolving Value Claims by Examining Consequences

When a dispute over values arises, it is often helpful to ask what the consequences are of adhering to this or that value, or of defining the value in a particular way. What are the consequences, you might ask, of locking people up for being found in possession of a so-called dangerous drug? How is it dangerous, and for whom? For the user, perhaps, but who else is directly affected? Should people be punished for harming only themselves? But if we lock up drug users, mightn't this set a dangerous precedent? If, on the other hand, we were to decriminalize use of the drug, mightn't this bring its users out into the open, making them more likely to go for treatment?

Asking about consequences often shifts the locus of a controversy to more resolvable questions of fact or belief. Sometimes, of course, we discover that we do not have the answers to our own questions, but then at least we know what to look for in conducting further research.

Resolving Value Conflict by Attachment to Higher-Order Values

All values have some merit for potential audiences. Persuaders, however, are not limited to the intrinsic value of their proposals. Instead, any given value can gain credence by attachment to more centrally held values. The right to pray in schools, for example, gains considerably if the audience believes that not having the right undermines society's freedom of religion. Similarly, a woman's decision to have an abortion increases in significance if that decision is attached to the right to choose, or the right to maintain autonomy over one's body. Values, then, become relatively stronger if you can associate them with higher-order values.

Resolving Value Conflicts by Identifying Common Assumptions

Common assumptions often underlie conflicting value propositions. If you can identify the common assumption, the only remaining task is to determine which value better protects it. Take the example of censorship in the high schools. Advocates of censorship argue that parents' rights to control their children's education must be protected, while opponents maintain that the right to read is paramount. Though seemingly inconsistent, both values could depend upon the underlying assumption that children must be protected. Parental control is necessary to ensure that the individual needs of the child are met. A censorship advocate might argue that the child will never learn to make the proper choices without the experienced guidance of the parent. The right to read is essential to expose children to counterarguments that challenge their most cherished beliefs. Only with this exposure, a censorship opponent might argue, can the child develop an adequate defense of his or her primary values.

Once the common assumption is identified, the question becomes what best protects children: restricted exposure through parental control, or broad exposure through the right to read? By identifying such underlying assumptions, the conflict shifts from a value confrontation to one of how best to fulfill a shared goal.

Resolving value conflicts is not an easy task. For most of us, the basic values that we hold dear exist in a precarious state of balance. We want freedom but also order, spontaneity but also control, property rights but also human rights, stability but also change, what is equitable but also what is profitable. We may believe that the value we are defending is important, while at the same time recognizing that opposing values may have merit. By failing to examine value conflicts, we are apt to apply our value choices inconsistently from case to case. Examining the conflicts cannot guarantee consistency either, but it might show us the consequences or benefits of choosing a particular value, or show us that no relevant conflict existed in the first place.

Thinking about Beliefs

In Chapter 2, I characterized *beliefs* as judgments, held with varying degrees of certainty, that a given object possesses certain attributes. Beliefs are fundamental to persuasion. We offer beliefs in support of value and policy judgments, and we undergird these claims with yet additional belief assertions. At bedrock are claims of the "How do I know?" variety:

My intuition tells me it's so.

My tipster rarely fails me.

The authority quoted in the article I read is very knowledgeable.

The majority is usually right.

Since I said it, it must be so.

Propositions of Fact and Value

Propositions are debatable assertions, and *propositions of fact* (sometimes called propositions of belief) are belief claims about what is true or false, probable or improbable. Propositions of fact are *supportable* (made to seem more or less plausible) by facts, but they are not in themselves facts. Rather, they are interpretations. The statement that many people believe in extrasensory perception is a fact. The statement that many people are capable of ESP is a proposition of belief. Predictions, causal assertions, legal claims about guilt or innocence, controversial historical claims—these are examples of propositions of belief.

Compared to value judgments, belief claims tend to elicit greater agreement on the meaning of key terms. Here are some examples of propositions of fact and value:

Proposition of Fact

1. Cutbacks in the welfare program have helped widen the gap between the rich and the poor.
2. Mandatory seat belts will reduce traffic fatalities by 20 percent.
3. The USSR denies its people freedom of worship.
4. Censorship of literature only increases its sales.
5. On the average, the top hitters in baseball get paid more than the top pitchers.

Proposition of Value

1. Widening the gap between the rich and the poor is immoral.
2. Seat belts don't feel good around the body.
3. It's better to be dead than Red.
4. It's not the government's job to regulate morals.
5. In baseball, hitting is more important than pitching.

Relationships among Belief, Value, and Policy Questions

I will say a good deal more in Chapter 10 about supporting belief claims. Here, suffice it to remind you of Fishbein and Ajzen's (1975) theory that attitudes toward proposed policies are influenced jointly by beliefs that a given attitude object possesses certain attributes, and by value judgments concerning those attributes. As regards the question of whether a policy is needed to correct alleged discrimination against women paying higher rates for life insurance, here is an example of the belief-value-policy relationship. The hypothetical responses are to the charge that women currently pay higher life insurance rates than men:

	Respondents			
	1	2	3	4
Question of belief: Do women pay higher rates?	Yes	Yes	No	Yes
Question of value: Is paying higher rates unfair?	Yes	No	Yes	Yes
Conclusion: Is there a problem?	Yes	No	No	No

In this example, only respondent 1 believes there is a problem, but respondents 2 and 3 remain unconvinced for very different reasons. Respondent 2 doesn't view women paying higher rates than men negatively. Respondent 3 doesn't believe the assertion is true. Note that respondent 4 may actually see a problem in women *not* paying higher rates than men.

Sometimes controversies turn on belief questions and at other times on value questions. In these cases, it may be perfectly appropriate to prepare a speech or essay dealing just with questions of belief or just with questions of value. In justifying the plan of action, other belief and value considerations will come into play. For example, you might propose to ameliorate the problem of (alleged) past discrimination against women by requiring that life insurance companies that charged women higher rates in the last ten years provide compensation to them or their families. As a part of the justification for your proposed plan, you might maintain that insurance companies should be able to afford the compensations you envision (belief) and that they ought ethically to pay the compensations (value).

The defense of a proposed policy may be built on several subpropositions of fact and value. In arguing for a policy, you might wish to show that there is more than one problem occasioning its need. Each such claim would constitute a separate subproposition. For example, an opponent of the federal government's stringent economic policies maintained in a magazine editorial that these policies were causing the poor to go hungry, the unemployed to give up hope of reemployment, and the elderly to fear for their economic security. Each such belief claim needed a separate defense. The editorialist implied, furthermore, that the federal government's policies were immoral. Defenders of the policies would no doubt take issue with her, perhaps insisting that it is not the government's role to provide full economic support to the needy. It is a good bet that she and they would disagree as to what they meant by "immorality." That is the way it is with questions of value.

Marshaling Support for Your Position

This discussion should give you a great deal to think about as you investigate your topic. It should point you to the types of issues you will probably have to contend with and their relationships. It should also help you to formulate a defensible position, and perhaps to address the issues imaginatively as well.

Whatever the effect of the investigative process, there is a point at which research for inquiry's sake must give way to research for advocacy's sake. Recognizing that no position is without flaws, ask yourself which of the alternatives is "least worst," and then become its impassioned champion. Shift now to a search for evidence and arguments that will support your position. Gather other support materials that will help you generate audience interest and excitement, and that will facilitate their learning and remembering of your ideas. Polish your speech or essay for maximum impact. Articulate some of your remaining uncertainties if you think that appropriate, but not to the point of appearing confused or ambivalent.

A particularly memorable example of the problem of balancing responsible investigative research with effective advocacy involved a former student named Veronica. Upon taking a job in the psychology department's animal laboratory,

Veronica was initially shocked at what appeared to be her callous disregard on the part of the laboratory technicians toward the lives and feelings of the animals they worked with. Veronica was convinced that many laboratory experiments were unnecessary, and her convictions were strengthened upon reading that laboratory scientists had developed new methods of research which reduced the need for lethal or pain-causing injections of animals and other seemingly inhumane treatments. But further inquiry led to indecision. Much of the research performed in her department's animal laboratory was for training purposes. She could not argue with the need for training. What Veronica initially perceived as disinterest toward the animals on the part of the technicians turned out in some cases at least to be genuine concern mixed with a sense of resignation at the inability to do anything about the problem. Veronica herself reacted less emotionally to the apparent pain and suffering of the animals the longer she worked at the lab.

Still, Veronica was convinced that some correctives were possible, and she set out now to find out about how animals were treated at other psychology laboratories. The result of her search was a more balanced presentation, bolstered by testimony in support of her proposal from other laboratory workers. The correctives Veronica finally came up with were far less sweeping than the plan she initially conceived, but they were also a lot easier to defend.

Locating Supporting Materials

Having decided upon the claim you wish to make, you should now gather additional supporting hierarchy. You will usually be able to find everything you need, or almost everything you need, in a library. Good sources of information include books, periodicals, newspapers, and government documents. Each of these resources provides unique information about your topic. You should therefore avoid overreliance on or exclusion of any one of them.

Books are useful for general background reading and for specialized, detailed information. Although you are probably most familiar with the card catalog, *Books in Print, Forthcoming Books in Print,* and *Paperback Books in Print* may also help identify books on your subject. Before reading any book in its entirety, you may want to read a short review about the book. You can find such reviews, complete with a short summary and evaluation of the book, in *Book Review Digest, Book Review Index,* and *Current Book Review Citations.*

Should you want to find more recent or more concise information about your topic, periodical research will be helpful. Hundreds of periodical indexes exist, usually arranged according to subject matter. *The Reader's Guide to Periodical Literature,* for example, indexes news magazines such as *Time* and *Newsweek,* and journals of opinion such as *The New Republic.* Sociological literature may be found in the *Social Science Index* and *Sociological Abstracts.* You will find information on major public policy issues in the *Public Affairs Information Service,* on psychological issues in *Psychological Abstracts,* on educational issues in *Education Index,* and on legal issues in *The Index to Legal Periodicals,* the *Current Law Index,* and *The Index to Periodical Articles Related to the Law.* If you can find only one promising source on your topic, check the *Social Science Citation Index* for all articles in which your author has been cited.

This list of periodical indexes is by no means comprehensive. Your library may have indexes that are specific to your topic. While doing research on a prime television show, for example, a former student discovered *The Complete Directory to Prime Time Network Television Shows, Total Television: A Comprehensive Guide to Programming from 1948 to 1980,* and *Television Drama Series Programming: A Comprehensive Chronicle, 1959–1975.* By using indexes that deal specifically with your subject, you will be able to locate articles not readily available from the more general indexes. To locate these more obscure indexes, check the index catalog in your periodical reference room.

If your goal in research is to have the most up-to-date information, or to understand the facts surrounding your topic, newspaper indexes are frequently the best choice. A few of the national newspapers, such as the *New York Times,* the *Wall Street Journal,* and the *Washington Post,* have their own indexes in which they arrange stories according to subject. Articles from a variety of newspapers may be located in *Editorials on File.* As the name implies, these articles will be more opinionated than the common news story. *Editorials on File* is published every two weeks, so the information remains current.

If your topic deals with a subject of interest to the federal government, government documents may be your most useful research tool. Both the *Monthly Catalog of United States Government Publications* and the *Congressional Information Service* index congressional documents, reports, and hearings according to subject. The *Congressional Record Index* provides a semi-weekly account of each of the legislative sessions. The *American Statistical Index* reviews all statistical publications of the United States government.

If you are looking for the complete text of a speech to analyze, you might begin by looking at the numerous anthologies available at most libraries. More recent speeches may be located in *Vital Speeches of the Day* or the *New York Times.* If you are interested in presidential speeches, compilations of all presidential addresses are also available in your library's government documents department.

SUMMARY

This chapter was designed to advance your thinking and research about questions of policy, fact, and value. Cases for proposed policies are built on subpropositions of fact and value, and they depend in turn on support for other belief claims. Unlike tests for factual or belief claims, no consensus exists on how to evaluate the strength of a value. By showing that adherence to one value will lead to consequences or attachments to more centrally held beliefs, you have taken a first step. Perhaps more effective, though, would be to search for a way of arguing that a conflict never existed.

Particular attention is necessary to the processes of thinking about problems and alternative solutions. From an objectivist perspective, speeches or essays on policy issues should address proposals to the causes of empirically demonstrated problems. Alternatives to that perspective include Schön's ideas about problem-setting, the comparative advantages approach, and Watzlawick et al.'s cybernetic approach. The need to put aside preconceptions and to move beyond conventional judgments in doing investigative research is always important, as is the need at some point to move from research for inquiry's sake to research for advocacy's sake.

EXERCISE

1. For a policy issue of your own choosing, reframe the way the problem is ordinarily thought about by telling a story containing a new generative metaphor. Show what consequences for policy follow from the story.

2. For a policy issue of your own choosing, formulate two versions of a brief speech or essay, one using a need-plan approach, the other using a comparative advantages approach.

3. A recent study of "Best Places To Live," commissioned by the Rand-McNally Corporation (Philadelphia Inquirer, March 12, 1985), found Pittsburgh; Boston; Raleigh–Durham, N.C.; San Francisco; Philadelphia; Nassau-Suffolk, N.Y.; St. Louis; Louisville; Norwalk, Ct., and Seattle "best" in that order among 329 metro-areas. What do you think of these findings? How might you gather evidence and assemble arguments challenging the exclusion of your favorite metropolitan area or the inclusion of one of the areas on the list?

Chapter *10*
Argument and Evidence

This chapter, like the last one, is concerned with how argument and evidence may be adapted to the types of rhetorical situations persuaders typically confront. Its focus is on tests of argument and evidence for typical rhetorical situations. Recall that persuasion deals in matters of judgment rather than certainty and that the issues tend also to be ego-involving and emotion-arousing. Complicating matters further are constraints of time or space on how much can be said, as well as pressures on decision-makers to formulate judgments and take action before all the facts are in. Add to these problems the fact that audiences may be ill-informed or ill-equipped to process the information and the arguments presented to them. These conditions are hardly ideal for rational deliberation, and it is therefore not surprising that scientists, mathematicians, and others in a more fortunate position tend to scoff at the argumentation displayed in such typical rhetorical arenas as the courtroom, the legislative chamber, and the bull session among friends. Still, one cannot always choose one's issues or the circumstances in which they will be addressed. Assuming you want to do more than simply put one over on your audiences, how can you make a reasonable case?

The Place of Argument and Evidence in Co-Active Persuasion

One way of thinking about argument in our culture is as a fight or a war (Lakoff and Johnson, 1980). Witness such expressions as the following:

They *resisted* the speaker's arguments, but in the end found them *overpowering*.

He *lost* the argument; she *won* the argument.

There is no way of *getting around* the argument.

You'll be *defeated* if you *advance* that argument.

She *shot down* her opponent's arguments with *powerful* statistics.

That argument was a real *blockbuster*.

It is also possible to think of argument as a cooperative activity—as something we can do *with* others. This, of course, is the co-active approach to argumentation, and it is the one that will be emphasized here. What counts from a co-active perspective is winning belief rather than winning arguments, and this depends on whether the audience is willing to travel with you as you attempt to move their thinking along from premises to conclusions and from one set of conclusions to another.

The process of argument by which we derive conclusions from premises is called *deductive reasoning*. Deductive reasoning is considered *valid* when the conclusions *follow from* the premises. It is considered *sound* when the reasoning is *valid* and the premises are *true*. If all we needed to be concerned with was the validity of deductive reasoning, we would find that there are very precise rules to guide us. But everyday argument is typically couched in vague or ambiguous language, and there is reason as well to question the truth probability of its premises. *Inductive* reasoning is concerned with truth probability—with whether the evidence presented is *believable*, and with whether the evidence is *an index to what we want to know*. Its tests are far less precise than those of formal, deductive logic, but because most arguments in typical rhetorical situations are of the informal variety, we will need to be at least equally concerned with these tests as well.

In this chapter I will deal with each in turn, beginning with a discussion of formal, deductive reasoning, then moving to a consideration of informal argument, including tests of evidence used in inductive reasoning. Having presented various tests of argument and evidence, I want to comment further on what the concept of "reasonableness" might mean as applied to rhetorical situations. Several suggestions are offered in that section on a handy logical shortcut known as the *enthymeme*, and on the appropriate use of emotional appeal in persuasion. Finally, I will illustrate many of the concepts presented in this chapter by showing how they might be applied to a speech—in this case, Richard Nixon's well-known "Checkers" speech.

Formal Argument

Formal argument involves *deductive* reasoning. The most typical expression of deductive reasoning is the syllogism. A *syllogism* posits premises from which a conclusion can be drawn. For example:

All human beings are mortal. (*premise*)

I am a human being. (*premise*)

Therefore, I am mortal. (*conclusion*)

The conclusion is necessary given the rules of grammar and the unambiguous meaning of the key terms in the argument. The key terms may in fact be replaced by content-neutral symbols in very much the same way we treat a mathematical equation. Here is a syllogism of this general configuration:

All Xs are Y.

Z is an X.

Therefore, Z is Y.

Such a syllogism is said to be valid; its conclusion follows from its premises, whether or not the premises are themselves true. The syllogism

All Philadelphians wear purple socks.

Richard is a Philadelphian.

Therefore, Richard wears purple socks.

is perfectly valid even though its first premise is surely false.

The rules of deduction permit us to determine whether conclusions drawn from premises are valid or fallacious, but they provide no test of the truth-content of the premises. We cannot deny the syllogism "proving" Richard's purple socks in purely deductive terms; we must gather fresh evidence to disprove the truth of the premise asserting that all Philadelphians wear purple socks. The conclusion is a product of deduction, but the premises are the product of induction.

Formal Fallacies

Errors in deductive reasoning are called *formal* fallacies. Fallacious syllogisms are always invalid, whether their premises, or even their conclusions, are true. Although we would probably accept the premises in the following syllogism as true, there is no formal, interconnecting link between the premises that allows us to draw the conclusion:

The United States is a great agricultural power.

The United States is a great power.

Therefore, the United States is great because of its agriculture.

The following argument assumes fallaciously that an object is a member of a class simply because it shares one characteristic of the class. To glimpse the fallacy, imagine if Brownie were a cat, or an elephant, or even the name of a favorite table:

Dogs have four legs.

Brownie has four legs.

Therefore, Brownie is a dog.

A related fallacy consists in assuming that because two categories of objects share a common characteristic, they must be equivalent:

Dogs have four legs.

Cats have four legs.

Therefore, dogs are cats.

Lest this type of fallacy seem too obvious, here is a fairly commonplace example of the same type:

The rebels are for land reform in Central America.

The communists are for land reform in Central America.

Therefore, the rebels are communists.

The differences between valid and fallacious reasoning are vividly illustrated in the case of hypothetical, "if-then" arguments. Using the "if" portion of the statement as an *antecedent*, and the "then" portion as a *consequent*, we can identify two valid logical relationships and two invalid ones. The valid relationships are *affirming the antecedent* and *denying the consequent*. The invalid relationships are *affirming the consequent* and *denying the antecedent*. An example of each follows.

Affirming the antecedent—valid
If Representative O'Hare is a supply-sider, she wants to lower taxes.
O'Hare is a supply-sider.
O'Hare wants to lower taxes.

Denying the consequent—valid
If Richard is a member of AA, he will refuse alcohol.
Richard does not refuse alcohol.
Richard is not a member of AA.

Affirming the consequent—invalid
If Richard is a member of AA, he will refuse alcohol.
Richard refuses alcohol.
Richard is a member of AA.

Denying the antecedent—invalid
If Representative O'Hare is a supply-sider, she wants to lower taxes.
O'Hare is not a supply-sider.
O'Hare does not want to lower taxes.

Thus far we have examined individual syllogisms in isolation. It is typically the case, however, that they are strung together in interconnected chains known as *sorites*. Not uncommonly, a syllogism that seems invalid taken in isolation can be shown to be valid in the context of other arguments with which it is linked. The following syllogism presents us with a general class of formal fallacies called a *non sequitur;* that is, the conclusion seems to bear little or no relation to its premises:

All scientific rationalists place humans over God.

Tyler is a scientific rationalist.

Therefore, we should always reject Tyler's arguments.

It is possible, however, to build a reasonable case against Tyler by constructing a sorites in which prior conclusions are used as starting points for further argument:

All arguments that place humans over God are mistaken.

We should always reject mistaken arguments.

We should reject arguments that place humans over God.

All scientific rationalists place humans over God.

Tyler is a scientific rationalist.

Tyler always argues from the perspective of scientific rationalism.

Therefore, we should always reject Tyler's arguments.

Informal Fallacies

Problems arising from the definition of terms in a claim or from the relevance of the premises in an argument are called informal fallacies. Some informal fallacies are discussed immediately below, while others are discussed in the section on tests of evidence. Note that there is no universally accepted classification of fallacies, so that it is entirely possible that you may find the following listed by other names in other texts. The types illustrated in this chapter, while highly common, do not comprise an exhaustive list.

Arguments "Against the Person"—Ad Hominem. In this type of fallacy, the communicator attacks the character of her opponent as a way of diverting attention from the opponent's arguments or as justification for rejecting the opponent's arguments:

"Mr. Jones claims to fight for freedom of speech, but Mr. Jones is a pornographer. Surely we can't sit still while a pornographer tries to lecture the good citizens of this township on the subject of public morality!"

Here the character of the opponent serves as a reason not for direct rejection of the claim, but for shifting the discussion to an analysis of the opponent per se. It is this sort of *ad hominem* attack that brings charges of mudslinging in political contests.

Equivocation. An argument exhibits the fallacy of equivocation when the same word carries different meanings in the same argument:

"Why do you doubt the miracles described in the Bible when you've witnessed miracles like man landing on the moon?"

In this example, "miracle" first means something that defies the law of nature and then means something that you would not have thought possible. That the moon landing occurred does not make the Biblical kind of miracle any more likely.

The charge of deliberate equivocation is not always easy to substantiate. A political advertisement supporting Rudy Boschwitz for U.S. Senate was head-lined: "Wendell Anderson says he doesn't have the second worst voting record in the U.S. Senate. The Congressional Record says he does." The ad then goes on to show Anderson to have had a 48 percent attendance record, placing him 99th among 100 senators. Assuming these facts to be true, the question remains whether the *quality* of Anderson's voting record was second worst. At best, the admakers are vague in their use of the word "worst."

Begging the Question. This occurs when a questionable or controversial premise is merely assumed to be true:

"Hockey must surely be the best sport, because no other sport is as aggressive."

If the value of aggressiveness is not defended in this example, the communicator has begged the question.

A common form of question-begging consists in positing the conclusion of an argument as the premise. We see a great many question-begging arguments on propositions of value. The statement "Education is good because education is beneficial" begs the question of the value of education. "Education is beneficial" is hardly distinguishable from the claim "Education is good." Similarly, consider "Morton is handsome because he is good-looking." Question-begging is a form of *circular argument* in which the reasons for believing a claim turn out to be the claim itself. Circular argument is also called *tautology.*

Complex Question. Sometimes claims are combined in such a way as to make it difficult or impossible to sort them out. Consider this question: "Don't you agree that it's about time for America to resume its rightful place as the leader of world democracy?" This question enjoins anyone saying "yes" or "no" to take a position on at least the following four issues: (1) whether America has at any time been the "leader of the world democracy"; (2) whether or not America has at any time lost its leadership ("resume" implies a lapse in that leadership); (3) whether or not America should lead world democracy; (4) whether or not America can lead world democracy.

These are themselves complex issues, at least one of which is likely to be slighted by a "yes" or "no" answer. Note that such an answer boxes a respondent into a very narrow position. Those answering with an unqualified "yes" would buy into a wealth of historical, policy, and value assumptions. Those answering "no" are likely to have their loyalty questioned, even though they may be intending only that America has maintained its leadership of world democracy (whatever that is).

False Dichotomy. The false dichotomy demands an either-or choice when such a harsh decision is not necessary. A politician who claims "You can vote for me, or you can get another four years of high taxes" implies that voting for her or him will automatically create low taxes, and that not voting for her or him will automatically result in continued high taxation. In most such cases, there are in fact alternatives that fall between either extreme. The false dichotomy tries to obscure those choices.

Even though the material above comes under the heading of fallacy, you will see these techniques used time and again by persuaders. The frustrating thing for the critic is to recognize that informal fallacies often work perfectly well and, in some contexts, at least, do not seem all that unreasonable. I shall return to this point later in the chapter.

Reasoning from Evidence: The Process of Induction

How serious is the food shortage problem in Eritrea? Why is it that so many people in Elizabeth, New Jersey, have cancer of the gall bladder? Which candidate for governor is likely to win in November? What is the best way to deal with the problem of traffic fatalities?

Each of these questions requires evidence for its answer. Each also requires an inference from the evidence to a large generalization—what is known as an *inductive leap. Induction* is the process by which we derive generalizations, and perhaps predictions as well, from the evidence presented. Although the truth of an inductive generalization can never be established with certainty, there are reasonable grounds for selecting evidence and for drawing inferences from it.

Recall that evidence may consist of examples, statistics, testimony, or some combination thereof. As regards the seriousness of the food shortage problem in Eritrea, we might turn to statistics supplied by an authoritative source such

A perfect appeal for price-minded car-renters. Note how this example of compara-tive advertising incorporates the principle of *repetition with variation*. It is an effective use of evidence. *(Courtesy of Romann & Tannenholz Advertising. Copywriters: G. Romann and Barry Tannenholz.)*

as UNESCO or the World Bank. Or we might describe actual instances of hunger and malnutrition in a particularly hard-hit community. Or we might depend for our judgments of the seriousness of the problem on the opinions of experts, rather than on any evidence they present to us. Better still, we might combine these different forms of evidence, for each offers distinct advantages and disadvantages.

Statistics tend to be the most comprehensive but also the most distanced from the actual object of study; one would not necessarily get a feeling for what hunger and malnutrition are like in Eritrea from the numbers alone. Examples help illustrate a phenomenon, but if they are all that is presented, it is easy to dismiss them as isolated or atypical cases. Expert opinion is often all we have to go on highly controversial issues, but it is precisely on such issues (judgments of legal insanity; judgments of how to heal a sick economy) that the experts tend to disagree and to nullify each other's testimony.

Tests of Factual Claims (Examples and Statistics)

The first question one should ask about factual claims is whether the alleged facts are true. Here all manner of subsidiary questions may be asked about the reliability and validity of the evidence. One may ask, for example, whether the findings are consistent, or whether there are many exceptions and counterinstances. If factual claims are based on secondhand reports—from reporters or witnesses—are the sources of the reports reliable, competent, unprejudiced? Did they actually observe the event? Were they physically and mentally capable of accurate reporting? Were they detached and unbiased? Were their reports verified by others?

Problems in Questionnaire Data. Answers to questions are only as good as the questions themselves. Consider in this connection some of the difficulties pollsters confront. A typical electoral poll question might look something like the following: Suppose that an election for governor of————were to be held today. Which candidate would you vote for, Candidate Fuzz or Candidate Blurp? The question seems appropriate enough, but pollsters have learned from experience not to trust their own subjective impressions. In limiting the alternatives to a choice between two candidates, perhaps they are discouraging respondents from naming third-party candidates. In posing the question directly rather than open-endedly, perhaps they are eliciting fewer "don't knows" than if they had simply asked respondents to list their choice of candidates. In asking them who they would vote for, perhaps they are prompting respondents who did not intend to vote to answer as though they did. In supplying the names of the candidates, perhaps they are calling attention to who is running, rather than to party affiliation. In listing Fuzz first and Blurp second, perhaps they are inadvertently favoring one candidate over the other.

Each of these potential obstacles to accurate polling has in fact been shown to be a real problem in studies of opinion polling. In one study, designed to demonstrate people's tendencies to "yeasay" rather than "naysay," respondents in a national survey were asked the trick question: Do you think incest is good for the economy? Seventy percent said yes!

Problems in Secondhand Reporting. An outstanding example of problems in secondhand reporting concerns war reporting. In the early years of the war in Vietnam, seasoned reporters would return from visits to that troubled nation with glowing accounts of the progress of the South Vietnamese regime at beating back the Vietcong guerrillas. Usually, however, they would rely for their information on what government officials told them. These officials, in turn, would rely on reports from the front. Thus, for example, the journalists might be told that the "kill ratio" in a recent battle was 10 Vietcong for every government soldier. Little did they realize at the time that combat officers were grossly misrepresenting the facts and that government officials were distorting them further. Clearly, an accurate picture of progress in the war could not be gained from press briefings in Saigon.

But even when reporters ventured out into the countryside to observe a military operation, the impressions they received were bound to be inaccurate. In the presence of the military, villagers tended to express support for the Saigon regime, but their real sympathies usually lay with the Vietcong. It took some time to recognize that villages in the South tended to be government-controlled by day and Vietcong by night.

The second set of questions one should ask concerns the leap from the evidence. Are the facts presented relevant and representative, and are there enough of them to warrant the generalization or prediction? Put another way, are the facts an index to what we want to know?

We have seen that examples are often dismissed as atypical or unrepresentative in number. Statistics too may lead to faulty inferences, as when the sampling is unrepresentative, or when the statistical unit is inappropriate, or when a comparison is being made between noncomparable data, or when causal generalizations are drawn from correlational data alone. Here are some examples.

Unrepresentative Sample. A magazine known as the *Literary Digest* now has an infamous place in the annals of opinion polling. In the 1936 contest between presidential incumbent Franklin Delano Roosevelt and Republican challenger Alf Landon, the *Digest* polled a representative sampling of persons listed in telephone directories and concluded, erroneously, that Alf Landon was the probable winner. He actually carried only two states. The problem, of course, was that many more Republicans than Democrats had telephones at that time.

Inappropriate Statistical Unit.

> The workers at ACME Bank are paid very well. On average, they earned $57,200 in 1986.

A figure like this was probably derived by computing the *mean*—adding all employee salaries together, including the bank president's, and then dividing by the number of employees. The problem here, as with all unbalanced or skewed distributions, is that the arithmetical average is disproportionately influenced by just a few extreme cases. A better statistical average for skewed distributions is the *median*—the point above or below which 50 percent of the cases fall.

Here is another example:

> Unemployment isn't really very high. Only 6 percent of the nation's bread-winners were among those laid off and still seeking work last month.

Or conversely:

> Unemployment is extremely high. In the last year some 15 percent of the work force was unemployed at one time or another. I of course include here all potential workers: retirees seeking to supplement their pensions, teenagers looking for summer work, college students seeking part-time employment, workers who had been fired or who had quit, others who were laid off and have since given up on seeking additional employment, still others contributing marginally to their family incomes, and, yes, laid-off breadwinners still seeking work.

The first obviously counts too few categories of jobless persons as unemployed; the second example counts too many. Example 1 is based on figures for a particular month; example 2 takes an entire year as its time unit. A better statistic would present a seasonally adjusted average unemployment figure per month for a given year, and it would include more than laid-off breadwinners, while excluding pensioners, temporaries, part-timers, and the like.

Noncomparable Units or Inappropriate Units. A former student, Michael Caulfield, used his background as an insurance actuary to undermine a full-page newspaper advertisement put out by the National Organization of Women (NOW) on June 1, 1982, in which NOW argued that women are short-changed by gender-linked insurance premiums. Here are some excerpts from his speech:

> The ad asks why women should pay more for health insurance when they have shorter average hospital stays than men. It fails to mention that they have 40 percent more hospital stays.
> The ad asks why women should pay more for disability insurance when they have lost fewer workdays. It fails to mention that they have indeed lost fewer workdays, but to injuries alone. When illness is included they have actually lost more workdays.
> The ad quotes the president of the Society of Actuaries as saying that female mortality rates are approximately 60% of a male's, and then concludes that the premiums should also be 60% of a male's. This ignores the fixed expenses of doing business and fails to recognize that more than mortality costs are included in the premium. For example, could you buy a pint of milk for half the price of a quart of milk? I think not.
> The ad then labels as "folklore" the fact that women outlive men, generally, and uses some pretty impressive statistics to back this up. It says that—get this— 85% of all women live no longer than 85% of all men. You may be thinking just what I was thinking when I read this: "Huh? What does that mean?" So let's examine the claim and see what it means. . . . What has been done is that the best of one category has been compared with the worst in another category and then inferences are drawn as to equality. Like comparing a good Chevy with a bad Cadillac.

Noncomparable Statistical Units or Inappropriate Statistical Unit.

> Oakland's police department reports a higher rate of crime for the city than does Philadelphia's. I conclude that Philadelphia is a safer place to live in.

This may be the case, but you had better be sure that the reports were of comparable accuracy and that the same practices were counted as crimes in each city. Suppose Oakland counts public drunkenness and gambling as crimes, but Philadelphia does not. In any case, so-called crimes such as public drunkenness and gambling, as well as white collar crimes such as bank fraud, are not really evidence of safety or danger. A more revealing comparison would be between major street crimes.

Data No Longer Relevant.

Taussig calculated the annual death rate from abortion at between 5,000 or 10,000 per year. This is proof that abortion is a very dangerous medical procedure.

Proof that it *was* dangerous, perhaps, but Taussig's study was reported in 1932, well before the advent of antibiotics, frequent transfusions, legalization of hospital-performed abortions, and the like. The risks of death have been drastically reduced.

Spurious Correlation or Unidentified Countercauses.

Whether smoking is harmful to society is questionable. Since 1900, cigarette sales in the United States have risen from fewer than three billion cigarettes annually to more than 620 billion. During this period, for many reasons, average life expectancy has increased from 47 to 72 years. (Quoted from *The Smoking Controversy: A Perspective*, A Statement by the Tobacco Industry, 1978)

Here the pamphlet's grounds for suggesting that cigarette smoking may not be harmful are highly questionable. Neglected by the claim is the very real possibility that unidentified countercauses, such as improved nutrition, more than compensated for smoking's adverse effects.

Still, the pamphlet reminds us of an important lesson, that correlational data alone are never in themselves proof of causation. Consider this example:

As smoking has increased, so has the divorce rate. It may be, therefore, that smoking contributes to marital unhappiness.

Or that marital unhappiness contributes to smoking. Or neither, or both. Here is another example:

A majority of U.S. senators are millionaires. What better proof that wealth creates power?

This additional example is presented here because this error is so common. We do not know in this case about the time order of occurrence of variables; perhaps power was a source of wealth. We also do not know what other factors may have been operative. Perhaps a third factor, such as intelligence or education, led to power *and* wealth.

Post Hoc Fallacy. This is the fallacy that assumes that which preceded an event must have caused it.

> Most heroin users smoked marijuana first. It is therefore reasonable to conclude that marijuana smoking causes heroin use.

Like the previous examples of spurious correlations, a good way to expose this fallacy for what it is is to take it to an extreme:

> Most heroin users drank milk first. Therefore, milk drinking causes heroin use.

Here is another example:

> Before I assumed the mantle of the presidency our economy was in a mess. Since implementing changes in economic policies, the economy has recovered its health. I'd say our policies have worked.

This is a more muted form of the post hoc fallacy, but it is the fallacy nonetheless. Note that had the president given *reasons* why he thought his policies turned the economy around, he would not have been guilty of the fallacy. The fallacy is evidenced only when the mere fact of precedence is taken as proof of causation.

Improperly Drawn Conclusion.

> The richest 25 percent of the world's nations use more than 75 percent of the world's resources. This is proof that energy resources are unfairly distributed.

Strictly speaking, it is true only that energy use is unequally distributed. The question of fairness involves additional considerations. Note, however, that there is no way of proving such things as fairness. Leaps from the data must be made nonetheless.

Tests of Expert Testimony

Enthusiasts of science boast that science knows no authority; all opinion, including expert opinion, must be subject to challenge. That may be fine for science, but few of us have the resources to check matters at first hand. We must therefore rely on expert opinion. Whereas some logicians oppose the use of all appeals to authority, I urge only that you subject the testimony you are considering using to certain tests of authoritativeness: Are the alleged authorities relatively free from prejudice or exaggeration? Are they in a position to render informed judgments on the matter at hand (e.g., Did they make a study of the subject?)? Are they not only experienced but also characteristically wise and prudent?

The decision as to which persons qualify as authoritative in any given case is often a very difficult one to make; if we knew, we probably wouldn't need their testimony in the first place and could substitute our own. Nevertheless, it is possible to illustrate the tests of authoritative opinion with some examples.

Appropriate Appeal to Authority.

> John Dokes deserves the promotion. I'm a specialist in his line of work and I've supervised him for two years. I haven't always liked John, and in fact he's still not someone I'd choose for a friend, but I have to admit that he's very capable.

Here the supervisor's credibility is bolstered by the fact that he does not like John but would recommend him for promotion anyway. This is akin to the credibility of reluctant witnesses in a courtroom; we are especially prone to honor their testimony because it runs counter to their prejudices. Here is another example:

> When it comes to recommendations for technical assistance to the farmers of Bangladesh, there is no one we can trust more than Dr. J. D. Dykes. Before coming to the university, Professor Dykes did field studies of peasant communities throughout Asia. He is the author of several books on the subject and dozens of research monographs. He spent three years in Bangladesh interviewing villagers, farmers, and government officials. I think we can take seriously what Dykes says about the capacity of Bangladesh farmers to apply techniques of. . . .

Often, as in this example, you can make a reasonable case to your audience for citing one expert source rather than another. Dykes sounds impressive.

Inappropriate Appeal to Authority.

> A majority of doctors think the morals of young people have declined.

The problem here, of course, is that this is not a medical issue. Here is another example:

> Jane Fonda doesn't think much of nuclear power. Neither do the Beach Boys. It must be bad.

Here again, the persons cited are not particularly expert on the issue.

Adapting Arguments and Evidence to Rhetorical Situations

At a debriefing conference following the 1984 presidential election, a seasoned political analyst was asked why it was that Ronald Reagan managed to do so well yet say so little, while his opponent, Walter Mondale, addressed a wide range of issues with carefully developed arguments and evidence, yet failed miserably. Was this not proof of the irrationality of the American electorate?

The analyst conceded that the standard Reagan campaign fare fell far short of accepted standards of argumentation, but he cautioned the questioner not to dismiss that rhetoric as empty or irrational. Reagan, after all, had a consistent message, and having repeated it often over a period of years, he was able to summon up whole strings of argument in the listener's mind merely by offering synoptic phrases and anecdotal evidence. Above all, said the analyst, Reagan and his people understood the nature of campaigning through television, in which neither candidate is likely to get more than 27 words on the evening news. Reagan understood "the dominant limit of not having time."

At the outset of this chapter, I raised the question of whether special allowance needs to be made in applying rules of argument and evidence to the distinctive nature of rhetorical situations, such as election contests. It is time we confronted this question directly, recognizing that our conceptions of what might be called "rhetorical proof" may sometimes fall far short of our ideals of scientific proof or formal deductive logic. While there is value in using science and formal logic as models of argument and evidence, we need to remember that most persuasion is different in important ways from scholarly discourse. It operates under very real constraints of time and space and availability of information. It builds on drama and excitement, and not just information. Given the issues with which it is concerned, its tests must be those of reasonableness or plausibility rather than incontestability.

Consider, for example, whether persuaders should ever use anecdotal evidence to support their claims. By strict standards of evidence and argument, such evidence ought to be disqualified. And yet, as Schön so eloquently testified, the stories people tell about problems and their solutions, and the metaphors embedded within these stories are every bit as important as the statistics they use to establish the existence of a problem or the workability of a solution.

Similar questions were raised above about the use of expert testimony. By strict scientific standards, all arguments from authority are of dubious merit. What counts are direct tests of empirical claims under controlled conditions. Yet who among us has the time or the ability to conduct such studies over the range of issues of interest to us? And even if we could perform such research, would we not still need help in resolving value and policy questions? As regards issues that cannot possibly be resolved by appeals to fact alone, are we not better off with such tests of expert testimony as were provided earlier than dismissing all argument from authority as illogical and inadmissable?

Let us take the argument one step further. If the testimony of experts is of dubious merit, surely arguments based on popularity (known as *ad populum* appeals) are without foundation. Just because "more people prefer Budweiser" doesn't make it better than other beers. Just because IBM is the leading manufacturer of computer software doesn't make it the best manufacturer. Fifty million Frenchmen *can* be wrong! Yet suppose you are traveling through a town you've never been in before. Is it so unreasonable to pass up an empty restaurant at lunchtime for one that seems to be quite popular with the townspeople? Or suppose that you knew nothing about beers. Wouldn't Budweiser's popularity be reason enough to try it under the circumstances?

The point is not to denigrate the role of formal logic or scientific proof, but to emphasize the variety of considerations that must inform a successful advocate's approach to an issue. Formal deductive arguments are elaborate and painstaking. They must posit precise premises—many of which we would otherwise take for granted—and they must conform to a staggering array of technical demands. Most people do not have the time or the expertise to argue in such a fashion, and in fact, a great many propositions are not suited to formal deductive treatment. Moreover, questions about the truth probability of premises cannot be settled deductively. Deductive arguments require agreement on the premises, but on many controversial issues the kinds of statements that marshal enough support to serve as shared premises are so general that they mean very little.

Similar arguments can be made about the limitations of the scientific model. A privileged audience of scientists might not want to hear anecdotal accounts of time spent with cancer patients when coming to a decision on smoking. They would probably find much more credible reports of carefully controlled statistical studies on the relationship between smoking and cancer. On the other hand, however, dock workers in Baltimore might not give a hoot for the statistical reports, but could be powerfully persuaded by the story of a buddy dying in the hospital.

This leads us right back to the concept of co-active persuasion, which emphasizes the importance of the audience for a given argument. Some audiences share unique experiences that make some types of argument particularly easy to use, and other types particularly difficult. Americans who lived through the Great Depression are more likely to listen to arguments centering on the importance of economic security than Americans who have never lived through a national economic crisis. The process of proof on economic security for the older audience would not take a great deal of effort. On the other hand, the advocate addressing the younger crowd might need much more time just to establish the importance of the issue.

The Logical Shortcut

The idea of logical shortcuts that depend upon information and opinion already internalized by the audience is admirably expressed in the concept of the enthymeme. The *enthymeme* is a rhetorical syllogism in which one or two elements of an argument are suppressed on the assumption that the audience will fill in the missing material. A recent automobile advertisement showed a car in a snowstorm with the legend, "You notice that the car is not stuck." This advertisement is designed to sell the car enthymematically. The writers assumed the audience would be able to fill in personal experience on the difficulty of driving in the snow, and the consequent desirability of owning an automobile that can drive through a Swedish snowstorm. We could reconstruct a kind of argument implicitly embodied in the commercial:

Good cars can travel in rough weather. (*implicit*)

The Saab can travel in rough weather. (*explicit*)

You should purchase a Saab.

An example of an enthymeme. *(Courtesy of Saab Scania and Ally & Garganzo, Inc., Advertising)*

Note that this is not a formally valid argument; it leaves too many assumptions dangling without support. It is, however, an effective scheme for persuasion, because we can enthymematically fill in the missing steps. We know that we want to buy good cars, that we have been offered an example of a good car, that the Saab normally performs in the way depicted, and so on.

Do not forget that the persuasive force of the enthymeme depends on prior audience beliefs. If you try to use an enthymematic format when the ground is not prepared, the argument will probably fail. For example, in the presidential campaign of 1984, Walter Mondale ran an advertisement showing a father digging a hole in the backyard while children played around him. Words ran up the screen in a crawl, quoting an undersecretary of Defense to the effect that Americans could survive a nuclear war "with enough shovels." The purpose of the advertisement was to demonstrate the danger of nuclear war with Ronald Reagan in office. However, in order to reach that conclusion, the audience would have had to supply the following assumptions: (1) that the views of the undersecretary of defense were in fact dangerous; (2) that the views of the undersecretary reflected Reagan's own views; (3) that the views of the undersecretary were mistaken—that we could not survive a war. Furthermore, to make the claim "actionable" in electoral terms, the public would need to fill in the solution as well: that Walter Mondale would be a safer president. Many analysts feel that Mondale was unsuccessful in making this series of claims stick, a failure due in part to the tortured enthymematic structure.

Emotional Appeal

Having made a case for the judicious use of enthymematic shortcuts, let us turn now to the question of the place of emotional appeal in persuasion. There is a tendency in our culture to bifurcate fact from value, reason from emotion, and to decide that only questions of fact and logic can be addressed rationally. Correspondingly, there is a tendency to denigrate all appeals to emotion and all expressions of emotion as being in some sense irrational. This may be one reason that the scientifically minded often object to the use of factual illustrations; they tug at the heartstrings, sometimes eliciting emotional responses in place of coolheaded analysis. While we ought not to allow emotion to stand in place of reason or to overwhelm reason, we are obligated to provide our audiences with a feeling for problems and not just a dry accounting of them. We are also entitled to appeal to emotion when moving beyond questions of fact or logic to issues of value or policy.

On the first of these points, McCroskey (1969) concluded from a summary of 21 experiments, many of them his own, that factual evidence can be a powerful force in persuasion, particularly if the evidence is new to the audience; if it is perceived as reliable, representative, and comprehensive; and if it is presented by a source whose own credibility is not so high that it alone can carry the day. McCroskey added, however, that the evidence should not only be new, it should also, if possible, be dramatic and even shocking to the audience.

Where the facts are not in themselves dramatic or shocking, they can be made so by anecdotes that vividly portray what a problem is like. It has been said that while statistics may tell us the percentage of a workforce that is employed, those who are out of work are 100 percent unemployed. What does it mean to sit idly by while others are earning a living? What does it feel like to return to employment agencies again and again, only to be told that business is slow or that you lack the requisite skills or that you're too young or too old for the jobs available? A well-told story helps put things in context for the audience. They are able to see relationships between immediate events and the conditions that brought them about, and between the case at hand and other, analogous situations. Rather than bifurcating fact and value, logic and emotion, factual illustrations perform an integrative function.

An example of use of dramatic evidence. *(Courtesy of Minneapolis Star & Tribune and Bozell & Jacobs, Inc. Art Director: Ron Anderson. Copywriter: Tom McElligott.)*

We also need to distinguish between appropriate and inappropriate appeals to emotion. There is a class of fallacies called *motive in place of support* (Cederblom and Paulsen, 1982) that includes *appeals to pity* and *appeals to consequences*. Suppose that an unemployed breadwinner should stand charged in court with having robbed a grocery store to get food for his family. The defense attorney asks for acquittal, saying that the question of whether the man robbed the store is less consequential than the fact of his desperation. The prosecution asks for a verdict of guilty on the ground that robbers of any kind are a threat to society and ultimately to the jury itself.

Strictly speaking, both the appeal to pity and the appeal to consequences are inappropriate to the jury's task of determining guilt or innocence. Here it is the facts that count, and not the reasons for the act or the consequences of the decision. However, these same appeals would surely be appropriate at sentencing time, after a determination of guilt or innocence had been made.

Here is where the judge and/or the jury would need to move beyond questions of fact and logic to judgments of value and policy. In these circumstances, appeals to emotion are quite appropriate.

In general, logic and emotion are not antithetical. It used to be thought that a persuasive appeal could either be logical or emotional, as if logic and emotion occupied separate boxes in a receiver's psyche. Now it is recognized that an effective argument may be 100 percent logical and 100 percent emotional. An argument for seat belts, for example, may appeal to the emotion of fear, while being inductively and deductively sound. Although it is true that logical reasoning may be impaired under conditions of high emotional arousal, moderate degrees of arousal may actually facilitate thought. In any case, it is not necessarily "illogical" to be emotional.

Case Study
Argument and Evidence in Nixon's "Checkers" Speech

The same principles of reasoning suggested in this chapter as guides to rhetorical practice can also be used in analyzing the rhetorical practice of others. Nixon's "Checkers" speech (see end of chapter) offers a useful object for analysis. At the time of its presentation on September 23, 1952, then Senator Nixon had already been nominated as the Republican candidate for vice-president. But there was tremendous pressure on him to resign from the ticket in the face of charges that he had accumulated a secret $18,000 "slush fund" for personal use in return for favors to the California businessmen who contributed to it. Even Nixon's running mate, Dwight David Eisenhower, considered Nixon a liability and wanted him off the ticket.

The "Checkers" speech is a classic of its kind. You might wish to compare it with Senator Edward Kennedy's apologia on Chappaquidick, reproduced in Chapter 14. The speech was clearly effective, but it also contained a great many vague terms, begged questions, and specious arguments.

Consider, for example, Nixon's use of a false dichotomy at the very outset of the speech. By Nixon's enthymematic logic, if a politician doesn't respond in detail to charges of wrongdoing, his integrity deserves to be questioned. Never mind the possibility that the charges might be constructed out of whole cloth, and hence be unworthy of a reply. Or that others might have answered the charges in the politician's stead. For Nixon, there are but two alternatives, and they point to a presumption of guilt unless innocence has been established. Indeed, by the third paragraph, giving details becomes equated with telling the truth, which in turn is equated with telling Nixon's side of the case. Not giving details is, by implication, not telling the truth, a good example of the fallacy of *denying the antecedent*:

If you give details, you are telling the truth.

You are not giving details.

Therefore, you must not be telling the truth.

Begged in the next paragraph is the question of the relationship between the test of immorality and illegality. Nixon seems to suggest that the test of immorality is the more strenuous one; passing that test automatically means passage of the illegality test as well. But are laws based solely on ethical considerations? Are there not moral acts (e.g., speeding past red lights to get someone to a hospital) that are nevertheless illegal? Left undefended is the possibility that Nixon's "slush fund" might have been illegal, even if morally justified.

Particularly specious are the arguments Nixon uses to turn the tables on his Democratic opponents. Since the fundamental issue in the speech is Nixon's own guilt or innocence, Nixon's accusations of wrongdoing amount to little more than *non sequiturs*.

By now, the form of the denial of the antecedent fallacy should be readily apparent. Here is yet another example:

> Mr. Sparkman and Mr. Stevenson should come before the American people as I have and make a complete financial statement as to their financial history. And if they don't, it will be an admission that they have something to hide.

You should also be able to identify the following as a *post hoc* fallacy:

> Seven years of the Truman-Acheson Administration and what's happened? Six hundred million people lost to the Communists, and a war in Korea in which we have lost 117,000 American casualties.

Nixon is implying that, since these tragic events occurred during Truman and Acheson's term of office, they are responsible for having brought them about. And again:

> We hear a lot about prosperity these days but I say, why can't we have prosperity built on peace rather than prosperity built on war?

Assuming, even, that the Democrats could be shown to have been responsible for the war in Korea simply because they were in office when it started, Nixon would still need to show that it was the war economy that had produced the country's prosperity; that question remains *begged* in this speech.

The very next paragraph presents us with yet another denial of the antecedent: Nixon offers three criteria for immorality, and then, having argued that he is not guilty of immorality on any of those counts, he concludes that he should not be held guilty at all.

Let us assume for the moment that Nixon's evidence that he was not guilty on any of these charges ought to be believed. (I say "assumed" because the evidence on the secrecy and favoritism counts is embarrassingly scant.) Even so, we would still be left with the possibility of a fourth or a fifth criterion of immorality. Suppose, for example, that the donations were offered in return for special favors to be provided *after* Nixon had been elected vice-president. The sum and substance of Nixon's argument here may be reduced as follows:

If A_1, A_2, A_3, then B.

Not A_1, A_2, A_3.

Therefore, not B.

There are other fallacies in this speech, but the one type used most conspicuously is *inappropriate appeal to pity*. Nixon plays effectively on the audience's heartstrings in references to his parents and to his modest beginnings as a lawyer. He is especially effective in the "Checkers" story and in the account of the woman with the $10 check. Yet none of these tales bears directly upon his guilt or innocence.

Having identified numerous fallacies in the "Checkers" speech, let us conclude with a plea for fairness in our judgments of it. Given the pressures he was under to resign if he did not win belief, Nixon was understandably emotional in this speech. But not all his appeals to emotion were inappropriate, surely not the basic appeal for sympathy at having had to defend his honor so publicly. Nixon's three tests of immorality might have constituted an incomplete list, but they were not unreasonable criteria. Although Nixon begged the question of the relationship between morality and legality, he could be reasonably sure that his critics would be effectively silenced if he could answer those three criteria. No doubt Nixon begged other questions in the speech, but given the time limits, he surely did not have much choice in the matter. Again we ought not to make our tests of argument and evidence too stringent, or none of us will pass them.

SUMMARY

In the less than perfect conditions for rational exchange that co-active persuaders must typically confront, they must still make a reasonable case. This involves moving *inductively* from evidence to generalizations and *deductively* from premises to conclusions. Deductive reasoning is sound if its premises are true and if the conclusions follow validly from the premises. This was illustrated in the examples given of various syllogisms. The evidence used in inductive reasoning should be believable and relevant. It may include examples, statistics, and/or testimony.

This chapter provides a basic introduction to the varieties and tests of argument and evidence, with the recommendation that readers consult a good textbook on critical reasoning (such as Cederblom and Paulsen, 1982) for more information. Noted in particular were typical problems in reasoning, among them vagueness, formal fallacies, and fallacious inductive reasoning. Among the fallacies illustrated were affirming the consequent, denying the antecedent, equivocation, *non sequitur*, begging the question, false dichotomy, false analogy, *post hoc* reasoning, and inappropriate appeals to pity and to consequences. Also identified were common problems in the use of evidence, including unrepresentative sampling, inappropriate statistical units, noncomparable units, and spurious correlation in the leap from statistical data to empirical generalizations, and the use of inexpert sources of unreliable, secondhand reports in generalizations based on testimony.

Given the special nature of rhetorical situations, however, reasoning and evidence often must be adapted to fit the particular circumstance. Speaking enthymematically and making appropriate use of emotion while still arguing reasonably are valid techniques for the persuader in most cases.

EXERCISES

1. In this chapter, the definition of "reasonableness" in persuasion is not very precise. Can you suggest a more precise definition? Should we equate reasonable arguments with "winning" arguments—as in the Checkers speech? On the other hand, should we demand of politicians, editorialists, and other prototypical persuaders that they adhere to the same standards of argumentation as those exhibited in scholarly exchanges among philosophers or scientists?

2. In your view, should we adhere to the same standards in judging the speeches and writings of others as we do when preparing our own arguments, or should we have one set of standards for practice, another for analysis?

3. Evaluate the following argument from the Checkers speech:

   Let me say this: I don't believe I ought to quit because I'm not a quitter. And, incidentally, Pat's not a quitter. After all, her name was Patricia Ryan and she was born on St. Patrick's Day, and you know the Irish never quit.

4. Find examples of exceptionally good and exceptionally poor reasoning in the Op-Ed columns or Letters to the Editor of a newspaper. Justify your choices.

5. Illustrate ten of the problems in reasoning and evidence identified in this chapter through examples of your own.

6. Construct a reasonable set of arguments on a proposition of your own choosing.

7. Prepare a brief speech or essay on a proposition of value or policy that relies exclusively on the following facts, compiled recently by the IRS, and reported in the Philadelphia Inquirer, March 5, 1985, p. 1. Try to include as many of these facts as you can.

   a. 2.8 percent of the nation's population controls 28 percent of America's personal wealth.

   b. That 28 percent is worth approximately $2.4 trillion.

   c. The number of millionaires doubled between 1976 and 1982, the years for which the statistics were compiled.

   d. Nearly 4.4 million people had assets in excess of $300,000.

   e. The typical wealthy woman has more money than the typical rich man.

   f. More than one-third of the wealthy live in California, Texas, Florida, and New York City.

   g. Real estate is the favorite asset of the rich.

   After you have prepared your message, compare it with what others have come up with. Have you reached the same conclusions? Why or why not?

My Side of the Story

My Fellow Americans: I come before you tonight as a candidate for the Vice Presidency and as a man whose honesty and integrity have been questioned.

The usual political thing to do when charges are made against you is to either ignore them or to deny them without giving details.

I believe we've had enough of that in the United States, particularly with the present Administration in Washington, D.C. To me the office of the Vice Presidency of the United States is a great office, and I feel that the people have got to have confidence in the integrity of the men who run for that office and who might obtain it.

I have a theory, too, that the best and only answer to a smear or to an honest misunderstanding of the facts is to tell the truth. And that's why I'm here tonight. I want to tell you my side of the case.

I am sure that you have read the charge and you've heard that I, Senator Nixon, took $18,000 from a group of my supporters.

Was It Wrong?

Now, was that wrong? And let me say that it was wrong—I'm saying, incidentally, that it was wrong and not just illegal. Because it isn't a question of whether it was legal or illegal, that isn't enough. The question is, was it morally wrong?

I say that it was morally wrong if any of that $18,000 went to Senator Nixon for my personal use. I say that it was morally wrong if it was secretly given and secretly handled. And I say that it was morally wrong if any of the contributors got special favors for the contributions that they made.

And now to answer those questions let me say this:

Not one cent of the $18,000 or any other money of that type ever went to me for my personal use. Every penny of it was used to pay for political expenses that I did not think should be charged to the taxpayers of the United States.

It was not a secret fund. As a matter of fact, when I was on "Meet the Press," some of you may have seen it last Sunday—Peter Edson came up to me after the program and he said, "Dick, what about this fund we hear about?" And I said, Well, there's no secret about it. Go out and see Dana Smith, who was the administrator of the fund. And I gave him his address, and I said that you will find that the purpose of the fund simply was to defray political expenses that I did not feel should be charged to the Government.

And third, let me point out, and I want to make this particularly clear, that no contributor to this fund, no contributor to any of my campaign, has ever received any consideration that he would not have received as an ordinary constituent.

I just don't believe in that and I can say that never, while I have been in the Senate of the United States, as far as the people that contributed to this fund are concerned, have I made a telephone call for them to an agency, or have I gone down to an agency in their behalf. And the record will show that, the records which are in the hands of the Administration.

What for and Why?

But then some of you will say and rightly, "Well, what did you use the fund for, Senator? Why did you have to have it?"

Let me tell you in just a word how a Senate office operates. First of all, a Senator gets $15,000 a year in salary. He gets enough money to pay for one trip a year, a round trip that is, for himself and his family between his home and Washington, D.C.

And then he gets an allowance to handle the people that work in his office, to handle his mail. And the allowance for my State of California is enough to hire thirteen people.

And let me say, incidentally, that that allowance is not paid to the Senator— it's paid directly to the individuals that the Senator puts on his payroll, that all of these people and all of these allowances are for strictly official business. Business, for example, when a constituent writes in and wants you to go down to the Veterans Administration and get some information about his GI policy. Items of that type for example.

But there are other expenses which are not covered by the Government. And I think I can best discuss those expenses by asking you some questions. Do you think that when I or any other Senator makes a political speech, has it printed, should charge the printing of that speech and the mailing of that speech to the taxpayers?

Do you think, for example, when I or any other Senator makes a trip to his home state to make a purely political speech that the cost of that trip should be charged to the taxpayers?

Do you think when a Senator makes political broadcasts or political television broadcasts, radio or television, that the expense of those broadcasts should be charged to the taxpayers?

Well, I know what your answer is. The same answer that audiences give me whenever I discuss this particular problem. The answer is, "no." The tax-payers shouldn't be required to finance items which are not official business but which are primarily political business.

But then the question arises, you say, "Well, how do you pay for these and how can you do it legally?"

And there are several ways that it can be done, incidentally, and that it is done legally in the United States Senate and in the Congress.

The first way is to be a rich man. I don't happen to be a rich man so I couldn't use that.

Another way that is used is to put your wife on the payroll. Let me say, incidentally, my opponent, my opposite number for the Vice Presidency on the Democratic ticket, does have his wife on the payroll. And has had her on his payroll for the ten years—the past ten years.

Now just let me say this. That's his business and I'm not critical of him for doing that. You will have to pass judgment on that particular point. But I have never done that for this reason. I have found that there are so many deserving stenographers and secretaries in Washington that needed the work that I just didn't feel it was right to put my wife on the payroll.

My wife's sitting over here. She's a wonderful stenographer. She used to teach stenography and she used to teach shorthand in high school. That was when I met her. And I can tell you folks that she's worked many hours at night and many hours on Saturdays and Sundays in my office and she's done a fine job. And I'm proud to say tonight that in the six years I've been in the House and the Senate of the United States, Pat Nixon has never been on the Government payroll.

There are other ways that these finances can be taken care of. Some who are lawyers, and I happen to be a lawyer, continue to practice law. But I haven't been able to do that. I'm so far away from California that I've been so busy with my Senatorial work that I have not engaged in any legal practice.

And also as far as law practice is concerned, it seemed to me that the relationship between an attorney and the client was so personal that you couldn't possibly represent a man as an attorney and then have an unbiased view when he presented his case to you in the event that he had one before the Government.

And so I felt that the best way to handle these necessary political expenses of getting my message to the American people and the speeches I made, the speeches that I had printed, for the most part, concerned this one message— of exposing this Administration, the communism in it, the corruption in it— the only way that I could do that was to accept the aid which people in my home state of California who contributed to my campaign and who continued to make these contributions after I was elected were glad to make.

No Special Favors

And let me say I am proud of the fact that not one of them has ever asked me for a special favor. I'm proud of the fact that not one of them has ever asked me to vote on a bill other than as my own conscience would dictate. And I am proud of the fact that the taxpayers by subterfuge or otherwise have never paid one dime for expenses which I thought were political and shouldn't be charged to the taxpayers.

Let me say, incidentally, that some of you may say, "Well, that's all right, Senator; that's your explanation, but have you got any proof?"

And I'd like to tell you this evening that just about an hour ago we received an independent audit of this entire fund.

I suggested to Gov. Sherman Adams, who is the chief of staff of the Dwight Eisenhower campaign, that an independent audit and legal report be obtained. And I have that audit here in my hand.

It's an audit made by the Price, Waterhouse & Co. firm, and the legal opinion by Gibson, Dunn & Crutcher, lawyers in Los Angeles, the biggest law firm and incidentally one of the best ones in Los Angeles.

I'm proud to be able to report to you tonight that this audit and this legal opinion is being forwarded to General Eisenhower. And I'd like to read to you the opinion that was prepared by Gibson, Dunn & Crutcher and based on all the pertinent laws and statutes, together with the audit report prepared by the certified public accountants.

"It is our conclusion that Senator Nixon did not obtain any financial gain from the collection and disbursement of the fund by Dana Smith; that Senator Nixon did not violate any Federal or state law by reason of the operation of the fund, and that neither the portion of the fund paid by Dana Smith directly to third persons nor the portion paid to Senator Nixon to reimburse him for designated office expenses constituted income to the Senator which was either reportable or taxable as income under applicable tax laws. (signed) Gibson, Dunn & Crutcher by Alma H. Conway."

Now that, my friends, is not Nixon speaking, but that's an independent audit which was requested because I want the American people to know all the facts and I'm not afraid of having independent people go in and check the facts, and that is exactly what they did.

But then I realize that there are still some who may say, and rightly so, and let me say that I recognize that some will continue to smear regardless of what the truth may be, but that there has been understandably some honest misunderstanding on this matter, and there's some that will say:

"Well, maybe you were able, Senator, to fake this thing. How can we believe what you say? After all, is there a possibility that maybe you got some sums in cash? Is there a possibility that you may have feathered your own nest?"

Financial History

And so now what I am going to do—and incidentally this is unprecedented in the history of American politics—I am going at this time to give to this television and radio audience a complete financial history; everything I've earned; everything I've spent; everything I owe. And I want you to know the facts. I'll have to start early.

I was born in 1913. Our family was one of modest circumstances and most of my early life was spent in a store out in East Whittier. It was a grocery store—one of those family enterprises. The only reason we were able to make it go was because my mother and dad had five boys and we all worked in the store.

I worked my way through college and to a great extent through law school. And then, in 1940, probably the best thing that ever happened to me happened. I married Pat—sitting over here. We had a rather difficult time after we were married, like so many of the young couples who may be listening to us. I practiced law; she continued to teach School. I went into the service.

Let me say that my service record was not a particularly unusual one. I went to the South Pacific. I guess I'm entitled to a couple of battle stars. I got a couple of letters of commendation but I was just there when the bombs were falling and then I returned. I returned to the United States and in 1946 I ran for the Congress.

When we came out of the war, Pat and I—Pat during the war had worked as a stenographer and in a bank and as an economist for a Government agency—and when we came out the total of our savings from both my law practice, her teaching and all the time that I was in the war—the total for that entire period was just a little less than $10,000. Every cent of that, incidentally, was in Government bonds.

Well, that's where we start when I go into politics. Now what have I earned since I went into politics? Well, here it is—I jotted it down, let me read the notes. First of all I've had my salary as a Congressman and as a Senator. Second, I have received a total in this past six years of $1,600 from estates which were in my law firm at the time that I severed my connection with it.

And, incidentally, as I said before, I have not engaged in any legal practice and have not accepted any fees from business that came into the firm after I went into politics. I have made an average of approximately $1,500 a year from nonpolitical speaking engagements and lectures. And then, fortunately, we've inherited a little money. Pat sold her interest in her father's estate for $3,000 and I inherited $1,500 from my grandfather.

We live rather modestly. For four years we lived in an apartment in Park Fairfax, in Alexandria, Va. The rent was $80 a month. And we saved for the time that we could buy a house.

Now, that was what we took in. What did we do with this money? What do we have today to show for it? This will surprise you, because it is so little, I suppose, as standards generally go, of people in public life. First of all, we've got a house in Washington which cost $41,000 and on which we owe $20,000.

We have a house in Whittier, Calif., which cost $13,000 and on which we owe $10,000. My folks are living there at the present time.

I have just $4,000 in life insurance, plus my G. I. policy which I've never been able to convert and which will run out in two years. I have no life insurance whatever on Pat. I have no life insurance on our two youngsters, Patricia and Julie. I own a 1950 Oldsmobile car. We have our furniture. We have no stocks and bonds of any type. We have no interest of any kind, direct or indirect, in any business.

What Do We Owe?

Now, that's what we have. What do we owe? Well, in addition to the mortgage, the $20,000 mortgage on the house in Washington, the $10,000 one on the house in Whittier, I owe $4,500 to the Riggs Bank in Washington, D.C. with interest 4½ per cent.

I owe $3,500 to my parents and the interest on that loan which I pay regularly, because it's the part of the savings they made through the years they were working so hard, I pay regularly 4 per cent interest. And then I have a $500 loan which I have on my life insurance.

Well, that's about it. That's what we have and that's what we owe. It isn't very much but Pat and I have the satisfaction that every dime that we've got is honestly ours. I should say this—that Pat doesn't have a mink coat. But she does have a respectable Republican cloth coat. And I always tell her that she'd look good in anything.

One other thing I probably should tell you because if I don't they'll probably be saying this about me too, we did get something—a gift—after the election.

A man down in Texas heard Pat on the radio mention the fact that our two youngsters would like to have a dog. And, believe it or not, the day before we left on this campaign trip we got a message from Union Station in Baltimore saying they had a package for us. We went down to get it. You know what it was.

It was a little cocker spaniel dog in a crate that he sent all the way from Texas. Black and white spotted. And our little girl—Trisha, the 6-year-old—named it Checkers. And you know, the kids love the dog and I just want say this right now, that regardless of what they say about it, we're gonna keep it.

It isn't easy to come before a nation-wide audience and air your life as I've done. But I want to say some things before I conclude that I think most of you will agree on. Mr. Mitchell, the chairman of the Democratic National Committee, made the statement that if a man couldn't afford to be in the United States Senate he shouldn't run for the Senate.

And I just want to make my position clear. I don't agree with Mr. Mitchell when he says that only a rich man should serve his Government in the United States Senate or in the Congress.

I don't believe that represents the thinking of the Democratic party, and I know that it doesn't represent the thinking of the Republican Party.

I believe that it's fine that a man like Governor Stevenson who inherited a fortune from his father can run for President. But I also feel that it's essential in this country of ours that a man of modest means can also run for President. Because, you know, remember Abraham Lincoln, you remember what he said: 'God must have loved the common people—he made so many of them.'

Courses of Conduct

And now I'm going to suggest some courses of conduct.

First of all, you have read in the papers about other funds now. Mr. Stevenson, apparently, had a couple. One of them in which a group of business people paid and helped to supplement the salaries of state employees. Here is where the money went directly into their pockets.

And I think that what Mr. Stevenson should do should be to come before the American people as I have, give the names of the people that have contributed to that fund; give the names of the people who put this money into their pockets at the same time that they were receiving money from their state government, and see what favors, if any, they gave out for that.

I don't condemn Mr. Stevenson for what he did. But until the facts are in there there is a doubt that will be raised.

And as far as Mr. Sparkman is concerned, I would suggest the same thing. He's had his wife on the payroll. I don't condemn him for that. But I think that he should come before the American people and indicate what outside sources of income he has had.

I would suggest that under the circumstances both Mr. Sparkman and Mr. Stevenson should come before the American people as I have and make a complete financial statement as to their financial history. And if they don't it will be an admission that they have something to hide. And I think that you will agree with me.

Because, folks, remember, a man that's to be President of the United States, a man that's to be Vice President of the United States must have the confidence of all the people. And that's why I'm doing what I'm doing, and that's why I suggest that Mr. Stevenson and Mr. Sparkman since they are under attack should do what I am doing.

Now, let me say this: I know that this is not the last of the smears. In spite of my explanation tonight other smears will be made; others have been made in the past. And the purpose of the smears, I know, is this—to silence me, to make me let up.

Well, they just don't know who they're dealing with. I'm going to tell you this: I remember in the dark days of the Hiss case some of the same columnists, some of the same radio commentators who are attacking me now and misrepresenting my position were violently opposing me at the time I was after Alger Hiss.

To Continue Fight

But I continued the fight because I knew I was right. And I can say to this great television and radio audience that I have no apologies to the American people for my part in putting Alger Hiss where he is today.

And as far as this is concerned, I intend to continue the fight.

Why do I feel so deeply? Why do I feel that in spite of the smears, the misunderstandings, the necessities for a man to come up here and bare his soul as I have? Why is it necessary for me to continue this fight?

And I want to tell you why. Because, you see, I love my country. And I think my country is in danger. And I think that the only man that can save America at this time is the man that's running for President on my ticket— Dwight Eisenhower.

You say, "Why do I think it's in danger?" and I say look at the record. Seven years of the Truman-Acheson Administration and what's happened? Six hundred million people lost to the Communists, and a war in Korea in which we have lost 117,000 American casualties.

And I say to all of you that a policy that results in a loss of 600,000,000 to the Communists and a war which costs us 117,000 American casualties isn't good enough for America.

And I say that those in the State Department that made the mistakes which caused that war and which resulted in those losses should be kicked out of the State Department just as fast as we can get 'em out of there.

And let me say that I know Mr. Stevenson won't do that. Because he defends the Truman policy and I know that Dwight Eisenhower will do that, and that he will give America the leadership that it needs.

Take the problem of corruption. You've read about the mess in Washington. Mr. Stevenson can't clean it up because he was picked by the man, Truman, under whose Administration the mess was made. You wouldn't trust a man who made the mess to clean it up—that's Truman. And by the same token you can't trust the man who was picked by the man that made the mess to clean it up—and that's Stevenson.

And so I say, Eisenhower, who owes nothing to Truman, nothing to the big city bosses, he is the man that can clean up the mess in Washington.

Take Communism. I say that as far as that subject is concerned, the danger is great to America. In the Hiss case they got the secrets which enabled them to break the American secret State Department code. They got secrets in the atomic bomb case which enabled 'em to get the secret of the atomic bomb, five years before they would have gotten it by their own devices.

And I say that any man who called the Alger Hiss case a "red herring" isn't fit to be President of the United States. I say that a man who like Mr. Stevenson has pooh-poohed and ridiculed the Communist threat in the United States—he said that they are phantoms among ourselves; he's accused us that have attempted to expose the Communists of looking for Communists in the Bureau of Fisheries and Wildlife—I say that a man who says that isn't qualified to be President of the United States.

And I say that the only man who can lead us in this fight to rid the government of both those who are Communists and those who have corrupted this Government is Eisenhower, because Eisenhower, you can be sure, recognizes the problem and he knows how to deal with it.

Now let me say that, finally, this evening I want to read to you just briefly excerpts from a letter which I received, a letter which, after all this is over, no one can take away from me. It reads as follows:

"Dear Senator Nixon,

"Since I'm only 19 years of age, I can't vote in this Presidential election but believe me if I could you and General Eisenhower would certainly get my vote. My husband is in the Fleet Marines in Korea. He's a corpsman on the front lines and we have a two-month-old son he's never seen. And I feel confident that with great Americans like you and General Eisenhower in the White House, lonely Americans like myself will be united with their loved ones now in Korea. "I only pray to God that you won't be too late. Enclosed is a small check to help you in your campaign. Living on $85 a month it is all I can afford at present. But let me know what else I can do."

Folks, it's a check for $10, and it's one that I will never cash.

And just let me say this. We hear a lot about prosperity these days but I say, why can't we have prosperity built on peace rather than prosperity built on war? Why can't we have prosperity and an honest government in Washington, D. C., at the same time. Believe me, we can. And Eisenhower is the man that can lead this crusade to bring us that kind of prosperity.

And, now, finally, I know that you wonder whether or not I am going to stay on the Republican ticket or resign.

Let me say this: I don't believe that I ought to quit because I'm not a quitter. And, incidentally, Pat's not a quitter. After all, her name was

Patricia Ryan and she was born on St. Patrick's Day, and you know the Irish never quit.

But the decision, my friends, is not mine. I would do nothing that would harm the possibilities of Dwight Eisenhower to become President of the United States. And for that reason I am submitting to the Republican National Committee tonight through this television broadcast the decision which it is theirs to make.

Let them decide whether my position on the ticket will help or hurt. And I am going to ask you to help them decide. Wire and write the Republican National Committee whether you think I should stay on or whether I should get off. And whatever their decision is, I will abide by it.

But just let me say this last word. Regardless of what happens I'm going to continue this fight. I'm going to campaign up and down America until we drive the crooks and the Communists and those that defend them out of Washington. And remember, folks, Eisenhower is a great man. Believe me. He's a great man. And a vote for Eisenhower is a vote for what's good for America.

Chapter *11*
Forms and Functions of the Persuasive Speech

In a speech before an advertising group in the midst of the 1981–82 recession, then Secretary of the Treasury Donald T. Regan began:

> I am delighted to be here today with so many who know the power of advertising, a market science dedicated to the proposition that businesses that insist on hiding their light under baskets have a whole chapter devoted to them—Chapter Eleven.
>
> In my own business career I've had the pleasure of meeting a great many dedicated advertising professionals. I've got to admit that at times their single-minded devotion to their calling could be a bit frightening, as witness the tale of two account executives who met over lunch. One mentioned that a colleague had passed away.
>
> "Good Lord," his friend said: "That's terrible. What did he have?"
>
> "Oh nothing much," said the other. "Just a small toothpaste account and a beer client. Nothing worth going after."
>
> I know the recession has meant difficult times for corporate leaders everywhere—and borrowing has been very difficult with high interest rates. But I still wish that more businessmen had adopted that principal lesson of advertising—putting the best foot forward, or at least moving it—with regard to the 1981 tax bill.
>
> It's like the story of a fellow whose business had fallen on hard times. He was a devout person, and had given generously to his church for many years. He figured that perhaps there were accounts receivable he hadn't pursued. So he went to church and asked God to let him win the lottery. He waited, expectantly, but nothing happened. So he returned to church, somewhat upset. Once again he

pled his case. And once again, nothing. The next time, angry, he shouted at the Almighty: "Why don't you give me a break?"

Suddenly, a great wind swept through the church, and a deep powerful voice said, "Give *you* a break? Why don't you give *me* a break? At least buy a ticket!"

The 1981 tax bill contains unprecedented incentives to invest and rebuild. Yet I note that industrial production fell another 0.5 percent in August. And a recent Commerce Department survey shows that businesses now plan to spend 4.4 percent less this year, after inflation, on new plant and equipment than last year. I learn every time I go up on Capitol Hill that I'm definitely not the Almighty, but let me say to you anyway: "Buy a ticket!"

Secretary Regan's opening remarks illustrate many of the speech forms and functions to be discussed in this chapter, and they also exhibit evidence of rhetorical polish. The first paragraph combines getting attention with building rapport by means of such standard devices as reference to the occasion, a compliment to the audience, and humor. Humor is accomplished by means of a *double entendre*, a sophisticated play on the use made by advertising firms of Chapter Eleven of the federal bankruptcy code to avoid paying taxes. This ironic allusion serves as well to bind speaker and audience together as "with it" people, able to understand and enjoy the joke's subtlety.

As befits the occasion, a dinner, and the role expectations associated with the genre of the after-dinner speech, Regan follows the first paragraph with two humerous anecdotes that simultaneously lead into his subject and also express identification with his audience. Never mind that the audience has probably heard these or similar stories many times before. Their telling has a ritual quality; they affirm at a relational level a sense of shared values—of being members of the same club. Moreover, their conversational style sets an informal tone for the speech that should make more digestible to this already satiated audience the many statistics Regan will be serving up in the body of the speech.

Between anecdotes, Regan manages to commiserate with his audience, while at the same time expressing in the most general terms his central thesis, that business should be investing more—"putting the best foot forward, or at least moving it—with regard to the 1981 tax bill." The punch line to the anecdote that follows provides Regan with a memorable way of restating his central thesis. It is a metaphor, a figure of speech, used to make the idea come alive: "Buy a ticket!"

The Regan speech is not a brilliant oration, but it is a polished one—far more polished, as you will see, than the 1980 Carter acceptance speech, examined in some detail in Chapter 14. The difference between a polished speech and an ordinary effort is in its evidences of careful attention to stylistic details. The typical speech fulfills its requisite functions formulaically; the polished one employs what might be called "good form." Regan's opening evidences good form by its choice of humor, by its economy of language, and by the way it combines the introductory functions of attention-getting, rapport-building, and orienting of the audience.

Functions of the Introduction

Getting Attention

It is a truism that audiences selectively expose themselves to messages and selectively attend to those they see or hear. Countering these tendencies often requires careful planning and great ingenuity. The job of getting attention may begin months before a speaking event through whatever steps are taken to publicize it. For an important revival meeting, such as those that used to be staged by Dwight Moody before the turn of the century (Huber, 1955), preparations would begin with the announcement that the renowned minister would be coming to town.

Excitement might be generated by construction of a huge tabernacle in the city to be visited and by the news that special trains had been arranged to travel to the site across specially laid tracks. Local ministers would be asked to build expectations for the revival meetings in regular Sunday services. Tickets printed in different colors (to increase feelings of status—the colors had no significance in themselves) would be distributed. At the start of the meeting, Moody would remain in the background until prayers were said and hymns were sung by local ministers and choirs. Only then would he appear to deliver his sermon. As he well knew, his first moments on stage were important not only for the words he uttered, but also for the impression nonverbal cues would be making: his appearance, his voice, his gestures, the attention given him by the dignitaries on stage, and so on. Efforts to maintain attention were continued throughout the speech and even afterward, as additional hymns were sung and meetings arranged for those who "saw the light."

Even with a "captive" audience, and even when the social context is conducive to careful listening, the speaker must often fight his or her way past apathy and competing stimuli. Consider the job of a visiting speaker at a campus convocation. At first the listener makes a *physical* adjustment. Books are placed under the seat. A sweater is pulled off. The student leans on one buttock, then decides to try the other. Next comes the *social* adjustment, and this may go on for several minutes. "Hi Freddy, Hi Louise. Guess who I saw at the cafeteria this morning. . . ." In the midst of all this is the guest lecturer, all but forgotten on the stage.

A list of "openers" for a formal speech should probably include the humorous anecdote, the brief quotation, the pithy reference to the audience or the occasion, and the factual illustration. Because so many stimuli compete for attention at the beginning of a speech, some persuaders also use startling statements or other shock techniques. A favorite story concerns Robert G. Ingersoll, the notorious nineteenth-century lecturer who, as a confirmed agnostic, had a penchant for engaging crowds of Fundamentalists smack dab in the middle of the Bible Belt. Ingersoll was not much for common ground techniques. After an open-air crowd had been assembled, he would turn to his audience and say, "If there is a God, let him strike me dead in 40 seconds."

Remember that every message about substantive matters is also an image of projection. What images do these speakers project? *(Top left, Richard Wood/The Picture Cube; top right, Elizabeth Crews; bottom, Art Braitman)*

And he would pull out a large stopwatch, gaze up at the sky, and begin a verbal countdown. Wary of the inevitable thunderbolt, the crowd would back away and Ingersoll, with a triumphant smile, would yell: "What's the matter? Don't you trust God's aim?"

In fairness to the faithful, let it be said that the religious leaders of Ingersoll's day were no slouches at the same shock techniques. A contemporary of Ingersoll's, Henry Ward Beecher, visited many of the same towns as the infidel. Among his favorite topics for a sermon was blasphemy. It was therefore quite a shock to one of his church audiences when he bellowed out: "Goddamnit, it's hot!" After sufficient disbelief was registered, Beecher leaned forward and said, "Yes, ladies and gentlemen, that's the phrase I heard from the mouths of many of you as I ambled through your town this afternoon."

Building Rapport

We have seen how Donald Regan used humor to build rapport with an essentially sympathetic audience. A far more difficult rapport-building task was faced by Palmer Hoyt, former editor and publisher of the Denver *Post*, in a speech to the Arkansas Press Association. Here humor was used to defuse hostility.

During the autumn of 1957, Little Rock, Arkansas, became the symbol of the South's resistance to court-ordered desegregation of public schools. In compliance with the Supreme Court's landmark decision three years earlier, the School Board of Little Rock set in motion a plan for gradual integration. This was resisted, however, by the townspeople, most of the state's newspapers and politicians, and especially the governor, Orval Faubus, who called in the National Guard in the name of states' rights. In response, President Eisenhower brought in federal troops to enforce the desegregation ruling.

Given the climate of events, it should not be surprising that advocacy of school integration was a not-too-popular position in Little Rock on January 10, 1958, the day Hoyt addressed the press of Arkansas. Complicating matters was the fact that the "head lion," Orval Faubus, was sitting conspicuously in the audience.

The speech to a hostile audience poses the greatest challenge to persuaders, requiring, particularly in the introduction, that they build goodwill and common ground in preparation for the inevitable clash over issues. Reproduced here is the introduction to Hoyt's speech. Consistent with the principles of co-active persuasion introduced in Chapter 7, Hoyt emphasizes membership group similarities, refers to sources his audience can accept, wisely refrains from an explicit statement of his position, employs the yes-yes method of establishing major premises, and orients the audience to view the conflict from a broad pragmatic perspective. See if you can identify the techniques he employs.

Hoyt's Speech

Mr. President, Governor Faubus, members of the Arkansas Press Association, ladies and gentlemen, I am glad to be here tonight to talk to such a distinguished group of fellow newspapermen. And I am happy to have, at long last, the opportunity to meet one of America's most controversial figures—your own governor, the Honorable Orval Faubus.

My father was a Baptist preacher, and I was brought up on the Bible.

One of my favorite Bible stories was that of a gentleman, name of Daniel, who with a little urging, sauntered into a lion's den one day.

As a child, I used to wonder how old Daniel felt when the gate clanged shut and he found himself alone with those lions. Now I know. Because here I am. I'll have to agree that you are a nice-looking bunch of lions. Furthermore, I doubt if Daniel had the pleasure of being introduced by the head lion. But even so, it occurs to me that, lest I be devoured, I had best make my position clear.

You know, first, that I am a newspaperman. As such, over a period of almost four decades, I have worked for better human relations but I have learned that good human relations cannot be legislated. They are the product of time, education, and effort.

Some of you may look upon me as a "damnyankee." May I say, parenthetically, that I was 25 years old before I knew "damnyankee" was only one word.

A few of you, and I hope it is only a few, may regard me as a carpetbagger.

I would be less than realistic if I didn't concede that newspapermen, damnyankees and carpetbaggers, all three, seem at the moment to be fairly unpopular in this great commonwealth.

Before embarking on my main thesis tonight, may I say—this I do believe: No man can reflect upon the incident known as "Little Rock" without feelings of compassion for the people intimately and personally involved. A community within a Nation that is troubled by internal dissension, harassed by external critics and humiliated by internal civil disorder is no less a sorry spectacle than a nation itself in the grip of civil war.

Let the millions of Americans outside of Arkansas ask themselves if they, under similar provocation from within or without, could comport themselves with greater poise or restraint.

I shall not presume to levy judgment upon your gracious governor, Orval Faubus. What transpired here, after your school board set in motion a gradual program of integrating your public schools, has been exhaustively discussed by Arkansas' own press.

The facts have been widely and painfully appraised.

And, it seems to me that Little Rock's Arkansas Gazette, under the guidance of my friends, J. N. Heiskell and Harry Ashmore, reported accurately on the news of conditions within this city when the Arkansas National Guard was called into action. It is my personal view that the Gazette's editorial position has reflected great journalistic statesmanship. I have noted that the same is true of some other Arkansas papers.

It is not for me, as a newspaperman, damnyankee, carpetbagger, or whatnot, to evaluate the motives of any party to this case. I am, as you will see, less interested in motivation than in effect.

I have accepted your president's invitation to speak to you as a fellow American, and as such to point out what seem to me to be certain inescapable facts and conclusions.

The first is, that you and I and all of us in the free world are in a mess. If we don't do something about it soon, there will be no laws to squabble about and no way of life to preserve.

The second point is that we have all—our leaders and ourselves—had a hand in making this mess. We have been complacent about our ability to defend ourselves; selfishly materialistic and appallingly unconcerned with the consequences of our behavior upon the rest of the world—particularly the effects on the minds of men.

Suddenly we are awakened by the beeping of satellites, the flash of rockets not our own, and the unpleasant sound of angry words of men who do not love us.

And this is the background against which we may be on stage and performing an American tragedy in three acts.

As I have said, all three acts concern all of us, but one of them concerns you especially.

What are the acts of this unfolding, this implied tragedy?

The first is the effect and the impact of such episodes as the Little Rock case on our own respect for law and on our leadership of the free world.

The second act involves the economic challenges raised against the American people by the evil, if dedicated, geniuses in the Soviet Union.

The third act, and perhaps the climax of our tragedy, is built around the fundamental question of survival. Survival against internal economic collapse; survival against the threat of thermonuclear war or international blackmail in the age of the rocket, the missile and the platform in outer space.

Orienting the Audience

"First I tell 'em what I'm gonna tell 'em. Then I tell 'em. Then I tell 'em what I told 'em."

Why follow the example of the minister quoted above? Why not simply "tell 'em"? Although persuaders may sometimes wish to mask illogic behind a veil of ambiguity, at least some understanding of a message is almost always a prerequisite to acceptance of a proposition. Orienting an audience by telling them what you are going to tell them is the starting point from which audience understanding may be achieved.

The orienting functions that you *might* perform include: (1) stating a thesis, (2) indicating what you will not be talking about, (3) defining key terms, (4) providing background information, (5) suggesting first premises, (6) offering analyses and explanations, and (7) previewing main points. Just which functions you *do* cover will depend on time and circumstances. In a 90-second television editorial, orienting the audience may consist of no more than declaring the existence of a problem, stating a thesis, and providing a brief explanation. Here is the introduction to an editorial by a former student:

> Teens are having sex. It is time we stop denying that fact. It should be obvious to all of us from the rising number of teenage pregnancies.
>
> Fortunately, many young women are responsible enough to take precautions for their actions. We should not condemn them for having sexual relations. Instead we should commend them for the adult way they have chosen to handle themselves by acquiring effective contraceptives.
>
> On February 22, Secretary Richard Schweiker proposed a regulation that states all family planning clinics would be required to notify the parents of teens who visit the clinics. The confidentiality teens now enjoy would be violated.

In a longer and more complex treatment of a subject, it is essential that you prepare the audience thoroughly for what is to come. Still, you will need to be strategic in deciding how to orient your audience. Here, for example, are some factors to consider in orienting an audience on the subject of no-fault auto insurance.

Indicating Subject and Position. Listeners should generally have a clear notion of *what* it is you will be discussing, and *why*. As indicated in Chapter 8, communicators run a risk if they leave their position implied or conceal it until the very end of the message. Not knowing what they are driving at— where their logic is heading—audiences may misperceive intent or lose interest in the message. Generally speaking, positions should be stated *in terms of the reaction desired from the audience.* As precisely as possible, you should indicate what you want your audience to believe, feel, desire, and do, even if the details of the proposal must await exposition in the body of the message. Rather than saying: "I think something should be done about auto insurance costs," one might say: "I'm here to ask your support for a no-fault insurance plan for our state that will cut your auto insurance costs by at least 20 percent."

Exclusions. The counterpart of revealing what will be talked about is indicating what will be excluded from your speech or essay. Statements of subject and position are often misleading until they are qualified. Continuing with the example just given, the speaker might now say: "Now, I'm not here to advocate just any no-fault plan—certainly not the kinds of plans that many have rightly called unconstitutional, those that deny citizens the right to sue a company for extra damages in case of severe injury or death. What I'll be asking you to support is the Denenberg plan put forth by former Insurance Commissioner Herbert Denenberg of the Commonwealth of Pennsylvania. . . ."

Definitions of Key Terms. What is no-fault insurance? On almost any controversial issue such as this one, there are bound to be key terms that need defining. The most familiar form of definition is the dictionary definition. It names something, puts it into a category, and then separates it from members of that category. No-fault insurance might be defined as "a system of auto insurance that provides immediate and automatic payment, regardless of fault, to all persons who suffer injuries or property damage in auto accidents."

In and of themselves, dictionary definitions tend to be too abstract. Often it is helpful to supplement them with other types, such as definitions by example and definitions by contrast. Persuaders should recognize, however, that in adding color to a definition, they may also be introducing bias. Definitions should ordinarily be unobjectionable. They should be regarded as ground rules that must be accepted by the players if the game of communication is to proceed. To supplement the dictionary definition, the communicator might proceed as follows:

> Let's suppose that you run into someone on a rain-slicked highway who failed to signal that he was turning. Who's at fault? Chances are that if anyone claimed injury, the case would go to court under the present system. Lawyers for the victor would get one-third to one-half the settlement fee; the victor would get the rest. "No-fault" insurance largely eliminates the role of the lawyer. Injury and property settlements are based on formulas and they are awarded directly to both parties. The idea is to reduce insurance premiums by reducing legal fees, at the same time providing increased protection to drivers.

Background Information. In a 10-minute speech, a persuader might well want to introduce historical or other background material before entering upon the body of the message. How many states have no-fault insurance at present? How did the idea originate? What other states are considering it? These are just some of the factual questions that might be discussed briefly in the introduction.

Acceptable First Premises. In addition to the other benefits to be derived from emphasizing source-receiver commonalities on underlying assumptions, values, or other first premises, these attempts at establishing common ground serve to orient receivers to the types of arguments that will be presented later. Like the vacuum cleaner salesperson in an earlier example, the advocate of no-fault insurance might set the audience up by suggesting general criteria against which any system of auto insurance should be evaluated. Later in the speech or essay, he or she might reintroduce these criteria and show that the system compares favorably with other alternatives.

Analysis and Explanations. Chances are that the body of a speech or essay on no-fault insurance will begin with an indictment of the present system: its manifest evils, and the reasons that it must be replaced rather than simply repaired. Such an indictment assumes that there is something wrong with the system in principle, that the alleged evils stem from the very nature of the system rather than from particular practices associated with it. But what is "the system"? What are its underlying principles? Often, the basic principles of the system are not at all obvious. An indictment of the present auto insurance system might well be preceded by analyses and explanations of its underlying principles—its inherent assumption, for example, that every accident is caused by a "guilty" party to the accident.

Let us consider another example. Suppose you favor a right-to-work law, a law on the books in several states that prohibits compulsory unionism. Suppose, further, that you believe many unions to be corrupt. What is inherently or intrinsically wrong with compulsory unionism? Is it the fact that unions are corrupt? Certainly not. Many unions that require membership as a condition for continued employment are not at all corrupt. Analysis of the system must proceed further lest a listener decide that corruption needs to be eliminated, but not compulsory unionism. Part and parcel of compulsory unionism, however, is the principle that even if a union is corrupt, workers must belong to it without choice. An explanation of this subtle but important distinction in the introduction of a speech or essay would go a long way toward making later indictments believable.

Preview. A well-organized speech or essay is likely to increase source credibility and be easier to understand (McGuire, 1969). Although the research evidence on the relationship between organizational structure and comprehension is surprisingly inconclusive (Thompson, 1967), until additional evidence is forthcoming it is undoubtedly safer to assume that a tightly structured message will be better understood than a poorly structured one. Minimally, a well-organized speech or essay subordinates minor ideas to major ideas, avoids overlapping, divides (and subdivides) material in terms of a single significant principle, and allows ideas to flow in a logical progression.

Whatever the structure of the body of a speech or essay, it is generally useful to preview it in the introduction. Thus, you might indicate that you will first discuss evils in the present system, then their causes, and then their solutions. Or you might preview only the first section of the body of the message, identifying the three or four inherent evils that will constitute your indictment of the present auto insurance system and the order in which they will be discussed. Previews provide attention sets; they key receivers to main ideas and their logical relationships.

Interest-Maintaining and Orienting Functions in the Body of the Speech

Making Ideas Come Alive

The language of the body of the speech should be alive, vivid, exciting, robust. Main ideas can be made memorable by use of slogans, mottoes, aphorisms, alliterative and rhythmic statements, and parallel phrasing. Supporting materials may be made more interesting by rounding out statistics, paraphrasing long or dull quotations, using analogies, contrasts, and metaphorical language, and by judicious use of humor. Interest in the speech can also be sustained by utilizing such natural attention-getters as conflict, suspense, curiosity, novelty, and contrast throughout the message.

Factual Illustrations. Persuaders can profit from examination of the interest-sustaining devices used by weekly news magazines such as *Time* and *Newsweek*. The difference between the same story in a newspaper and in a news weekly is often a difference between news made brief and news made interesting. The newspaper reader wants the essential facts first and the details later, if at all. Hence, the job of the reporter is to present the "four Ws and the H" of an event in the lead paragraph: the Who, What, When, Where, How and sometimes the Why. The readers of a news weekly ask for and get a writing style that captures attention from first page to last. In addition to the other devices we have named, the weeklies make heavy use of *factual illustrations*. A factual illustration contains the same "four Ws and an H" that are found in the first paragraph of a news story, but it adds concrete and vivid *imagery*. A one-paragraph statement about an assault on a kibbutz in Israel might become a story about two children and the horror they experienced, complete with names, family background, minute descriptions of their living quarters following the attack, a full paragraph of the sounds made by the mortars, and so on. Because it builds drama, conflict, concreteness, novelty, and other such factors into the story, the factual illustration is especially compelling as an interest-getter. And it can serve as a form of evidence and clarification as well.

Personalizing. Attention has already been directed to the value of a co-active, conversational style, one that communicates *with* the audience, rather than *at* them. Part and parcel of that style is the transformation of dry, abstract statistics into terms audiences can understand on a personal level. Here is an example from Regan's speech to the advertisers:

> Where government took 13 cents of every dollar earned in 1929, in 1950 that had more than doubled to 29 cents. And by 1960, it had increased to 34 cents. By 1970 it was 37 cents. And last year you and I shelled out 41 cents of every dollar to all levels of government.

A bit later in the speech Regan launches a comparison between the Reagan revolution and the Roosevelt revolution that serves as the focus of the body of his speech. The style, once again, is personal, conversational; the audience is invited to eavesdrop on his thinking process:

> A few weeks ago I came across a book with an interesting title. Written by a Cornell Professor, that book is called: *The Roosevelt Revolution.* And then last week the Urban Institute released a report on the Reagan Presidency which concluded that we are producing the greatest revolution in government since Franklin Roosevelt.
> I started to think about that conclusion, and what it represents.

N,E,S,C. It should be emphasized that orienting is not something that should stop once the introduction to the speech has ended. Audiences need *transitions* to remind them of where you have been and where you are going: For example, "Now that the time-saving features of no-fault have been discussed, let's talk about cost savings." They can almost always profit from clear statements of main points, and they may also need reviews of difficult sections of the speech—called *internal summaries*. Moreover, for any given main point, you might well find it necessary to provide additional definitions, explanations, or other clarifications. Drilled into my head by my old debate coach were the letters N,E,S,C:

*N*ame it.

*E*xplain it.

*S*upport it.

*C*onclude it.

Here is an example from the Regan speech:

> The third fundamental difference, and it is an important one, between the Roosevelt and the Reagan Revolutions involves two different suffixes to the root word: "flation."
>
> During the Roosevelt period the struggle was against a very painful affliction called deflation. Indeed, an early piece of New Deal legislation was actually entitled the Farm Relief and Inflation Act. It was designed to produce some inflation. There's really nothing mysterious about that. There are very few individuals or groups that enjoy deflation. To be sure, prices drop, but so do incomes and wages. Mortgage payments remain fixed, but real estate values fall. You can buy more, but somehow you feel poorer.
>
> Not so with the more dangerous affliction that confronted this Administration. Inflation is not immediately painful. In fact, the pain doesn't appear until an awful lot of inflation has been ingested. It's like a kind of tranquilizer. And so we must undertake the difficult task of ending the psychology of inflationary expectations.

And here is another:

> A fourth difference is constituencies.
>
> When Franklin Roosevelt took office there was no constituency for depression and deflation. For every financier who purportedly made a fortune by selling stock short and buying Scotch long, millions were losing life savings, taking huge cuts in pay (if they had a job at all), facing bankruptcy or foreclosure.
>
> But the bureaucracies built to deal with those problems often built their own constituencies as well.
>
> Some groups and individuals came to depend on this or that government program as a form of life support. Others grew to perceive each particular form of government assistance as a mandate from Jehovah.
>
> Thus, while Roosevelt could tell the nation that it had nothing to fear but fear itself, he obviously had never faced a lobbying blitz from several hundred trade associations.

Concluding the Persuasive Speech

The conclusion to the persuasive speech should be short and to the point. It may exhort the audience to action, it may specify how they should act, and it may visualize the future for them once they act; but whether or not it urges overt action, it should tie the ideas of the speech together for the audience, packaging them, if possible, with a memorable synoptic statement. Regan's closing statement restates his main ideas, but it isn't very memorable. It sounds like he was in a hurry to get off the platform:

> These are the elements of the Reagan Revolution. It will not come easy or fast. But it will come every day with new spending decisions, every year with new budgets, and hopefully every quarter with new corporate statements that show American business to have the animal spirit that leads to profit and prosperity.
> Thank you.

Much more effective is the closing statement in the student's editorial on the Schweiker proposal. The editorial observes the extremely important principle of providing repetition with variation. Its final exhortation is particularly memorable:

> We must realize that teens will continue to have sexual relations, whether their parents are aware or not. Secondary to that fact is that without the services family planning clinics can now provide for responsible young women, they will be forced to turn to less effective birth control methods, or no methods at all. More teen age girls will get pregnant. Getting pregnant seems like a rather high price to pay for a lack of family communication—that may not even be the teen's fault.
> Please write to Secretary Schweiker and oppose his regulation. Do not punish a responsible young woman for being responsible. The address is:

Secretary Richard Schweiker
300 Independence Avenue
Department of Health and Human Services
Washington, D.C. 20201

Figures of Speech

Metaphor

The title of Secretary Regan's speech is "The Reagan Revolution." The title of Palmer Hoyt's speech is "Civil Rights: The Eyes of the World Are upon Us." Not by accident, both speeches are entitled by metaphors. Like its close cousin, the *simile*, a *metaphor* is a comparison of sorts, a way of seeing one thing in terms of another. However, metaphors are nonliteral comparisons, and for that reason they tend to be more powerful expressions. In the metaphorist's hands, for example, Gertrude Stein's "love" would not be *"like* a red, red rose;" it would *become* a red, red rose.

Some metaphors serve only to add force or drama or life to a description (*screaming* headlines, *yellow* journalism), but others serve also to direct or redirect thought on a matter. In Chapter 9, we saw how generative metaphors such as paintbrush-as-pump could trigger productive new thinking on a matter. Other such metaphors may serve also to suggest the need for new courses of action.

Consider, for example, the many uses that have been made by former presidents of the "This means war" metaphor. President Lyndon Johnson declared a War on Poverty. Ford pledged on all-out War on Inflation. And Carter insisted that the energy problem presented us with "the moral equivalent of war." As Lakoff and Johnson (1980) observed, the "war" metaphor was not simply an emotionally loaded term: It structured thought and directed action. As regards Carter's use of the term, for example,

> The WAR metaphor generated a network of entailments. There was an "enemy," a "threat to national security," which required "setting targets," "reorganizing priorities," "establishing a new chain of command," "plotting new strategy," "gathering intelligence," "marshaling forces," "imposing sanctions," "calling for sacrifices," and on and on. The WAR metaphor highlighted certain realities and hid others. The metaphor was not merely a way of viewing reality; it constituted a license for policy change and political and economic action. The very acceptance of the metaphor provided grounds for certain inferences: there was an external, foreign, hostile enemy (pictured by cartoonists in Arab headdress); energy needed to be given top priorities; the populace would have to make sacrifices; if we didn't meet the threat, we would not survive. It is important to realize that this was not the only metaphor available. (pp 156–157)

The artful use of metaphor is an important mark of the polished speech, but finding just the right metaphor isn't always easy. Wayne Booth (1978) has provided this particularly stunning example of reframing by metaphor:

> A lawyer friend of mine was hired to defend a large Southern utility against a suit by a small one, and he thought he was doing fine. All of the law seemed to be on his side, and he felt that he had presented his case well. Then the lawyer for the small utility said, speaking to the jury, almost as if incidentally to his legal case:
>
> So now see what it is. They got us where they want us. They holding us up with one hand, their good sharp fishing knife in the other hand, and they sayin', "You sit still, little catfish, we're just going to gut ya'." (p. 179)

In this example, a contest between relative equals is transformed into a saga of David versus Goliath. Moreover, the speaker not only manages to link himself with his audience in opposition to the lawyer for the larger utility, he also redirects attention from the substantive issues toward the personalities involved. Note how every last detail of this seemingly casual remark, from its Southernisms and "down home" grammatical style to the choice of a catfish (as opposed, say, to a carp) serves to support the frame the lawyer is trying to create. Imagine, says Booth, that the speaker had tried to frame the picture of victimization using a different metaphor:

> The big utilities just expect us to stand around helplessly while they sap our vital forces.

or

> And so the big utility is trying to disembowel the company I represent, right before our very eyes.

Clearly, the catfish motif is superior.

Other Figures of Speech

Metaphor is an example of a *figure of speech*, a twist or turn of phrase that departs from ordinary or "normal" ways of saying something. We ordinarily associate figurative language with highly stylized messages—with oratorical eloquence—but, as in the foregoing example, effective figures of speech can also be folksy and conversational. *Irony* is another figure of speech (sometimes called a *trope*) that depends for its effect on a recognition by the listener that what was said was not literally intended. By the same token, the successful ironist can trade on the sense of intimacy created by the sharing of its intended meaning.

Of course, figures of speech are used a great deal in platform oratory; witness their use by politicians. One test of a good figure, suggests language expert William Safire (1984), is its freshness. When, at the 1984 Democratic Convention, Jesse Jackson said, "If there were occasions when my grape turned into a raisin and my joy bell lost its resonance . . . ," Safire thought that fresh; but when Jackson said, "In 1980 many . . . saw a light at the end of the tunnel in Reaganism," that was stale. Similarly, Safire liked Ronald Reagan's references in a Fourth of July oration to America as not just a word, but "a hope, a torch shedding light to all the hopeless of the world." However, he thought Reagan's description of America as "a rocket pushing upward to the stars" a bit trite. Better than all these metaphors, suggested Safire, was John F. Kennedy's evocation of a small boy challenging himself in "America has tossed its cap over the wall of space." This new-age metaphor captured the spirit of the space venture.

Commenting on a resurgence of eloquence in the speechmaking at the 1984 Democratic National Convention, Safire provided examples of a number of other figures of speech.

> *Allusion*—indirect reference without attribution, as in Senator Gary Hart's reference to a well-known phrase from *Macbeth:* "His rhetoric about jobs is but sound and fury signifying nothing."

Antithesis—the juxtaposition of sharply contrasting ideas in balanced or parallel words and phrases. Representative Geraldine Ferraro combined allusion with antithesis in paraphrasing a well-known antithesis of John F. Kennedy's: "The issue is not what America can do for women, but what women can do for America."

Alliteration—the recurrence in a line or phrase of words beginning with the same sound. Senator Edward Kennedy derided the "California Coolidge" whose advisers "practice polarization politics."

Apostrophe—addressing a person not present. Governor Mario Cuomo declared: "There is despair, Mr. President, in faces you never see, in the places you never visit in your shining city."

Anaphora—repetition of a word or phrase to begin several successive lines. Geraldine Ferraro repeatedly intoned, "It isn't right"; Gary Hart used "At issue in this campaign" several times.

These are among the most widely used figures of speech. To these could be added metonymy and caricature, among others that will be covered in Chapter 15. The "I-could-but-I-won't" technique, by the way, is another figure of speech, known as *apophasis*—saying something by artfully declining to say it.

SUMMARY

This chapter has identified requisite functions of the introduction, body, and conclusion to the persuasive speech, and it has also identified forms and figures appropriate to the fulfillment of these functions.

The essential functions of the introduction are getting attention, building rapport with the audience, and orienting them. Attention-getters include the humorous anecdote, the factual illustration, quotations, references to the audience or occasion, and startling statements. Humor may also be a rapport-building device, as may other of the co-active devices discussed in Chapter 7. Orienting the audience may include a thesis statement, exclusions, definitions, background information, first premises, analyses and explanations, and a preview.

These functions of the introduction are continued in the body of the speech, along with the provision of support for the position or proposal. Interest may be sustained through the use of figurative language, vivid illustrations, and personalized interpretations of facts and statistics.

The conclusion to the persuasive speech may urge action and specify how to act, but it should in any case tie things together for the audience and send them home with a verbal package they can remember and recite to themselves.

Mention of "verbal packages" leads directly to figures of speech, the last subject discussed in this chapter. Particular attention was directed to metaphor, the "trope of tropes." A metaphor, metaphorically speaking, is a lens, a filter, a screen, a frame; not only does it vivify ideas, it may also generate and structure them. Other figures of speech discussed in the chapter include irony, allusion, antithesis, alliteration, apostrophe, and anaphora. The use of devices such as these is one mark of polished speech presentations. However, polished addresses not only observe these forms, they also display "good form."

EXERCISE

Survey several speeches in one issue of the magazine *Vital Speeches of the Day*, paying particular attention to introductions. What devices do speakers use to fulfill the functions of attention-getting, rapport-building, and orienting the audience? Also, how many of the figures of speech discussed in this chapter can you identify in the speeches?

Chapter *12*
Leading Persuasive Campaigns

It has been repeatedly emphasized in this book that significant changes in audiences are unlikely to come about through a single speech, essay, or other "one-shot" communication; hence the reason for *persuasive campaigns*—organized, sustained attempts at influencing groups or masses of people through a series of messages. Some campaigns are mammoth undertakings, involving a large variety of spokespeople, media, channels, messages, and audiences. Such efforts are not without their special problems.

Campaigns may be categorized in various ways. Some campaigns seek to elicit specific behaviors: a vote for candidate X, the purchase of brand Y, a contribution to charity Z. Others are less concerned with specific behavioral payoffs than with influencing beliefs and values. They vary from public relations campaigns that aim at fostering more favorable images of a group or organization to indoctrination campaigns that seek to resocialize individuals so as to get them to endorse entire ideologies and life styles. Clearly in the latter category are missionary efforts at religious proselytizing, citizen education programs for new immigrants, and "thought reform" programs for political prisoners in totalitarian countries. Under the heading of efforts to "resocialize" individuals we might also include Alcoholics Anonymous, psychoanalysis, and other such "treatment" programs. Finally, there are *institutional change* campaigns of the kind practiced by local citizen's groups, special interest lobbies, and reform-oriented protest movements. The aim here may be to change personnel (e.g., hire more black police officers, fire the police chief), practices (e.g., stricter enforcement of housing codes), policies (e.g., university policies of "publish or perish"), institutional values and priorities (rewarding research by faculty over quality of teaching).

This chapter will focus on characteristics of campaigns that are not simply extensions of principles covered in earlier chapters. It will focus, in other words, on unique features of persuasive campaigns: both the greater potential for influence that comes from being able to approach audiences developmentally and the greater potential for problems that can arise from such efforts. Special attention will be directed to campaigns for institutional change.[1] As the title of this chapter implies, we will be concerned primarily with campaigns in which you may be likely to take a leadership role—relatively small-scale campaigns such as those limited to a local community or an institution such as a university. Chapter 16 is primarily concerned with analyzing campaigns and presents commentary on political campaigns, product advertising campaigns, and indoctrination campaigns.

Campaigns in Stages: A Developmental Model

Charles Larson (1983), has observed that campaigns

> . . . do not run on the same level or pitch throughout. They do not repeatedly pound away on the same pieces of information. They do not always have the same strategy at various times in their existence. Instead, they grow and change and adapt to audience responses and to the emergence of new issues. (p. 167)

What Larson is saying, of course, is that campaigns proceed developmentally, through stages, each stage building on the last, yet exhibiting a life of its own. The following outline of stages and their respective components is intended to be quite general, so as to encompass a wide variety of campaign types. As indicated in Figure 12.1, the stages in the model do not terminate as each next stage begins; planning, for example, is a continuous process throughout any campaign.

Planning

Although plans for a campaign must periodically be modified in light of new developments, certain steps must be taken at the outset.

Goal-Setting. To be considered here are intended primary effects (the basic purpose or purposes of the campaign), as well as secondary effects (for

---

[1] Although the term *institution* is sometimes used to refer to an established law, custom, or practice (constitutional law, the Miss America Pageant, Fourth of July orations), I use the term in its organizational sense to refer to a relatively enduring, publicly sanctioned collectivity, empowered by law or custom to perform societal functions. Examples include educational institutions, governments and government agencies, established political parties, business organizations, and mainstream religious denominations. When uninstitutionalized groups act in concert to change institutions from without, we may speak of the collectivity as a *social movement*. The discussion of institutional change campaigns in this chapter will include (but not be restricted to) moderate protest movements, those utilizing essentially co-active strategies of persuasion. It will largely exclude, however, the efforts of more militant collectivities. A discussion of their efforts at campaigning, if we can call them such, belongs more properly in the next chapter.

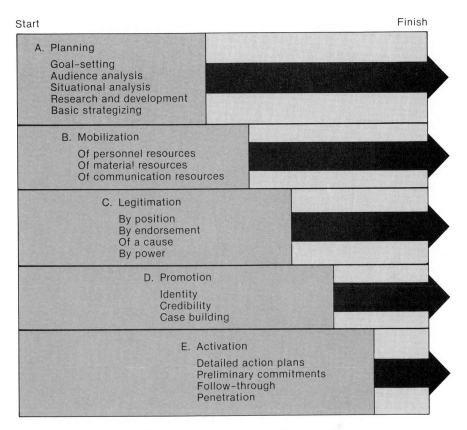

Figure 12.1 Campaign Stages and Components Model (CSCM).

example, effects on the image of the campaign organization); immediate goals as well as long-range goals; goals for the campaign as a whole, as well as subgoals for each stage. Generally speaking, it is well to formulate primary goals at several levels: (a) what you would ideally like to achieve; (b) what you expect to achieve; and (c) the bare minimum that would still make your campaign worthwhile. Often the large-scale campaign is of questionable value when measured against the amount of time, effort, and money expended. According to one study, for example (Etzioni, 1972), driver education campaigns have saved lives at the cost of $88,000 per life. Compare this with the introduction of mandatory seat belts and other safety accessories in new cars, estimated to cost only $87 per life saved!

Audience Analysis. Especially important in campaigns is analysis of the many audiences that are targeted for persuasion in terms of their varied reasons for support or opposition. The Department of Communication at a large university sought to have its course in public speaking made mandatory for all undergraduates. To the College of Business, it appealed in terms of practical benefits. To colleagues in education, it characterized public speaking as especially

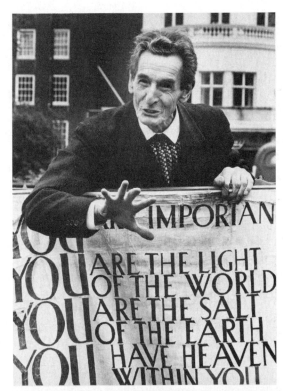

Some campaign perennials. Top left: *Union group campaigning for increased wages and benefits (Ken DeBlieu).* Bottom left: *Political campaign rally (Paul Conklin).* Top right: *preaching (EKM-Nepenthe).* Bottom right: *''Fire the coach'' (Bill Watkins, Philadelphia Magazine).*

relevant for teachers and their students. The department recognized, however, that these appeals would cut little ice in its own College of Liberal Arts, which prided itself on maintaining traditional academic values in the face of pressures for practicality and relevance. Accordingly, the chairman of the department circulated to his colleagues in liberal arts a long and scholarly memo on the humanistic rhetorical tradition that characterized public speaking training as a venerable practice which began with the preparation of citizen-orators in ancient Greece and Rome. They were dutifully impressed.

Situational Analysis. More so even than for a single speech, careful attention must be paid to prior situational factors, to the climate prevailing at the onset of the campaign, and to events as they are likely to unfold. On April 30, 1973, Richard Nixon launched a campaign to restore some measure of public confidence in himself and his beleaguered administration. Nixon knew not only that he would have to account for recent incriminating disclosures, but that the stage was set for a more thoroughgoing investigation by a special prosecutor and for the opening of hearings by the Senate Select Committee on Watergate on May 15. Some people wondered why Nixon did a turnabout in his speech by praising the news media. It may well be that he anticipated the need for a favorable—or at least not unfavorable—press in the months ahead.

Research and Development. What management experts refer to as the R&D function of business organizations has its counterpart in persuasive campaigns. It involves the gathering of arguments and evidence to be used in building persuasive messages, as well as the development of knowhow for implementation. The failure to take these necessary steps is common among amateur campaigners. One well-intentioned student attempted to launch a campaign to require bicycle safety education in the public schools. Intuitively, he decided that the best way to get action was to testify at a meeting of the Philadelphia School Board. Unfortunately, he had not yet come up with a plan for such a program or discovered how and where decisions of this kind are made in the school system or sought to determine whether there were any groups that might have been interested in aiding his campaign or even developed documented proof of the existence of a problem.

Basic Strategy. Although campaign strategies must frequently be revised in light of new developments, it is nevertheless possible at the outset to formulate global strategies. Should the politician run a high-visibility campaign or maintain a "low profile"? Should the candidate engage in image-building or run a "negative" campaign of attack on the opponent? Is it more advantageous to remain mute or ambiguous on highly controversial issues, or to attempt to enlarge one's constituency by seeking to convert the skeptical?

Basic strategies must, of course, be formulated with the other planning factors we have identified clearly in mind. Advertisers for Eastman Kodak ran a camera-purchasing campaign aimed at families with expectant mothers; they did so on the basis of evidence that these families were least likely to own cameras and most likely to purchase them. A Midas Muffler campaign zeroed in on the inadequacies of ordinary service stations; it did so on the basis of evidence that these stations were their stiffest competition and were vulnerable to attack. In the same way, groups seeking institutional change must formulate strategies with an eye toward maximizing their resource capabilities.

Mobilization

Mobilization consists in locating, acquiring, developing, and exploiting the resources necessary to run the campaign.

Personnel Resources. Persuasive campaigns require organization. The effectiveness of any campaign organization depends on adherence to its program, loyalty to its leadership (or active commitment to shared leadership), a collective capacity and willingness to work, energy mobilization, and member satisfaction. A hierarchy of authority and division of labor must be established in which campaign workers are persuaded to take orders, to perform menial or time-consuming tasks, and to forego social pleasures.

The problems of personnel mobilization are more acute for the leaders of voluntary organizations such as charities, political parties, and self-help groups, especially those seeking institutional change. Whereas commercial sales organizations, for example, may induce productivity through tangible rewards and punishments, volunteer organizations must rely on ideological and social commitments from their members. These commitments may endow the group with great energy for a period of time, but commitments of this kind are difficult to sustain.

There is no simple way to mobilize volunteers for sustained efforts. A spirited, energized membership is the strength of many voluntary campaigns, yet morale cannot be secured through abdications of leadership or of leadership tasks. Members may feel the need to participate in decision-making, to undertake pet projects on their own initiative, to put down leaders or other followers, to obstruct meetings by socializing, or to disobey directives. The leadership cannot ignore these needs—especially today, when members are likely to be well educated, independent, given to "doing their own thing." Still, they cannot accede to all of them either.

Material Resources. A clever group can work toward fulfilling several campaign requirements simultaneously. At Temple University, several students sought to organize a consumer action group in the Ralph Nader image. The leadership recognized that they would need money, lots of it, to build and maintain the organization and advance its goals. Conceivably, a foundation grant might have been forthcoming, but they sought another fundraising approach, one that would help legitimize the group and promote its values at the same time. A "mini-campaign" was launched for a campus referendum on whether money should be raised for the group by means of a voluntary dues checkoff on student tuition bills. The vote was favorable, and the group went next to the administration with a strongly worded request that it execute the checkoff—or be in the embarrassing situation of opposing an organization that had widespread student support. Not surprisingly, the administration proved anxious to please.

There are often hidden costs associated with acquiring material resources. Yet favoritism toward large donors is the rule, not the exception, in politics, and it extends to other voluntary organizations. The power of the purse often dictates or influences policies of colleges and universities, social welfare lobbies, and charity organizations. Campaign leaders must frequently ask themselves whether the courtship of "fat cat" contributors is worth the price of a loss of independence.

Communication Resources. One need for money in large-scale campaigns is to purchase or control communication resources. They include access to channels of influence and to the mass media, as well as basic information and knowhow needed to communicate effectively. Commercial organizations have long purchased market analyses, mailing lists, media expertise, and media time. According to one estimate, media advertising constitutes 50 to 90 percent of the budget for major political campaigns (Blumenthal, 1980). The modern political campaigner, of course, now purchases these same resources.

Legitimation

To say that someone has legitimacy is to say that others have conferred upon that person the right to exercise authoritative influence in a given area or to issue binding directives. These others, meanwhile, tacitly acknowledge a corresponding obligation to take him or her seriously or to follow his or her directives. Scientists have enormous legitimacy—to the point where, in psychological experiments on legitimacy, even the psychologists have been astounded.

Simply on the basis of such instructions as "The experiment requires that you continue," Milgram (1963) was able to persuade subjects to administer what they believed were dangerous electrical shocks to their peers. Pepitone (1955) encountered little resistance in getting subjects to sort out waste baskets filled with disgusting debris. Frank's (1944) subjects continued for a full hour in attempts at balancing a marble on a small steel ball. Orne (1962) has commented despairingly on his inability to find tasks so noxious that subjects would not perform them. Indeed, in one experiment (Orne and Evans, 1965), subjects picked up what they believed were poisonous snakes, while others agreed to place their hands in nitric acid and to throw it in the face of a lab assistant. Seldom, of course, do campaigners have that degree of legitimacy.

Legitimations are the grounds upon which legitimacy is established. A campaign or campaign organization may be legitimated in any of several ways.

Legitimacy by Position. A common type of legitimacy is that which inheres in a role or position within government, business, or some other established institution. Without knowing anything about the surgeon general of the United

States, we may heed the advice offered in an antismoking campaign sponsored by that individual because the position confers a certain authority.

Groups seeking institutional change are often well advised to secure positional legitimacy by attaching themselves, if they can, to some established institution—a church, a university, perhaps even the very institution they seek to change. Community organizers speak of the importance of being invited into the communities they seek to influence, and students seeking campus change often find it useful to get appointed to university committees or commissions.

Legitimacy by Endorsement. The next best alternative to the power of positional legitimacy is endorsement by those who have it. Bettinghaus (1981) speaks of "checking in with the power base," which for him includes not only those in official positions of power, but also informal opinion leaders:

> The role of the legitimizer is a peculiar one. He is seldom active in the early stages of a social-action campaign. He does not make speeches in favor of the proposal. He does not write letters to the newspaper, and he frequently will ask that his name not be associated with the new idea. He may not want to give a formal approval to a new proposal. But he can effectively block the adoption of a new idea by saying, "No!" If he simply agrees that a proposal is a desirable one he may well clear the way for future operations by the change agent and eventual adoption of the proposal. (p. 257)

Legitimacy of a Cause. Those seeking minor reforms in an institution or the adoption of innovations in a community may well be granted positional legitimacy or at least the blessings of key legitimizers. But those seeking more widespread changes are likely to threaten and be threatened by the institution or community's sanctions and taboos: its laws, its maxims, its customs governing manners, decorum, and taste, its insignia of authority, and so on.

Still, the change-minded group may utilize co-active persuasion to establish its legitimacy by representing its cause as one that any virtuous individual must endorse. Programs may be defended in the name of God or the Founding Fathers or the Constitution or Natural Law. Here the promotion and legitimation stages are merged.

Legitimacy by Power. The last resort for campaigners is to establish legitimacy by sheer power. A discussion of this alternative properly belongs in the next chapter. The point is that groups seeking change must often fight for the right to be heard or to negotiate in their own interests.

Promotion

Once a campaign group has taken effective steps to plan, mobilize resources, and secure legitimations, it is in a powerful position to promote its cause before a wider audience. Effective promotion, in turn, should open doors for the group that may have been closed before in terms of personnel, material, and communication resources, as well as endorsements by key influentials (Jamieson and Campbell, 1983).

In the ideal persuasive campaign, there is continuity from beginning to end of the promotion process. An advertising campaign may "go public" with messages somewhat mysteriously alluding to a new product that is soon to appear on supermarket shelves. Mystery may continue as a theme once its identity is revealed, the product somewhat humorously being described as having magical qualities, its label and packaging reinforcing that concept. Rather than the usual endorsements by attractive celebrities or "just plain folks," subsequent ads may feature testimonials by actors associated with suspense theater. Should the product become an established competitor in its field, later ads may tone down the mystery theme, playing now, perhaps, on its reputation for dependability.

This example illustrates, once again, the importance of having an overall campaign strategy at the promotion stage. Larson (1983, p. 175) speaks here of providing audiences with an "invitation to the drama." He argues that it is the dramatic which compels major interest in any campaign; that the materials of the drama should be enacted through deeds, rather than pedantically stated; and, above all, that the "plot" of the drama should provide unity to the campaign. The "plot" may be the familiar underdog saga of the honest politician fighting the "pols" against overwhelming odds. Or it may be Richard Nixon as the Good Sheriff in 1968, with plans for peace abroad and law and order at home. Or it may be the Camelot theme, as in the Kennedy campaign of 1960. In campaigns for institutional change and in self-help campaigns, the drama often has a negative focus and is embodied in religious metaphors: a crusade against evil or evil persons, or a quest for "purification" of the evil in ourselves.

Various steps have been proposed by different campaign theorists as substages within the promotion stage.

Identity. Political candidates are nowhere without name recognition. Commercial advertisements do better getting negative attention than no attention. Worthy charities must somehow stand out from others making a claim on the public's generosity. So it is that campaign managers work assiduously at formulating memorable slogans, devising labels and catchy jingles, and finding clever ways to build repetition of the same campaign themes.

Effective identification symbols are those which serve members of the campaign organization (giving them an identity), as well as the larger public. Some groups choose identification symbols mostly to promote ingroup solidarity. These may include special songs, handshakes, flags, ceremonies, hair styles, and speech patterns. Where once the Democrats and Republicans featured ingroup images at their party conventions (party emblems and flags, pictures of party heroes), now, with the conventions televised, the emphasis is on identification symbols that link the party with the people and that even make a pitch for members of the opposition.

Credibility. Moving beyond the creation of a favorable and memorable identity, the campaign leadership must establish its own believability as well as the credibility of the group as a whole. The first step for leaders is to promote respect, trust, and attraction from their own followers. Here, especially, deeds are important, not just words. Occasionally, followers will be taken in by a charismatic firebrand, but for the most part they will want concrete evidence that this individual has their interests at heart, is capable of delivering, and possesses such qualities as intelligence and expertise, honesty and dependability, maturity and good judgment.

Establishing personal or group credibility to the satisfaction of suspicious outsiders may be considerably more difficult. On this score, Zimbardo (1972) has offered a number of suggestions to college students on how they might canvass door to door in behalf of controversial or hostility-arousing positions. His pointers on establishing credibility (paraphrased below) bear close resemblance to those offered in earlier chapters. With some modification, they may be adapted to other campaigns.

1. Impress the target with your expertise, concern, and dedication, being forceful but not overbearing.
2. Make some points which are against your own best interest; indicate the sacrifices you have made and would be willing to make.
3. Have a respected person introduce you.
4. Begin by agreeing with what the audience wants to hear.
5. Minimize your manipulative intent until you ask for commitment.
6. Avoid group situations where the majority are known or expected to be against you.
7. Socially reinforce target persons by listening attentively to what they have to say, by maintaining eye contact and close but comfortable physical proximity, by individuating them (using proper names, for example) and helping them to individuate you (through appropriate personal anecdotes), by nodding or saying "good" or "that's interesting" on specific points, by smiling to reinforce more general classes of behavior, and in general by showing respect and appreciation for them.
8. Show genuine enthusiasm and concern for the issues.
9. To reduce the natural resentment accorded to college student types, differentiate yourself from audience stereotypes by a neat appearance, by showing respect, even awe, for how hard the target persons work, and by intimating, through offhand examples, that you are not privileged and spoiled.
10. Work in pairs that differ in some obvious characteristic such as temperament, age, or sex, but that provide the bases for similarities by one or both with the target persons.

Case-Building. Campaigners generally attempt to build a case within the framework of the need-plan approach discussed in Chapter 9. A need is established, and the candidate, product, charity, self-help program, or what have you is claimed to be capable of filling that need. In campaigns, of course, persuaders have the advantage of being able to pound home the same message repeatedly (using the principle of repetition with variation) or to stretch out a suspicion-arousing case over a series of stages—focusing on problems and principles in the beginning, for example, and pushing their own favorite solution in subsequent messages.

The main case-building principle we wish to emphasize here is embodied in the saying: "Different strokes for different folks." Particularly when campaigning for institutional change, separate attention must be given to three different groups: campaign participants, members of the general public, and organizational decision-makers.

Campaign participants. It is a truism of voluntary campaign organizations that they fail as often from fragmentation from within as from resistance from without. Within these organizations, factional conflicts invariably develop over questions of value, strategy, tactics, or implementation. Purists and pragmatists clash over the merits of compromise. Academics and activists debate the necessity of long-range planning. Others enter the campaign with personal grievances or vested interests. Preexisting groups that are known to have divergent ideological positions are nevertheless invited to join or affiliate with the campaign because of the power they can wield.

These and other differences may be reflected at the leadership level as well. Rarely can one campaign leader handle all the leadership roles and tasks of the campaign. Hence the need for a variety of leadership types: theoreticians and propagandists to launch the campaign, political or bureaucratic types to carry it forward. There may also be cleavages between those vested with positions of authority in the campaign, those charismatic figures who have personal followings, those who have special competencies, and those who have private sources of funds or influence outside the campaign.

The problems of building a case before the general public without offending one or another faction within the campaign organization were well illustrated by Key '73, a religious crusade that was supposed to have combined the evangelical thrust of some 140 denominations, 250,000 congregations, and 100 million Christians (*Time*, February 19, 1973). As might be expected, this amorphous group was compelled to deal in generalities and deliberate ambiguities, avoiding doctrinal issues or questions about the role of the church in respect to social injustices or political oppression. Quite obviously, this is an extreme case, since the campaign membership allegedly included half the nation's population, but it can be a considerable problem for other campaign organizations as well.

Community activist Saul Alinsky (1971) was a long-time proponent of what might be called *bottom-up* tactics of reform, as opposed to the *top-down* tactics typically practiced by business leaders, church officials, and other elites within the community. Crucial to the success of the bottom-up approach in the impoverished neighborhoods where Alinsky often did his organizing was sustaining a sense of solidarity among the members of the group.

Alinsky suggested several things that could be done to solidify community action organizations, not all of them applicable to other campaign types or less militant campaign styles. First was the familiar tactic of focusing on a common enemy. Second, he suggested that it is often expedient to lead your people in a "cinch fight," one that will demonstrate to them their success capabilities. If at all possible, he advised, the actions they take in advancing the group's cause should not drag on too long and should be enjoyable. Also important is the need to revitalize the membership by periodically introducing new issues and varying the tactics employed. Above all, he suggested, "Never go outside the experience of your people . . . [and] whenever possible, go outside the experience of the enemy" (p. 127).

My own "rule" for the leaders of voluntary campaigns is more general: Whatever case you construct for persuading outsiders, build with an eye toward solidifying campaign participants.

General public. The case taken before the public must vary, of course, with the type of campaign and the nature of the audience being addressed. We focus once again on campaigns for institutional change, but highlight less militant tactics than those proposed by Alinsky.

Bettinghaus (1981) has suggested a series of steps in building a case before the general public: establishing a need for the social systems involved, identifying and defining goals for relevant individuals and groups, securing agreement on methods to accomplish change, and constructing a formal plan of work to be accomplished.

With respect to need, Bettinghaus identifies several techniques that can be used. First, there is basic education. Through face-to-face contacts and exploitation of the available mass media, the change-oriented group can lay out its facts and its arguments. Second, the group may conduct questionnaire surveys. In addition to aiding the group's efforts at audience analysis, questionnaires may in themselves be persuasive documents, compelling reflection by people who might not otherwise have perceived the existence of a problem, and generating survey data which, if favorable to the group's cause, may be used to convert fence-sitters. Third, Bettinghaus advises demonstrations or trials—pilot projects that may evidence both need and feasibility. Fourth, the group may call attention to precedents for the proposed action within the community or institution, as well as envy-arousing precedents in other communities. The need for a new high school gymnasium may be argued, for example, on the grounds that several schools in nearby towns have added new gym facilities. Finally, the group may exploit crises that develop by building on the immediately felt need.

With respect to goals, methods, and work plans, Bettinghaus advocates an essentially participatory pattern of persuasion, one in which members of the general public share in the development of project proposals or at least are asked to play a policy confirmation role. Here the campaigner must be politically sensitive. The ideal solution may be unacceptable; the politically feasible solution may be one that provides a little something for everyone.

Key decision-makers. Locating those with real power or influence in organizations is not always easy. Groups seeking institutional change are often referred to minor functionaries with fancy titles who are assigned to hear out complainants and, if possible, to soothe their ruffled feelings. Unless change-oriented groups understand how influence flows and where the buck stops in a given institution, they are liable to be given the runaround. Often, moreover, key decision-makers are not identifiable by their titles. One such person at Temple University, for example, held the modest title of registrar. Another was secretary to a dean. Both exerted more influence than several university vice-presidents.

A general rule of institutional change—to be discussed more fully in the next chapter—is that key decision-makers are unlikely to take significant action on conflict-arousing issues unless direct or indirect pressure is applied. Proposals for innovations designed to improve the overall efficiency of the institution are likely to be greeted with open arms; proposals in support of group interests at the expense of other group interests are likely to be resisted unless accompanied by a show of strength. This is not to say that co-active appeals will have no effect. The campaign group may call attention to the endorsements it has received or to its other sources of legitimacy. Moreover, if the decision-makers are personally impressed with a proposal, they may act within the limits of their freedom and perhaps even stretch those limits.

Still, they are likely to be subject to cross-pressures that constrain them from taking major action. University presidents, for example, are not simply power holders; they are also power brokers who must balance the conflicting demands of students, faculty, alumni, parents, community leaders, and so on. Co-active persuasion used to incite the student body to action may constitute just the right sort of indirect pressure needed to influence the president. Secretly, a given president may welcome the pressure; without it, it might be virtually impossible to present a case to other key decision-makers, such as trustees or state legislators.

Activation

Building a compelling case is not enough. Unless the campaigner seeks only to communicate information or to modify attitudes, it is necessary to make special provisions for the action stage.

Detailed Action Plans. Campaigns often fail because the campaign target lacks specific information on how to act. Voters must be told where to vote and how to vote. People with problems must learn how to get help. In the case of campaigns for institutional change, there are bound to be misinterpretations unless plans for action are made concrete. Bettinghaus (1981) has enumerated the types of detail needed in a proposal for a community innovation such as a new recreation center:

> The formal plan of work will include decisions about financing, operational steps to be taken in implementation, the time sequence that has to be followed, and most important, the specific tasks which each individual associated with the implementation will have to perform. Making these decisions will result in an organizational structure charged with actually carrying out the operations. This structure will provide for appropriate lines of authority, a detailed task description for each individual, and the relation of the operational group to other community groups and institutions. (p. 268)

Preliminary Commitments. Professional campaigners have learned that it is wise to secure partial, preliminary commitments from people before the final action is taken. Short of obtaining cash donations, the charity solicitor may work toward obtaining campaign pledges. Short of securing even verbal agreements to purchase new cars, the automotive sales organization may provide all sorts of inducements to get people to the showrooms. If at all possible, the preliminary commitment should be of a public nature and should entail some effort on the part of the individual. The attitude of the individual should be strengthened by the act of overt commitment. Zimbardo (1972, p. 90) also suggests that the campaigner "provide several levels of possible behavioral alternatives for the person." The campaign pledge card, for example, may list several monetary alternatives: $1, $5, $10, $100. Says Zimbardo, "pushing the most extreme is likely to get a greater level of compliance even if the extreme is rejected."

Follow-Through. On Election Day, each major party mobilizes a large campaign organization for poll-watching, telephoning, chauffeuring, babysitting, and so on. Advertisers seek to make buying a habit among those who have made initial commitments. Revivalist campaigns work at translating instant "conversions" into weekly church attendance.

Campaign organizations seeking institutional change may be granted authority and resources to put programs into operation themselves (at least on a trial basis), or they may get promises of action from the institution itself. In the latter case, more than one externally initiated program has failed for lack of administrative follow-through. The campaign organizations have been at least partially to blame for not maintaining the pressure. A good rule of institutions is that institutional policies are what their administrators do about them. Often, it is precious little.

In the case of programs administered initially by the campaign organization itself, there is a similar danger that once the innovation has been effectively sold, campaign activists will become lazy or indifferent or begin caring more about their reputations than about the persons they claim to be serving. At some point, the new innovation must be institutionalized, and this is another juncture fraught with potential problems. Several years ago, a group of students at Temple University helped form a voluntary organization named Conscience that successfully ran a day camp for disadvantaged children. For three summers the organization endured, even thrived on, its poverty, its dearth of trained leaders, and its lack of formal ties to the university. Then, with the members' consent, the university began providing large amounts of money, facilities, and technical assistance. The support was now there, but the spirit was gone. The appropriate socioemotional adjustments for institutionalization had not been made.

Penetration. In the ideal campaign, those reached directly become persuaders themselves. Advertisers dance for joy when radio listeners begin humming aloud the jingle they have heard in the commercial. New converts to a religious group are often asked to proselytize in its behalf. And political campaigners often rely on opinion leaders to carry their television messages to others. In each case there is *penetration* beyond the initial receivers to their own interpersonal networks.

The effective conclusion to a campaign for institutional change occurs not simply when the change is put into practice, but when others begin hearing about it, speaking favorably about it, and even attempting to emulate it. Serving as a model for others is often a small campaign group's most important accomplishment.

Case Studies

A. Extending the Model of Stages and Components: Case Study of a Successful Antismoking Campaign

Several years ago I was persuaded to give up smoking as a result of a sophisticated campaign by SMOKENDERS, one that illustrates the model of campaign stages and components, as well as a number of behavioral principles of persuasion introduced in earlier chapters. Research and development and basic strategy by the SMOKENDERS organization were done well in advance of the treatment program. Its campaign planners were aware that smokers are a varied lot, some of them hooked for physical reasons, others in need of a psychological "fix," still others habituated but not addicted. Essential to the success of the campaign was knowledge of belief structures sustaining smoking, as well as beliefs and values that could be appealed to in helping smokers extinguish their habits. Potential appeals to stop smoking included guilt (setting a bad example for the children), shame (embarrassment at having an addiction), fear (of lung cancer), as well as positive inducements such as social support for trying to stop. However, not all these appeals are equally salient to all smokers. Thus, for example, in organizing support groups within the class, teachers found it useful to secure belief and value profiles of class members.

Because it relies for the most part on paid staff, SMOKENDERS does not experience the problems that typically arise in strictly voluntary organizations. Yet its teachers are all former smokers and program graduates, and hence have an unusual degree of commitment to what they are doing, which they communicate to their students.

Among SMOKENDERS' most important resources are the endorsements it receives from hospitals, private physicians, universities, major corporations, and entertainment stars, which it uses to legitimize its efforts. SMOKENDERS has no difficulty legitimizing its cause; that, after all, is a recognized social good. But there are all manner of programs in competition with SMOKEN-DERS, many of them promising faster, cheaper, less painful cures. Hence, legitimation remains an extremely important campaign stage.

At the time I joined up for a SMOKENDERS course, its identity was well known. I learned about it from a psychologist, but its more than 100,000 graduates are apparently a major source of word-of-mouth advertising. Still, the organization needed to promote its programs through the mass media, and to indicate when and where they were to be held.

The promotion stage builds on the principle of "different strokes for different folks" through its use of a variety of educational and behavior modification techniques. A two-hour class might balance informational and rational appeals with testimonials by class members and participation in small group discussions. For some class members, rational appeals were highly persuasive. For others, it was psychological support from the group or the teacher that counted most. For still others, it was information about how to quit that was of greatest significance.

SMOKENDERS traded on the principle that time, money, effort, and so on, freely given, are dissonant with thoughts of discontinuing the program. Attending a free trial class created some dissonance. Paying to stay in the class created more. Participating actively in the program, and especially going through the difficult withdrawal process, created still more. Students were told to expect feelings of resistance and hostility, including rejection of the teacher. The latter was minimized in part by the presentation of threatening information in a deniable form—on harmful effects of smoking as something *other* programs emphasize, *not* SMOKENDERS. Fear appeals were also paired with assurances that the harmful effects of smoking could be reversed with its cessation.

Particularly effective was the activation stage of the campaign, which began at Week Five with limited withdrawal and ended weeks after students had stopped smoking altogether. The process of withdrawal began with the toughest periods—after meals and during work breaks, for example—and were extended from there. Students could smoke freely during "legal" periods, but they had to keep detailed records of when and how often they smoked, which they were required to turn in to their instructor. The records themselves served as a form of feedback and self-reinforcement.

During the activation stage, old habits were upset, new ones begun. Students switched brands, switched hands, switched eating and drinking habits, acquired routines of carrying a toothbrush and mouthwash with them at all times, brushing after each meal, engaging in daily exercises. Once they had stopped smoking entirely, they were helped to prevent backsliding. Desires to return to smoking as well as negative effects of cessation such as weight gain and irritability were anticipated and dealt with, in some cases by reframing a negative effect such as dizziness as a healthy sign of bodily adjustment. Each class member was required to keep a diary, and these were consulted during times of stress. One of my entries recalled the first day of the class when everyone was encouraged to smoke at will—which we did, to the point that all of us were made terribly uncomfortable. I thought about that day many times during the withdrawal period.

B. Combining Top-Down and Bottom-Up Strategies of Social Change: Case Study of a Planning Analysis

I have maintained throughout this book that practice and analysis go hand in hand. This is nowhere more true than in the planning stages of a campaign, which depends for its strategy formulation on careful analysis of goals and problems.

The following are excerpts from a report which I prepared for a committee of the National Research Council which was advising the federal government's Occupational Safety and Health Administration (OSHA) on informational campaigns it might help organize as part of an overall effort to prevent occupational cancer. The key recommendation of the report, one I expected would not be tremendously popular with OSHA officials, was that they sponsor *bottom-up* efforts at social change, along with *top-down* efforts. OSHA was alarmed, and quite properly so, at recent statistics on the number of incidents and harmful consequences of occupational cancer (Brodeur, 1973), and it also recognized the need to communicate to workers about the problem, relatively independent of its consequences, so as to honor what had become recognized in law as the worker's "right to know." Hence, OSHA sought to instill awareness, to secure compliance with health and safety recommendations, and to encourage workers to initiate corrective actions of their own. However, it tended, as do many other groups, to treat persuasion largely as information-giving, and information as a commodity that can be transmitted to others like a gift package. The sorts of bottom-up tactics recommended by Saul Alinsky and practiced by community action and other social movement organizations seemed to me to be a useful companion to the more typical top-down educational efforts for this problem as well.

The report that follows is organized in outline form around the requirements-problems-strategies (RPS) framework. It is intended in part as a way of showing how the concepts and research generalizations presented in this book may be brought to bear on the formulation of strategies for large-scale campaigns.

Report to the National Research Council Symposium on Public Information in the
Prevention of Occupational Cancer
SUBJECT: Campaign Strategies

CAMPAIGN MESSAGE PREPARATION
by

Herbert W. Simons
Department of Speech, Temple University

Requirements:
A Typology of Intended Effects

Awareness	Compliance	Initiation of Action
Awareness of carcinogenic materials in the workplace	Adherence to safety regulations	Encouragement of adherence by others to safety and health recommendations
Awareness of danger signs	Medical checkups	
Awareness of carcinogenic effects	Adherence to medical advice	Reports and official complaints about dangers
Awareness of action alternatives	Receptivity to new information and suggestions: e.g., attendance at safety meetings	Demands for information from authorities (e.g., generic chemical names)
Awareness of the consequences of actions vs. inaction		Demands for action (e.g., safer chemicals, technological safeguards)

General Principles of Communication

The following principles are in the nature of truisms about communication. They apply to all of the above tasks. Adherence to these principles is a "must" for any educational program.

I. Communication takes place on the recipients' terms.
   A. It is the received message that counts, not the sent message.
   B. Coverage of materials does not equal learning of materials.
   C. Messages must be adapted to different audiences, in terms of their beliefs, values, attitudes, knowledge, interest, norms, etc.
   D. Attention, accurate perception, and appropriate motivation are prerequisites to awareness, voluntary compliance and initiation of action.

II. Campaigns of communication are more effective than one-shot messages.
   A. Multiple sources, messages, media, and channels are more effective than reliance on one source, medium, etc.
   B. Effective campaigns employ the principle of repetition with variation.
   C. Effective campaigns work through opinion leaders—initial recipients and early adopters of innovations who serve, in turn, to educate and persuade others.
   D. Effective large-scale campaigns consist of a series of integrated small-scale campaigns, adapted to different goals and audiences.

III. Every message has multiple effects.
   A. The forms of messages communicate, not just their content.
   B. Messages have primary effects (i.e., adherence to a given safety recommendation) as well as secondary effects (e.g., belief that safety is primarily a matter of worker responsibility) that may or may not be intended.
   C. Substantive messages simultaneously communicate about the source of the message: his/her competence, trustworthiness, good will towards the audience, etc.

IV. The believability of a message depends significantly on the credibility of the source.
   A. Technical information is best transmitted by persons believed to be competent and trustworthy; attractiveness is less important.
   B. Motivational appeals are best transmitted by persons perceived to be trustworthy and attractive; competence is less important.
   C. The ideal source is a "super-representative" of the audience; attractive to them by dint of similar occupation, interests, background, etc., but different in that he/she is perceived to have greater knowledge, competence, trustworthiness, etc. Especially effective are behavioral models—persons who can offer first-hand testimony or whose behavior can serve as an exemplar for others.

V. Recipients of messages combine emotion and logic in forming judgments and taking action.
   A. The mix of emotion and logic is highly variable from recipient to recipient and from one message to another.
   B. Recipients are "hedonistic calculators": they weigh costs against benefits in forming judgments and taking action. Decisions are not always "rational," although seemingly "irrational" actions (e.g., emotional defenses) are often realistic responses to a threatening environment.

VI. Educational campaigns require reciprocal feedback.
   A. Recipients learn and are persuaded best through active participating; i.e., when they have opportunities to ask questions, test their perceptions with others, etc.
   B. Campaigns require constant reevaluation and revision based on feedback from recipients.

General Implications for Education About Occupational Cancer

It is not difficult to draw general implications from the foregoing principles about how to educate workers about occupational cancer. Needed is a large-scale campaign that utilizes, in a series of integrated small-scale campaigns, different sources (industrial authorities, safety and health experts, union personnel, OSHA staff, nonprofit agencies, employee representatives, etc.), different media and channels (films, pamphlets, orientation meetings, on-the-job training, mass media advertising, news exposés, etc.), and different messages (informational messages, motivational messages, reminders, etc.) to achieve different effects. The question is not whether to employ one or another source, message, medium, etc., but how to *combine* them most effectively, and how to adapt them to different audiences. That, in turn, requires audience analysis and periodic feedback to determine how best to "get through" to recipients. Effective campaigns will not rely on one-way communications: they will involve worker participation in the development of programs, in the transmission of ideas and information to other workers, in demonstrations of appropriate and inappropriate action, and in the cultivation of positive group norms among work teams. Communicators must demonstrate potential benefits from receipt of information and recommendations, and they must overcome potential objections. Intended effects must be considered in relation to each other, and multiple effects, including unintended effects, must be anticipated. So as to derive more specific programmatic implications, it will be helpful to identify the peculiar problems involved in communicating about occupational cancer.

Problems Involved in Communicating About Occupational Cancer

Subject Matter Problems

1. Lack of consensus on what is a carcinogen: e.g., untested and inadequately tested materials; lack of agreement on test criteria;
2. Highly technical information;
3. Ambiguous terms (e.g., variation in names of chemical compounds);
4. Variability in subject matter required for different audiences;
5. Ambiguous danger signs (e.g., "colorless, odorless gases");
6. Difficulties in communicating about latency effects;
7. Inexact information about consequences of action and inaction;
8. Threatening nature of the information.

Resistance by Workers

1. Emotional defenses: fatalism, denial ("it can't happen to me"), sense of futility, resignation, rationalization;
2. Ignorance of legal rights and of opportunities to prevent cancer or reduce harmful effects;
3. Mistrust of sources of information (see below);
4. Habit and inertia;
5. Social pressures against learning (e.g., prevailing "macho" norms within work groups);
6. Fear of loss of income or job benefits from learning that one has cancer or is prone to it (e.g., possible loss of job or downward transfer to a safer job);
7. Fear of reprisal from company or negative group pressures for issuing reports, complaints and demands.

Inadequate Sources and Communication Channels

1. Many companies are apparently motivated to withhold information and resist change. Profit motive, indifference, concerns about generating anxiety, and other factors have led companies in some cases to:
   a. classify information about generic names of chemicals;
   b. fail to share reports on occupational hazards with workers;
   c. conduct half-hearted programs of health and safety education;
   d. resist introducing costly technological safety innovations;
   e. resist external pressures for change.
   (Note: Where these problems exist they are serious impediments to "top-down" educational efforts. We have not been able to determine, however, the extent of these problems, and suspect that most companies are simultaneously motivated to prevent occupational cancer.)
2. OSHA staff inadequate and too removed from problems; same is true of most other outside agencies;
3. Unions for only ¼ of workers; some unions ineffective or unmotivated;
4. Cheapest, most easily developed media provide one-way communications; little evidence of widespread exposure or utilization of materials;
5. Sources perceived as expert not always perceived as trustworthy or interpersonally attractive (e.g., medical officers in a company); sources perceived as trustworthy and attractive not always perceived as expert (e.g., employee representatives at monthly safety meetings).

Goal Incompatibilities (examples below)

1. Too much fear arousal (through greater awareness) may inhibit compliance;
2. Readiness to comply with safety recommendations may inhibit actions against companies guilty of code violations;
3. Overuse of formal complaint mechanisms may overtax OSHA staff from fulfillment of systematic inspection responsibilities;
4. Medical checkups may provide false sense of security;
5. Adversary stance toward companies may inhibit cooperation on safety matters and lead to conflict on other matters.

Overcoming Problems and Fulfilling Goals: Major Findings and Recommendations

Not all of the foregoing problems can be overcome by educational programs; and not all goals are likely to be achieved for substantial numbers of workers. The short-term effects of any educational program are likely to be minuscule and significant long-term effects cannot be guaranteed. Realism dictates that success be measured in relative terms (e.g., comparison of percent compliance in companies benefiting from educational programs versus those not exposed to them), rather than against an absolute, ideal standard. Moreover, even modest successes will require a highly ambitious and expensive large-scale campaign. The findings and recommendations offered here are designed to augment the earlier section of this report on General Implications for Education About Occupational Cancer.

I. Reconciling "Top-Down" versus "Bottom-Up" Approaches to Education
   A. Most educational programs are of the "top-down" variety.
They presuppose:

1. a passive, potentially acquiescent worker,
2. who needs to be appropriately informed and motivated,
3. in a cooperative, problem-solving context,
4. by benevolent, competent, higher status authorities (e.g., company safety officers; medical doctors; OSHA professionals),
5. mostly via one-way communications (pamphlets, films, lectures, etc.),
6. so as to secure awareness and compliance goals.

B. A relatively few educational programs (e.g., UPA, PhilaPosh) are of the "bottom-up" variety. They presuppose:
   1. that workers must be motivated primarily to initiate action on their own behalf;
   2. the need for a conflict orientation toward companies (assumption that, on their own, companies will sacrifice workers for profits);
   3. the need to organize workers for collective action;
   4. the need for "consciousness-raising" among workers;
   5. that workers will act in their own best interests if given a genuine opportunity to do so.

C. Both "top-down" and "bottom-up" approaches can be useful to workers, and both should therefore be supported by OSHA.
   1. The "bottom-up" approach is more consonant with the General Principles of Communication, outlined above, but it is unlikely, in the immediate future, to reach large numbers of workers, or to provide basic information needed to fulfill awareness and compliance goals (see above). Its principal function will be to goad companies and some unions into appropriate "top-down" actions.
   2. The "top-down" approach can be greatly improved by more regular adherence to sound communication principles. It can provide greater expertise and other resources, and it can reach larger numbers of people. Companies must be provided with greater incentives for appropriate action and information-giving.

II. "Top-Down" Communications: Creating Awareness and Compliance
   A. Educational aids (e.g., pamphlets, films, slide shows, etc.)
      1. Educational aids should be used in conjunction with, rather than as a substitute for, two-way, interpersonal communications.
      2. As important as educational aids is their ready availability in the workplace and the existence of incentives such as released time to read and discuss them.
      3. Visual media are generally more effective than print media.
   B. Both educational aids and oral communications with workers can be improved by greater efforts at attention-getting and comprehension. The following findings from communication research are relevant here.
      1. The less effort required by recipients, the greater their attention and comprehension.
      2. Attention is given almost involuntarily to stimuli that are novel, colorful, contrasting, dramatic, visual, and voluntarily to stimuli that appeal to curiosity, vital interests, and threats to perceived freedom.
      3. Recipients seek out supportive information but do not necessarily avoid nonsupportive information. However, resistance to information about occupational cancer is likely to be greater than to other information which communication researchers have studied.
      4. Messages are more likely to be understood when: (a) they are spaced rather

than massed; (b) they are organized around two to five main points; (c) they motivate interest; (d) they abound with colorful illustrations; (e) examples, statistics, etc. are presented vividly; (f) main points are repeated for retention purposes.

C. Awareness goals are more likely to be realized when tied explicitly to goals of compliance and/or initiation of action.

D. Fear appeals to motivate awareness and compliance
   1. Fear appeals are likely to be ineffective or counter-productive unless accompanied by messages indicating: degree of harm from inaction, how to act, that actions can be taken easily, that recommended action will prevent the problem, reduce its likelihood, or contain or solve it once it arises.
   2. Appeals to fear for family and friends are often more effective than appeals to fear for self.

E. Changes in behavior do not always follow upon changes in beliefs, attitudes or intentions.
   1. Needed are situational incentives for conformity and absence of situational disincentives;
   2. Recipient must be able to comply, both physically and psychologically;
   3. Compliance is facilitated by: (a) group meetings to change social norms; (b) material incentives for compliance awarded to teams rather than individuals; (c) appeals to supportive reference groups; (d) threats by authorities (as a last resort); (e) use of opinion leaders in work groups (provide special training and material rewards for safety education); (f) use of behavior models— persons who can set examples for others to follow.

F. Overcoming Worker Resistance
   1. Findings
      a. Ego-defensiveness (i.e., fight and flight mechanisms such as denial and fatalism) is especially resistant to persuasion.
      b. Defensiveness must be overcome therapeutically. Egos must be supported. There must be opportunities for airing workers' fears and examining each seriously. Persons who can serve as behavior models are especially effective in this regard.
   2. Recommendations
      a. One-to-one counselling and small group discussions;
      b. Support groups among workers for consciousness-raising;
      c. Transfer of highly defensive persons to nonhazardous jobs;
      d. Public service TV advertising;
         (1) to get ego-defensive attitudes out in the open;
         (2) to get occupational cancer discussed within families;
         (3) to provide the telephone number of a "hotline" for further information.

III. "Bottom-Up" Communication: Emphasis on Initiation of Action
   A. Reports, complaints and demands by workers are increased when workers perceive:
      1. a gap between perceived realities and expectations,
      2. that action will bring positive benefits,
      3. that action will not bring reprisals.
   B. The bottom-up approach involves a *chaining out* process:
      1. A relatively small number of workers sets an example for others to follow;
      2. Education and action programs are imitated by other small groups when the initial groups demonstrate that they can achieve results;
      3. Education and action programs are legitimized by successes, endorsements

from influential outside groups (OSHA?) and adoptions by major union organizations;

    4. Escalated pressures for change by worker collectives provide goads to companies and governmental bodies for top-down change;

    5. Changes initially resisted by companies become formal programs that they now positively evaluate as evidence of how progressive they are.

C. Reaching small numbers of rank and file workers can be accomplished by trade unions or ideologically minded, nonprofit organizations.

    1. Workers can be attracted to education programs by means of news media exposure of dangerous conditions, leafleting outside plants, union newsletters, word-of-mouth, etc.

    2. Meetings of workers from different companies should stress

        a. Consciousness-raising—e.g., awareness that workers in different companies have similar problems.

        b. Company culpability and possibilities for change.

    3. Education and action are integrally related (for example)

        a. Workers are asked, as part of their educations, to request information from supervisors that supervisors are likely to withhold (e.g., generic names of chemicals). Inability to get information through individual requests teaches need for collective action;

        b. Collective actions that meet with success demonstrate possibilities for change, provide motivations for sacrifice, acceptance of discipline, induce esprit de corps among worker collectives.

    4. Bottom-up efforts are dependent on many of the same teaching aids (e.g., pamphlets on safety hazards) as top-down efforts.

D. Bottom-up efforts at initiation of action about occupational cancer should become an important part of the larger contemporary movement for improvement of working conditions by trade unions. It should eventually have important awareness and compliance effects as well.

Summary of Main Recommendations

1. Use of "bottom-up" educational programs in addition to "top-down" programs.
2. Use of concrete recommendations and reassurances in conjunction with use of fear appeals.
3. Use of opinion leaders, especially those who can serve as behavioral models.
4. Worker input in development and appraisal of educational programs.
5. Research to determine what works, rather than reliance on abstract principles or general research findings.

SUMMARY

Utilizing a model of campaign stages and components, this chapter has focused on the unique characteristics of persuasive campaigns: both the greater potential for influence that comes from being able to approach audiences developmentally, and the greater potential for problems that can arise from such efforts. Given special attention were relatively small-scale campaigns for institutional change, of the kind likely to be engaged in by readers of this book.

Typical treatments of persuasive campaigns focus on the promotion stage. Planning, mobilization of resources, and efforts at legitimation must precede promotion of the product, candidate, and so on before the general public, and must continue through the final campaign stage: activation. Voluntary campaigns especially tend to falter at the mobilization stage for lack of inducements to discipline and cohesion. And voluntary campaigns for institutional change tend to fail also from insufficient pressure on key decision-makers or from lack of follow-through at the activation stage.

A persistent theme in this chapter has been the importance of the dramatic. Few campaigns succeed solely on the basis of the information they provide or the didactic arguments they offer. Information is important, but it must be embedded in symbols and actions that spark the imagination and invite participation from a public that seeks excitement and psychological gratification as much as it does hard evidence and material satisfaction.

Although special emphasis was placed on the unique characteristics of campaigns, this does not mean that principles of persuasion discussed earlier in the book do not apply. This was illustrated in the discussion of door-to-door canvassing and in the case studies presented in the chapter.

EXERCISE

1. Do a planning analysis for a campaign of your own imagining, preferably a small-scale campaign that you might lead or help carry out. If there is time, try to implement the campaign and provide a record of your experiences.
2. Do a case study of an institutional change campaign using the model of stages and components outlined in this chapter.

Chapter *13*
Persuasion In Social Conflicts

What are social conflicts? How are they different from disagreements or differences of opinion? What techniques of persuasion are appropriate to interpersonal conflicts between persons having relatively equal power? To asymmetrical interactions where power is unevenly distributed? To conflicts between protest movements and established institutions? What are the relative merits in conflict situations of co-active forms of persuasion as opposed to more combative alternatives?

Nature of Social Conflicts

In Chapter 5, I defined a *conflict* as a clash of interests in which one party's relative gain is another's relative loss. An explanation of that definition should make clear why persuasion in social conflicts warrants a separate chapter in this book—why, that is, the techniques of persuasion prescribed for nonconflict situations are not always applicable to conflict situations.

First, a social conflict is not simply a misunderstanding or semantic confusion or communication breakdown; it goes deeper than that. Situation comedies are rife with apparent crises between husband and wife or boss and employee in which the source of tension is an error of fact or interpretation that is easily correctable with a bit of dialogue. These might more accurately be labeled *pseudoconflicts*.

Second, the notion of a clash of interests presupposes something more than a disagreement, difference of opinion, or academic controversy. This point deserves considerable emphasis, since there is a widespread tendency to minimize or wish away conflicts by treating them as though they were mere disagreements. To underscore the point, picture the difference between a newspaper columnist arguing that the auto workers deserve higher wages and the same argument coming from the head of the United Auto Workers in the midst of a collective-bargaining session. The columnist would have been arguing a controversial position, it is true, but it is questionable whether he or she would have had anything more than an academic and passing interest in the matter. The union leader, by contrast, is quite clearly involved in a social conflict, evidenced by a clash over incompatible interests. Similarly, two people—even two intimates—may subscribe to divergent religious principles without necessarily being in conflict. Their interests might well become incompatible, however, if one felt morally compelled to convert the other, or if, as in a marriage, both had to decide how to rear offspring. (Note that conflicts over principles arise whenever one party makes unacceptable claims upon the other, or when, in the face of divergent goals, their activities must be coordinated.)

To have an interest in something, then, is to covet or value it personally, whether it be an item of scarcity such as money, or a principle such as equal pay for equal work. For two people (or groups) to have *incompatible interests*, each must stand as an obstacle to maximum realization of the other's interests. Two people may disagree on the market value of a house that is up for sale without necessarily being in conflict. But should the disputants be seller and potential buyer, they would indeed be in conflict. (Note that they might well reach an amicable compromise and still have been in conflict; as in any such bargaining situation, each party's relative gain over what he or she could have paid or received is the other party's relative loss.)

Third, the same persons may be embroiled in a conflict on one level and in a controversy or disagreement on another level. Consider the case of two undergraduates engaged in a classroom debate over Israel's annexation of Arab territories. To the extent that either party may receive a poor grade or suffer loss of reputation from doing badly in the debate, they are indeed engaged in a conflict. But the conflict is not over Israel's relationship with its Arab neighbors! *That* remains a disagreement or difference of opinion. A conflict may involve value differences or personal animosities or competition for scarce resources, but once again, *the personal interests of one party must be threatened by the other party.*

Already it should be clear that appeals to reason or common ground may not be sufficient to resolve social conflicts; indeed, in such conflicts as between labor and management, buyer and seller, husband and wife, Israel and Egypt, the combatants might well have reason to remain antagonistic. Let us now turn to the fourth point, which is that, to a greater degree than in classroom discussions or bull sessions between friends, attitudes in conflict situations are linked to beliefs about relative power capacities.

In a college debate, one has the luxury to decide that such and such is what two conflicting parties *ought* to do, irrespective of the nature of the context and of each side's willingness and capacity to reward or punish the other. The realities of conflict situations generally militate against agreement on ideal solutions. Trust levels tend to be low, ego-involvement high, channels of communication closed or restricted, and neither side able to enforce its conception of an ideal outcome. Hence, "peace with honor" may be a truce agreement following a military stalemate. What is considered "honorable" or "desirable" is necessarily what one can hope to get *under the circumstances*. Correspondingly, the conflicting parties may struggle to alter the other's circumstances as a way of modifying the other's beliefs and attitudes. What emerges most often is an implicit or explicit *compromise*.

Cooperation and Competition in Mixed-Motive Conflicts

One of the paradoxical features of practically all social conflicts is that the adversaries are motivated simultaneously to cooperate and compete with each other. Seldom is either party served by annihilating the enemy, or taking all his money, or totally incapacitating him. Real-life conflicts, in this sense, are not like foot races or games of chess or poker. Instead, they are of the *mixed-motive* variety. To understand this fact of social conflicts is to understand why purely combative strategies of influence seldom make sense.

Consider, once again, the case of a labor-management conflict over wages. Admittedly, it is in the interests of labor to get as much as possible, and it is likewise in the interests of management to give as little as possible. Each, moreover, has combative weapons available (prolonged strikes, layoffs, and so on) by which to punish or cripple the enemy. Why don't they use them more often?

The obvious answer is that they have much to lose by acting combatively and much to gain through cooperation. Morality aside, let us examine the interests of labor and management in terms of the potential costs and benefits exchanged by acting combatively or cooperatively.

First, we should remember that purely coercive influence entails relatively high *delivery costs*. To punish another, or even to threaten effectively, one must mount an offensive capability. Co-active persuasion, on the other hand, may cost little or nothing. Second, because conflicts involve reciprocal influence, each side must calculate the repercussions of its actions in terms of possible *retaliation costs*. The use of force may carry the day, but only at the price of incurring the wrath of the adversary, who may strike back with even greater fury. Third, the use of purely combative strategies over an issue such as wages may block the resolution of other, subsidiary, issues. The ensuing buildup of antagonisms may so impede communication and reduce trust as to make what once were considered trivial questions into significant and unresolvable matters of principle. Fourth, strategies of a purely combative nature often enrage nonadversaries, who then bring their own influence to bear on the situation. Some combative acts are punished by law, others are vilified by the press, and still others cause backlash reactions from the public.

Thus far, I have stressed the costs involved in employing purely combative strategies, but there are also benefits possible from employing cooperative, co-active means of influence. Conflict theorists like to speak of benefits in terms of a hypothetical *benefits pie*, and they are fond of pointing out that the size of the pie is by no means finite. Should a labor-management conflict escalate beyond control, the size of the pie is reduced. On the other hand, should the two sides find a way to increase productivity and profits, the size of the pie is increased. Cooperation on one issue can breed a spirit of harmony on other issues and reduce the need for offensive capabilities.

So what is the optimal influence strategy for mixed-motive conflicts? The answer is that there is no single answer. It depends on one's interests: on whether one is more interested in short-term or long-term benefits, in getting a larger share of the pie (but perhaps, along with it, a smaller pie) or in increasing the size of the pie. It depends, too, on one's power capacity relative to one's opponents—on whether, for example, they can outlast you or you can outlast them should push come to shove, as in a prolonged labor strike.

Symmetrical versus Asymmetrical Conflicts

A conflict between persons or groups with relatively equal power to reward or punish the other is called a *symmetrical* conflict. A conflict between antagonists having unequal power is an *asymmetrical* conflict. There are, of course, degrees of asymmetry, and relative power may vary as well from one situation to another. Parents have the upper hand in most families most of the time, but children are not without their own resources, including the capacity to withhold love at precisely the moments when their parents are most in need of it. Employers tend to be "one-up" on their employees, but the imbalance is usually reduced and sometimes reversed as a result of unionization.

Conflict Orientations. How one feels about conflict and how one deals with it once it arises are partly a function of one's role in an organization. Within large-scale social systems such as universities and business organizations, symmetrical conflicts routinely develop between competing members of the system, and asymmetrical conflicts take place between rank-and-file members of the system and representatives of the system as a whole. The former are called *actor-actor* conflicts; the latter are *actor-system* conflicts. For example, student organizations often engage in *actor-actor* competitions for new members, and they occasionally become embroiled in *actor-system* conflicts with university administrators over issues of student rights.

Within their spheres of authority, administrators of every kind tend to be system-oriented. For these system representatives, there is an understandable preference for conflict prevention and for speedy resolutions of conflicts once they arise. For example, college deans try to discourage competition for funds among the departments they supervise. They tend to identify more with the need for order and stability in the college as a whole than with the interests of any one component of the system. Likewise, the president of the United States tends to look askance upon strikes by organized labor. Like the dean of a college, he tends to be system-oriented rather than actor-oriented.

These orientations are manifested in recurring patterns of talk about conflict—i.e., in *genres* of conflict rhetoric. Those with system orientations tend to downplay the need for conflict within their organizations and to label conflicts as mere disagreements or misunderstandings. Their emphasis in public statements is on the benefits that can accrue to all from cooperation. And, of course, they tend to reserve their harshest criticisms for the "troublemakers" who initiate actor-system conflicts. From an actor orientation, on the other hand, conflict is necessary, natural, and in any case inevitable—not something to be prevented or wished away. From the perspectives of those who lead movements in behalf of students' rights, for example, protests may be necessary, even if disruptive, because they call attention to injustices. A good deal more will be said about protest movements later in the chapter.

Symmetrical Conflicts and the Prisoner's Dilemma. Consider now the question of whether to cooperate or compete in a symmetrical conflict. Recall that here the power to reward and punish is roughly the same for both sides. Many of the essential features of mixed-motive conflicts are illustrated in what has come to be known as the *prisoner's dilemma* game (PD). Figure 13.1 presents what is known as a *payoff matrix*. Player Y has two possible moves, *a* and *b*. If Y plays *a* he receives either $+1$ or -2 units of reward, depending on X's move. If Y chooses *b*, he gets $+2$ or -1 units of reward, depending on X's move. X's payoffs are similarly determined by a combination of both players' moves. If Y plays *a* and X plays *d*, for example, X gets $+2$. But if Y had played *b* while X played *d*, each would have received -1. Note that two players must choose simultaneously. As can be seen, each player has a possible cooperative choice (*a* or *c*) and a possible competitive choice (*b* or *d*). Each knows that the competitive choice is best personally, for it offers the possibility of the greatest gain. But—and this underscores the interdependent nature of mixed-motive conflicts—if both players make the competitive choice, both lose.

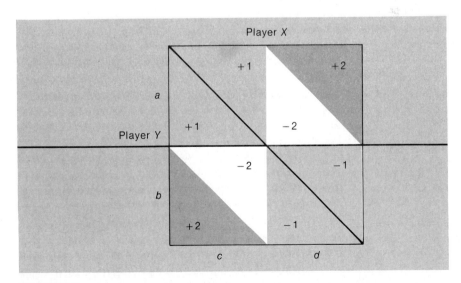

Figure 13.1.

One of the advantages of games such as this one is that they help us to understand a great variety of conflicts, from marital squabbles to labor-management contests. In both types of conflicts, for example, goals often remain ambiguous over the life of the relationship, each party alternating between mutual accommodation (the *ac* combination) and victory at the expense of the other. (In some bad marriages, each side willingly suffers -1 outcomes for the perverse joy of seeing the other experience -1 outcomes.) At the same time, of course, the game necessarily oversimplifies situations. In real life, for example, each side may have more than two options; moves may alternate, rather than occurring simultaneously; payoffs are not known in any quantitative sense; and the distribution of rewards and punishments may vary from that presented in the figure. Nevertheless, the game captures the ambiguities and paradoxes of conflict interactions, and that is no small accomplishment.[1]

The Audiences for Social Conflicts

Even if it were assumed (however erroneously) that purely combative strategies are required for dealing with an adversary, it should be remembered that the leadership of conflict groups such as labor and management must address a variety of audiences besides the opposition; indeed, that co-active persuasion with some of these audiences is necessary in order to constrain or coerce the adversary. Co-active persuasion has a place even in the most embittered clashes between adversaries.

Figure 13.2 presents a simplified model of actors, reactors, and communication patterns in a mixed-motive conflict characterized by two competing groups. In the figure we show five pairs of messages (each leadership component sends comparable types of messages) directed to five different audiences:

1. *Leader to supporters.* In industrial conflicts, international conflicts, conflicts between political parties, and so on, there are generally people who sympathize with one side or the other without functioning as active members. Co-active persuasion is used primarily to recruit and indoctrinate these supporters. The larger and more committed the following, the larger the power base. Hence, leaders seek to foment a sense of grievance, a feeling of collective identity among the following, a belief in the legitimacy of the group and its leaders, hostility toward the opposition, and confidence in the ingroup's power to succeed.
2. *Leader to hard-core members.* The same co-active rhetoric used to recruit

---

[1] Before you read on in this chapter, try the PD game with others to see what the experience is like. For research purposes, the game is usually played with elaborate restrictions on interactions, but you can play it more informally. Try playing it in three stages: (1) For 50 trials (each trial involves one simultaneous move by each player), all talk between you should be prohibited. After the 50 trials are over, compute total scores for each. The scores will themselves be a form of communication about how each of you plays the game. (2) For the next 50 trials, verbal communication should again be prohibited. This time, however, each side's move should be revealed after each trial. (3) For the next 25 trials, you may verbally communicate before each trial. Pay careful attention to the ploys and counterploys used in making threats and promises.

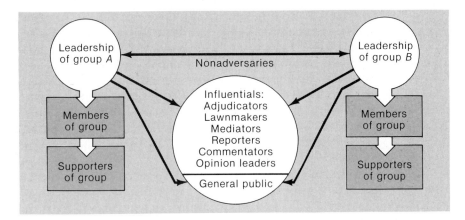

Figure 13.2 Leader-generated messages and their audiences in a mixed-motive conflict between two groups.

and indoctrinate supporters is also used to intensify the commitments of hard-core members, but in addition they must be mobilized to do the hard work of the adversary group.

3. *Leader to general public.* If significantly awakened, the general public can tip the balance in social conflicts, either by constraining one or the other side or by bringing indirect pressure on the adversaries via lawmakers, the courts, and so on. Hence, the leaders of adversary groups engage in public relations campaigns aimed at justifying their means and ends and delegitimizing the opposition. In some cases, the leadership may use combative methods of influence on the general public as a way of exerting indirect pressure on adversaries or influentials.

4. *Leader to influentials.* Each side regularly courts these persons, and in regulated conflicts may be bound by the decisions of adjudicators or reciprocally influenced by mediators. Combative influence may also be employed here as a way of bringing indirect pressure on adversaries.

5. *Leader to leader.* In rough-and-tumble conflicts between adversaries, direct co-active persuasion between leaders may be highly restricted, but it may still take place via messages to nonadversaries. As conflict escalates, messages ostensibly directed at other leaders may actually be meant for the ears of nonadversaries or followers, as a way of confirming the rigidity or stupidity or immorality of the opposition. It may also be used, of course, to get the opposition's attention and willingness to negotiate and compromise.

Persuasion in Interpersonal Conflicts: Win-Win versus Win-Lose Orientations

As a general rule, it is a good idea to employ co-active forms of persuasion before employing more combative measures. Deutsch (1969) speaks in this connection of the need for an essentially cooperative, *win-win* approach to conflict as opposed to a competitive, *win-lose* approach. The latter, he maintains, is apt to have mutually destructive consequences (*lose-lose*), as when, in the PD game, each player opts for the competitive move and winds up getting −1.

In the course of these lose-lose conflicts, says Deutsch, there is an expansion of the size and number of motives and participants implicated, of the size and number of principles and precedents believed to be at stake, of the costs participants are willing to bear, of the norms each side is willing to exempt itself from, and of the intensity of hostility toward the other. Cooperation is driven out by suspiciousness and combativeness. There is increasing reliance on power and on tactics of threat, coercion, and deception. There is a corresponding shift away from persuasion and tactics of conciliation and rapport-building. Communication becomes impoverished and unreliable. Channels are either not used, or used to mislead and intimidate. Reliance is placed on espionage or on other circuitous routes for gathering information.

As a consequence, says Deutsch, little confidence is placed in information provided directly from the other, and opportunities for error and selective perception are enhanced. The range of perceived alternatives is reduced. There is a reduced time perspective, a focus on the immediate. Thought is polarized, reduced to either-ors and stereotyped responses. There is greater susceptibility to fear- or hope-inspired rumors and increasing pressure toward social conformity. One's own behavior is seen as more benevolent and legitimate, and there is a corresponding assumption that differential legitimacy should be differentially rewarded. Once committed, there is a tendency to justify past actions and to mobilize further with each successive response by the adversary.

If, after reading Deutsch's impressive list, you remain unconvinced of the dangers of combativeness, there is additional evidence from recent research using the Prisoner's Dilemma game: One ought not only to begin a long-term relationship co-actively, one ought always to signal a willingness to return to cooperation any time the relationship takes a turn toward destructive conflict. Most prior research on Prisoner's Dilemma involved a limited, prespecified number of trials, and in these situations, an essentially competitive approach is often more successful than a mixed or largely cooperative approach.

Robert Axelrod (1984) conceived the idea of inviting 14 professional game theorists to enter the equivalent of a PD tournament by each submitting one set strategy for unlimited, extended use against the other players. The clear winner of the tournament, mathematician Anatol Rapoport, devised a system that always cooperates on the first playing of the game (choosing *a* or *c*, depending on whether one is X or Y), then mimics what the other player did the last time around on each successive play. If your opponent competed in the last move, you now compete. If your opponent cooperated, you cooperate as well—perhaps indefinitely, so long as the opponent is also willing to maintain this *win-win* approach.

One of the advantages of Rapoport's "tit-for-tat" system is that it is simple and thus sends a clear message. Often in real-life conflict situations our words are garbled and our actions difficult to read. A second advantage is that it is "nice." It always begins with cooperation and never "holds a grudge." Third, it is "tough" when it needs to be tough. It doesn't "turn the other cheek" in the face of persistent competition; it lets the opponent know instead that competition (in the form of a *b* or *d* move) will always be met by competition.

Interestingly, Rapoport's system was victorious in a second tournament, this one involving experts as well as readers of popular computing magazines. Like Rapoport's, the systems that did well all began cooperatively, whereas the poorest systems began competitively. The latter did very well against the few entries that consistently turned the other cheek, but they suffered disastrously against each other. Axelrod speculates on the possibility that the evolution of cooperation in human as well as nonhuman species may have developed through experiences offering "lessons in life" similar to those provided in his tournaments.

Dealing with Resistance and Hostility

One reason conflicts escalate beyond the intentions of either party is that neither knows how to cope with the resistance and hostility displayed by the other. Often attempted solutions only exacerbate the problem as, for example, when we suggest to others that the conflict could easily be resolved if only *they* would be more reasonable. On presenting students with Deutsch's characterization of the process of conflict escalation, they have had no difficulty finding examples from their own experiences where, try as they might, they could not reverse a pattern of destructive conflict. After months of nagging at her apartment mate to share equally in the performance of household chores, Chris thought she had hit upon a perfect solution: a "contract" with Becky that would specify who would do what, when, and with what penalties for nonperformance. But when Becky was presented with the proposal, she rejected it outright as another of Chris's efforts at imposing her way of doing things on the relationship.

In recalling the details of a conflict episode or of a conflictual relationship, it is all too easy to present matters solely from one's own point of view. One student complained, for example, that his impending marriage was placed in jeopardy even before it had begun by his fiancee's invocation of her father's "dumb opinions" to back up her own. While upbraiding his fiancee for failing to listen to (his) reason, he at least acknowledged that she might have had legitimate complaints about his tendency to respond on an intellectual level to the conflicts that divided them, when what was most needed were direct expressions of affection and respect.

Sometimes conflicts such as these cannot be resolved without outside intervention. The internal relationship takes on the properties of a "game without end." Not uncommonly, the battle is waged over issues that are only symptomatic of the real cause of concern—over whose turn it is to wash the dishes, for example, rather than over who is to control the rules of the relationship.

Many of the techniques for overcoming resistance and hostility were discussed in previous chapters. Differences can be bridged co-actively by reaching out to the other, emphasizing common bonds and shared experiences as well as areas of agreement on the matter in question. Humor, too, can defuse hostility. In heated conflicts, where misperception and misunderstanding are the rule rather than the exception, showing that you can understand and even appreciate the other's perspective is especially important. Taking the perspective of the other may include:

1. Probing their perceptions—asking nonjudgmentally how they see you and how they see you seeing them
2. Articulating their perspective to *their* satisfaction—if necessary, asking for their help in enlightening you
3. Indicating that you can respect their feelings even if you cannot agree with them entirely

On being subjected to criticism, asking for more information rather than becoming immediately defensive is especially effective. At a large university, according to Frost and Wilmot (1978), the boss of one of the divisions initiated a process of calling each of the department heads in for unscheduled private conferences at which he made known a long list of criticisms he had been accumulating.

> Finally, Shirley was called in. When the boss mentioned that "people weren't getting all the work done and they were spending too much time on coffee breaks," Shirley asked for more information. She said, "Have you been unhappy with some part of my work?" The boss said he could not think of anything right then. The boss, who was really not angry or upset at Shirley at all, mentioned a few things, which Shirley accepted, and then they turned their attention to other matters in the office. (p. 138)

Whenever possible in a conflict situation, you should try to preserve the other's sense of decisional freedom (Brehm, 1962). In the example provided earlier, Chris would probably have been better off using (1) an *implicit* approach—encouraging Becky to participate in the formulation of Chris's recommendation; (2) the *method of residues*—broaching her recommendation only after joint consideration of a variety of less attractive options; (3) *providing behavioral alternatives*—indicating a range of solutions to the problem that she could accept.

In Chapter 6 *reframing* was described as a particularly useful technique for overcoming resistance and hostility. A supervisor of a multisection course in public speaking used this technique with two graduate assistants who had been experiencing a great deal of conflict in teaching one of the sections together. Initially the supervisor merely listened as the co-teachers ventilated their frustrations at having to work with a partner who was so inept, so irresponsible, so mean, and so on. She then observed wryly that the patterns of their talk were almost identical. Each alternated between blaming and defending. Evidently they had much in common; perhaps they could now put their heads together to figure out how to alter the pattern.

Note that the supervisor's comment reframed in two ways: (1) It shifted the *terms* of the conflict from one of fault-finding to one of joint responsibility; (2) it shifted the *level* of the conversation from talk about this or that substantive matter to metacommunications about the relationship, as manifested in the co-teachers' own pattern of talk.

Often the size and severity of the conflict can be redescribed so as to make it easier to deal with. What had been labeled a racial conflict can be relabeled a conflict between two people who happen to be of different races. "Being treated unfairly" can become "being treated unfairly on a particular occasion." An issue of principle might be reframed as a question of how best to apply a principle.

The techniques of co-active persuasion described in Chapter 7 and elaborated on in subsequent chapters are not unlike those Gibb (1961) found to be characteristic of verbal behaviors that tended to reduce defensiveness. His list included: (1) *neutral descriptions*, without implied need for change; (2) a *problem-orientation*, a desire to collaborate in defining a mutual problem and seeking its solution without predetermined opinions; (3) *spontaneity*, honest and straightforward motives and spontaneous responses; (4) *empathy* for the feelings and attitudes of the listener; (5) *equality* as reflected in mutual respect and minimization of differences in skill, position, IQ; and (6) *provisionalism*, investigating and suggesting rather than being dogmatic and arbitrary.

When two people begin to approach a conflict as *their* problem, noted Deutsch, their talk is often lively, intense, impassioned, but at the same time creative, engaging, satisfying, and even entertaining. In "productive" conflicts, he observes, positions are stated directly, and there is allowance for expressions of anger as something normal and expected, even helpful. There are likely to be expressions of warm feelings as well, but care is taken to avoid premature agreement, since this only masks the underlying problem. Often it helps to fractionate the conflict—to divide it into parts and begin discussion of the more easily resolvable issues. Success in solving these problems breeds success with others. It also serves as a reminder of positive qualities in the other and of common bonds. And it may lead to the realization that there is room for compromise. In fractionating the conflict, the two parties may even discover that their different values make tradeoffs possible, each party "giving" on one issue so as to "get" on another.

Dealing from a One-Down Position

What should you do if your use of cooperative, co-active methods of persuasion does not succeed at overcoming resistance and hostility? What *can* you do, moreover, if the other person has much greater power than you—if, in other words, you are in a *one-down* position?

A largely cooperative approach to interpersonal conflicts assumes a *symmetrical* relationship between the contending parties, one in which power is fairly equally distributed. In *one-up* relationships to another, those in which you hold greater power, it is possible to gain compliance and even change attitudes by use of coercion and material inducements. One-up persons may also exploit perceptions of high status, expertise, or personal attractiveness. In psychotherapy, according to Gillis (1974), long waiting lists, high fees, unreasonable hours, diplomas, jargon, and references to famous colleagues all contribute to the prestige of the therapist and consequently enhance and maintain high treatment expectations on the part of the client. Within therapy, Gillis continues, interventions can be directed toward establishing the therapist's "command power" (powerful arguments, esoteric interpretations, confusion tactics) or "friendship power" (flattery, stressing similarities, empathy statements, joining against a common enemy).

Consider now the often desperate situation of persons in a one-down relationship of long duration, the child at the mercy of rejecting parents, the army recruit suffering at the hands of a sadistic drill instructor, the wife bound dependently to an abusive husband, the employee who must answer to an authoritarian boss. In these situations, says Deutsch, protestations of unfairness are likely to be met defensively. Those to whom the appeal is addressed may deny the problems, or try to ignore them, or blame others, or combine sham cooperation with counteraggression, or propose substitute solutions rather than needed solutions. What then?

One obvious solution to the problem of persistent abuse is to leave the relationship. Another is to band with others experiencing the same or similar problems to fight unfair treatment. Yet another is to secure third-party support. However, these solutions are not realistically available in a great many situations. For example, the abused wife may have few job skills and a large family to care for. Meanwhile, she is unlikely to have much in the way of positive or negative "chips" to bargain with. One source of potential power that low-power persons can sometimes call upon is the refusal to cooperate authentically until such time as the other is willing to negotiate on equal terms. This can be paired with the promise of increased cooperation should the other agree to discuss matters equitably.

In encounters such as these, style or mode of presentation becomes extremely important. On a continuum from passive to aggressive, one's confrontative tone should be somewhere in the middle—*assertive,* in the sense of being forceful and direct about one's own feelings, but not in such a way as to demean or denigrate the other. In a long-term relationship, where many of the conflict-engendering issues have been debated *ad nauseam,* it is sometimes helpful to make plain your wants and then say no more, letting your supporting arguments hang enthymematically as unstated premises. Yet learning to be assertive does not generally come easy to persons accustomed to being one-down in relationships.

Sometimes, paradoxically, one can also exercise control by appearing to have lost control. Examples of this are common. A bored partygoer may announce that she has developed a severe headache that compels her to leave early. A seducer may claim that his advances are motivated by uncontrollable passions. How, according to conflict theorist Thomas Schelling (1969), might driver A convince driver B to surrender efforts to seize a bridge toll lane that they were each competing for? Not by rational persuasion in the usual sense, but by opening the car window and screaming that the brakes have failed; or by advancing the car while looking away from the other driver; or by acting insane, inebriated, or retarded; or by acting as though seizure of the lane were a matter of principle.

Loss of control may be externally imposed for tactical reasons. A union may constrain its negotiators from being able to postpone a strike deadline, thus, in effect, rendering the negotiator immune to counterinfluence from the opposition. Similarly, professors at some schools are not allowed to change a grade once it has been written into the official record. And, as I learned to my dismay, the Philadelphia police are forbidden from retracting parking tickets once they have written them, even if they have made a mistake.

Perhaps the most convincing way of showing that you mean business is actually to lose control. The seducer may actually get carried away, and the partygoer may actually get a headache. Taking the traffic lane example to its extreme, the driver bent on victory might place a brick on the accelerator and climb on to the back seat. Actual loss of control is common among persons who have been subjected to persistent degradation. Watzlawick et al. (1967) have argued that the schizophrenic's symptoms are an unconscious way of warding off perceived threats from the outside world. They function in this sense as rhetorical strategies. A phenomenon known as *learned helplessness* has received increased attention in studies of low-power persons. Demonstrated experimentally in psychological research on lower-order animals (Seligman, 1975), it consists in a loss of apparent capacity and eventual abandonment of initiative as a function of external reinforcements. Abandoning pride or personal possessions as a way of showing that you have nothing to lose is yet another "power of the powerless."

While loss of control tactics "work" up to a point, they are obviously far from the ideal of talk that cements relationships as it solves immediate problems. And they are risky as well. Suppose the other driver is also a lunatic? Suppose the union negotiator is dealing with a company that would welcome a strike? More to the point of this section, suppose the abusive husband gets satisfaction from his wife's helplessness? Appearing helpless and developing other symptoms as strategies are clearly last-ditch efforts.

Should even these tactics fail, what then? It is at this point that Deutsch reluctantly acknowledges the necessity for low-power persons and groups to engage their adversaries combatively through such harassment techniques as ensnarling bureaucracies in their own red tape, and being excessively friendly and cooperative. The risks of escalation and further humiliation are great, he admits, but then, what else can one do? Deutsch confronts us once again with the limits of co-active persuasion. We are left with the paradoxical conclusion that productive outcomes are unlikely to be achieved unless we are sometimes willing to risk destructive outcomes. With this observation, we may better understand not just battles for recognition and equality and fair treatment in interpersonal relationships, but also the actions of militant social movements.

Persuasion by Social Movements

Social movements are sustained efforts in behalf of a cause by noninstitutionalized collectivities, groups such as the rebels of El Salvador, the dissidents of the Soviet Union, the various minority rights organizations that have flourished from time to time in the United States.

Movements may seek to resist change or to promote it. The former may be further divided into *resistance* movements seeking to prevent change, and *restorative* movements seeking a return to old values and practices (Simons, Mechling, and Schreier, 1984). Among movements that seek to promote change, Aberle (1966) distinguished four types: (1) *transformative* movements seeking total change in the social structure, (2) *reformative* movements seeking partial change in the social structure, (3) *redemptive* movements seeking total change in individuals, and (4) *alternative* movements seeking partial change in individuals. Aberle warns that any given case may be difficult to classify. For example, Jerry Falwell and many of his followers in the Moral Majority began with the purpose of changing individuals, but wound up seeking institutional reforms.

Many of the issues we have been examining in this chapter find dramatic illustration in the rhetoric of social movements. What I have been referring to as co-active versus combative forms of persuasion translate, in movement terms, into moderacy versus militancy, respectively. The two approaches will be contrasted in some detail. My purpose in this section is partly to illustrate principles already covered in the chapter and partly to provide change-oriented readers with a sense of the options they have available. In the final section of this chapter we will consider another alternative, the *expressive* approach.

Moderates versus Militants

As applied to protests against institutional policies or practices, moderates are the embodiment of reason, civility, decorum. Moderates collect petitions, send telegrams to their congressional representatives, write books, picket and march peacefully, organize voting blocs, file lawsuits, and so on. Exuding earnestness, charm, and an aura of competence, they get angry but do not shout, issue pamphlets but never manifestos, inveigh against social mores but always in the value language of the social order. Their "devil" is a condition or a set of behaviors or an outcast group, never the persons they are seeking to influence. Those persons are assumed to be capable of "listening to reason."

To the extent that moderates are successful at garnering mass support for their positions, their actions might well threaten those in power and might thus constitute a kind of combative persuasion, but their threats are generally muted or implied, and they always operate within limits prescribed by "the system." For the most part, moderates seek to reduce the psychological distance between the movement and those outside it by speaking the listeners' language, adjusting to their frame of reference, adapting to their needs, wants, and values. Jesse Jackson's Rainbow Coalition provides an example of a once militant movement that has sought legitimacy by working within the framework of traditional electoral politics.

If co-active persuaders assume or pretend to assume an ultimate identity of interests between the movement and its antagonists, militant combative persuaders act on the assumption of a fundamental clash of interests. In mixed-motive conflicts, each can lay claim to a part of the truth and each can boast support from proud philosophical traditions. The moderate's commitment to co-active persuasion is rooted in the Greco-Roman democratic tradition, in Judeo-Christian conceptions of the brotherhood of man, in Emerson's faith in human educability, in John Stuart Mill's conviction that truth will survive any open competition of ideas, and in the writings of countless others. Militants, by contrast, are inclined to be mistrustful of ordinary citizens or to assume that the systems they oppose are likely to be intractable. With Marx, they are apt to believe that the masses have lost sight of their "real" interests or that those in power are unlikely to surrender it willingly. Although Machiavelli wrote for princes and not for protestors, the militant is inclined to accept that writer's view of persuasion as an adjunct to force rather than its alternative. Likewise, the militant would probably go along with Henry James when he wrote that "Life *is*, in fact, a battle. Evil is insolent and strong; beauty enchanting but rare; goodness very apt to be weak, folly very apt to be defiant; wickedness to carry the day; imbeciles to be in great places, people of sense in small, and mankind generally unhappy."

This is not to say that militants offer no appeals to shared values. They do, indeed, but in ways that call into question other widely held values. In general, the militant tends to express greater degrees of dissatisfaction (Stewart, Smith, and Denton, 1984). Whereas the moderate tends to ask "how" questions, the militant asks "whether" questions. Whereas the moderate sees "inefficiencies" in existing practices, the militant sees "inequities." Whereas the moderate might regard authority figures as "misguided" though "legitimate," the militant would tend to regard these same figures as "willfully self-serving" and "illegitimate." Whereas both might pay homage to law, the militant is more apt to derogate human laws in the name of "higher" laws. Thus, for example, some anti-abortionists have interpreted biblical writ as justification for bombings of abortion clinics.

The actions of militants are not all of a piece by any means. The practice of classic civil disobedience, for example, borders on being intermediate between militancy and moderacy. To test the constitutionality of a law, that law is violated. However, the law in question is violated openly and nonviolently, no other laws are breached in the process, the rights of innocent persons are not interfered with, and, if found guilty, the law violator willingly accepts punishment. Contrast this strategy with acts that can more clearly be labeled combative in nature: confrontational acts, strikes, boycotts, riots, political bombings and kidnappings—all the way to organized guerrilla warfare. By means of verbal polemics and direct action techniques, protestors who practice combative persuasion threaten, harass, cajole, disrupt, provoke, intimidate, coerce. Al-

Two views of abortion. *(Ira Wyman/Sygma)*

though the aim of pressure tactics may be to punish directly (strikes, boycotts), more frequently they are forms of "body rhetoric," designed to dramatize issues, enlist additional sympathizers, delegitimize the established order, and— except in truly revolutionary situations—force reconsideration of existing laws and practices, or pave the way for negotiated settlements.

Indeed, even the most militant acts of protestors are likely to have rhetorical elements. At the very least, militants must establish the credibility of their threats and alter their target's perceptions of what is expedient under the circumstances. Beyond that, their symbolic acts of force may well engender support from those outside the movement, and even if they are not initially inclined to support the movement's programs, changes in their behavior produced by "forced compliance" might well lead them to modify their attitudes. Consider in this context the ghetto riots of the sixties. Many theories have been offered to account for these riots, some of them alleging that they were simply a form of entertainment, or that the rioters were interested only in what they could steal. Yet the evidence suggests that the rioters were fairly representative of the communities in which they lived; that they enjoyed widespread support from other residents; that riot targets were selective; and, most significantly, that the majority of riots occurred immediately following the assassination of

Martin Luther King (Fogelson, 1971; Skolnick, 1969). On this basis, those more in sympathy with the rioters characterized their acts as rhetorical. Whatever their intent, it is clear that the riots called attention to grievances, fostered community solidarity, and provided ammunition for lawmakers who had been pushing for antipoverty legislation. Coser (1967) has described the Watts uprising as a kind of "collective bargaining by riot."

Advantages and Disadvantages of Moderate and Militant Approaches

So different are the rhetorical conceptions of moderate and militant strategists that it strains the imagination to believe both approaches may work. Yet the decisive changes wrought by militant rhetorics on the left and the right in recent years give credence to the view that co-active persuasion is not the only alternative. Let us compare, in general terms, the strengths and limitations of moderate and militant approaches.

1. Militant tactics confer visibility on a movement; moderate tactics gain entry into decision centers. Because of their ethos of respectability, moderates are invited to participate in public deliberations (hearings, conferences, negotiating sessions) even after militants have occasioned those deliberations by prolonged and self-debilitating acts of protest.

2. For different reasons, militants and moderates must both be ambivalent about success and failures. Militants thrive on injustice and ineptitude displayed by their targets. Should the enemy fail to implement the movement's demands, militants find themselves vindicated ideologically, yet frustrated programmatically. Should some of the demands be met, they are in the paradoxical position of having to condemn them as palliatives. Moderates, by contrast, require tangible evidence that the larger structure is tractable in order to hold followers in line; yet too much success belies the movement's reason for being. Not uncommonly, militants and moderates escalate their demands when faced with the prospect of success, but this makes them vulnerable to charges of bad faith. Self-proclaimed militants can avoid this problem by demanding at the outset considerably more than the system is willing to provide, but should self-proclaimed moderates do likewise, they invite charges of being "too militant."

3. Militant supporters are easily energized; moderate supporters are more easily controlled. Strong identification by members with the goals of a movement—however necessary to achieve *esprit de corps*—may foster the conviction that any means are justified and breed impatience with time-consuming tactics. The use of violence and other questionable means may be prompted further by restrictions on legitimate avenues of expression imposed by the larger structure. Such was the case, many have argued, with the Solidarity movement in Poland. Countering these pressures may require that the leaders mask the movement's true objectives, publicly disclaim the use of tactics they privately advocate, promise what they cannot deliver, exaggerate the strength of the movement, and so on. A vicious cycle develops in which militant tactics invite further suppression, which spurs the movement on to more extreme methods.

Having aroused their following, however, the leaders of a militant movement may become victims of their own creation, unable to contain energies within prescribed limits or to guarantee their own tenure.

On the other hand, leaders of moderate groups frequently complain that their supporters are apathetic. As Turner and Killian (1957) have pointed out: "To the degree to which a movement incorporates only major sacred values its power will be diffused by a larger body of conspicuous lip-service adherents who cannot be depended upon for the work of the movement" (p. 337).

4. Militants are effective with power-vulnerables; moderates are effective with power-invulnerables; neither is effective with both. Targets of protest may be labeled as power-vulnerables to the degree to which (a) they hold possessions of value and therefore have something to lose (for example, property, status, high office); (b) they cannot escape from a source's pressure (unlike suburbanites, for example, who could escape, physically or psychologically, from the ghetto riots of the sixties); (c) they cannot retaliate against a source (either because of normative or physical constraints). Such targets as university presidents, church leaders, and elected government officials are highly vulnerable—especially if they profess to be "high-minded" or "liberal"—compared to the mass of citizens who may lack substantial possessions, be able to escape, or feel no constraints about retaliating.

As leaders of institutions allocate priorities in the face of conflicting pressures from other groups, they are unlikely to act on the programmatic suggestions of protest groups—even when they are sympathetic—unless pressured to do so. Hence, co-active strategies alone are likely to be ineffectual with them, whereas combative strategies should stand a better chance of modifying their attitudes. On the other hand, combative strategies are likely to be less effective with power-invulnerables than co-active strategies, and they might well invite backlash effects. Where the movement and the larger structure are already polarized, the dilemma is magnified. However much they may wish to plead reasonably, wresting changes from those in public positions requires that leaders build a sizable power base. And to secure massive internal support, leaders must at least *seem* militant.

Intermediate Strategies

It should be clear that in choosing between co-active and combative strategies of persuasion, the protest leader faces a series of dilemmas: neither approach is likely to meet every rhetorical requirement nor resolve every rhetorical problem; indeed, the introduction of either approach may create new problems.

So it is that the leadership of a protest movement may attempt to resolve or avoid the aforementioned dilemmas by employing intermediate strategies, admittedly a catchall term for those efforts that combine militant and moderate patterns of influence. They may alternate between appeals to common ground and threats of punishment, or speak softly in private and stridently at mass gatherings. They may form broadly based coalitions that submerge ideological differences or utilize speakers with similar values but contrasting styles. They may stand as "conservative radicals" or "radical conservatives," espousing extreme demands in the value language of the social order or militant slogans in behalf of moderate proposals. In defense of moderacy, they may portray themselves as brakemen holding back more militant followers.

Intermediacy can be a dangerous game. Calculated to energize supporters, win over neutrals, pressure power-vulnerables, and mollify the opposition, it may end up antagonizing everyone. The turned phrase may easily appear as a devilish trick, the rationale as a rationalization, the tactful comment as an artless dodge. To the extent that strategies of intermediacy require studied ambiguity, insincerity, and even distortion, perhaps the leaders' greatest danger is that others will find out what they *really* think.

Still, some strategists manage to reconcile differences between militant and moderate approaches and not simply maneuver around them. They seem able to convince the established order that bad-tasting medicine is good for it and seem capable, too, of mobilizing a diverse collectivity within the movement. The key, it would appear, is the leader's capacity to embody a higher wisdom, a more profound sense of justice: to stand above inconsistencies by articulating overarching principles. Few will contest the claim that Martin Luther King, Jr., epitomized the approach. Attracting both militants and moderates to his movement, King could win respect, even from his enemies, by reconciling the seemingly irreconcilable. The heart of the case for intermediacy was succinctly stated by King himself: "What is needed," he said, "is a realization that power without love is reckless and abusive and love without power is sentimental and anemic. Power at its best is love implementing the demands of justice, and justice at its best is power correcting everything that stands against love."

The major protest movements of the sixties all seemed to require combinations of militant and moderate approaches. Militants were counted upon to dramatize the Vietnam issue, moderates to plead forcefully within inner circles. Threats of confrontation prompted city and state governments to finance the building of new schools in ghetto areas, but it took reasonableness and civility to get experienced teachers to volunteer for work in those facilities. Demands by revolutionary student groups for transformations of university structures helped impel administrators to heed quasi-militant demands for a redistribution of university power. Support for the cause by moderate groups helped confer respectability on the movement. Thus, however much they might have warred among themselves, militants and moderates each performed important functions.

A Brief Look at the "Expressive" Alternative

As indicated earlier, many young people believe that neither militant nor moderate (nor intermediate) approaches to protest are realistic. Yet if asked whether they sought significant changes in society's institutions, they would respond affirmatively and might even label themselves "revolutionaries." Proponents of the approach include many holistic health people, gay liberationists, back-to-nature advocates, and others concerned fundamentally with matters of life style. An important component of the viewpoint is the doctrine of expressivism, a kind of "anti-rhetorical rhetoric." Although I am by no means convinced that the approach can be applied to all arenas of protest, I recognize it as a viable approach to some issues and believe that its proponents offer a significant critique of conventional approaches to protest. Here is a brief summary of the position as it has been argued.

In their preoccupation with strategies of persuasion, militants and moderates are really barking up the wrong tree. Institutions do not change until people change, and people do not change as a result of the machinations of movement strategists. They change when an idea is ripe for the times, and when they have come to that idea as a result of direct personal experiences. Amitai Etzioni (1972) speaks of an "iron law of sociology that states that the fate of all popular movements is determined by forces they do not control" (p. 35). He is probably not too far from the truth.

In point of fact, moderates and militants are really cut from the same cloth, and most ironically, they are not very different from the social order they seek to change. Scratch at the source of our society's ills and you will find a set of dehumanizing values that are also reflected in conventional protest groups. Like the society at large, moderate and militant leaders scheme, manipulate, exploit—even their own followers. And when they get caught up in their own manipulations, their only solution is to manipulate some more. Ultimately it is a self-defeating mentality because, in addition to dominating other people and the surrounding physical environment, protest leaders begin to think of their cause as a set of cold abstractions.

That is why life-style movements are truly revolutionary. Their target is not so much particular laws or practices, but the values giving rise to society's institutions. Only when these values are changed can the institutions of our society be changed.

The alternative to conventional strategies, then, is an honest, unstructured, leaderless, nonmanipulative exchange of ideas and feelings among people, as exemplified by consciousness-raising sessions among women or meditation groups among Eastern religionists. It is not simply a compromise between the way of the moderate and the way of the militant, but a genuine alternative.

So much for the expressionist approach. While this is not the place for a full-scale debate over its merit, we should at least consider some counter arguments:

1. It is not necessarily true that institutions do not change until the masses of people change. It was shown earlier, in fact, that the reverse may occur: Changes in behavior compelled by new laws or edicts may lead to changes in the public's attitudes.
2. While it is true that claims of success by the leaders of conventional movements are frequently overstated, it is also true that movements of this kind have exerted considerable influence in recent years. Witness, for example, the substantial triggering and catalytic effects of the civil rights movement. If anything, these movements could have profited from greater attention to matters of rhetorical strategy.

3. It is true that the leaders of moderate and militant movements tend to be manipulative, and in this sense no different from "exploiters" in the larger society. There is great danger in this, especially if power considerations come to outweigh all others. But just as one movement may lose sight of its values, another may become so preoccupied with value questions that it becomes impotent. The question is one of balance, and here proponents of expressivism are faced with the same conflicts among rhetorical requirements as conventional movements.

SUMMARY

A social conflict is a clash over incompatible interests in which one party's relative gain is another's relative loss. Conflicts are not simply misunderstandings, semantic confusions, or communication breakdowns; nor are they disagreements, differences of opinion, or controversies—they are always something *more than that*. Divergent interests are at stake, interests important to one or both parties.

At the same time, however, that the antagonists are prompted to oppose each other, they also find it necessary to cooperate with each other. Hence the use of co-active persuasion in these *mixed-motive* conflicts, combined with the marshaling and occasional deployment of power resources.

The focus of this chapter has been on the relative costs and benefits of alternative ways of responding to various types of conflict. Conflicts between power equals are called *symmetrical* conflicts; they are typified by the Prisoner's Dilemma game. Conflicts between unequals are *asymmetrical;* by definition, they involve one party who is one-up in the relationship and another who is one-down. For long-term symmetrical conflicts, we saw that Rapoport's *tit-for-tat* approach was most workable, at least in the context of the PD game. We also examined ways of dealing with conflict and hostility that reduce the likelihood of *lose-lose* outcomes. For asymmetrical conflicts, we focused in particular on the plight of one-down, low-power persons and identified a range of alternatives for them, including assertive refusals of cooperation, loss of control techniques, coalition formation, and harassment. In the course of the discussion of types of conflict, we saw that there were recurrent *actor-oriented* and *system-oriented* patterns of response to conflict, each constituting a distinct rhetorical genre.

We moved then to a detailed comparison of co-active and combative persuasion as means by which protest movements may secure institutional change. As applied to protest movements, these terms actually refer to a range of choice on a continuum from ultramoderate to ultramilitant. Moderates and militants differ in terms of the degree to which they are willing to work within the system, the scope and intensity of the "devils" they attack, and the extent to which they rely on appeals to common ground or, on the other hand, find it necessary to bolster appeals and arguments with displays of power or delegitimizing techniques such as confrontation. Perhaps the fundamental difference between the two is in terms of orientation. Whereas co-active persuaders assume or pretend to assume an ultimate identity of interests between the movement and its antagonists, militants act on the assumption of a fundamental clash of interests. Since most conflicts are of the mixed-motive variety, involving combinations of common and conflicting interests, each can lay claim to a part of the truth.

Choosing between moderate and militant approaches is far from easy. Militant tactics confer visibility on the movement and open the doors for negotiation, but it is the moderate who frequently gains entry into the actual negotiations. Militant supporters are easily energized; moderate supporters are more easily controlled. Militants are effective with power-vulnerables; moderates are effective with power-invulnerables; neither is effective with both. Some movements attempt to combine the attractive features of moderate and militant approaches by use of intermediate strategies. Other movements have looked askance at both moderate and militant approaches and have sought to develop alternative strategies that are essentially *expressive* in nature. In general, I would not recommend the use of combative strategies *unless* more moderate methods have been found wanting, the situation requires immediate and drastic action, and there is strong likelihood that these strategies will be at least partially successful.

EXERCISES

1. Do a case study of persuasion in a social conflict of your own choosing. Drawing on concepts introduced in this chapter, characterize the conflict by type, nature of participants, modes of influence employed, patterns of escalation, and so on. How was persuasion different in this conflict than it would have been had the conflicting parties been engaged in a mere difference of opinion? Had you been one (or both) of the interactants, what would you have done differently?

2. The following case study, presented by novelist Lois Gould (1973), first appeared in *Ms. Magazine*. On the surface, it concerns a problem of bedmaking. Ms. Gould's husband gets up after she does and hastily tosses the covers back on the bed—a practice she finds extremely annoying.

The immediate question for Ms. Gould is how to get her husband to make the bed unlumpily. However, she realizes that lumpily made beds are often symptomatic of the larger question of who is to have what power in the relationship. Her "rhetorical analysis" of her husband's behavior is as follows:

I. My husband's habitual act is symbolic in nature.
　　A. He is competent to make the bed unlumpily.
　　　　1. He made his own bed in the army.
　　　　2. He made his own bed in camp.
　　　　3. He taught his children to make their beds neatly.
　　　　4. Skills like these do not rust from disuse.
　　B. He has as much time to make unlumpy beds as I do.
　　C. He, as much as I, cares that the house is kept neat.
　　D. Only with great reluctance did he begin making the bed at all.
II. The act symbolizes an interest in perpetuating power and privilege.
　　A. Before acceding (with great fanfare) to my request that he make the bed at all, he offered the following arguments:

    1. Who makes the bed is unimportant.

    2. Making the bed would make me late for work.

    3. You do it faster and more efficiently.

    4. Why don't you hire a maid?

B. Once he gave in, he said "There, I made the bed for you."

C. If confronted over the bed's lumpiness, he would probably say:

    1. "What, for that matter, is a decent bed?"

    2. Why are you getting hung up on household sociology?

    3. Surely, you have better things to do than carp at me, now that you don't have to make the bed.

D. These arguments give contextual meaning to the lumpy bed.

Viewed in context, the lumpy bed is a way of saying:

    1. I'm a very important person.

    2. You're not a very important person.

    3. I therefore have a right to dominate in this relationship.

What strategies of influence are most appropriate in situations like this? Discuss this case with others and ask yourself what Gould should have done. Suppose, as she reports, she had already tried a variety of strategies, including reviewing with her husband how beds ought to be made, demonstrating with iron-clad logic why her husband ought to make the bed properly, and outright pleading. What should she do next?

No doubt you have been in situations similar to this one. Write a brief description of the conflict and indicate how, in retrospect, you think you should have handled it.

   3. Keep a careful record of your behavior in conflicts that arise between you and intimate friends or relatives over a period of a week. Then analyze your behavior in terms of its costs and benefits. How often do you:

    a. Directly communicate your feelings on a matter

    b. Carp, blame, or ascribe motives of badness or madness

    c. Use such "loss of control" techniques as developing a physical symptom or claiming ignorance, innocence, or incompetence

    d. Pout or sulk when frustrated or charged with wrongdoing

    e. Seek common ground for possible compromises or reconciliations

    f. Compliment or humor as a way of defusing hostility

    g. Blame yourself and beg forgiveness

    h. Threaten punishments for noncompliance

    i. Promise rewards for compliance

    j. Objectify or intellectualize the conflict, as though feelings were irrelevant to the matter

   4. Analyze the rhetoric of a social movement using concepts introduced in this chapter.

Part Three
Analysing Persuasion

We may think of the critic in a sense as a prism: filtering, defining and analyzing the light shed by a rhetorical event. Not only the light but the prism itself is an object of rhetorical interest. As the prism turns, different colors and shades are brought to our attention, each having a single source but each so fused in the single source that only the prism may articulate it. On the other hand, the critic is not an inanimate object, like a prism, with only the capacity for passive reflection. The critic's humanity is necessarily inherent in his work. His critical act is constituted of and by his choices and judgments.

From the Report of the Committee on the
Advancement and Refinement of Rhetorical Criticism
(Bitzer and Black, 1971, p. 224)

Chapter *14*
Doing Rhetorical Criticism

Why is it that Lincoln's Gettysburg Address is so memorable? If you were to give that speech, how would you do it differently? Would Ibsen's *A Doll's House* be any better if it were less rhetorical? What do first-grade primers tell us about sex-role stereotypes in our culture? Is there a predictable pattern in concession speeches by candidates who lose elections? Is there really a consistent relationship between the number of footnotes in a scientific article and its chances of being published? Why is it that so many people fall for Bayer Aspirin advertisements? Since stylistic simplicity is so highly valued in our culture, how is it that Jesse Jackson is able to get away with a highly ornate style?

Each of these questions and thousands more like them constitute legitimate starting points for critical analyses of rhetorical happenings. Critics or analysts (I use the terms interchangeably) may be motivated by outrage at an apparent misuse of language or logic, or a pretension to objectivity that is belied by the facts. Their critical impulse may spring from a pragmatic interest in persuading others or in determining how others attempt to persuade them. They may have an irreverent streak and thus be inclined to demythify claims or claimants to universal truth. They may appreciate a rhetorical effort and want to know why it was so admirable. Or they may simply be puzzle-solvers by temperament who enjoy unraveling some of the mysteries of persuasion. In each case, they will attempt to make sense of the rhetorical act or event, either as an object of interest in its own right or because it helps illuminate some larger issue, problem, or theoretical question. Criticism serves consummatory functions when it stops at evaluation or explanation of a rhetorical effort. It performs instrumental functions when it focuses on persuasive discourse as case-study material in the service of a larger end such as theory-building or theory-testing.

It should be apparent that we have no choice but to be rhetorical critics if we are to function intelligently as consumers of persuasive communications; furthermore, postmortems on our own rhetorical efforts and on the efforts of others can help sharpen our skills as practitioners of persuasion. The motive for criticism need not be selfish, of course, and in fact the best criticism speaks to a wide audience. Focusing on a significant rhetorical object or issue, it corroborates commonplace observations, or makes the nonobvious apparent, or provides justification for an evaluation or theoretical interpretation. In all cases, it does more than describe a work or the critic's gut reaction to it. Like the objects of their analyses, critics are themselves persuaders with cases to present and defend. We may not entirely agree with the analysis, but we must respect it if the case has been well argued.

You ought to try your hand at writing rhetorical critiques or analyses, if for no other reason than that the act of applying principles covered in this book will help you better assimilate them. This chapter and the two chapters that follow offer suggestions on how to proceed, as well as sample analyses. Featured in this chapter are critical applications of the requirements-problems-strategies framework (RPS) introduced in Chapter 5.

Choosing a Topic or Question

The critic has wide latitude in terms of topic selection. The object of analysis may be written or oral, verbal, or nonverbal. It may be a historical remnant that has enduring significance, or a contemporary event of ephemeral interest. The critical analysis may be confined to a speaker or speech or even to a segment of a speech. On the other hand, it may extend to a comparison of speakers or speeches, or to an entire campaign or movement, or to an identification of rhetorical patterns in a form or genre of persuasion such as public service advertising or debate in Congress.

Depending on the scope of the project, you might fasten on minute details or paint the rhetorical canvas with broad brushstrokes. Microscopic analysis can often help us to discover meanings in commonplace objects that had previously gone unnoticed. Here, for example, is Lloyd Brown's (1974) analysis of a simple billboard advertisement:

> The scene is Main Street, Any City, U.S.A. The likeness of Colonel Sanders beams benevolently down on snarled traffic from a large, well-lit billboard which he shares with the inevitable bucket of Kentucky Fried Chicken and with an eye-catching phrase in bold lettering. "Woman's Liberation." Once again, the motivation seems straightforward enough—a very popular talking-point becomes the huckster's attention-getter. But note, too, how subtly significant shifts and distortions in images and language have simultaneously effected a selling pitch on the ideological level. "Women's Liberation"—the collectivist associations of the original phrase have been replaced by an individual emphasis that evokes "freedom." And, equally important, the exhortatory and prophetic connotations of the origi-

nal rallying cry have been shoved to the background of our consciousness by the concrete, three-dimensional presence of that imposing bucket: liberation is now, it is of the present, it is already here. The almost tangible physicality of the Colonel and his bucket is a reassurance of incontrovertible facts: the fact of Kentucky Fried Chicken restaurants, the fact of "secret recipes," "herbs," "spices," warm succulence, and not least, the established fact that the little woman has been "liberated" from the stove this evening—just as she has been freed from drudgery by all the gadgetry of a marvellous technological paradise. The gastronomic image confronts and transforms the feminist's rhetoric—no need for exhortatory threats and prophecies about liberation for "women"; "woman" is already a "liberated" individual, emancipated, enfranchised, and packaged like so many Kentucky fried breasts and legs for our (male) consumption. As for those who agitate for humanistic rather than merely physical liberation, the patriarchical features of the benign Colonel are a sufficient rejoinder—it is a man's world. (p.34)

You should find ample materials in this book to help guide your analysis. If it is *interpretive* criticism that you are engaged in, you might make use of one or another theory, model, or conceptual distinction presented earlier. For example, the RPS approach might be used in studying image-management techniques used by job applicants in hiring interviews or by job supervisors in handling employee grievances. Rank's model or Fishbein and Ajzen's theory might be used in analyzing product advertising campaigns. Schein's model of unfreezing and refreezing (to be discussed in Chapter 16) might be used to analyze the proselytizing efforts of a religious cult. Schön's observations on problem-setting and Watzlawick et al.'s model of reframing might be used in analyzing policy-oriented rhetoric. Deutsch's generalizations about patterns of destructive conflict could be brought to bear upon studies of interpersonal or intergroup conflicts. The comparison in Chapter 13 of moderate and militant styles of protest could be applied to contemporary social movements.

If you wish to go beyond interpretive analysis in providing an evaluation of a given work, you might apply, singly or in combination, standards of artistry or ethics. The test of *artistry* is how inventively the persuader adapted to a given situation. Note that this is not the same as asking whether a given message achieved its intended effect. That is less an evaluative issue than an interpretive one. It requires that we get actual evidence of effects—from surveys, election results, news reports, and the like. Evidence of effects may be brought to bear upon judgments of rhetorical artistry, but the latter, strictly speaking, is solely concerned with whether a message *ought* to have been effective, given what we know about the situation and about principles of persuasion appropriate to that situation. By that standard, a well-crafted but essentially unsuccessful speech presented under very trying circumstances (e.g., Edward Kennedy's speech on Chappaquiddick) might well be judged artistic, while another that succeeded despite itself would not. To derive inferences about what is rhetorically appropriate in a given situation, the critic often engages in generic analysis as well as analysis of unique situational characteristics.

Judgments of ethics are typically based on criteria of *soundness, self-*

consistency, or *social consequences*. Recall from Chapter 10 that soundness of argumentation is actually based on two subtests: Are the premises true? Does the conclusion follow from the premises? Here the critic evaluates the evidence presented in support of the premises, as well as the quality of reasoning displayed in the message. We know, of course, that perceptions of truthfulness and logical rigor depend not only on soundness of argumentation, but also on how well the persuader exploits the "resources of ambiguity" in language to create impressions of objectivity. Chapter 15 offers advice on analyzing ostensibly objective claims, both in terms of artistry and of soundness. It also illustrates applications of the next criterion to be introduced, *self-consistency*.

Advertisers, publicists, academics—persuaders of all kinds—often make claims about themselves and their rhetoric that they do not, perhaps cannot, live up to. The critic is then in a position to hoist the persuader by his or her own petard. The structure of self-consistency critiques is fairly straightforward. To make a case, the debunker begins by citing the persuader's publicly stated claims to purity. This persuader claims that her discourse is purely objective. That persuader claims his administration has only the students' interests at heart. That persuader purports to be interested only in the esthetics of her art, and not in how others see it. Next, the critic sets forth criteria for accepting or rejecting the persuader's claims. If the persuader is purely objective, for example, presumably there should be no distortion, concealment, or misrepresentation of factual data.

Applying these criteria, the critic now uses the persuader's own words to debunk her. Evidence is presented to show that she is not what she purports to be; that she has not only dealt in appearances, as any persuader does, but in illusions, deceptions, and hypocrisies. Frequently, the critic introduces a theatrical metaphor: Having looked at the public performance of the persuader, let us see what she is really like by going backstage. There we will discover that the exterior is only a façade.

The final criterion concerns long-term *social consequences*. I argued in Chapter 5 that advertisers, sitcom producers, and other purveyors of popular art and entertainment can hardly disclaim responsibility for the effects of their work on cultural values and stereotypes. Whether or not we hold communicators responsible for the social consequences of their actions, we may nevertheless attend carefully to those consequences and pronounce judgments on their utility for our society. Recall, for example, the discussion in Chapter 5 of gender displays in advertising. Sometimes it takes a series of messages to establish a pattern of ethically questionable persuasion. Feminist Erica Jong (1973) has assembled a revealing array of ad slogans and added commentary on their cumulative effects:

> "Be kind to your behind." "Blush like you mean it." "Love your hair." "Want a better body? We'll arrange the one you've got." "That shine on your face should come from him, not from your skin." "You've come a long way, baby." "How to score with every female in the universe." "The stars and sensual you." "To a man they say Cutty Sark." "A diamond is forever." "If you're concerned about

douching. . ." "Length and coolness come together." "How I solved my intimate odor problem." "Lady be cool." "Every woman alive loves Chanel No. 5." "What makes a shy girl get intimate?" "Femme, we named it after you."

What all the ads and all the whorescopes seemed to imply was that if only you were narcissistic *enough*, if only you took proper care of your smells, your hair, your boobs, your eyelashes, your armpits, your crotch, your stars, your scars, and your choice of scotch in bars—you would meet a beautiful, powerful, potent and rich man who would satisfy every longing, fill every hole, make your heart skip a beat (or stand still), make you misty and fly you to the moon (preferably on gossamer wings), where you would live totally satisfied forever. (p. 9)

Must rhetorical criticism be confined to paradigm cases of persuasion, such as those that have occupied most of our attention in this book? To the contrary, analyses of peripheral cases are often more rewarding. Here the critic can teach us something merely by showing *that* a given item or pattern of discourse is rhetorical. A critic can advance the thesis, for example, that ostensibly objective high school history textbooks tend to be rhetorical in the sense that they manifest a consistent ideological bias. Or that a poem we would ordinarily not regard as rhetorically inspired actually constitutes a plea for recognition by the author.

Where a given work is obviously rhetorical, the critic of peripheral cases can still perform a service by showing us *how* it persuades—how the illusion of scientific rigor is created in a dietary manual; how forms and colors are used to make a rhetorical statement in Picasso's *Guernica;* how theatrical devices are used to propagandize in Odets's *Waiting for Lefty.*

Virtually no human act or artifact need escape rhetorical attention, although it should be acknowledged that other perspectives on the object of analysis may be equally valid. A poem, for example, might be examined syntactically, or as a historical curiosity, or as an exemplar of literary form. None of these analyses would be rhetorical, however. *The rhetorician's distinctive task would be to examine the poem in terms of the implicit or explicit appeals and arguments it offers and its potential or actual effects on particular audiences.* A report of a Speech Communication Task Force on rhetorical criticism (in Bitzer and Black, 1971) made this same point when it argued that rhetorical criticism was definable not in terms of any special object of study, but in terms of the special set of lenses worn by the rhetorician (p. 220). In this way, too, it is distinguishable from syntactical analysis, historical analysis, literary criticism, or what any of a number of other disciplines might do by way of analyzing a human act or artifact.

Because rhetorical criticism has a way of growing like topsy, you should probably bite off less than you think you can chew. Rather than examining every speech made by your favorite politician, try focusing on one speech, or perhaps on a small segment of it. The remainder of this chapter offers suggestions on using generic analysis for purposes of assessing rhetorical artistry. Featured, as promised, is the RPS approach.

Assessing Rhetorical Artistry: Kennedy at Chappaquiddick

One week after the drowning of Mary Jo Kopechne at Chappaquiddick, Senator Edward Kennedy went before the American people to explain his role in the tragic affair. The speech, delivered July 25, 1969, on all three major networks, is of a type known as the *apologia*, discussed in Chapter 3. Recall that speeches of this type are designed to defend public personages against charges of wrongdoing. In identifying the speech as an example of a given genre, we have an immediate clue to its purpose and to what might be appropriate in situations of that type. At least we know how others have handled like situations.

A copy of the Kennedy speech is presented on pages 294–297. Your assessment of Kennedy's rhetorical artistry should probably begin with an analysis of factors extrinsic to the speech text itself: the historical context, the audience, the immediate occasion, and the speaker's goals and aspirations. How had the news media reported and characterized the sequence of events leading up to the speech? What did people know (or think they knew) about these events, and how much interest had the events aroused? In particular, what competing "theories" or collective impressions had been built up in the public's mind about Kennedy's role in the Kopechne drowning? What did the general public think of Kennedy, both before and after Chappaquiddick? Was he trusted? respected? liked? envied? feared? What was his standing among state and national politicians? What prompted the speech at that time? Was his own explanation of the sequence of events coming under increasing scrutiny? And what of the future? To what extent, for example, did Kennedy's long-range political ambitions influence his speech purposes and strategies?

The second step is message-centered and involves a preliminary assessment of the speech in light of the nature of the situation. In formulating an initial assessment of the speech, ask yourself what Kennedy could have done under the circumstances. Among the options Ware and Linkugel (1973) identify for the apologia are *denial* ("I didn't do it"), *differentiation* ("I did it, but I didn't intend it"), *bolstering* ("Look also at the good things I've done"), and *transcendence* ("Let's look at my actions in a larger context than merely one of guilt or innocence"). Other theorists name options of *ignoring the charges* and of *accusing the accusers*, perhaps impugning their motives for bringing the charges. Clearly not all these strategies would have been appropriate in this case.

From an examination of the speech itself, we may gain additional insights into the speaker's motives and stylistic decisions. Billed as a "Statement to the People of Massachusetts," the speech was aired on national television. Does this suggest additional motives for its delivery? By constituting his audience as the people of Massachusetts, was Kennedy attempting to get the entire nation to accept their verdict as *its* own, knowing full well that a "jury" of his own direct constituents would be most sympathetic? Was his self-portrayal particularly well suited to the largely Roman Catholic "jury" that resides in Massachusetts—a Joblike character seeking absolution from bad acts (venial sins), but adamantly insisting on what the theology values most: good intentions? The brevity of the speech befitted a man who was too traumatized by an event to discuss it at length. But was it too concise—suggesting a possible coverup?

Before rendering a final assessment of the speech, you might search also for tangible evidence of effects of the speech and reasons for those effects. An examination of newspapers and magazines from the period might reveal, for example, that thousands of letters of support flowed in from Kennedy's constituents; that Kennedy held his own among newspaper columnists; that the general public reacted sympathetically, especially to Kennedy's references to his long-suffering family; that Kennedy continued to stand well among Democratic politicians and retained a high popularity rating in the Gallup polls. But, on the other hand, years after the event most people still believed his chances of becoming president had been hurt by Chappaquiddick and investigative reporters were still raising serious questions about it.

With this evidence in hand, try now to present a reasoned evaluation of the speech. Indicate not only why you think it was artistic or inartistic, but what the speaker could have done to improve the speech, given the circumstances.

An Illustration of the RPS Approach: Jimmy Carter's 1980 Acceptance Speech

The requirements-problems-strategies approach involves much the same considerations as those discussed above in connection with the Kennedy speech, but it also offers a way of bringing greater structure and clarity to analyses of a message. Its focus, as you will recall, is on how strategies are adapted to problems growing out of the unique nature of the persuader's situation, as well as conflicting rhetorical requirements that inhere in messages of a given generic type. (Review the discussion of RPS in Chapter 6 before reading the analysis that follows.)

As a final illustration of the RPS framework, we apply it to the genre of the presidential acceptance speech and, more specifically, to Jimmy Carter's presidential acceptance speech before the Democratic National Convention at Madison Square Garden in New York, August 14, 1980. A copy of the speech is found on pp. 297–306. From what we know about the typical situational context for speeches of this kind, we can begin to formulate rhetorical requirements.

Requirements

We know, for example, that the nominee's ultimate goal is to win in November and that, to do so, he will need all the help he can get from within and outside his party. We know too that the acceptance speech is scheduled as the culmination of the convention proceedings and that the convention itself occurs at a symbolically significant transitional point between the highly conflictual presidential primaries and the upcoming election contest. From these facts alone,

Carter giving his acceptance speech. *(UPI/Bettmann Newsphotos)*

it should be possible to begin our list of rhetorical requirements.

In his acceptance speech, the nominee should attempt to heal the wounds of battle within the party. Differences in outlook that might have threatened to divide the party must now be submerged and subordinated to principles of unity and loyalty and sacrifice. The nominee must make conciliatory gestures to adversaries and enlist their cooperation for the battle ahead. He must remind them that his opponents, and their opponents, are now outside the party rather than within. And he must sound the themes that will be echoed in the months ahead—themes that can provide a rallying cry for the party faithful; themes that can also appeal to opinion leaders and ordinary citizens outside the party.

We know too that the acceptance speech has a significant ritual component to it, growing out of a long tradition. There are the balloons and the placard-waving and the dancing in the aisles after the nominee has been introduced as "The next President of the United States." And there are the nominee's gestures of appreciation, his call for quiet, and his opening words of thanks to the delegates and of tribute to the party and to its past leaders. At ceremonial events in general, speakers have an excellent opportunity to display themselves favorably by the manner in which they perform the appropriate rituals. As the nominees go through the motions of evoking their party's traditions at this event, they will be attempting to look and sound presidential.

We know also that the acceptance speech is televised to many millions of people. That the speech will be heard by a significant cross-section of the populace represents a great opportunity, but it also poses something of a challenge, for we know in general that what pleases some audience segments will inevitably alienate others. One consequence of acceptance speeches being televised should be a slight modification of the rituals. For example, instead of invoking only the memories of past leaders from within one's own party, now the nominees should quote past heroes of both major parties in an effort to appeal to a broader spectrum of opinion.

But the acceptance speaker still must persist in giving primary attention to his convention audience because of the curious relationship between the convention audience and the larger television audience. Many in the television audience, particularly those with little involvement in politics, will probably take their cues about how well the nominee is doing from their assessment of the convention audience's assessment. We know that the television networks frequently assist the viewer by showing pictures of reactions to the speech by those in attendance at the convention. Thus the presidential nominee must play to the smaller convention audience because of its influence on the larger television audience.

This, then, is an illustration of what we can learn about what a persuader must do from an assessment of situation alone. This assessment contains some hypotheses that probably ought to be checked against studies comparing actual speeches (Hart, 1984; Ritter, 1980). But even assuming that no such studies were available, we might still feel confident in formulating prescriptive rules for the genre on the basis of our situation-based theoretical assessment. Here is a capsule summary of requisite functions and subfunctions emerging from that assessment:

1. Healing the wounds of battle within the party
   a. Enlisting the cooperation of former opponents
   b. Redirecting energies toward the new "enemy"
   c. Looking and sounding like the leader of the entire party
2. Preparing party activists for the upcoming campaign
   a. Identifying themes around which party stalwarts can mobilize
   b. Inspiring effort and dedication
   c. Looking and sounding like a winner
3. Winning the support of opinion leaders and ordinary citizens outside the party
   a. Articulating campaign themes that have broad-based appeal
   b. Impressing the television audience that the "live" convention audience has been duly impressed
   c. Looking and sounding "presidential"

This list provides a set of benchmarks for rhetorical analysis of any given acceptance speech, but it ought not to be a stopping point for the analyst. With

Ritter (1980), for example, the critic might note that the burdens for the acceptance speech fall somewhat differently upon the incumbent president than upon his challenger. Carter had a White House record to defend. He could no longer attack the "mess in Washington" as he had done in 1976. The challenger, on the other hand, has to convince people that he is sufficiently experienced to perform the job competently. Carter had to fulfill other rhetorical requirements as well which were unique to his situation, but these can be identified as we move to the second stage of application of the RPS framework: problem identification.

Problems

The rhetorical problems of persuaders consist of competing pressures arising from the need to fulfill conflicting rhetorical requirements and other constraints on goal accomplishment that stem from characteristics of the persuader, audience, topic, or occasion. Having a clear grasp of these problems makes the rhetorical choices of persuaders more comprehensible and provides grounds for evaluating alternative message strategies.

Many of the competing pressures on the presidential acceptance speaker are already implicit in the foregoing analysis, but these and other cross-pressures need to be identified in greater detail, as they apply to the particular case. As you have seen, the acceptance speaker has to perform multiple roles as party leader, election campaigner, and dignified statesman. These roles may not be entirely harmonious, and they were not in Carter's case. For, in attempting to placate opponents within his own party, he risked humiliating himself in the eyes of the voters.

For each such role, moreover, there are the familiar problems of balancing ethics and effectiveness, long-range versus short-range objectives, the need for flexibility and the need to appear consistent. Having cultivated an image of truthfulness and consistency, would Carter create unwittingly an image of insincerity and inconsistency by shifting from positions previously taken to those that might have greater appeal in the upcoming campaign? Or, in hewing uncompromisingly to positions previously taken, would he leave voters with an impression of inflexibility, thus endangering his reelection chances even more?

Compounding these problems is the fact of having to deal with multiple audiences. The Democratic party is heterogeneous enough—a loose and uncomfortable amalgam of forces that includes "boll weevil" conservatives from the South, northern liberals, feminists, blacks, Hispanics, the remnants of a blue-collar, Catholic constituency, retirees, and other such voting blocs. Appealing *through* representatives of these groups to a larger and even more diverse television audience is a rhetorical nightmare. It is no wonder that Carter looked and sounded nervous as he appeared before the podium. At one point, his intended reference to that "great man who should have been president" became "Hubert Horatio Hornblower," rather than "Hubert Horatio Humphrey." This, quite clearly, was one ritual Carter did not handle appropriately.

Our knowledge of the rhetorical requirements for the acceptance speech genre helps point to the problems Carter faced, but it could not help us to predict their severity: his extraordinarily low approval rating as president; his inability to resolve the festering problems of inflation and of American hostages in Iran or to reverse the long-term trend toward conservatism in America. In crafting an effective oration, Carter was constrained further by the apparent popularity of his chief opponent—so much so that he rarely referred to Ronald Reagan by name, choosing instead to speak of "others," or of "the new leaders of the Republican party," or of "the Republican nominee."

But the chief problem for Jimmy Carter was in the person of his archrival for the nomination, Senator Kennedy. Kennedy had refused to capitulate during the primaries after it had become clear that Carter had the nomination sewn up. He had embarrassed Carter by coming on strong in the late primaries. He had demanded and received the opportunity to mold significant portions of the Democratic platform. And he had exploited the unusual occasion of a rival's speech to the delegates to upstage Carter with what everyone agreed was a brilliant oration, a simulacrum of the acceptance speech he would have given had he been nominated, and perhaps a model of the type of speech Carter himself should have given. Now Kennedy was demanding as the price of even token cooperation that Carter publicly plead for his support and register his endorsement of those portions of the Democratic platform with which Kennedy was most identified.

I suggested earlier that the acceptance speaker must enlist the cooperation of past opponents. This, it should now be clear, is not always easy. Kennedy had good reason for remaining distant. Carter had scorned Kennedy in the past, even to the point of bragging to the media *before the primaries* that "I'm going to whip his ass." Kennedy, quite legitimately, was concerned lest the principles he stood for be abrogated. And he was anxious to preserve a power base for 1984 and beyond. Carter was aware that the price for cooperation from the Kennedy forces would be high. But how high?

Strategies

The Carter acceptance speech exhibits an argumentative structure common to other speeches of its type, which Ritter (1980) has labeled the *political jeremiad*. Like the religious jeremiads delivered during colonial times by Puritan preachers, the political jeremiad presents an image of America as having a special destiny and an image of the candidate and his party as having a special role in the fulfillment of that destiny. It draws sharp contrasts between "us" and "them," maintaining that the other party is responsible for much that is wrong with America and that the election of their choice of candidates would lead America further astray from its divinely inspired mission. The election, then, is a Judgment Day, a critical moment in history when, from the vantage point of the "in-party" nominee, the people must decide between a continuation of the progress made by the party toward fulfillment of America's historic purposes, or a retrogression paralleling the fall from grace that occurred when the opposing party was last in power.

That Carter should have opted for a political jeremiad made good strategic sense. Its use was consonant with audience expectations for occasions of this type and was particularly well suited to the public's image of Carter as a deeply religious man. Most listeners would no doubt have judged Carter as sincere when, in the characteristically religious vocabulary of the political jeremiad, he described his experience as a political campaigner as "a total immersion in the human reality of America."

The question, however, is the manner in which Carter constructed his jeremiad. The speech was long—much longer than Reagan's and much longer than most speeches of its kind. For the largest part of the speech, Carter provided numerous one- or two-line contrasts between Democrats and Republicans, preferring evidently to appeal separately to each voting bloc within the Democratic party, rather than hammering away at a few unifying themes. This contributed to the excessive length of the speech and probably was responsible for the obvious lapses of attention among many in the convention hall.

Moreover, the overall form of Carter's "cafeteria" approach stresses a difference between "two futures," with Carter playing the dual roles of campaigner and prophet. That Carter should have chosen to contrast futures rather than actual records of accomplishment was understandable, given his low ratings at the polls. But by the same token, his low credibility, combined with his obvious biases as a candidate, should have made his vision of the future somewhat suspect.

I question, too, whether Carter should have avoided attacking Ronald Reagan by name. Reagan was popular, but he was also vulnerable to attack as an actor and political extremist. Surely the occasion of an acceptance speech at a political convention permits, even encourages, hard-hitting personal attacks. And surely the Democrats needed someone to rally against if they could not find someone to rally around. Remember too that many in the television audience would be judging Carter's speech by the reaction it received from those present at the convention. The convention audience would react favorably to a biting attack by Carter, as they had to Kennedy's attack.

That Carter's attack on Reagan was muted was part of the overall hesitant tone of the speech. In place of crisp comparisons that would project an image of decisiveness, Carter drew out his sentences, often selecting two nearly synonymous terms in place of a single well-chosen one. Carter found it necessary, for example, to question the "commitments and policies" of his opponent as though policies did not entail commitments. He pledged defense increases that would be "prudent and rational," as though a prudent increase could ever be irrational.

Carter's murky tone is nowhere more evident than in his references to Kennedy. In this, the most crucial moment of the speech, Carter could have brought the audience to its feet with an eloquent plea for Kennedy's support. The salute to Kennedy need not have been exaggerated, but it should not have been garbled—as Carter's was. Carter first places Kennedy in the company of an also-ran, Governor Jerry Brown, a tactic unlikely to win the hearts of the Kennedy people. His subsequent references are complimentary, but they lack zing. Kennedy is said to be a "tough competitor and a superb campaigner"— note the redundancy once more. After praising Kennedy's speech before the convention—again in multiple terms—Carter declared himself to be "reaching out" to Kennedy and his supporters, as though the fact of his appealing for their support needed to be announced and not just demonstrated. The next lines are trite and perhaps a bit condescending. Carter himself, and not simply the party, needs Kennedy's "idealism and . . . dedication working for us." And, in an allusion to Kennedy's continuing presidential ambitions, "there is no doubt that even greater service lies ahead of you." He then follows these cliché expressions with the vaguest possible images of America's future—"good life," "secure nation," "just society," and so on, to which he and Kennedy are committed and which presumably warrant their forming a "partnership" together. The reference to a partnership founded on a shared commitment to vague generalities would be self-deprecating were it believable, but it surely is not believable.

I conclude that Carter failed to respond appropriately to the demands of the situation. Carter appealed for the support of his former opponent, but he did so unconvincingly. He directed energies away from past conflicts within the party, but he did not provide a credible object to rally around or against. He neither sounded like a winner, nor made Reagan sound like a loser. In attempting to mobilize party stalwarts, Carter sounded too many themes. In attempting to win over the highly heterogeneous television audience, he spread himself too thin. Carter was ultimately done in by the problem of image. In attempting to overcome his initial image problems, he probably compounded them by sounding defensive, indecisive, and unconfident.

A Final Comment: On Writing the Critical Analysis

"Whatever else it may be," insists Wayne Brockriede (1974, p. 165), "*useful* rhetorical criticism . . . must function as an argument." Where scientific methods such as content analysis are employed, the weight of the argument is carried substantially, though not entirely, by the hard data presented. But what of the critic who subjectively interprets or evaluates a given work or derives implications for theory from a single case? Here the eye of the critic is not simply a camera lens that reflects the light cast by the rhetorical object, but a complex prism that refracts it in idiosyncratic ways. How does the artistic critic get us to see what he or she sees, and more than that, to accept his or her vision of the symbolic reality as valid or correct?

The answer, it seems apparent, has something to do with linguistic sensitivity. Like any other persuader, the critic has functions to perform of a rather mundane nature. The introduction must identify a topic or thesis and justify it as significant. Orienting materials must be provided in the form of background information, previews or partitions, definitions and explanations. Attention and interest must be captured and sustained throughout. The body of the essay must be structured strategically and clearly. Arguments must be offered and evidence adduced in support of them. And in the conclusion the critic must tie things together, summarizing major generalizations offered within the body of the critique and suggesting possible implications and applications.

But these bare bones of the critical essay in no way hint at the communication

skills required of the artistic critic. We get a better glimpse of the art of
criticism when we see good critics at work at the task of re-creating the
rhetorical event for their readers. Here critics offer more than a scorecard of
players and acts; they order, yes, but in ways that lead inexorably to the
inferences and judgments they will be making. In Mailer's (1968) essay on the
tumultuous 1968 Democratic National Convention, the scene opens with a long
description of the Chicago stockyards. Page after page describes pigs taken to
be slaughtered and dragged howling through the assembly line. There we meet
Mailer's archtypical Chicagoan, a wide-nostriled, blood-stained ethnic who
resembles nothing so much as the animals he is butchering. Yet we learn soon
that Mailer respects these human carnivores: their wide nostrils were fashioned,
after all, to do the hard work of our society. Then the scene shifts to O'Hare
Airport, where delegates and demonstrators in support of Eugene McCarthy
are filing down the gangplank. Suddenly we see the inevitability of the violence
that was to erupt on the streets of Chicago that August. For McCarthy's
supporters are the paper-wielding, intellectual, narrow-nostriled denizens of
our society. Chicago, 1968, hints Mailer, is symbolized by the nostrils of its
antagonists. It is a tragic encounter because neither side can appreciate the
virtues of the other.

As in Mailer's essay, good artistic criticism uses metaphors as linguistic
economies. Global images are wrought from snatches of dialogue or from
nuances of gesture. Here, for example, is Garry Wills' (1974) description of
John Ehrlichman, a powerful figure in the Nixon administration who was now
defiantly standing trial in connection with the attempted theft of papers belonging
to Daniel Ellsberg's psychiatrist:

> While St. Clair implied at the Court that Presidents are above the law, John
> Ehrlichman was arguing at his own trial that the President's men are above it
> too. He came into the courtroom cocky with an assurance that had grown from
> the trial's first stage, when David Young proved to be an unimpressive witness
> for the prosecution. On the stand, Ehrlichman suffered a momentary catch of
> nervousness in his throat—and put that rebellious member in its place. Ostenta-
> tiously, he poured water and drank, ran it around his mouth, swallowed, drew
> his top lip up, ran tongue across teeth, adjusted his jaw line back and forth to
> the proper firmness, then raised his eyebrows at the jurors—a whole toilette in
> ten seconds. Here, clearly, was a man in charge. (p. 17)

Even as evidence of the effects of a message is presented, the skilled artistic
critic manages to avoid tedious accountings. Note, for example, how Marie
Nichols (in Scott and Brock, 1972) interweaves historical materials to create a
composite picture of immediate reactions by witnesses to Lincoln's first inaugural
address:

> As Lincoln read on, the audience listened respectfully, with "intense interest,
> amid a stillness almost oppressive." In the crowd behind the speaker sat Horace
> Greeley, momentarily expecting the crack of the fire. At one point he thought it
> had come. The speaker stopped. But it was only a spectator crashing down
> through a tree. Otherwise, the crowd in the grounds "behaved very well."

Buchanan sat listening, and "looking as straight as he could at the toe of his right boot." Douglas, close by on Lincoln's right, listened "attentively," showing that he was "apparently satisfied" as he "exclaimed, *sotto voce*, 'Good,' 'That's so,' 'No coercion,' and 'Good again.' " Chief Justice Taney did not remove his eyes from Mr. Lincoln during the entire delivery. Mr. Cameron stood with his back to the President, on the opposite side of Mr. Douglas, "peering off into the crowd." Senator Seward and the other Cabinet officers-elect "kept themselves in the background." Senator Wigfall of Texas, with folded arms, "leaned conspicuously in a Capitol doorway," listening to the inaugural, plainly wearing "contempt, defiance, derision, on his face, his pantomimic posture saying what he had said in the Senate, that the old Union was a corpse and the question was how to embalm it and conduct the funeral decently." Thurlow Weed moved away from the crowd, reporting to General Scott at the top of the slope, "The Inaugural is a success," as the old general exclaimed, "God be praised! God in his goodness be praised." (pp. 78–79)

These fragments suggest that communication skills are an indispensable part of the artistic critic's methodological equipment. Like poets, artistic rhetorical critics capture the elusiveness of human experience. Simultaneously, they present arguments, erecting a logical structure that will support their contentions. And that, of course, is a fair description of what any persuader must do.

SUMMARY

A colleague, Trevor Melia, likens the various academic disciplines to observers, each on a different mountain top, looking down on the same valley of subject matter. From their vantage point atop Rhetoric Mountain, rhetorical critics or analysts are inclined to see as rhetorical not only paradigm cases of persuasion, but also borderline or peripheral cases such as news reports, scientific discourse, plays and poetry, expressive acts, and ostensibly coercive acts. The scope covered by an analysis may range from a series of persuasive campaigns all the way to a small excerpt from a 10-minute speech.

Messages may be examined interpretively or evaluatively, and as illustrative examples or as objects worthy of attention in their own right. Interpretive analysis often seeks to explicate a case by means of some larger theory or model or conceptual distinction, and/or to illustrate the utility of the theory or model by means of the case. The skilled critic often attempts to probe beneath the surface to reveal hidden meanings, inexplicit strategies, and nonobvious motives.

Evaluative criticism not only describes or explains a work, it pronounces judgment upon it based on criteria the critic identifies and defends. The work may be described as inartistic or as illogical, for example, or as having promoted undesirable consequences. Debunking is a popular form of evaluative criticism in which the critic cites a persuader's claims to "purity" of motive and then undermines those pretensions. This chapter featured the requirements-problems-strategies approach in an evaluation of a presidential nomination acceptance speech.

EXERCISES

1. Do an RPS analysis of a nationally televised speech. After you have completed your analysis, compare it with newspaper and magazine commentaries on the speech.

2. Ghostwrite the message you think a persuader should have given but didn't; then justify your choices. What, for example, should Edward Kennedy have said on Chappaquidick? What should Carter have said about Kennedy in his 1980 acceptance speech?

3. Compare the Kennedy speech with Nixon's "Checkers" speech, presented in Chapter 10. Which conforms more closely with the characteristics of the mass media *apologia* proposed by Rosenfield (see discussion in Chapter 3)?

Statement to the People of Massachusetts

My fellow citizens:

I have requested this opportunity to talk to the people of Massachusetts about the tragedy that happened last Friday evening.

This morning I entered a plea of guilty to the charge of leaving the scene of an accident. Prior to my appearance in court it would have been improper for me to comment on these matters.

But tonight I am free to tell you what happened and to say what it means to me.

On the weekend of July 18, I was on Martha's Vineyard Island participating with my nephew, Joe Kennedy—as for thirty years my family has participated—in the annual Edgartown Sailing Regatta.

Only reasons of health prevented my wife from accompanying me.

On Chappaquiddick Island, off Martha's Vineyard, I attended on Friday evening, July 18, a cook-out I had encouraged and helped sponsor for a devoted group of Kennedy campaign secretaries.

When I left the party, around 11:15 P.M., I was accompanied by one of these girls, Miss Mary Jo Kopechne. Mary Jo was one of the most devoted members of the staff of Senator Robert Kennedy. She worked for him for four years and was broken up over his death. For this reason, and because she was such a gentle, kind, and idealistic person, all of us tried to help her feel that she still had a home with the Kennedy family.

There is no truth, no truth whatever, to the widening circulated suspicions of immoral conduct that has been leveled at my behavior and hers regarding that evening. There has never been a private relationship between us of any kind.

I know of nothing in Mary Jo's conduct on that or any other occasion—the same is true of the other girls at that party—that would lend any substance to such ugly speculation about their character.

Nor was I driving under the influence of liquor.

Little over one mile away, the car that I was driving on an unlit road went off a narrow bridge which had no guard rails and was built on a left angle to the road.

The car overturned in a deep pond and immediately filled with water. I remember thinking as the cold water rushed in around my head that I was for certain drowning.

Then water entered my lungs and I actually felt the sensation of drowning. But somehow I struggled to the surface alive. I made immediate and repeated efforts to save Mary Jo by diving into the strong and murky current but succeeded only in increasing my state of utter exhaustion and alarm.

My conduct and conversations during the next several hours to the extent that I can remember them make no sense to me at all.

Although my doctors informed me that I had suffered a cerebral concussion as well as shock, I do not seek to escape responsibility for my actions by placing the blame either on the physical, emotional trauma brought on by the accident, or on anyone else.

I regard as indefensible the fact that I did not report the accident to the police immediately.

Instead of looking directly for a telephone after lying exhausted in the grass for an undetermined time, I walked back to the cottage where the party was being held and requested the help of two friends, my cousin, Joseph Gargan, and Phil Markham, and directed them to return immediately to the scene with me—this was some time after midnight—in order to undertake a new effort to dive down and locate Miss Kopechne.

Their strenuous efforts, undertaken at some risk to their own lives, also proved futile.

All kinds of scrambled thoughts—all of them confused, some of them irrational, many of them which I cannot recall, and some of which I would not have seriously entertained under normal circumstances—went through my mind during this period.

They were reflected in the various inexplicable, inconsistent, and inconclusive things I said and did, including such questions as whether the girl might still be alive somewhere out of that immediate area, whether some awful curse did actually hang over all the Kennedys, whether there was some justifiable reason for me to doubt what had happened and to delay my report, whether somehow the awful weight of this incredible incident might in some way pass from my shoulders.

I was overcome, I am frank to say, by a jumble of emotions, grief, fear, doubt, exhaustion, confusion, and shock.

Instructing Gargan and Markham not to alarm Mary Jo's friends that night, I had them take me to the ferry crossing. The ferry having shut down for the night, I suddenly jumped into the water and swam across, nearly drowning once again in the effort, and returned to my hotel about 2:00 A.M. and collapsed in my room.

I remember going out at one point and saying something to the room clerk.

In the morning, with my mind somewhat more lucid, I made an effort to call a family legal adviser, Burke Marshall, from a public telephone on the Chappaquiddick side of the ferry and belatedly reported the accident to the Martha's Vineyard Police.

Today, as I mentioned, I felt morally obligated to plead guilty to the charge of leaving the scene of an accident. No words on my part can possibly express the terrible pain and suffering I feel over this tragic incident.

This last week has been an agonizing one for me and the members of my family, and the grief we feel over the loss of a wonderful friend will remain with us the rest of our lives.

These events, the publicity, innuendo, and whispers which have surrounded them and my admission of guilt this morning—raise the question in my mind of whether my standing among the people of my state has been so impaired that I should resign my seat in the United States Senate.

If at any time the citizens of Massachusetts should lack confidence in their Senator's character or his ability, with or without justification, he could not in my opinion adequately perform his duty and should not continue in office.

The people of this state, the state which sent John Quincy Adams and Daniel Webster and Charles Sumner and Henry Cabot Lodge and John Kennedy to the United States Senate, are entitled to representation in that body by men who inspire their utmost confidence.

For this reason, I would understand full well why some might think it right for me to resign. For me this will be a difficult decision to make.

It has been seven years since my first election to the Senate. You and I share many memories—some of them have been glorious, some have been very sad. The opportunity to work with you and serve Massachusetts has made my life worth while.

And so I ask you tonight, People of Massachusetts, to think this through with me. In facing this decision, I seek your advice and opinion. In making it, I seek your prayers. For this is a decision that I will have finally to make on my own.

It has been written a man does what he must in spite of personal consequences, in spite of obstacles and dangers and pressures, and that is the basis of all human morality.

Whatever may be the sacrifices he faces, if he follows his conscience—the loss of his friends, his fortune, his contentment, even the esteem of his fellow man—each man must decide for himself the course he will follow.

The stories of the past courage cannot supply courage itself. For this, each man must look into his own soul.

I pray that I can have the courage to make the right decision. Whatever is decided and whatever the future holds for me, I hope that I shall be able to put this most recent tragedy behind me and make some further contribution to our state and mankind, whether it be in public or in private life.

Thank you and good night.

Carter's Nomination Acceptance Speech

Fellow Democrats, fellow citizens:

I thank you for the nomination you've offered me, and I especially thank you for choosing as my running mate the best partner any President ever had, Fritz Mondale.

With gratitude and with determination I accept your nomination, and I am proud to run on the progressive and sound platform that you have hammered out at this convention.

Fritz and I will mount a campaign that defines the real issues, a campaign that responds to the intelligence of the American people, a campaign that talks sense. And we're going to beat the Republicans in November.

We'll win because we are the party of a great President who knew how to get reelected—Franklin Delano Roosevelt. And we are the party of a courageous fighter who knew how to give 'em hell—Harry Truman. And as Truman said, he just told the truth and they thought it was hell. And we're the party of a gallant man of spirit—John Fitzgerald Kennedy. And we're the party of a great leader of compassion—Lyndon Baines Johnson, and the party of a great man who should have been President, who would have been one of the greatest Presidents in history—Hubert Horatio Hornblower—Humphrey. I have appreciated what this convention has said about Senator Humphrey, a great man who epitomized the spirit of the Democratic Party. And I would like to say that we are also the party of Governor Jerry Brown and Senator Edward Kennedy.

I'd like to say a personal word to Senator Kennedy. Ted, you're a tough competitor and a superb campaigner, and I can attest to that. Your speech before this convention was a magnificent statement of what the Democratic Party is and what it means to the people of this country and why a Democratic victory is so important this year. I reach out to you tonight, and I reach out to all those who supported you in your valiant and passionate campaign. Ted, your party needs and I need you. And I need your idealism and your dedication working for us. There is no doubt that even greater service lies ahead of you, and we are grateful to you and to have your strong partnership now in a larger cause to which your own life has been dedicated.

I thank you for your support; we'll make great partners this fall in whipping the Republicans. We are Democrats and we've had our differences, but we share a bright vision of America's future—a vision of a good life for all our people, a vision of a secure nation, a just society, a peaceful world, a strong America—confident and proud and united. And we have a memory of Franklin Roosevelt, 40 years ago, when he said that there are times in our history when concerns over our personal lives are overshadowed by our concern over "what will happen to the country we have known." This is such a time, and I can tell you that the choice to be made this year can transform our own personal lives and the life of our country as well.

During the last Presidential campaign, I crisscrossed this country and I listened to thousands and thousands of people—housewives and farmers, teachers and small business leaders, workers and students, the elderly and the poor, people of every race and every background and every walk of life. It was a powerful experience—a total immersion in the human reality of America.

And I have now had another kind of total immersion—being President of the United States of America. Let me talk for a moment about what that job is like and what I've learned from it.

I've learned that only the most complex and difficult task comes before me in the Oval Office. No easy answers are found there, because no easy questions come there.

I've learned that for a President, experience is the best guide to the right decisions. I'm wiser tonight than I was 4 years ago.

And I have learned that the Presidency is a place of compassion. My own heart is burdened for the troubled Americans. The poor and the jobless and the afflicted—they've become part of me. My thoughts and my prayers for our hostages in Iran are as though they were my own sons and daughters.

The life of every human being on Earth can depend on the experience and judgment and vigilance of the person in the Oval Office. The President's power for building and his power for destruction are awesome. And the power's greatest exactly where the stakes are highest—in matters of war and peace.

And I've learned something else, something that I have come to see with extraordinary clarity: Above all, I must look ahead, because the President of the United States is the steward of the Nation's destiny. He must protect our children and the children they will have and the children of generations to follow. He must speak and act for them. That is his burden and his glory.

And that is why a President cannot yield to the shortsighted demands, no matter how rich or powerful the special interests might be that make those demands. And that's why the President cannot bend to the passions of the moment, however popular they might be. That's why the President must sometimes ask for sacrifice when his listeners would rather hear the promise of comfort.

The President is a servant of today, but his true constituency is the future. That's why the election of 1980 is so important.

Some have said it makes no difference who wins this election. They are wrong. This election is a stark choice between two men, two parties, two sharply different pictures of what America is and what the world is, but it's more than that—it's a choice between two futures.

The year 2000 is just less than 20 years away, just four Presidential elections after this one. Children born this year will come of age in the 21st century. The time to shape the world of the year 2000 is now. The decisions of the next few years will set our course, perhaps an irreversible course, and the most important of all choices will be made by the American people at the polls less than 3 months from tonight.

The choice could not be more clear nor the consequences more crucial. In one of the futures we can choose, the future that you and I have been building together, I see security and justice and peace.

I see a future of economic security—security that will come from tapping our own great resources of oil and gas, coal and sunlight, and from building the tools and technology and factories for a revitalized economy based on jobs and stable prices for everyone.

I see a future of justice—the justice of good jobs, decent health care, quality education, a full opportunity for all people regardless of color or language or religion; the simple human justice of equal rights for all men and for all women, guaranteed equal rights at last under the Constitution of the United States of America.

And I see a future of peace—a peace born of wisdom and based on a fairness toward all countries of the world, a peace guaranteed both by American military strength and by American moral strength as well.

That is the future I want for all people, a future of confidence and hope and a good life. It's the future America must choose, and with your help and with your commitment, it is the future America will choose.

But there is another possible future. In that other future I see despair— despair of millions who would struggle for equal opportunity and a better life and struggle alone. And I see surrender–the surrender of our energy future to the merchants of oil, the surrender of our economic future to a bizarre program of massive tax cuts for the rich, service cuts for the poor, and massive inflation for everyone. And I see risk—the risk of international confrontation, the risk of an uncontrollable, unaffordable, and unwinnable nuclear arms race.

No one, Democrat or Republican either, consciously seeks such a future, and I do not claim that my opponent does. But I do question the disturbing commitments and policies already made by him and by those with him who have now captured control of the Republican Party. The consequences of those commitments and policies would drive us down the wrong road. It's up to all of us to make sure America rejects this alarming and even perilous destiny.

The only way to build a better future is to start with the realities of the present. But while we Democrats grapple with the real challenges of a real world, others talk about a world of tinsel and make-believe.

Let's look for a moment at their make-believe world.

In their fantasy America, inner-city people and farm workers and laborers do not exist. Women, like children, are to be seen but not heard. The problems of working women are simply ignored. The elderly do not need Medicare. The young do not need more help in getting a better education. Workers do not require the guarantee of a healthy and a safe place to work. In their fantasy world, all the complex global changes of the world since World War II have never happened. In their fantasy America, all problems have simple solutions—simple and wrong.

It's a make-believe world, a world of good guys and bad guys, where some politicians shoot first and ask questions later. No hard choices, no sacrifice, no tough decisions—it sounds too good to be true, and it is.

The path of fantasy leads to irresponsibility. The path of reality leads to hope and peace. The two paths could not be more different, nor could the futures to which they lead. Let's take a hard look at the consequences of our choice.

You and I have been working toward a more secure future by rebuilding our military strength—steadily, carefully, and responsibly. The Republicans talk about military strength, but they were in office for 8 out of the last 11 years, and in the face of a growing Soviet threat they steadily cut real defense spending by more than a third.

We've reversed the Republican decline in defense. Every year since I've been President we've had real increases in our commitment to a stronger Nation, increases which are prudent and rational. There is no doubt that the United States of America can meet any threat from the Soviet Union. Our modernized strategic forces, a revitalized NATO, the Trident submarine, the Cruise missile, the Rapid Deployment Force—all these guarantee that we will never be second to any nation. Deeds, not words; fact, not fiction. We must and we will continue to build our own defenses. We must and we will continue to seek balanced reductions in nuclear arms.

The new leaders of the Republican Party, in order to close the gap between their rhetoric and their record, have now promised to launch an all-out nuclear arms race. This would negate any further effort to negotiate a strategic arms limitation agreement. There can be no winners in such an arms race, and all the people of the Earth can be the losers.

The Republican nominee advocates abandoning arms control policies which have been important and supported by every Democratic President since Harry Truman, and also by every Republican President since Dwight D. Eisenhower. This radical and irresponsible course would threaten our security and could put the whole world in peril. You and I must never let this come to pass.

It's simple to call for a new arms race, but when armed aggression threatens world peace, tough-sounding talk like that is not enough. A President must act responsibly.

When Soviet troops invaded Afghanistan, we moved quickly to take action. I suspended some grain sales to the Soviet Union; I called for draft registration; and I joined wholeheartedly with the Congress and with the U.S. Olympic Committee and led more than 60 other nations in boycotting the big propaganda show in Russia—the Moscow Olympics.

The Republican leader opposed two of these forceful but peaceful actions, and he waffled on the third. But when we asked him what he would do about aggression in Southwest Asia, he suggested blockading Cuba. [*Laughter*] Even his running mate wouldn't go along with that. He doesn't seem to know what to do with the Russians. He's not sure if he wants to feed them or play with them or fight with them.

As I look back at my first term, I'm grateful that we've had a country for the full 4 years of peace. And that's what we're going to have for the next 4 years—peace.

It's only common sense that if America is to stay secure and at peace, we must encourage others to be peaceful as well.

As you know, we've helped in Zimbabwe-Rhodesia where we've stood firm for racial justice and democracy. And we have also helped in the Middle East.

Some have criticized the Camp David accords and they've criticized some delays in the implementation of the Middle East peace treaty. Well, before I became President there was no Camp David accords and there was no Middle East peace treaty. Before Camp David, Israel and Egypt were poised across barbed wire, confronting each other with guns and tanks and planes. But afterward, they talked face-to-face with each other across a peace table, and they also communicated through their own Ambassadors in Cairo and Tel Aviv.

Now that's the kind of future we're offering—of peace to the Middle East if the Democrats are reelected in the fall.

I am very proud that nearly half the aid that our country has ever given to Israel in the 32 years of her existence has come during my administration. Unlike our Republican predecessors, we have never stopped nor slowed that aid to Israel. And as long as I am President, we will never do so. Our commitment is clear: security and peace for Israel; peace for all the peoples of the Middle East.

But if the world is to have a future of freedom as well as peace, America must continue to defend human rights.

Now listen to this: The new Republican leaders oppose our human rights policy. They want to scrap it. They seem to think it's naïve for America to stand up for freedom and democracy. Just what do they think we should stand up for?

Ask the former political prisoners who now live in freedom if we should abandon our stand on human rights. Ask the dissidents in the Soviet Union about our commitment to human rights. Ask the Hungarian Americans, ask the Polish Americans, listen to Pope John Paul II. Ask those who are suffering for the sake of justice and liberty around the world. Ask the millions who've fled tyranny if America should stop speaking out for human principles. Ask the American people. I tell you that as long as I am President, we will hold high the banner of human rights, and you can depend on it.

Here at home the choice between the two futures is equally important.

In the long run, nothing is more crucial to the future of America than energy; nothing was so disastrously neglected in the past. Long after the 1973 Arab oil embargo, the Republicans in the White House had still done nothing to meet the threat to the national security of our Nation. Then, as now, their policy was dictated by the big oil companies.

We Democrats fought hard to rally our Nation behind a comprehensive energy policy and a good program, a new foundation for challenging and exciting progress. Now, after 3 years of struggle, we have that program. The battle to secure America's energy future has been fully and finally joined. Americans have cooperated with dramatic results. We've reversed decades of dangerous and growing dependence on foreign oil. We are now importing 20 percent less oil—that is $1\frac{1}{2}$ million barrels of oil every day less than the day I took office.

And with our new energy policy now in place, we can discover more, produce more, create more, and conserve more energy, and we will use American resources, American technology, and millions of American workers to do it with.

Now, what do the Republicans propose? Basically, their energy program has two parts. The first part is to get rid of almost everything that we've done for the American public in the last 3 years. They want to reduce or abolish the synthetic fuels program. They want to slash the solar energy incentives, the conservation programs, aid to mass transit, aid to elderly Americans to help pay their fuel bills. They want to eliminate the 55-mile speed limit. And while they are at it, the Republicans would like to gut the Clean Air Act. They never liked it to begin with.

That's one part of their program; the other part is worse. To replace what we have built, this is what they propose: to destroy the windfall profits tax and to "unleash" the oil companies and let them solve the energy problem for us. That's it. That is it. That's their whole program. There is no more. Can this Nation accept such an outrageous program?

AUDIENCE. No!

THE PRESIDENT. No! We Democrats will fight it every step of the way, and we'll begin tomorrow morning with a campaign for reelection in November.

When I took office, I inherited a heavy load of serious economic problems besides energy, and we've met them all head-on. We've slashed Government regulations and put free enterprise back into the airlines, the trucking and the financial systems of our country, and we're now doing the same thing for the railroads. This is the greatest change in the relationship between Government and business since the New Deal. We've increased our exports dramatically. We've reversed the decline in the basic research and development, and we have created more than 8 million new jobs—the biggest increase in the history of our country.

But the road is bumpy, and last year's skyrocketing OPEC price increases have helped to trigger a worldwide inflation crisis. We took forceful action, and interest rates have now fallen, the dollar is stable and, although we still have a battle on our hands, we're struggling to bring inflation under control.

We are now at the critical point, a turning point in our economic history of our country. But because we made the hard decisions, because we have guided our Nation and its economy through a rough but essential period of transition, we've laid the groundwork for a new economic age.

Our economic renewal program for the 1980's will meet our immediate need for jobs and attack the very same, long-range problem that caused unemployment and inflation in the first place. It'll move America simultaneously towards our five great economic goals—lower inflation, better productivity, revitalization of American industry, energy security, and jobs.

It's time to put all America back to work—but not in make-work, in real work. And there is real work in modernizing American industries and creating new industries for America as well.

Here are just a few things we'll rebuild together and build together:

—new industries to turn our own coal and shale and farm products into fuel for our cars and trucks and to turn the light of the sun into heat and electricity for our homes;
—a modern transportation system of railbeds and ports to make American coal into a powerful rival of OPEC oil;
—industries that will provide the convenience of futuristic computer technology and communications to serve millions of American homes and offices and factories;
—job training for workers displaced by economic changes;
—new investment pinpointed in regions and communities where jobs are needed most;
—better mass transit in our cities and in between cities;
—and a whole new generation of American jobs to make homes and vehicles and buildings that will house us and move us in comfort with a lot less energy.

This is important, too: I have no doubt that the ingenuity and dedication of the American people can make every single one of these things happen. We are talking about the United States of America, and those who count this country out as an economic superpower are going to find out just how wrong they are. We're going to share in the exciting enterprise of making the 1980's a time of growth for America.

The Republican alternative is the biggest tax giveaway in history. They call it Reagan-Kemp-Roth; I call it a free lunch that Americans cannot afford. The Republican tax program offers rebates to the rich, deprivation for the poor, and fierce inflation for all of us. Their party's own Vice Presidential nominee said that Reagan-Kemp-Roth would result in an inflation rate of more than 30 percent. He called it "voodoo economics". He suddenly changed his mind toward the end of the Republican Convention, but he was right the first time.

Along with this gigantic tax cut, the new Republican leaders promise to protect retirement and health programs and to have massive increases in defense spending—and they claim they can balance the budget. If they are serious about these promises, and they say they are, then a close analysis shows that the entire rest of the Government would have to be abolished, everything from education to farm programs, from the G.I. bill to the night watchman at the Lincoln Memorial—and their budget would still be in the red. The only alternative would be to build more printing presses to print cheap money. Either way, the American people lose. But the American people will not stand for it.

The Democratic Party has always embodied the hope of our people for justice, opportunity, and a better life, and we've worked in every way possible to strengthen the American family, to encourage self-reliance, and to follow the Old Testament admonition: "Defend the poor and the fatherless; give justice to the afflicted and needy." We've struggled to assure that no child in America ever goes to bed hungry, that no elderly couple in America has to live in a substandard home, and that no young person in America is excluded from college because the family is poor.

But what have the Republicans proposed?—just an attack on everything that we've done in the achievement of social justice and decency that we've won in the last 50 years, ever since Franklin Delano Roosevelt's first term. They would make social security voluntary. They would reverse our progress on the minimum wage, full employment laws, safety in the work place, and a healthy environment.

Lately, as you know, the Republicans have been quoting Democratic Presidents. But who can blame them? Would you rather quote Herbert Hoover or Franklin Delano Roosevelt? Would you rather quote Richard Nixon or John Fitzgerald Kennedy?

The Republicans have always been the party of privilege, but this year their leaders have gone even further. In their platform, they have repudiated the best traditions of their own party. Where is the conscience of Lincoln in the party of Lincoln? What's become of their traditional Republican commitment to fiscal responsibility? What's happened to their commitment to a safe and sane arms control?

Now, I don't claim perfection for the Democratic Party. I don't claim that every decision that we have made has been right or popular; certainly, they've not all been easy. But I will say this: We've been tested under fire. We've neither ducked nor hidden, and we've tackled the great central issues of our time, the historic challenges of peace and energy, which have been ignored for years. We've made tough decisions, and we've taken the heat for them. We've made mistakes, and we've learned from them. But we have built the foundation now for a better future.

We've done something else, perhaps even more important. In good times and bad, in the valleys and on the peaks, we've told people the truth, the hard truth, the truth that sometimes hurts.

One truth that we Americans have learned is that our dream has been earned for progress and for peace. Look what our land has been through within our own memory—a great depression, a world war, a technological explosion, the civil rights revolution, the bitterness of Vietnam, the shame of Watergate, the twilight peace of nuclear terror.

Through each of these momentous experiences we've learned the hard way about the world and about ourselves. But we've matured and we've grown as a nation and we've grown stronger.

We've learned the uses and the limitations of power. We've learned the beauty and responsibility of freedom. We've learned the value and the obligation of justice. And we have learned the necessity of peace.

Some would argue that to master these lessons is somehow to limit our potential. That is not so. A nation which knows its true strengths, which sees its true challenges, which understands legitimate constraints, that nation— our nation—is far stronger than one which takes refuge in wishful thinking or nostalgia. The Democratic Party—the American people—have understood these fundamental truths.

All of us can sympathize with the desire for easy answers. There's often the temptation to substitute idle dreams for hard reality. The new Republican leaders are hoping that our Nation will succumb to that temptation this year, but they profoundly misunderstand and underestimate the character of the American people.

Three weeks after Pearl Harbor, Winston Churchill came to North America and he said, "We have not journeyed all this way across the centuries, across the oceans, across the mountains, across the prairies, because we are made of sugar candy." We Americans have courage. Americans have always been on the cutting edge of change. We've always looked forward with anticipation and confidence.

I still want the same thing that all of you want—a self-reliant neighborhood, strong families, work for the able-bodied and good medical care for the sick, opportunity for our youth and dignity for our old, equal rights and justice for all people.

I want teachers eager to explain what a civilization really is, and I want students to understand their own needs and their own aims, but also the needs and yearnings of their neighbors.

I want women free to pursue without limit the full life of what they want for themselves.

I want our farmers growing crops to feed our Nation and the world, secure in the knowledge that the family farm will thrive and with a fair return on the good work they do for all of us.

I want workers to see meaning in the labor they perform and work enough to guarantee a job for every worker in this country.

And I want the people in business free to pursue with boldness and freedom new ideas.

And I want minority citizens fully to join the mainstream of American life. And I want from the bottom of my heart to remove the blight of racial and other discrimination from the face of our Nation, and I'm determined to do it.

I need for all of you to join me in fulfilling that vision. The choice, the choice between the two futures, could not be more clear. If we succumb to a dream world then we'll wake up to a nightmare. But if we start with reality and fight to make our dreams a reality, then Americans will have a good life, a life of meaning and purpose in a nation that's strong and secure.

Above all, I want us to be what the Founders of our Nation meant us to become—the land of freedom, the land of peace, and the land of hope.

Thank you very much.

From "Public Papers of the Presidents of the United States: Jimmy Carter 1980–81." United States Government Printing Office, 1982, pp. 1532–1540.

Chapter 15
Analyzing Persuasion in the Guise of Objectivity

That there is value in analyzing virtually all discourse rhetorically has been a persistent argument of this book. This chapter presents a guide to the analysis of ostensibly objective messages: those, such as news articles, scientific reports, historical narratives, and the like, that purport to be unbiased and impartial; and those much more manifestly rhetorical documents, such as reports to shareholders and pharmaceutical advertisements which, although more obviously rhetorical in their aims and convictions, nevertheless purport to provide objective "fact," "information," "logic" in support of their claims. The guide directs your attention to the way messages are framed by the communicator, and to the way definitions, illustrations, comparisons, contrasts, and other message elements may be used to conceal or reveal, magnify or minimize, elevate or degrade, sharpen or blur, link or divide, simplify or complexify in presenting a picture of the external world. After presenting the guide in bare outline, I then illustrate how it may be applied to cases.

Guiding Questions

    I. *How the Message Is Framed*
       A. *Message Classification*
          1. How does the communicator classify the message?
          2. How, from your perspective, should the message be classified? Is its designation appropriate, or is it misleading in some way? Is the communicator promoting in the guise of being informative? Offering ideology in the name of science? Indoctrinating in the guise of

training? If so, is this mere innocent "hype," or is the communicator guilty of an "immoral rhetoric of identity deception"?

B. *Message Purpose*
  1. How does the communicator represent the goals of the message? What reaction(s) is he or she seeking from the audience? Why is he or she seeking them?
  2. What, from your perspective, are the communicator's "real" message purposes? Are the alleged goals and motives credible?

C. *Image Management*
  1. How does the communicator represent self in relationship to audience? How, in particular, does the communicator metacommunicate images of competence, trustworthiness, attractiveness, and goodwill? Consider here such clues to image management as the following:
     a. Self-reference
     b. References to audience
     c. Relational references
     d. Style or tone
  2. What is your perception of what the communicator is really like? Is the communicator's presentation of self essentially fair and accurate, or has the communicator projected a persona that highlights favorable qualities while hiding or obscuring unfavorable ones? Are there negative qualities that show through despite the communicator's best efforts to obscure them?

II. *How the Message Pictures the External World*
  A. *Choice of Terms.* What perceptions and associations are triggered by labels used to designate the key phenomena being referred to in the message, and by other terms used in definitions, illustrations, comparisons and the like? Of particular interest here are the following:
    1. Euphemisms and pejoratives
    2. Metonymy
    3. Metaphor
    4. Caricature
    5. Obfuscations
  B. *Treatment of Key Terms and Ideas*
    1. *Message structure.* What perspective on the subject matter is suggested by the manner in which the message is organized?
    2. *Alignments and divisions.* What is the structure of alignments and divisions among key terms in the message? What is identified with what, and what is opposed to what?
    3. *Attributions of causation.* What causes are singled out in descriptions or explanations of a phenomenon? How else might the phenomenon be reasonably described or explained? What is magnified or minimized by the account?
    4. *Balance/imbalance.* Are there imbalances in the selection and arrangement of arguments and evidence? Is the presentation one-sided? If two-sided, are arguments that might run counter to the communi-

cator's conclusions given equal weight? Is the appearance of fairness created by giving ground on trivial issues while holding firm on major ones? Is bias reflected in the placement of arguments, or in the way opposing views are represented, or in the treatment of pertinent facts? Are some relevant facts glossed over or concealed entirely?

Using the Guide: Explanations and Examples

The guide may be used informally to analyze the messages you come across on a day-to-day basis, or it can help you in the preparation of extended analyses. In preparing your analysis, remember that what you say will itself be an act of persuasion. Be convincing. Try to go beyond the obvious, but be sure to support your nonobvious claims. Do not try to cover everything in your analysis. Use only those critical tools that seem most relevant to your purposes and to the discourse you are examining.

Decide, then, what you are trying to accomplish. Are you trying to show how audience perceptions are shaped by the strategic uses of language? Is it your thesis that the message offers judgments, inferences, suggestions, or interpretations that are not fully warranted by the facts and logic presented? Or are you claiming, much more ambitiously, that the message displays evidences of deliberately disguised persuasive intent, and perhaps of deliberate obfuscation or distortion? Also ask yourself: Is the message an object of interest in its own right, or am I using it to illustrate something about persuasion as a whole or about messages of that type?

Having determined what you are trying to accomplish, decide which questions in the guide are most relevant to you. For example, several questions direct you to consider whether there is covert persuasive intent exhibited in messages that affect a stance of impartiality or neutrality. For many news reports or scientific articles or textbook selections, these may be the most important questions. But the message you happen to be analyzing may be of a different sort. Like the Mobil Corporation advertisement on p. 310, its claim to objectivity may consist not in the alleged absence of a thesis or point of view, but in its insistence on the unassailable logic of the viewpoint being expressed.

As you go to work on the message, put yourself in the position of the communicator. What was the speaker or writer trying to say? What obstacles stood in the way of goal accomplishment? Why this choice of language rather than some other? How else could the message have been stated? Before proceeding very far with the analysis, it is a good idea to gather as much background information as you can about the source, the medium, the audience, and the context. In terms of the Mobil Corporation advertisement, for example, you should know that Mobil is the second largest oil company in America, that it is involved in a number of energy and nonenergy areas (e.g., it owns Montgomery Ward), and that for several years prior to the ad's publication in 1978, Mobil and the other oil giants had been making enormous profits. This,

Business and the rational mind

Liberals, logical allies of business • The snobbery factor • A plea for independent thinking

We cannot, for the life of us, understand why so many liberals in this country are so hostile to private business, when in our opinion they should be working with business to achieve what should be their basic objectives.

Liberals have been among the prime movers in the enactment of much of this country's social legislation—Aid to Dependent Children, Social Security, housing for the poor and the elderly, school lunches, and other programs. All of these programs have to be financed by revenues derived mainly from taxes on individual and corporate income.

The greater these incomes—which is to say, the more prosperous American business is—the greater the tax revenues. When incomes drop, as in a recession, so do tax revenues. Social programs then have to be reduced accordingly or supported by deficit financing, which over any extended period means inflation. For the poor and for people living on fixed incomes, inflation is the cruelest tyranny of all.

It therefore would seem to us that in all logic liberals should be as pro-business as they are pro-social progress. And we believe many more of them would be if it were not so fashionable intellectually to be part of the "trendy left." Too many of them respond unthinkingly to social and academic pressures rather than engaging in clear, independent analysis.

Part of the problem appears to be snobbery, pure and simple. To many of what might be called the professional liberals, business—indeed, our whole industrial society—is impossibly vulgar. To some it is esthetically offensive. And because business can prosper only by serving the masses of people, some consider it unbearably plebeian.

Yet one of the continuing threads in the mainstream of liberal thought has long been a dedication to the democratic process and to the right of the masses of people to make their voice heard—and heard effectively. If people stop buying a company's goods or services on any large scale—or just make a credible threat to stop—that company's management tends to listen, and listen attentively. But if you think government is anywhere near as responsive, just recall your last encounter with your City Hall, or your maddening correspondence with a government agency.

Government can become so pervasive that it becomes virtually impossible for the citizenry to turn it around and change its course; indeed, ours may already have become so. But it's doubtful that business could ever get so big or so unresponsive, because it is subject to reaction in the marketplace and to public opinion generally, and to legislation that can curb an entire industry overnight.

What should be a tip-off to any thinking liberal is that an anti-business posture, complete with the cliches that too often substitute for thinking, is mandatory in many liberal circles and is not to be subjected to rigorous intellectual examination. It is a knee-jerk reaction, arising largely from conditions that ceased to exist many years ago and to some that never existed at all.

Lionel Trilling wrote: "It has for some time seemed to me that a criticism which has at heart the interest of liberalism might find its most useful work not in confirming liberalism in its sense of self-righteousness but rather in putting under some degree of pressure the liberal ideas and assumptions of the times."(*The Liberal Imagination: Essays on Literature and Society*, Charles Scribner's Sons, 1976.)

We find puzzling the extent to which liberals often seem impelled to weaken the economic structure on which not just social progress, but indeed our national livelihood depends. To them we suggest the following, oversimplified but nevertheless pointing up the heart of the matter:

Without adequate profits, no businesses.

Without businesses, no jobs.

Without jobs, no social programs.

Mobil

(© 1979 Mobil Oil Corporation.)

in keeping with other adverse publicity, had severely tarnished Mobil's corporate image.

Mobil and the other big oil companies had been accused during the seventies of creating artificial oil shortages, of monopoly control of oil resources, of windfall profits, of polluting air and water, of collusion with oil-producing nations, or bribing politicians in other lands, of making illegal campaign contributions, and of withholding information. But Mobil was also at this time riding the winds of change toward political conservatism in America, a trend manifested in part by shifts among some leading liberals toward the conservative camp. There was already a movement in Washington toward lower corporate taxes and deregulation—a movement, by the way, that Mobil executives claimed to have helped propel by ads like this one in the editorial sections of leading newspapers. These ads are not designed for ordinary citizens, but for the "movers and shakers" of society: politicians, business executives, college students, faculty, clergy, and so on.

How the Message Is Framed

Message Classification

How does the communicator classify the message? This question is especially important as regards persuasion in the guise of objectivity. Look for such favorable labels as "report," "study," "demonstration," "training," "teaching," "information," "science," "inquiry," "description," "explanation," "formal theory," "documentary film." Look for the conspicuous absence of such negatively valenced labels as "rhetoric," "propaganda," "argumentation," "opinion," "advertisement," "speculation," "inference," "ideology." Look too for bland, all-purpose classifications such as "conversation" or "discussion" that might serve to cover over persuasive intent without committing the communicator to the appearance of objectivity. Look finally for implicit classifications, as might be registered, for example, by a scholarly tone as opposed to a lighthearted one, or by the appearance of technical precision as opposed to a more casual style.

How, from your perspective, should the message be classified? Is its designation appropriate, or is it misleading in some way? Is the communicator promoting in the guise of being informative? Offering ideology in the name of science? Indoctrinating in the guise of training? If so, is this mere innocent "hype," or is the communicator guilty of an "immoral rhetoric of identity deception"?

The Mobil ad presents us with interesting questions of classification. It is editorial in style, but it is also an advertisement. It takes a partisan stance, but it acts as though its partisan stance is the only stance the "rational mind" can take. The ad is replete with suggestions that its claims are objectively grounded, but while the ad as a whole attempts persuasion in the guise of objectivity, there is nothing deceptive about it.

Contrast this ad with a series of Mobil ads that appeared on independent television stations not too long ago. Here Mobil voiced opinions similar to those in its Op-Ed advertisements, but it used the semblance of a television news program to do so. The viewer was presented with what looked like a television news room, replete with counter, anchorman in uniform, and global map in the background illuminated by flashing lights. The ads featured the Mobil logo in several places and the anchorman announced that he was from Mobil, but the messages were billed as issuing from Mobil's "Information News Center." These ads aroused charges of deceptive advertising.

Message Purpose

How does the communicator represent the goals of the message? What reaction(s) is she or he seeking from the audience? Why is she or he seeking them? A general sense of what the communicator is after is revealed through an analysis of message type, but here we want to get more specific. Is the communicator attempting to influence beliefs, values, attitudes, private actions, public actions? What specifically does he or she want us to think or do, and why? Is the message part of a campaign or movement? Is the communicator fulfilling a professional obligation? What are his or her alleged interests?

What, from your perspective, are the communicator's "real" message purposes? Are the alleged goals and motives credible? In its Op-Ed ad, Mobil is rather vague about its goals. It does not tell readers who the ad is aimed at, what reactions it is seeking, and why. Mobil purports to be "puzzled" by the attitudes of many liberals toward business, but is it really seeking to become enlightened? Mobil addresses liberals directly at the end of the ad, but is the ad really addressed only to them? Is another of Mobil's goals to impress conservatives and perhaps drive a wedge between traditional liberals and others more sympathetic to business? Besides influencing opinion and action about the issues raised, might Mobil also be interested in bolstering its image in the eyes of its readers?

Image Management

How does the communicator represent self in relationship to audience? How, in particular, does the communicator metacommunicate images of competence, trustworthiness, attractiveness, and goodwill? Consider here such clues to image management as the following:

1. *Self-references*—to background, interests, qualifications. "As you may know, I have for many years been concerned with the problems of carcinogens in the workplace."
2. *References to audience*—compliments, expressions of liking or of interest in audience. "I think this group has what it takes to dig deeply into the problem of occupational cancer and come up with effective solutions."
3. *Relational references*—to shared attitudes or interests. "We're here because we both want to see the problems of occupational cancer eliminated."
4. *Style or tone*—manner of presentation. Since many more metacommunicational cues are implicit rather than explicit, this last category is important. The communicator may talk down to us condescendingly or try to impress us by speaking over our heads. She or he may convey the right to *tell* us the truth by acting as the omniscient observer. Or, as in most scientific articles, she or he may convey the impression of *showing* the truth by letting the data "speak for itself." A principal element of style is grammatical *voice* (first person active, third person passive).

Any number of adjectives may be used to capture the style or tone of a message, and sometimes no single word will do. Campbell (1972) has offered such descriptors as "personal, direct, ironic, satirical, sympathetic, angry, bitter, intense, scholarly, dogmatic, distant, condescending, 'tough' or realistic, 'sweet' or euphemistic, incisive, elegant" (p. 15).

It should be emphasized that the appearance of objectivity need not be created by appearing disinterested, aloof, or impersonal. Communicators may create the impression of warmth, of interest in the audience, of concern, while still projecting an image of balance, fairness, open-mindedness. For example, the communicator may refer to self as "I" and to audience as "you" or to both as "we," rather than employing the third-person passive voice common to scientific articles. In scientific journals, where stylistic detachment is conventional, use of the "I" or of active verbs may even function as a "meta-metacommunication" which implies, in context, that the communicator's arguments are so convincing that he or she doesn't need to metacommunicate a sense of detachment. This "message about the message about the message" may create an even greater sense in the audience of the communicator's objectivity.

What is your perception of what the communicator is really like? Is the communicator's presentation of self essentially fair and accurate, or has the communicator projected a *persona* (a public image) that highlights favorable qualities while hiding or obscuring unfavorable ones? Are there negative qualities that show through despite the communicator's best efforts to obscure them?

In its Op-Ed ad about liberals, Mobil clearly attempts to communicate an image of the corporation as personlike ("the life of us") and of the corporation-as-person as committed to "rational," "independent thinking." But Mobil's invective against liberals seems so strongly worded as to belie its own persona of cool-headed rationality. Note such emotionally loaded terms as "unthinkingly," "professional liberals," "knee-jerk reaction." While those initially hostile to liberals would probably find no difficulty with these terms and might enjoy the verbal beating Mobil is giving liberals, those at all sympathetic to the liberal persuasion would probably feel that Mobil has gotten carried away.

As a final example of image management, consider this excerpt from a report to stockholders by Cybermatics, a New Jersey graphic arts firm with a reputation for creativity:

> Cybermatics, Inc. hit bottom in 1972. Now we're bouncing back. But you may not believe it. That red ink on the cover means what you think it means. It was a bum year, and we have too much respect for our stockholders to try to sugar-coat it.

The statement surely breaks with the tradition of dry, impersonal reports to stockholders, and it reinforces Cybermatics' image of creativity. But one wonders whether the firm is being a bit devious in claiming that its candor derives from great respect for its shareholders. From another perspective it is a disarming device, employed to minimize the adverse effects of information that the company is bound by law to provide in any case.

How the Message Pictures the External World

This section is concerned with choice and treatment of terms—with how names, definitions, illustrations, and other such message elements may be used to elevate or degrade, highlight or downplay, sharpen or blur.

Choice of Terms

What perceptions and associations are triggered by key labels, and by other terms used in definitions, illustrations, comparisons, and the like? Of particular interest here are euphemistic (positive) and pejorative (negative) labels, metonymy, metaphor, caricature, and obfuscations.

Euphemisms and Pejoratives. That words may carry positive or negative emotional loadings (lean/skinny, firm/obstinate, stable/rigid, unusual/abnormal) has already been amply illustrated. Emotionally loaded words such as these are often found in seemingly objective descriptions and definitions. Note, for example, that whereas most textbook writers on persuasion tend to distance persuasion from coercion while imbuing the latter with even worse connotations than it deserves, writers critical of persuasion tend to make it seem coercive by use of such pejoratives as "manipulation," "mind-bending," and "sophistry" in descriptions or definitions of the term. One is hard-pressed, as we have seen, to find synonyms for "persuasion" that are not emotionally loaded. This seems to be the case with respect to a great many concepts. One expert describes the "high" produced from marijuana as "mind-expanding." Another characterizes it as "reality distorting." Is there a completely neutral way of describing it? Probably not.

Nevertheless, some euphemisms or pejoratives may seem particularly noxious to you. Notorious to many critics was the United States government's use of terms to cloud the meaning of some of its ethically questionable actions during the war in Vietnam, while at the same time making them seem more palatable. In the absence of a war declaration from Congress, we were said to be engaged in a "police action." Peasants placed in internment camps against their will were said to be assigned to "New-Life Hamlets." Protesters jailed before formal charges had been filed were said to be in "protective detention." Other terms included "protective reaction strike," "surgical bombing," and "free-fire zone." These terms gave license to the massive and often indiscriminate bombing of areas populated by peasants.

Metonymy. Metonymy is a rhetorical device by which one entity is used to represent another that is related to it. The substitution of one entity for another may involve part for whole (e.g., "a new set of wheels" for "a new car"), face for person (e.g., "She's just a pretty face"), place for institution ("Wall Street's mood is grim"), institution for people ("Mobil said . . . "). These substitutions may also evoke positive or negative feelings.

Note how Mobil uses metonymy to support its "liberals" thesis. Business is represented in paragraph 6 as a company's "management," while government (used here as though it were a person) is represented by City Hall and by government bureaucrats. Imagine, by contrast, if government had been represented by a popular governmental building ("When the White House calls . . . "), while business had been represented as "corporate bureaucrats."

Metaphor. Recall that a metaphor is a device for seeing one thing in terms of another. It "brings out the thisness of a that and the thatness of a this"

(Burke, 1945). Earlier we examined the important role of *generative* metaphors in structuring thought on a matter. Consider, for example, the different implications of defining the human being metaphorically as a stimulus-response machine, a rat in a maze, a complex machine such as a computer, a swirling sea of only partially channeled energies, or a mental acrobat on a psychological tightrope.

Caricature. To caricature someone is to exaggerate or distort certain of his or her distinctive or peculiar features, usually for comic effect. Often a complex figure is made into a recognizable stock character from literature or the arts. The "professional liberal" is consistently caricatured in the Mobil ad as an unthinking fool, and in paragraph 5 he is likened to another stock character in our culture—in this case, ironically, the haughty dowager type who scoffs condescendingly at anything new or different. Who but such a snob would use such phrases as "impossibly vulgar," "esthetically offensive," "unbearably plebeian?"

Obfuscations. To obfuscate is to shroud in mystery or ambiguity that which could be stated more clearly. Obfuscations may be designed to impress, to conceal emptiness of thought, or to evade responsibility for illicit ideas or activities.

In the social sciences, obfuscation often takes the form of high-sounding jargon. Here is Edwin Newman (1975) in *Strictly Speaking:*

> "Siblings are conflicted in their interpersonal relationships" *means* children of the same parent don't like each other (p. 176).

> "Exogenous variables from the causal linkage that explains the poverty impact, the behavior modification and the intergroup dissonance in the target area" *means* that outside factors cause the poverty and the changes in people that lead to trouble in the neighborhood. (p. 176)

In the leaden vocabulary of obscurantist social scientists, says Newman, "boundaries are parameters, parts are components, things are not equal but co-equal, signs are indicators, and causes are exogenous variables." (p. 176).

One function of such jargon is, of course, to bolster the image of the communicator. That it can be effective was shown in an article in *Psychology Today* (Horn, 1980). Before an audience of professional psychologists, educators, social workers, and psychiatrists, a certain Dr. Myron L. Fox presented a one-hour talk, followed by a half-hour discussion, on the subject, "Mathematical Game Theory as Applied to Physician Education." The audience rated the lecture clear and stimulating, but the speaker was in fact a phony, a professional actor who had been instructed by researcher J. S. Armstrong to make up a lecture out of "bafflegab"—in this case, *non sequiturs* and contradictory statements taken from a *Scientific American* article, mixed with jokes and meaningless references to unrelated topics.

As reported by Horn (1980), the researcher conducted follow-up studies which further supported his hypothesis that "An unintelligible communication from a legitimate source in the recipient's area of expertise will increase the recipient's rating of the author's competence." In one study, 32 management professors rated passages from management journals "more competent" than rewrites of these passages that retained the essential content but made them more readable.

Treatment of Key Terms and Ideas

Message Structure. What perspective on the subject matter is suggested by the manner in which the message is *organized?*

The structure of the message provides clues to the way communicators see their subject matter, and more important, how they want others to see it. As Campbell (1972) has observed:

> A historical-chronological form emphasizes development over time. A narrative-dramatic form reflects an organic view of reality and assumes that vicarious sharing of integrally related experiences is essential to the understanding of a concept or situation. A problem-solution form emphasizes the need to discover a concrete policy in order to resolve a troublesome situation. A cause-effect form stresses the prediction of consequences. A topical form selects certain facts of the subject and suggests that others are relatively unimportant. A taxonomical form focuses on the interrelationships between the parts of a process or between the parts and the whole. Each structural form represents a choice of perspective that emphasizes certain elements of the material over others. (p. 16)

In its "liberals" ad, Mobil attempts to create the image of presenting incontrovertible deductive logic by the manner in which it organizes the material. If liberals want X, Y, and Z, as they say they do, then they should favor A, B, and C because A, B, and C lead to X, Y, and Z. Since not all liberals favor A, B, and C, these liberals are illogical and Mobil has a right to be puzzled.

Alignments and Divisions. What is the structure of alignments and divisions among key terms in the message? What is identified with what and what is opposed to what?

To summarize the main ideas of a message in a way that will point to nonobvious meanings, methods, and motives, Burke (1966) recommends a method known as *cluster analysis.* This involves searching out relationships of linkage and division among key terms in the message. In a typical message, says Burke, there is a cluster of favorable notions reflecting the communicator's *frame of acceptance,* and a subordinated cluster of unfavorable elements reflecting a *frame of rejection.* Ideas in each cluster are symbolically aligned and simultaneously distanced from those interlinked in the other cluster, the two clusters together thus forming a symbolic "equation" of antithetically balanced pairs.

A graphic illustration of clusters of "good" and "bad" opposing elements is found in this excerpt from the introduction to Martin Gardner's (1957) *Fads and Fallacies,* a book aimed at exposing such alleged "pseudosciences" as ESP, the flying saucer theory, Alfred Korzybski's general semantics, Velikovsky's "big bang" theory, astrology, and various dietary schemes. Gardner links "science" with "reputable investigators" and elevates both in relation to the promoters of "new and strange scientific theories." There is a further symbolic division between an "enlightened public" and the "less informed general public." Lest anyone believe that the line between "pseudo" and "real" is a fuzzy one, Gardner assures us that they typically are as different as "black and white." Thus, one can presumably be as confident of the differences between "real" science and "pseudo" science as one can about science itself. The key terms in this excerpt are represented below in clusters widely separated from one another. To the positive (+) and negative (−) clusters one might add other antithetical concepts, some of which are implied but not necessarily stated in the excerpt. These are given in parenthesis.

+ *Science*	− *Pseudoscience*
Reputable investigators	Incompetent and self-deluded investigators
Important matters	New and strange scientific theories
Busy doing	(Mostly talking)
(Leading)	Riding on coat-tails
Enlightened public	Less informed general public

One curious consequence of the current boom in science is the rise of the promoter of new and strange "scientific" theories. He is riding into prominence, so to speak, on the coat-tails of reputable investigators. The scientists themselves, of course, pay very little attention to him. They are too busy with more important matters. But the less informed general public, hungry for sensational discoveries and quick panaceas, often provides him with a noisy and enthusiastic following.

In the last analysis, the best means of combating the spread of pseudoscience is an enlightened public, able to distinguish the work of a reputable investigator from the work of the incompetent and self-deluded. This is not as hard to do as one might think. Of course, there always will be borderline cases hard to classify, but the fact that black shades into white through many shades of gray does not mean that the distinction between black and white is difficult (p. 7).★

Somewhat more complex is the Mobil Liberals ad, because it is built on two alleged ironies: (1) Those liberals who give the appearance of being most aligned with the needy are in fact seeking to divide the needy from their chief sources of financial support; (2) these same "professional" liberals align themselves with government and against business in the interests of democracy when it is business which is truly democratic. At issue fundamentally in this ad is the question of how these "unthinking" liberals think. The ad is about their own clusters of "good" and "bad," which Mobil places in its own negative

★ Martin Gardner, *Fads and Fallacies*, Dover Publications, Inc., New York, 1957. Reprinted through the permission of the publisher.

cluster, as shown below. Note that the key rhetorical strategy in this ad is one of "divide and conquer." Whereas liberals are typically identified one with another by way of a single cultural stereotype, they are here divided into two types, the better to vilify the "unthinking" liberal, while permitting Mobil the opportunity to woo "thinking" liberals.

+		−
Mobil		*"Professional" Liberals' Thinking*

	+	−
"Enlightened" liberals	Liberals	Conservatives
Independent thinking	Anti-business	Pro-business
	Government	
Responsiveness/democracy	Democracy	Anti-government/elitism
Helping the needy through business support		
	Helping the needy	Indifferent to the needy

Attributions of Causation. What *causes* are singled out in descriptions or explanations of a phenomenon? How else might the phenomenon be reasonably described or explained? What is magnified or minimized by the account?

Whenever a complex process is described, chances are that some causes will be selected over others. Upon observing conditions in a slum, a minister may see evidence of sinfulness, a police officer of lawlessness, a Marxist of the failure of capitalism. Burke (1945) speaks here of *Act, Scene, Agent, Agency, Purpose* as key elements in any well-rounded account of what people are doing and why they are doing it. And he suggests that one of these terms will generally be featured in causal explanations.

> In a rounded statement about motives, you must have some word that names the *act* (names what took place, in thought or deed), and another that names the *scene* (the background of the act, the situation in which it occurred); also, you must indicate what person or kind of person (*agent*) performed the act, what means or instruments he used (*agency*), and the *purpose*. Men may disagree about the purposes behind a given act, or about the character of the person who did it, or how the person did it, or in what kind of situation he or she acted; or they may even insist upon totally different words to name the act itself. But any complete statement about motives will offer *some kind* of answers to these five questions: what was done (act), when or where it was done (scene), who did it (agent), how he or she did it (agency), and why (purpose). (p. xv.)

The plasticity of these dramatic concepts—the way their ambiguity may be exploited by persuaders—is illustrated in the following case:

> The hero (agent) with the help of a friend (co-agent) outwits the villain (counteragent) by using a file (agency) that enables him to break his bonds (act) in order to escape (purpose) from the room where he has been confined (scene). In selecting a casuistry here, we might locate the motive in the agent, as were we to credit his escape to some trait integral to his personality, such as "love of freedom." Or we might stress the motivational force of the scene, since nothing is surer to awaken thoughts of escape in a man than a condition of imprisonment.

Or we might note the essential part played by the co-agent in assisting our hero to escape—and, with such thoughts as our point of departure, we might conclude that the motivations of this act should be reduced to social origins.

Or if one were given to the brand of speculative enterprise exemplified by certain Christian heretics (for instance, those who worshipped Judas as a saint, on the grounds that his betrayal of Christ, in leading to the Crucifixion, brought about the opportunity for mankind's redemption) one might locate the necessary motivational origin of the act in the *counter-agent*. For the hero would not have been prodded to escape if there had been no villain to imprison him. Inasmuch as the escape could be called a "good" act, we might find in such motivational reduction to the counter-agent a compensatory transformation whereby a bitter fountain may give forth sweet waters.

Pragmatists would probably have referred the motivation back to source in *agency*. They would have noted that our hero escaped by using an *instrument*, the file by which he severed his bonds; then in the same line of thought, they would have observed that the hand holding the file was also an instrument; and by the same token the brain that guided the hand would be an instrument, and so likewise the educational system that taught the methods and shaped the values involved in the incident. (p. xx)

Implicit in seemingly objective determinations of cause and effect are judgments of value and policy. As illustrated in the previous case, agent-centered explanations are preferred where one wishes to credit or blame; scenic explanations are typically offered to escape blame or to deny credit to one's enemies.

Attributions of causation frequently involve selecting an arbitrary starting point as the "cause" of a complex, continuing process of interacting causes and effects. Husband says that wife's nagging causes his alcoholism. Wife says that his alcoholism causes her nagging. Watzlawick, Beavin, and Jackson (1967) refer to this vividly as the *punctuation* of cause and effect. In the Gardner book, pseudoscientists are said to be ignored by the scientific community in part because they are "paranoid." Gardner does not consider the possibility that their "paranoia" may be caused, in part, by the scientific community's rejection.

Balance/Imbalance. Are there imbalances in the selection and arrangement of materials? Is the presentation one-sided? If two-sided, are arguments that might run counter to the communicator's conclusions given equal weight? Is the appearance of fairness created by giving ground on trivial issues while holding firm on major ones? Is bias reflected in the placement of arguments, or in the way opposing views are represented, or in the treatment of pertinent facts? Are some relevant facts glossed over or concealed entirely?

A training film by the Sun Corporation provides an interesting example of imbalance. It is a training film on how to handle asbestos that plays down the problem even as it addresses it. The film does not discuss the dangers of asbestos until a long introduction on the many risks of life (e.g., crossing the street, driving a car) is completed. This form of contextualizing has the effect of minimizing the dangers of asbestos. Little is said about what the company should do to prevent workers from exposure to asbestos dust. The emphasis is on what the workers should do. Asbestos and cancer from asbestos are classified as mere "occupational hazards," like pricking one's finger when sewing. The "hero" of the film is shown smoking and drinking coffee in the company cafeteria. He is not too smart, and he does not ask embarrassing questions, such as "How can I file a grievance over Sun exposing me to asbestos dust?" He is the model trainee viewers should emulate. The Sun film contrasts sharply with films on the subject by unions and by a government agency. In the union film, especially, the dangers of asbestos are played up and industry is blamed for ignoring the problem.

This completes the guide to persuasion in the guise of objectivity. However, many issues briefly touched upon here are discussed at greater length in other chapters. In particular, you should review Chapter 10 if you intend your analysis to cover not only questions of balance/imbalance in the presentation of evidence and arguments, but also questions about their quality. By the same token, you might well refer back to this chapter in analyzing messages of a clearly partisan nature. Many of the questions raised in the guide—about meta-communications, about choice and treatment of language—are relevant to virtually all persuasive messages.

Applying the Guide: Additional Examples

Case A: Scholarly Rhetoric

A rather fascinating rhetorical analysis was performed by Joseph Gusfield (1976). It focused upon 45 drunk driver studies, and in particular a study by Waller (1967) entitled "Identification of Problem-Drinking Among Drunken Drivers," which was selected by Gusfield for detailed analysis on the grounds that it had frequently been cited and exhibited rhetorical features typical of the other research papers. The Gusfield analysis points to many of the markers of persuasion in the guise of objectivity presented in the guide.

Gusfield's thesis in this analysis is twofold: (1) "To be scientific is to exercise a definite form over the language in use, to write in a particular way which shows that the writer is 'doing science.' " (2) "The artistic side of science is a significant part of the scientist's display of the external world" (pp. 17–18).

The first part of Gusfield's thesis takes us back to the discussion of image management. In the drunk driver studies, says Gusfield, the researchers maintain a tone of impersonal objectivity, revealed, for example, by their use of the passive, third-person, grammatical form ("It appeared that . . . ," "It was found," "The results indicated . . ."). The studies are all "placed" in established scientific or medical journals, thus lending them an air of respectability. Similarly, the authors signal their own competence by listing their professional roles and organizational affiliations. But having told the audiences of their professional competence, the authors move out of the limelight by establishing a reality outside the observer. This is accomplished by an emphasis on method which makes it appear as though anyone following the same regimen would have been led to the same conclusions. Similarly, there is a meticulous concern for detail in these studies that metacommunicates an image of great scientific integrity. In the Waller study, for example, percentages are given in decimals, such as 19.3 or 6.1 percent, rather than being rounded out. The language of the essay is emptied of feeling and emotion. Imagine, says Gusfield, that the title of Waller's article had been more journalistic ("He Couldn't Help Himself") or more literary ("The End of The Road"): Either title would have led to very different readings of the article. Finally, Waller metacommunicated subtly that he was on the reader's side—for example, in treating the issues primarily from the vantage point of how society might best be protected. In these ways Waller was said by Gusfield to project an image of *psychological distance* from his subject matter and *psychological proximity* toward his audience.

Many of these metacommunicational characteristics are reflected in the opening *"Abstract" of the Waller study*, reproduced below.

Information about previous contact with community agencies, particularly contact involving drinking problems, was compared for 150 drunken drivers, 33 accident-involved drivers who had been drinking but were not arrested, 117 sober drivers involved in accidents, 131 drivers with moving violations, 19 drivers with citations plus arrest warrants, and 150 incident-free drivers. Screening criteria for problem-drinkers were two or more previous arrests involving drinking or identification by a community agency as a problem drinker. These criteria were met by the following: drunken drivers, 63%; drivers with an accident after drinking, 50%; drivers with warrants, 30%; non-drinking drivers with an accident, 14%; persons with driving violations, 8%; and drivers with no incidents, 3%. High correlation was found between two or more arrests involving drinking and an impression of problem drinking. Eighty-seven percent of the drunken drivers were known to community agencies, most with multiple contacts starting before age 30. (p. 124)

For the second part of Gusfield's thesis, his claim that "the artistic side of science is a significant part of the scientist's display of the external world," Gusfield makes particular use of cluster analysis. In the Waller study, drinking drivers are classified as "problem drinkers" or "social drinkers." By Waller's use of language, observes Gusfield, these two types are presented as caricatures, the former conjuring up an image of a reeling, low-status drunk, the latter depicted as a solid citizen who just happens to take a drink now and then. The contrast between stock characters is magnified in many ways. For example, "problem drinkers" are disproportionately nonwhite, and nonwhite drinking drivers are said to have a greater number of arrests per person than whites. Only later does Waller acknowledge that the differences are not statistically significant. Thus, as Gusfield points out, the image of the nonwhite as problem drinker is introduced and then qualified, rather than being presented directly as a qualified or ambiguous image.

In these and countless other examples, we see that rhetorical choices can function to conceal or reveal, magnify or minimize, simplify or complexify, elevate or degrade, sharpen images or blur them, evoke links between things or divisions between them, create a sense of breadth or of specificity, and evoke varying connotative reactions.

Case B: Psychiatric Rhetoric

The next case illustrates the familiar problem in rhetorical criticism of demonstrating that one's own view of "the real" is any better grounded than the views one is trying to undermine. Claims of this kind are particularly difficult to defend when objectivity itself is called into question. To the charge that a communicator or group of communicators is pretentious and self-serving comes the retort: How do you know what things are *really* like?

Just such a response from the psychiatric community greeted Thomas Szasz's (1970) indictment of psychiatrists for practicing a secular theology in the guise of medical science. Citing parallels in religion to psychiatry's methods and purposes, Szasz claimed psychiatrists were religious shamans in disguise. His premise was that most so-called mental illnesses were really no more than problems in living, and were certainly not worthy of being labeled as illnesses in any medical sense. If people's mental illnesses were like medical ills, he maintained, they would be able to catch them, harbor them in tissues, and perhaps transmit them to others; that is, there would be a physiological basis for them.

As part of his critique of the psychiatric profession, Szasz maintained that psychiatrists "de-politicized" questions of "how to live" for devious purposes, posing as helpers of the so-called mentally ill, but actually committing many patients to mental institutions in the interests of the patients' families or of the society as a whole. Examples of persons unfairly labeled, by Szasz's account, were drug users and sexual deviants, persons who chose not to live by society's rules but who nevertheless could function quite effectively in society without harming anyone. Branding these people as "mentally ill," said Szasz, constituted a justificatory "rhetoric of oppression" that concealed the psychiatrist's partisan motives by treating the label as a merely technical one. The widespread use of the label was also self-serving, he said, for it legitimated an ever wider role in society for the psychiatric profession. And, since persons labeled "mentally ill" are often not listened to when they deny the validity of the classification, the label had the further effect of robbing them even of a language for expressing their victimization. Not all patients were opposed in the guise of supporting them, said Szasz. In the case of the neurotic who came for psychotherapy, the patient was often supported in opposition to the interests of others. But, in either case, said Szasz, the psychiatrist concealed his own partisan motives.

Szasz's writings have contributed to the de-institutionalization of mental illness and to restrictions on the use of the "illness" label by psychiatrists as applied to homosexuals and other so-called "deviants." But Szasz's views remain controversial. Were psychiatrists guilty of an "immoral rhetoric of identity deception" or did they simply hold to a different perspective than Szasz?

Case C: Rhetoric of This Chapter

A former graduate student, who happened also to be an oil company executive, did a rhetorical analysis of a miniversion of this chapter, maintaining that many of its examples and interpretations were ideologically biased against the big oil companies. Among his major objections were the following:

1. *Imbalance in the Sun Oil example.*

Simons mentions that the Sun film differs greatly from a film on the same subject made by the unions. He notes that in the union film the dangers of asbestos are highlighted, and that industry, in general, is blamed because they know the problem exists. Now the question I must raise is whether the union film shows all the problems, faults, bad habits, the ignoring of regulations, the years of fighting with management, that takes place on the part of the individual workers who refuse to wear their protective masks. This writer was personally involved in situations, when I was going through college, where I saw laborers working around asbestos and every day ignoring the equipment that was provided for them by management, and ignoring all the safety regulations that were posted every twenty to thirty feet in an area where the danger of asbestos was high. I am going to guess—and underscore that it is a guess—that I don't think the union film showed the workers' bad habits. I wouldn't expect them to do so! Also, I wouldn't expect Sun to show in their film a worker who is going to file a grievance! Of course an actor in Sun's film is not going to question how he can file a grievance against the company about asbestos; and of course an actor in a union film is not going to admit that he ignores the very safety rules that are imposed on him, for his protection, by the company. You might say that this is all obvious. But what is not obvious, and what is, in essence, persuasion, is that what Simons is communicating in his paragraph is that the Sun Company film, purporting to be an objective treatment of asbestos, actually contextualizes asbestos in order to downplay and minimize the alarm to you, the viewer. What Simons is not telling you is that by comparison the union film and the Government Agency films, on the same subject, of course are also contextualizing to best serve their ends.

2. *Mobil and the "Unsaid."*

One of the techniques that Simons gives us for objectively analyzing a message is to be sure to be aware of what is unsaid or concealed in the message. The example of this given in the paper concerns the ads of the Mobil Oil Company. Simons wants to be sure that we know that Mobil is the second largest oil company in America and that they have made enormous profits. But what exactly are enormous profits? It seems to me that the term is extremely subjective. While I would agree that anything in the millions of dollars is enormous to you and me, as individuals, would it really be enormous to Mobil? If I invest ten dollars in a bank account, and over a year's time earn one dollar on it, is the one dollar enormous? Most certainly not! If Mobil invests one hundred million dollars, and earns nine million dollars on it, is nine million dollars enormous? Well it obviously is a lot of money, but the point is that Mobil earned 9% on their investment and I earned 10% on mine. Did I earn more than Mobil? Are *enormous profits* going to be based on just the actual dollars themselves, or on the capital investment used to generate the dollars, or on the equity involved, or on the price of the stock; exactly how are you going to measure *enormous profits?* It seems to me that the term *enormous profits*, is, in today's jargon, somewhat pejorative, and most certainly introduces subjective elements in what is supposed to be an objective analysis. Even aside from the use of the term, *enormous profits*, and aside from the fact that we are reminded that Mobil is the second largest oil company and that we should keep this in mind when viewing their ads, we must question what is not said. Is it any more relevant, in viewing the Mobil ad, to keep in mind that Mobil is the second largest oil company, than it is that they employ one hundred thousand people, or that they give hundreds of millions of dollars to charity? I will leave the reader to answer that question. I do not know if these facts are any more relevant, but certainly in viewing the Mobil ads there is nothing that logically dictates that the only additional thing that I must know about Mobil is that they are the second largest oil company. It seems to me that what is left unsaid by Simons is any aspects that we might consider "good" qualities of Mobil.

3. *Alignments and Divisions in the Mobil Example.*

Another technique of objectively viewing a message is to be cognizant of the *clusters of alignments and divisions* within the rhetorical framework of the message. The very way in which a message is formed has a lot to do with what we perceive, both on the conscious and unconscious level. Again, in the paper by Simons, what we have is Mobil, and other big oil companies, being linked up with terms like: artificial oil shortages, monopoly, windfall profits, pollution, collusion, bribing, illegal contributions and withholding information. The point of reading the particular paragraph in question is to allow the reader to be sure that when he analyzes a message, he understands the underlying purpose that the creator of the message might have. Fair enough! But in giving examples of how one might objectively do this, and to use the example of an oil company that is linked with extremely inflammatory and pejorative terms, seems to me to align Mobil with breaking the law and cheating the public, on one pole and the rhetorician, the teacher, and the public on another pole. I think that someone who is unbiased when he begins reading Simons' paper would have to be negatively conditioned towards Mobil Oil Company at the conclusion of the paper, just because of the cluster of terms that Simons has associated with Mobil.

4. *Big Oil and Attributions of Causation.*

Many times the paper suggests that big business is after profits to such a degree they sacrifice ethics, morality, and the worker himself, as long as a profit is realized. The academic community many times views money making as "sinful" and tends to overreact against the profit motive (persuasive terms on my part). Throughout the paper Simons casts profits, economic growth, business executives, and capitalism in a negative light. Does the drive for corporate profits cause collusion, or breakdowns in the Welfare System, or the bribing of politicians? Are Simons' *attributions of causation*, illustrated in his paper, logical? Are politicians bribed because Mobil makes money? Are our social welfare programs in such dire straits because Mobil makes money? The point is that the reader might be persuaded, while not objectively shown, that an awful lot of what is wrong with our current society is somehow caused by Mobil, and other big oil companies, making money.

5. *"Windfall Profits as Buzz Word."*

Simons uses, a number of times in his paper, the term "windfall profits" when talking about the oil companies. I think this term is one of the most wonderful buzz words that has come into recent business and economic parlance. The "Windfall Profits" Tax actually does not exist as a tax under that name. It technically is an excise tax that was passed as part of the Tax Reduction Act in 1976. By the way, if you want to talk about obfuscation, how about a Congressional Bill, whose sole purpose was to gather more tax dollars for the Treasury, being labeled a "Tax Reduction Act." What this excise tax was supposed to do was to create revenue for the Government by taking the difference between oil that was discovered twenty-five and thirty years ago, which in essence cost two or three dollars a barrel but has a present selling value of twenty-eight dollars a barrel, and then tax that difference at very high tax rates. From the standpoint of rhetoric, what is most interesting is that the tax has nothing whatsoever to do with profits. Being a sales tax, it is levied on revenues, so, in essence, your company could be losing money but be paying this excise tax.

6. *Simons' Metacommunications.*

One last note on some metacommunicational cues that Simons gives us in his paper. We know that these cues are impressions of source credibility and serve to create impressions of objectivity in the message sender. In this case there is an obviously explicit message that we are given when we begin the paper because Simons tells us that he has written a book on the subject at hand. He explains how he used messages about content in his book and compares himself with other authors in the field. We are immediately put on notice that someone is talking to us who is an expert in his field. We are given implicit cues, as well, that serve as metacommunications. When someone (me?) writes a paper about the dangers of persuasion in the guise of objectivity, he adopts a stance that may be viewed as being more objective than the average man. That is, the author is seen as looking for objectivity, or looking for persuasion presented as objectivity in someone else. We receive cues, implicitly, about the author as being like a man performing the role for us of "omniscient observer." In addition to the implicit and explicit cues Simons gives us, we have an overall framework which houses the fact that we know, as readers of this paper, that Simons is the teacher of our course in persuasion. My goodness, if you ever were inclined to take something as objective, you probably couldn't think of a better case, because of all the metacommunicational cues, than to treat Simons' message as being objective. So, we have to be very, very careful when you have such an authority figure, supposedly objective, using examples about the oil business to an audience primed for, and geared to, receptivity toward that authority figure. In conclusion, I have attempted to look at the paper, "Persuasion in the Guise of Objectivity: A Framework for Analysis," to see whether or not there was, within the context of the paper, persuasion taking place regarding the oil companies. I think that there is persuasion in the paper. I think there is a great lack of objectivity, and a great lack of analysis of the facts, and a great deal of rhetoric, when it comes to discussion of the oil companies. We are told in the paper "Don't just assert; support your claims." Simons fails to do this in his comments concerning big business and oil companies. Our conclusion should be that we have to be very, very careful to keep a balanced view of all messages, even those messages that tell us to be very, very careful to keep a balanced view—like this one!

SUMMARY

Some messages purport to be unbiased and impartial, while others purport to provide objective support for more obviously rhetorical claims or objectives. This chapter has offered guiding questions and illustrations to help you analyze both types of persuasion in the guise of objectivity.

Broadly speaking, we may distinguish between the way messages are *framed* and how, by their choice and treatment of terms, they *picture* reality. In the first category are message classifications (e.g., "information," "education," "documentary"), declarations of purpose, and presentation of self in relationship to the audience. In the second category are the ways such basic rhetorical elements as labels, definitions, and illustrations could be used to conceal or reveal, magnify or minimize, sharpen or blur, and so on.

Raised here, as in Chapter 6, are questions about the appropriate critical stance of the rhetorician. If objectivity is unattainable, then surely the critic's own analyses of persuasion in the guise of objectivity are themselves suspect— themselves in need of rhetorical analysis. But if no critique can be said to provide the last word on a subject, this does not mean that all rhetorical judgments are arbitrary and without merit. To the contrary, there is great value in making the best case we can for a critical analysis.

EXERCISES

1. Some questions for thought and discussion: Is it possible to be objective in providing an analysis of persuasion in the guise of objectivity? If not, is there still value in examining ostensibly objective discourse from a rhetorical perspective? What is your evaluation of the "rhetoric" of this chapter? Do you agree with the analysis of the oil company examples by a former student? Should I have changed the examples? Should I have included the critique of the examples?

2. Using materials of your own choosing, do an analysis of persuasion in the guise of objectivity. For example, analyze one of the following:
   a. Ideological bias in American history books
   b. Religious indoctrination in Sunday School classes
   c. Quarterly reports to stockholders by corporations
   d. Supreme Court opinions on politically sensitive issues
   e. Investigative reports by regulatory agencies
   f. Orientation manuals for army recruits or new employees

3. The ad reprinted on page 145 was placed in a number of magazines by the R. J. Reynolds Tobacco Company as part of a major ad campaign. At first blush it appears as a balanced and fair-minded account of a controversy. Is it? Drawing upon relevant questions in the guide, provide an analysis of the ad's meanings, methods, and motives.

   Begin with an assessment of the motivations of the cigarette manufacturer. In your opinion, whose attitudes is the advertisement designed to change, and whose attitudes is it trying to reinforce? How might the message "from those who don't to those who do" be unbalancing or incongruous to those who don't smoke? What would you predict is its intended effect on those who do smoke? Why is the message in the left-hand column included? How, by putting words in the nonsmoker's mouth (and excluding other, perhaps more damning words) might the advertiser be trying to shape the nonsmoker's self-perceptions? And what of the counterbalancing of the two messages in one advertisement? What is the message metacommunicating? What is it designed to accomplish on a relational level, in terms of the readers' images of the R. J. Reynolds Tobacco Company? What associations are triggered by the ad's format—its simple and symmetrical black and white design? And how is the framing of the issue as a matter of "common courtesy" designed to alter perceptions?

Now consider in more detail the choice and treatment of key terms and ideas. Suppose the nonsmokers had been represented as saying:

> We're hopping mad.
> To us, the smoke from your cigarettes can be anything from a minor irritant to a real threat. . . .

And suppose that their message had gone on to mention the health dangers they attributed to secondhand smoke, not just the fact of their exposure to it.

By the same token, why are the smokers "on the spot"? Why is smoking for them a "choice" (not to mention a "very personal choice"), rather than an addiction?

Suppose a comparable ad had been prepared by the American Cancer Society. How would the ACS have crafted it?

Chapter *16*
Analyzing Campaign Rhetoric

Of the hundreds of persuasive messages with which we are typically bombarded in the course of a day, most are campaign messages. Among the major influences in our culture are political campaigns, product advertising campaigns, and indoctrination campaigns—each to be discussed in this chapter. Whereas the focus of Chapter 12 was on how to lead persuasive campaigns, the focus here is on how to analyze them.

In studying campaigns, you should be able to find an abundance of resources both in the library and in the community. It is especially exciting to get out into the field and interview campaign leaders, gather up campaign literature, and monitor the activities of a campaign as it unfolds. Some organizations are forever campaigning, but you can usually select particular efforts (e.g., a charity's fall solicitation drive, a business organization's campaign to defeat the passage of a particular bill) for detailed examination. Other campaign messages will, of course, be presented to you over the mass media. We look particularly here at the role of television in political campaigns.

Political Campaigns and the Electronic Media

No doubt many of you will wish to analyze one or another presidential campaign. Before analyzing any large-scale campaign, it is essential that you narrow your critical focus and decide how you will organize the analysis. Particularly helpful are models such as the model of campaign stages and components introduced in Chapter 12 (see Figure 12.1). Looking back on recent contests, we can see how the model might be applied in analyses of presidential campaigns. In the

1972 presidential contest, the Democratic hopeful, Senator George McGovern, was clearly no match for Nixon on just about every count imaginable. The Nixon effort was planned to perfection: a dramatic scenario calculated to win over disaffected Democrats by picturing the incumbent as being "above politics," and the contender as immoderate, inconsistent, and clumsy.

McGovern did exceedingly well at mobilizing resources during the primaries; soliciting millions in small donations through a direct-mail campaign, building a large army of volunteers, and capturing media attention by his early successes in the primaries (when McGovern walked into New Hampshire a month before the first primary, he had a 3 percent popularity rating in the polls and could not even muster an essential accoutrement of any major political campaign, a press bus). Still, he was no match for the Nixon organization, and with each evidence of failure at the promotion stage, there came a corresponding diminution in the generosity of his financial backers and in the ardor of his campaign staff.

A basic problem was legitimacy, and this was to hurt him grievously when he attempted to promote his candidacy. The convention left deep wounds among key decision-makers within the Democratic party, many of whom either bolted the party or sat out the election. McGovern had legitimacy by power and position, but he seemed unrepresentative of the party's mainstream and thus lacked legitimacy by endorsement.

Some of McGovern's promotional problems were stylistic. More serious, according to James Reston (*New York Times,* October 4, 1972), was his basic misreading of the American people—pushing them too far and too fast on gut issues. It is a truism of American politics that the successful campaigner is usually one who can capture the ideological center. Garry Wills (1972) has taken this principle one step further, arguing that political candidates must "not only 'out-middle' each other, but also engage in compensatory blandishments toward those who have least reason to trust them" (p. 37). McGovern appeared to have learned this lesson too late ("By the end of this year's campaign, McGovern could rhetorically out-policeman Nixon at home and out-Rabbi him abroad"—Wills), and his shifts on basic issues only served to undermine his initial base of support.

By early September, the die was cast. Over 60 percent of the American public had made preliminary commitments (often public commitments to friends and relatives; here the interpersonal network is important) for Nixon—or against McGovern. When the Watergate break-in was revealed in the press, the public could not assimilate it or connect it with Nixon; people had already been too well activated to alter their behavioral intentions.

The Image-Building Functions of the Electronic Media

This retrospective on the Nixon-McGovern contest should serve to illustrate how large-scale political campaigns may be incorporated within the model. Still, so far as these campaigns are concerned, the model makes insufficient provision for the role of the mass media, and particularly television.

At the very least, television makes it possible for a national candidate to appear "live" before many more millions of people than is possible by face-to-face communication. More than the other media, it can augment or diminish the effects of a candidate's messages by its reportage and its analyses and interpretations of the news. Even more impressive is television's capacity to build composite political images out of the bits and pieces of personality that a candidate's media and public relations experts may choose to expose to the voting public.

VOICE: Mr. President, what about the high cost of living?

EISENHOWER: My wife, Mamie, worries about the same thing, I tell her it's our job to change that on November 4.

In this, the first of the campaign-by-television spectaculars, Eisenhower turned to Madison Avenue for help in selling his grandfather image. Before that—even as late as the forties—although politicians had made widespread use of radio, the *forms* of their presentations over the electronic media constituted mere extensions of the platform speech styles they had habitually employed in the past. After that, politicians were almost invariably sold like pantyhose and popcorn:

CAMERA: Little girl picking daisies while babbling a countdown. Camera fades to a countdown at an atomic testing site. Scene dissolves into a mushroom-shaped cloud.

JOHNSON: These are the stakes: to make a world in which all God's children can live, or go into the dark. We must love each other or we must die.

The potential of television to create images that bear little or no relation to realities is perhaps best illustrated by a commercial in behalf of Clair Engle, an incumbent seeking reelection to the Senate in California in 1964. Engle had undergone brain surgery, had a paralyzed arm, and could barely walk or talk, but a carefully edited, repeatedly aired television commercial created an image of health. Fortunately for the voters, Engle died before the primary (Nimmo, 1970, pp. 141–42).

Romancing the Voter

Television also makes it possible for relative unknowns to become instant political contenders. Eugene McCarthy in 1968, George McGovern in 1972, Jimmy Carter in 1976, and Gary Hart in 1984 were each able to catapult themselves to prominence through television advertising and astute manipulation of television news.

Few politicians have made better use of television than did Jimmy Carter during the 1976 Democratic primaries. In the wake of Watergate, credibility became the watchword of political campaigns, and Carter sought to personify it with his ingratiating smile, his repeated promises that he would never lie to us, his background as farmer, engineer, populist governor, and devout Christian.

Strongly influencing the campaign was pollster Pat Caddell, whose theory of the alienated voter meshed well with the times and with Carter's persona, and whose sophisticated polling methods have set a precedent for subsequent campaigns.

Caddell conceives of alienation as a lack of trust in government and politicians to act in the voter's self-interest. One manifestation of it, he maintained, was the widespread support in 1968 for liberal Bobby Kennedy and conservative George Wallace by voters who saw in both an antipathy toward mainstream, Establishment politics. Caddell sought to land voters such as these in Carter's column through thematic messages rather than messages taking concrete stands on specific issues. Thus, for example, Carter was repeatedly pictured as a Washington outsider, and even as an "antipolitician." When voters became disaffected with the thematic appeals and began demanding more information, Caddell's polls were able to pick this up and adjust accordingly.

More than most pollsters before him, Caddell's methods were designed to profile strengths and weaknesses in rival candidates and to suggest needed adaptations, for particular voting segments, by the candidates he backed. A memo distributed within the upper echelons of the Ford campaign lamented that Caddell "always is in the field on a basis sufficient to disaggregate key states and constituencies from a national sample. Hence there is the possibility of a quick response to any new shifts in opinion and their immediate communication to the candidate. The Ford operation, by contrast, as befits a presidential staff operation, has double or triple the reaction time to new voter moods—a real disadvantage in a short campaign" (quoted in Blumenthal, 1980, pp. 37–38).

Political Cybernetics

Fine-tuning the electorate—determining what they want, devising messages tailored to those wants, testing those messages on sample voters before sending them out on a mass basis, surveying again to assess message effects, then using this information in devising new messages—was brought to a high art by the Committee to Elect Ronald Reagan in 1980. No organization—not the soap or the beer or the car manufacturers—spent more on television advertising that year, and the Reagan spots generally reflected sound audience analysis.

It is widely maintained that most voters, and especially those with low political involvement, get gratification from political campaigns chiefly because of the drama and entertainment they can provide (see Nimmo and Combs, 1980). For most people, the electronic media are about the only sources of political exposure. Television, especially, is said to fill a social void in people's lives. Campaigns by television provide objects on which they can project their wishes and illusions, fears and hostility. They become fans of political parties and candidates in much the same way they identify with football teams or baseball heroes. And rather than demanding hard information from newscasters, they insist upon "human interest" materials that will provide escape from duty and routine and items for small talk among friends. Says Edelman (1967):

> If political acts are to promote social adjustment and are to mean what our inner
> problems require that they mean, these acts have to be dramatic in outline and
> empty of realistic detail. In this sense publishers and broadcast licenses are telling
> the exact truth when they excuse their poor performance with the plea that they
> give the public what it wants. It wants symbols and not news. (p. 9)

In the presidential election contest of 1980, there were strong pressures
within Republican ranks to exploit television's character as an entertainment
medium by putting on a slick, highly entertaining advertising campaign.
Proponents of this strategy urged that professional actors be hired to create a
series of attack commercials that would display President Carter as a bumbling
incompetent.

Another faction within the Republican party, and ultimately the one that
prevailed, urged a positive campaign strategy, even at the risk of having the
ads appear dull. The essential requirement of the campaign, it was argued, was
that it play down qualities of the challenger perceived negatively by the voter,
such as his relative inexperience, and his reputation as an extremist. The ads
could attack the Carter record, but not the man himself. This meant that the
ads had to be factual and the facts well substantiated even if they appeared
somewhat dull. Emphasized by the Republican National Committee were ads
of the "talking heads" variety, featuring Reagan or some other leading figure
merely talking to the television camera and perhaps showing charts that
contrasted the campaign promises and the actual record of the Carter administration. Above all, the ads deflected attention from the negative image of
Reagan as a former actor by employing amateurs in testimonial roles and
allowing Reagan a few slips here and there in the delivery of his materials.
Focused interviews with Democrats who said they were independent revealed
that the ads were indeed perceived as dull, but they elicited favorable ratings
toward Reagan from the test sample.

The "Permanent Campaign"

The 1980 Reagan campaign defied political logic in other ways as well. Although
Reagan moderated his right-wing ideology somewhat, he made no bones about
his stands on a number of issues that even his own running mate feared would
land him in the soup. But Reagan was interested not just in catering to a
constituency, but in shaping a constituency. He wanted and received a mandate
for major legislative change. On the basis of his own strengths as a campaigner
and the weak showing of his rival, Reagan achieved his goals.

The term "permanent campaign" was used by Caddell in a memo urging
Carter to be working for his reelection from the moment he took office, but it
has been the Reagan administration and the conservative wing of his party
generally that have best exemplified Caddell's good advice. Reagan and his
conservative cohorts have been working for nothing less than a major realignment
of our political parties that will succeed in shifting the weight of the public
opinion toward conservative programs and politicians at least through this
century. Reagan's is a movement, and not just a campaign.

An important behind-the-scenes figure in the conservative movement is marketer Richard Viguerie. Viguerie specializes in direct-mail advertising. His treasure-trove of millions of names on computer tape constitutes a mobilizational base for the movement—a source of funds, of campaign volunteers, of information, and of votes. In the hands of Viguerie and his associates, the mails provide a vehicle not just for garnering support, but also for shaping opinion. As more and more people own personal computers, and as computers and telephones are hooked to two-way television technologies, the prospects for exercising political influence will be greatly increased. Intensive use of television, cybernetic adaptation, and permanence are sure to be hallmarks of the major political campaigns of the future.

Rhetorical Visions and the American Monomyth

One reason Ronald Reagan was able to get away with conspicuously ideological themes in 1984 was that he personally embodied what Nimmo and Combs (1980) have called the *American monomyth*. These authors argue that America's political mythology bears striking resemblance to themes running through its

How do scenes such as this one reinforce Reagan's monomythic image? *(AP/Wide World Photos)*

movies, its television series, its comic strips. As exemplified by such folk heroes as the Lone Ranger or Superman, or by such Hollywood cult figures as John Wayne and Gary Cooper, the American monomyth offers a recurrent plot of evil redeemed through heroic acts. The American hero is most often out of the West, a figure of humble origins such as Abe Lincoln who, hearing a call, responds reluctantly but forcefully to the necessity of leading a crusade against forces of evil that threaten the American Way.

This crusade, add the authors, has religious overtones. The American "quest" saga begins in Eden and ends in Eden. It is a story of a Fall and of eventual Redemption, involving cycles of sin, suffering, sacrifice, and salvation.

There have been numerous attempts to epitomize Ronald Reagan's mono-mythic status as folk hero, entertainment hero, and quasi-religious figure, but the best one I have found is in an account of the 1984 Republican convention by novelist V. S. Naipaul (1984). Said Naipaul of a film that was being used to tout the candidate:

> Once, before he became president, he was asked by a reporter, "Governor, whom are you patterning your life after?" Mr. Reagan said, "Oh, that's very easy. The man from—" After all the shots of John Wayne in "Ronald Reagan's America," and the emphasis on Mr. Reagan's own film past, one might have expected Mr. Reagan to say, "The man from Laramie." But what he said was, "The man from Galilee." And, oddly, during the convention week, the two did not seem dissimilar. (p. 30)

The term *rhetorical vision* was coined by critic Ernest Bormann (1972) to characterize a group's sense of mission—its collective conception of what it is about and what it needs to do to accomplish its goals. Rhetorical visions, said Bormann, are revealed in the metaphors organizations use to describe themselves, in the stories they tell about themselves, and particularly in their dreams about the future.

The 1984 presidential contest was marked by sharp differences in the rhetorical visions of the parties. Whatever the realities, the Republicans presented images of themselves as unified behind a strong leader, as efficient in their handling of campaign events, as astute in their use of television, as confident of their place in the political future. The Democrats, by contrast, seemed dispirited, disorganized, disunited. Whereas the Republicans paraded themselves as the vanguard of American politics, the Democrats complained publicly that they had lost their way. Thus the Republicans campaigned vigorously to register new voters, while the Democrats sought to hold together a patchwork coalition that was coming apart at the seams. Even by mid-October, the Democrats could not settle on an overarching theme for their presidential campaign, and they were unable to capitalize on Reagan's poor showing in the first debate.

Worse yet, the Democrats' rhetorical vision effectively prevented them from retooling. Whatever else they might be, they were not going to be like "those Republicans." One leading Democrat boasted of her party's relative lack of discipline. "They are like toy soldiers," she said; "we are like guerilla fighters." This same attitude carried over into their political strategizing. While the Republicans were fine-tuning their campaign messages in accordance with principles of political cybernetics, the Democrats went public with a pledge of a tax increase that they knew from their research would be highly unpopular. Mondale himself was by most accounts a good man, and he might have become a great president, but he was also an old-fashioned politician, a rally speaker ill at ease on television. While Ronald Reagan spoke conversationally to us in our living rooms, Mondale shouted. Even many of the Mondale commercials presented clips from rally speeches. It was almost as though the Mondale camp regarded the television medium itself as an intrusion.

This discussion has introduced a number of concepts that you might find useful in analyzing other campaigns:

1. What is the campaign organization's rhetorical vision? What are its dreams, its fantasies, its conceptions of an ideal future? What metaphors ("toy soldiers," "rag-tag guerillas") does it use to describe itself? How does it see itself in relation to its competition?
2. What are the bases for its rhetorical strategies? How does it learn about its target audiences, and about the probable effects of its campaign messages? Does it employ cybernetic (feedback) mechanisms for altering or fine-tuning its rhetorical strategies?
3. Has it adapted to modern-day campaign requirements? In campaigns for major political office, does it make effective use of television? Does it run a permanent campaign? Is its message consistent with the American monomyth?

Analyzing Product Advertising Campaigns

Many have argued that the selling of political candidates is not much different from the promotion of products. By the same token, you should be able to apply the campaign model to the analysis of advertising campaigns with relatively few modifications. The planning, mobilization, and legitimation stages of a television advertising campaign bring together a variety of talents: market researchers who supply data on consumer characteristics and product perceptions, idea people who develop storyboards (cartoonlike frame sequences and captions), agency producers who oversee the development of the ads, production companies that create the finished products, network liaisons who secure approvals and arrange showings (Seiden, 1976). The promotion and activation stages of the campaign include not just the product's advertising, but also its packaging and merchandising. Together, these influences should lead the consumer to try the product, but as Ehrenberg (1981) has argued, they by no means guarantee repeat purchasing. Except where there are few differences among products, it is the consumer's own experience with the product that is ultimately decisive. Ehrenberg would thus emphasize processes of trial and reinforcement at the activation stage, in addition to processes of persuasion at the promotion stage.

Image Marketing

Among the most fascinating aspects of product advertising is the exploitation of images, real or imagined, associated with the product, and linking the product with its potential purchasers. Through market research, advertisers discover the "positives" and "negatives" associated with a product, and they learn as well how different target groups perceive these image attributes in relation to themselves. The admakers are then in a position to play up the "positives," downplay the "negatives," and in some cases, to reframe perceptions so that what once was a "negative" is now a "positive."

Some products have intrinsic qualities that differentiate them from others. Others, however, are almost entirely image, and their images are constructed from research and seat-of-the-pants guesses about consumers and purchasing trends. Reported *Time Magazine* (December 11, 1978), costlier cosmetics may have more fish scales or triethaanolamine, but the difference between a $5 jar of cream and a $50 jar is mostly image. High price is in fact one of the selling points of cosmetics.

Some image-projection techniques are fairly obvious. They include flattery, snob appeal, plain folks devices, appeals to fears, wishes, and common concerns. Less obvious are appeals to self-concepts, including fantasies about the self called *self-ideals*. Our reasoning goes something like the following: I have (or like, or wish to have) qualities a, b, c, d, n; product X has these same qualities; therefore, I like product X. Sometimes the advertiser must first get you to *want* to have qualities *a* through *n*; more often, the task is simply one of convincing you that product X has these qualities, and perhaps that they can be made to rub off on you.

Product images are often geared to particular market segments. Perfume images, for example, include: (1) the irresistibly sexy woman, (2) the liberated woman, (3) the career woman who is also seductive, (4) the sweet-but-not-too-sweet teenager, (5) the sensuous woman, and (6) the traditional homemaker.

Mankiewicz and Swerdlow (1978) reported on a fascinating study by two Wharton School researchers at the University of Pennsylvania. They were able to demonstrate that people in surprising numbers could be made to feel strong preferences for some beers and strong dislikes for others, even though all the beer was identical. The researchers first classified regular beer drinkers into personality types, then asked 250 of them to rate four prospective new brands for Anheuser-Busch: Bix, Zim, Waz, and Biv. Each of these fictitious brands was described to the beer drinkers in storyboards allegedly prepared as part of the development of advertising campaigns. And each was matched to a personality type. For example, one series of drawings showed a working man arriving home from a hectic day, sitting down with one of the brands, and watching the cares of the world fade away. This was designed for those who drink beer as an escape from worldly pressures. Consistent with their hypotheses, the researchers found that the beer drinkers all perceived differences among the beers; a significant number selected one particular brand as their favorite; and many said that one brand or another was undrinkable. Yet all the beer came from the same vat!

Recall that, as an exercise in conjunction with Chapter 2, you provided comparisons of oranges and grapefruit on such traits as intimate-distant, sunny-cloudy, young-old, friendly-unfriendly. Many students are surprised when they discover that the survey results display a clear and consistent pattern. Motivational analyst Ernest Dichter (1960) has done image studies of many other items. He found, for example, that wood evokes images of warmth, throbbing, being live. Glass is mysterious and dangerous to people, yet tantalizing and strangely pleasurable.

There is virtually no limit to the analyses we can perform on the character of the products being sold to us. Here, for example, are critic Roland Barthes' observations about the properties we typically assign to laundry detergents:

> Chlorinated fluids have always been experienced as a kind of liquid fire, the action of which must be carefully estimated. Otherwise, the object itself would be affected, "burnt." The implicit legend of this type of product rests on the idea of a violent, abrasive modification of matter: the connotations are of a chemical or mutilating type; the product "kills" the dirt. Powders, on the other hand, are separating agents; their ideal role is to liberate the object from its circumstantial imperfection; dirt is "forced out" and is no longer killed. In the powder imagery, dirt is a diminutive enemy, stunted and black, which takes to its heels from the fine immaculate linen at the sole threat of the products' judgment. Products based on chlorine and ammonia are without doubt the representatives of a kind of absolute fire, a saviour but a blind one. Powders, on the contrary, are selective; they push, they drive dirt through the texture of the object, their function is keeping order, not making war. This distinction has ethnographic co-relatives: the chemical fluid is an extension of the washerwoman's movements when she beats the clothes, while powders rather replace those of the housewife pressing and rolling the washing against a sloping board.
>
> As for foam, it is well known that it signifies luxury. To begin with, it appears to lack any usefulness; then its abundant, easy, almost infinite proliferation allows one to suppose there is in the substance from which it issues a powerful germ, a healthy and powerful essence, a great wealth of active elements in a small original volume. Finally, it gratifies in the consumer a tendency to imagine matter as something airy, with which contact is effected in a mode both light and vertical, which is sought after like that of happiness in the gustatory category, in clothing, or that of soaps. Foam can even be the sign of a certain spirituality, inasmuch as the spirit has the reputation of being able to make something out of nothing (pp. 36–37).

Interpreting Advertising Messages

What are we to make of these observations about product attributes? In looking for nonobvious meanings, methods, and motives in advertisements, how can we be sure that the admakers are doing what we think they are doing? Although product advertisers are often loathe to reveal their campaign strategies, we may nevertheless make intelligent stabs at uncovering them through careful readings of their messages and of the contexts in which they are created. The trick is to search for that interpretation that best explains the ad. This assumes, of course, that the admakers know what they are about—a reasonable assumption in most circumstances. Television critic Mark Crispin Miller (1981) would have us approach an apparently well constructed television commercial in much the same way we would a work of literature. As regards one particularly clever commercial, he writes:

> Half-noticed, this commercial might seem just the usual empty allurement, merely one bright bubble from the great boiling cesspool of daily television. That inundation, however, is precisely what allows commercials to succeed: they come at us in stupefying numbers, each one overcharged and utterly forgettable, so that we find ourselves lulled into the receptive state of the well hypnotized. Although the process seems like an enormous imposition, it depends on our own complicity. "It's only a commercial," we say to ourselves, then settle back, watching without really watching, thereby letting each image make its deep impressions. Although we have learned to distrust commercials automatically, this sort of knee-jerk skepticism is a poor defense against the subtleties of advertising, which can affect you whether or not you believe their ostensible claims.
>
> We are accustomed to think of these subtleties in quasi-Pavlovian terms, as hidden stimuli that "turn us on" without our knowing it: nipples airbrushed into sunsets, lewd words traced into some ice cubes, etc. But this conception of the way ads work and of the way we apprehend them, is much too crude. They function, not mechanically, but poetically, through metaphor, association, repetition, and other devices that suggest a variety of possible meanings. The viewer, therefore, does not just watch once and start salivating, but senses gradually, half-consciously, the commercial's welter of related messages.
>
> And just as the viewer needn't recognize these subtleties in order to take them in, so, perhaps, the advertisers themselves may not know their every implication, any more than a poet or filmmaker is fully aware of all that his work implies. Of course, most of what we see in a good commercial was probably calculated by its makers, who are quite sophisticated, and who spend immense amounts of time and money on each 30- or 60-second bit. Nevertheless, some of these nuances might have been unconsciously intended, details that just "seemed right" as part of the commercial's general drift. Ultimately, however, these questions of intention are irrelevant. If criticism can demonstrate convincingly that a commercial uses certain strategies, then we can assume that those strategies are, in fact, at work, whether or not the advertisers might acknowledge them. (p. 29)

A Model for Indoctrination Campaigns

Thus far we have emphasized the similarities among campaigns of various types, but there are important differences as well. In a political campaign, says Republican consultant John Deardourff,

> [A]ll of the sales take place on the same day. The timing is important. You deliver on election day or it doesn't make a difference. In political advertising you are not interested in small market shares. The political advertiser can't be satisfied until he has 51% of the market. The political salesman—I hate that term—has got to find ways to communicate with all kinds of people. The

commercial advertiser knows how much money he will spend. But in a political campaign you almost never know. You improvise. (quoted in Blumenthal, 1980, p. 188)

Even sharper contrasts may be drawn between advertising campaigns and indoctrination campaigns. In the latter there is generally no equivalent of a product to purchase or a place such as a supermarket at which to purchase it. Ideologies, life styles, basic values can be experimented with, but at much greater cost than in trying out most products. Conversions to new ways of thinking and doing involve much greater commitments; and, of course, there are no money back guarantees. Sometimes, as with the molding of patriotic attitudes in children, the process of indoctrination is relatively painless, and is likely to go by some other name, such as education or training. But even in these cases, there are vast subject matter differences. Indoctrination campaigns attempt to establish systematic connections among a wide array of beliefs, usually by way of unifying principles. Advertising campaigns tend, by contrast, to have narrow and specific goals and to utilize whatever appeals are deemed necessary to evoke desired behavioral responses.

From time to time one hears news of indoctrination campaigns that effect nothing less than total transformations of the life styles and belief structures of seemingly normal individuals. The 1970s were rife with reports of the alleged "brainwashing" of newspaper heiress Patty Hearst by an urban guerrilla group known as the Symbionese Liberation Army, of massive conversions to religious cults such as the Moonies, and, most bizarre of all, of a mass suicide in Jonestown, Guyana, by followers of the charismatic firebrand, Rev. Jim Jones. Accounts of these proselytizing activities tend to be sensationalized, and the differences between them and institutionally approved efforts at indoctrination tend to be exaggerated. What gets labeled as "brainwashing" on the one hand, or merely as "resocialization" on the other, often depends on whether we approve of the ends being sought by a campaign, rather than the means. Nevertheless, the very necessity of having to go against culturally established values or beliefs does give the activities of outsider proselytizing groups such as the Moonies a distinctive—some say ominous—quality. And it also serves to highlight techniques of persuasion that are less noticeable in programs we approve.

Common to most efforts at "resocialization," says clinical psychologist Patrick Pentony (1981), is the undermining of a belief system or ideology. Pentony speaks of these as "theories" in the sense that they "do not allow inconsistencies either between their internal components or between the theory and accepted 'facts.' " The "theories" we hold dear are in these respects reality-defining and resistant to change. Often, he adds, they are adhered to without very much conscious awareness.

Schein, Schneier, and Barker (1971) label the process of undermining belief systems as *Demolition*, and they identify three components of this "unfreezing" stage: (1) *invalidation*, (2) induction of *guilt-anxiety*, and (3) the provision of *psychological safety* (see Table 16.1). In the attempted "brainwashing" of

TABLE 16.1 SUMMARY OF STAGES AND COMPONENTS IN SCHEIN et al.'s
RESOCIALIZATION MODEL

A. Demolition (unfreezing)
   1. Invalidation
   2. Induction of guilt-anxiety
   3. Provision of psychological safety
B. Transition
   1. New definitions of terms
   2. Broadened or altered perceptions of reality
   3. New standards of evaluation and judgment
C. Refreezing
   1. Integration
   2. Reconfirmation

American and European prisoners during the Korean War, invalidation involved a gradual chipping away of basic beliefs under highly controlled conditions, with sleep, social contact, exercise, and the like made contingent on "progress" at giving up long-held convictions. In less constricted environments where, for example, a college student might come to a meeting of a religious group "just to see what it's all about," the guiding ideology is likely to be more ripe for attack. Lofland (1977) characterizes the most susceptible targets for religious conversion as people experiencing enduring, acutely felt tensions, usually during a crisis or turning point in their lives, who tend in any case to see the world from a religious perspective.

The induction of guilt-anxiety is an adjunct to the process of invalidation. However troubled we are by apparent inadequacies in the "theories" we hold dear, we are much more likely to attempt to patch them up than to give them up. Thus, the change agent tends to tread lightly in challenging the target's beliefs, lest the target ignore these challenges, or reject them and derogate the change agent as well. Say Zimbardo et al. (1977), in their description of recruiting efforts by the Moonies: "Nonacceptable responses elicit an immediate uniform reaction from all members of the group; they are saddened, never angered, by deviant acts or thoughts. The consequence is the arousal of guilt for upsetting them by your disagreement" (p. 184).

Some sense of psychological safety would seem to be essential to the demolition process if the target is to internalize the recommended beliefs, rather than merely feign commitment. Pentony (1981) observes, however, that psychotherapists differ widely in the degree of supportiveness they provide, Rogerian, client-centered therapists making expressions of nonjudgmental positive regard a cornerstone of their therapeutic approach, other therapists so bent on destroying whatever remnants remain of their patients' sense of self-satisfaction that they deliberately drive them at the outset to utter despair. Awareness training groups and religious cults have tended in recent years to emphasize the positive aspects of the resocialization experience, and to use the group itself as a source of psychological safety. At a Moonie "farm" described by Zimbardo et al. (1977), "Potent social reinforcers are dispensed freely—smiles, approval, acceptance, praise, physical contact, and apparent love"

(p. 184). Recruits are asked only to keep an "open mind." However, say the authors, in the atmosphere of play and togetherness created at the farm, an "open mind" virtually means childlike submissiveness. Words themselves tend to take on new meanings in these contexts.

When the target's belief systems have been invalidated, they are ripe for the acquisition of a new structure of beliefs. This takes place during what Schein refers to as the transitional stage. By this time resistance is largely gone, and the targets are anxious to replace the premises that have failed them. This process involves (1) *new definitions of terms,* (2) *broadened or altered perceptions,* and (3) *new standards of evaluation and judgment.* The transitional process, says Schein, is largely cognitive: It is essentially an information-processing activity.

Yet, as Schein et al. observe, positive identification with the source of the information greatly facilitates the learning process. In psychotherapy, the patient is generally encouraged to identify strongly with the therapist and/or the group. In POW camps, there may be identification with the aggressor, a condition characterized by self-loathing and grudging admiration for one's persecutors. In still other situations, learning takes place not as a result of the teachings of any given change agent, but through an impersonal process Schein calls *scanning.*

A *refreezing* stage completes the resocialization process, according to Schein et al. Here the props that supported the old belief system—self-confidence, group support, belief consistency—are restored to be made serviceable for the new. Refreezing involves components of (1) *reintegration* and (2) *reconfirmation.* The new belief structure is incorporated into the larger personality pattern and into the individual's way of relating to others. Efforts are made at this stage to discourage backsliding and to encourage active, overt commitment to the new way of thinking. Lest convicts or mental patients revert to their old ways on being released from their institutions, they may be placed in halfway houses before being granted full freedom, or required to check back on a regular basis. Religious converts are often urged to engage in activities that will advertise and simultaneously reinforce their newly acquired beliefs.

In this section, I have emphasized common characteristics in efforts at political "thought reform," religious proselytizing, and psychotherapy. That indoctrination campaigns we approve and those we disapprove have much in common seems to be worth underscoring, for it raises profound ethical questions about what means of persuasion we should countenance.

We may go a step further. Zimbardo et al. (1977) have observed that the recruiting efforts of the Moonies form "an amalgam of virtually all the basic techniques and principles derived from the major theories of attitude and behavior change." The same can be said for other indoctrination efforts, including those with obvious benefits to their targets.

But, once again, there are also important differences, and these too need to be underscored. Just as there are some forms of psychotherapy that emphasize invalidation over psychological safety during the demolition stage, so there are forms of therapy concerned less with thoughts than with behaviors, less with eliminating causes of problems than with eliminating symptoms, less with

demolition than with reconstruction and reframing. These forms of psychotherapy bear a closer resemblance to what we discussed in Chapter 9 as
alternatives to the standard problem-cause-solution model than to Schein's
resocialization model. Pentony (1981) provides an excellent analysis and
comparison of methods of psychotherapy as modes of influence, and Frank
(1973) offers interesting insights on similarities and differences between psychotherapy and religious conversions.

Models, by their very nature, must oversimplify and in some respects
distort matters by ignoring differences. The campaign models presented here
and in Chapter 12 are no exception, and they should be used, combined,
modified, or discarded to suit the case at hand, rather than forcing the case to
fit the models. All this suggests the need for caution and a certain degree of
flexibility. While you might ordinarily wish to plan or analyze a political
campaign within the framework of the five-stage model presented here, Schein
et al.'s resocialization model would appear to be especially applicable to an
analysis of Reagan's 1980 campaign, with its heavy ideological emphasis.
Similarly, while Schein et al.'s model might ordinarily be used in studies of
traditional forms of psychotherapy, you might find the five-stage model more
useful in studies of other health education efforts, such as community mental
health campaigns. And it is of course possible to combine the models and to
introduce other models as well.

A Final Comment: The Question of Ethics

In the process of commenting on the practice and analysis of political, product
advertising, and indoctrination campaigns, this chapter has touched many times
on the problems of reconciling ethics and effectiveness. We have seen the power
of political persuaders to make a dying candidate seem very much alive; of
product advertisers to trade on unconscious associations; of religious proselyt-
izers to exploit personal vulnerabilities in their efforts at securing conversions.
We have seen too that ethically questionable rhetoric is not just practiced by
scoundrels. Indeed, you might well have some questions at this point about
practices recommended in this text.

One benefit of studying persuasion from the perspective of both the doer
of persuasion and the evaluative critic is that it should provide a greater sense
of balance about the extraordinary ethical dilemmas confronting persuaders.
Among practicing persuaders, there is a tendency to become excessively
Machiavellian—to be concerned with winning at all costs.

In the heat of a political contest or an advertising campaign or even a
classroom speech, there may well be a temptation to relax one's moral standards:
to fabricate evidence or to feign commitments or to deliberately draw unwar-
ranted inferences. Once having engaged in practices such as these, it is all too
easy to rationalize them—to decide, for example, that a classroom speech is
only an exercise and doesn't count in the real world; or that the fabrication of
evidence in this case is justified, since one could always find evidence just like
it if only one had the time to dig it out of the library.

Even among friends, there is a tendency to be selective and self-deceptive in applying moral standards. Says sociologist Morton Deutsch (1969), people tend in general to exempt themselves from moral standards they expect others to live up to. Since *my* objectives are worthwhile, reasons the persuader, often unconsciously, I'm entitled to bend the rules a bit. On the other hand, that other person had better toe the line. The tendency to apply moral precepts inconsistently is all the more persistent, observes Peter Berger (1963), because it is so often unconscious. By deceiving ourselves about our own tendencies to deceive others, says Berger, we manage both to protect our fragile egos and to appear sincere to others.

Once having rationalized an ethically questionable act, it is easy and tempting to fit new acts to the rule and, if necessary, to invent broader and more cynical rules. Here lie the seeds not just of occasional Machiavellian behavior, but of what psychologists refer to as the Machiavellian personality (Christie and Geis, 1970). We can decide, for example, that ethics are for the other guy; that if we don't con others, someone else will; that if we don't "get" others, they'll "get" us. Because Machiavellianism feeds on mistrust, it can become contagious, infecting entire professions and institutions.

Evaluative rhetorical criticism can provide a corrective to the excesses of Machiavellianism. Having carefully examined a message and the context in which it was presented, we may then pass judgment on the accuracy of its claims, the logic of its conclusions, and its probable social consequences. Not just the academic scholar, but also newspaper columnists and television commentators, media critics and magazines such as *Consumer Reports* provide valuable services in exposing shoddy claims, illegitimate inferences, dangerous consequences. Although not all communications from others must be guarded against like the plague, quite obviously there is a need for vigilance in the face of unscrupulous persuaders, and there is every reason to weigh and evaluate controversial assertions even when they emanate from those whom we trust.

But just as evaluative analysis provides a corrective to the excesses of Machiavellianism, so the critic's evaluative standards may also become excessive. As critics, we are often harder on persuaders than we would be if we were in their shoes. We heap scorn on Senator Sleazo, for example, when he ducks controversial issues, or presents us with a vague and confusing response to our questions, or when we learn that he has said different things to different audiences. Criticisms of this sort have their place, but they need to be tempered by the realization that Senator Sleazo would probably become Private Citizen Sleazo in short order, and perhaps be replaced by Senator Slimo, were he to follow our ethical prescriptions.

Rather than identifying exclusively with the interests of persuaders or persuadees, we need to practice a kind of *double empathy*. By a simple application of the Golden Rule, we need to correct for our Machiavellian tendencies as persuaders by putting ourselves in the place of our audiences and treating them the way we would want to be treated by them. That means, for example, that we should ordinarily observe such basic rules of fair play as the following:

ͺ cure the d,
blame the woman,
embarrassing to detail some
ͺptoms of her suffering, even to ͺͺ
ͺmily physician.

It was for this reason that years ago Mrs. Pinkham, at Lynn, Mass., determined to step in and help her sex. Having had considerable experience in treating female ills with her Vegetable Compound, she encouraged the women of America to write to her for advice in regard to their complaints, and being a woman, it was easy for her ailing sisters to pour into her ears every detail of their suffering. * * * * * *

No physician in the world has had such a training, or has such an amount of information at hand to assist in the treatment of all kinds of female ills.

This, therefore, is the reason why Mrs. Pinkham, in her laboratory at Lynn, Mass., is able to do more for the ailing women of America than the family physician. Any woman, therefore, is responsible for her own suffering who will not take the trouble to write to Mrs. Pinkham for advice.

This Advertisement of "Lydia Pinkham's Vegetable Compound" was Printed on June 27, 1905 (About Two Months Ago).

MRS. LYDIA E. PINKHAM'S MONUMENT
In Pine Grove Cemetery, Lynn, Massachusetts.
Mrs. Pinkham Died May 17, 1883 (22 Years Ago).

An early example of the consumer protection function. From Edward Bok, "Pictures that tell their own stories," *Ladies Home Journal,* September 1905, p. 15. Since passage of the Pure Food and Drug Act in 1906, advertisers have had to be more subtle in their deceptions.

1. Practice inquiry before advocacy. Be open to a variety of points of view before you embrace any one of them.
2. Know your subject. If what you say isn't based on first-hand knowledge, get the information you need from the library or from your own research.
3. Try to tell the truth as you perceive it. Don't deliberately invent facts or mislead audiences about your true opinions on a matter.
4. Appeal to the best motives in people, not their worst motives.
5. Be prepared to lose on occasion if winning means doing psychological harm to others and demeaning yourself in the bargain.

But, by the same token, we ought to temper our negative judgments of persuaders when functioning in the role of critics by asking ourselves what we would do were we in their shoes. Here, most important, we need to understand the circumstances under which persuasion takes place and the factors constraining rhetorical choices under those circumstances. This might lead us, for example, to be somewhat forgiving of our mythical Senator Sleazo. Politicians are expected to sacrifice clarity on issues for the sake of image. If they do not, we tend to reject them as incompetent. While we might insist that they risk image by staking out courageous positions on some controversial issues, we surely ought not to insist that their courage be taken to the extreme of foolhardiness. Surely they are entitled to dodge some verbal bullets by responding to direct questions with indirect replies. Hart (1982) asks: "Exactly what is it that a politician *can* say, knowing constantly that at least half of the information at his or her command will be alien to at least half of the audience and that a good portion of the remainder of the audience will disagree with almost any specific policy detailed for them? (p. 375) "Understandably," says Hart, "politicians climb the ladder of abstraction, searching for a suitably complex argot for their disagreeing, often disagreeable listeners." (p. 375)

EXERCISES

1. Apply the concepts introduced in the discussion of political campaigns to a political campaign of your own choosing. Try to structure your analysis in terms of one or another model or analytic framework provided in this book.
2. Do an analysis of a commonly advertised product—gasoline, toothpaste, beer, cigarettes, perfume—in a manner similar to Barthes' analysis of laundry detergents.
3. Use Schein et al.'s resocialization model in a comparison of a compulsory indoctrination campaign (basic training for army recruits) with a voluntary one used in more open institutions such as your own college or university. How are they different?
4. We have noted in this chapter the many respects in which product advertising campaigns are different from indoctrination campaigns. But what of the effects of multiple campaigns for products of the same type, such as medicinals? Do we not become "indoctrinated" to solve our health problems medicinally through repeated exposure to such messages? Consider too the effects of exposure to multiple campaigns for the same product over the course of a lifetime. Are we not "reared" on Coke advertisements as much or more than on Mother Goose and the Bible? Consider in particular the way the sexes or the races are depicted in ads of a certain type. This is an issue that has arisen at several points in the text, particularly in Chapter 5, and in the discussion in Chapter 14 of the social consequences of gender displays. Building on those discussions, compare the way the sexes or races are treated in 10 or more magazine ads for a commonly used product such as cigarettes, soft drinks, beer. What, if any, are the differences in the way the sexes or the races are depicted? Do you see evidences of sexism or racism? If so, who, if anyone, is to blame? Do you fault the advertisers for reinforcing stereotypes? Or are they just doing their jobs?

References

Abelson, R. P., and M. J. Rosenberg (1958). Symbolic psycho-logic: A model of attitudinal cognition. *Behavioral Science*, 3:1–13.

Aberle, D. (1966). *The Peyote Religion Among the Navaho*. Chicago: Aldine.

Ajzen, I., and M. Fishbein (1980). *Understanding Attitudes and Predicting Social Behavior*. Englewood Cliffs, NJ: Prentice-Hall.

Alinsky, S. (1971). *Rules for Radicals*. New York: Random House.

Anderson, N. H., and C. I. Hovland (1957). The representation of order effects in communication research (Appendix A). In C. I. Hovland (ed.), *The Order of Presentation in Persuasion*. New Haven, CT: Yale University Press.

Anisfeld, M., N. Bogo, and W. E. Lambert (1962). Evaluation reactions to accented English speech. *Journal of Abnormal and Social Psychology*, 65:223–231.

Aristotle (1932). *Rhetoric*. Trans. Lane Cooper. New York: D. Appleton Century.

Aronson, E., and J. Mills (1959). The effect of severity of initiation on liking for a group. *Journal of Abnormal and Social Psychology*, 59:177–181.

Aronson, E., J. Turner, and M. Carlsmith (1963). Communicator credibility and communicator discrepancy as determinants of opinion change. *Journal of Abnormal and Social Psychology*, 67:31–36.

Asch, S. E. (1952). *Social Psychology*. Englewood Cliffs, NJ: Prentice-Hall.

Atkinson, M. (1984). *Our Masters' Voices: The Language and Body Language of Politics*. London: Methuen.

Axelrod, R. (1984). *The Evolution of Cooperation*. New York: Basic Books.

Bailey, F. G. (1983). *The Tactical Uses of Passion: An Essay on Power, Reason, and Reality*. Ithaca, NY: Cornell University Press.

Bandura, A. (1977). *Social Learning Theory*. Englewood Cliffs, NJ: Prentice-Hall.

Barthes, R. (1972). Soap-powders and detergents. *Mythologies*, 36–38.

Becker, S. L. (1971). Rhetorical studies for the contemporary world. In L. Bitzer and E. Black (eds.), *The Prospect of Rhetoric*. Englewood Cliffs, NJ: Prentice-Hall.

Bem, D. J. (1965). An experimental analysis of self-persuasion. *Journal of Experimental Social Psychology*, 1:199–218.

———. (1970). *Beliefs, Attitudes and Human Affairs*. Belmont, CA: Brooks/Cole.

Berenda, R. W. (1950). *The Influence of the Group on the Judgments of Children*. New York: King's Crown Press.

Berger, P. L. (1963). *Invitation to Sociology—A Humanistic Perspective*. Garden City, NY: Anchor Books.

Berscheid, E. (1966). Opinion change and communicator-communicates similarity and dissimilarity. *Journal of Personality and Social Psychology*, 4:670–680.

Bettinghaus, E. P. (1981). *Persuasive Communication*. 3rd ed. New York: Holt, Rinehart and Winston.

Bettelheim, B. (1943). Individual and mass behavior in extreme situations. *Journal of Abnormal and Social Psychology*, 38:417–452.

Bitzer, L. F. (1968). The rhetorical situation. *Philosophy and Rhetoric*, 1:1–14.

Bitzer, L. F., and E. Black (eds.) (1971). *The Prospect of Rhetoric*. Englewood Cliffs, NJ: Prentice-Hall.

Black, E. (1965). *Rhetorical Criticism: A Study in Method*. New York: Macmillan.

Blumenthal, S. (1980). *The Permanent Campaign: Inside the World of Elite Political Operatives*. Boston: Beacon Press.

Bochner, S., and C. A. Insko (1966). Communication discrepancy, source credibility and opinion change. *Journal of Personality and Social Psychology*, 4:614–621.

Bonchek, V. (1967). Commitment, communicator credibility and attitude change. *Dissertation Abstracts*, 27:3929A–3930A.

Booth, W. (1974). *A Rhetoric of Irony*. Chicago: University of Chicago Press.

Booth, W. (1978). Afterthoughts on metaphor: Ten literal "theses." Critical Inquiry, 5:175–188.

Booth, W. C. (1971). The scope of rhetoric today: A polemical excursion. In L. B. Bitzer and E. Black (eds.), *The Prospect of Rhetoric*. Englewood Cliffs, NJ: Prentice-Hall.

Bormann, E. (1972). Fantasy and rhetorical vision: The rhetorical criticism of social reality. *Quarterly Journal of Speech*, 59:396–407.

Brehm, J. W. (1962). An Experiment on coercion and attitude change. In J. W. Brehm and A. R. Cohen (eds.), *Explorations in Cognitive Dissonance*. Englewood Cliffs, NJ: Prentice-Hall.

Brehm, J. W. (1966). *A Theory of Psychological Practice*. New York: Academic Press.

———, and A. R. Cohen. (1962). *Explorations in Cognitive Dissonance*. New York: Wiley.

Bridgeman, P. W. (1959). *The Way Things Are*. Cambridge, MA: Harvard University Press.

Brock, T. C. (1965). Communicator-recipient similarity and decision change. *Journal of Personality and Social Psychology*, 1:650–654.

Brockriede, W. (1974). Rhetorical criticism as argument. *Quarterly Journal of Speech*, 60:165–174.

Brodeur, P. (1974). *Expendable Americans*. New York: Viking.

Brown, L. W. (1974). The image-makers: Black rhetoric and white media. In J. L. Daniel (ed.), *Black Communication: Dimensions of Research and Instruction*. New York: Speech Communication Association.

Buckley, W. (1973). Impeach the speech, not the President. *The New York Times Magazine*, May 20, p. 30.

Burgoon, M., and E. P. Bettinghaus (1980). Persuasive message strategies. In M. E.

Roloff and G. R. Miller (eds.), *Persuasion: New Directions in Theory and Research.* Beverly Hills, CA: Sage.

Burhans, D. T., Jr. (1971). The attitude-behavior discrepancy problem: Revisited. *Quarterly Journal of Speech*, 57:418–428.

Burke, K. (1945). *A Grammar of Motives.* Englewood Cliffs, NJ: Prentice-Hall. (Reprinted 1969, Berkeley, CA: University of California Press. Page numbers in citations refer to this edition.)

———. (1966). *Language as Symbolic Action.* Berkeley: University of California Press.

———. (1969). *A Rhetoric of Motives*, Reprint. Berkeley: University of California Press. Originally published by Prentice-Hall, 1950. All references are to University of California edition.

Byrne, D. (1971). *The Attraction Paradigm.* New York: Academic Press.

Cacioppo, J. T., and R. E. Petty (1979). Effects of message repetitions and positions on cognitive response, recall, and persuasion. *Journal of Personality and Social Psychology*, 37:97–109.

Campbell, K. K. (1972). *Critique of Contemporary Rhetoric.* Belmont, CA: Wadsworth.

———. (1973). The rhetoric of women's liberation: An oxymoron. *Quarterly Journal of Speech*, 59:74–86.

———. (1982). *The Rhetorical Act.* Belmont, CA: Wadsworth.

———, and K. H. Jamieson. (1978). *Form and Genre: Shaping Rhetorical Action.* Annandale, VA: Speech Communication Association.

Cartwright, D., and F. Harary (1956). Structural balance: A generalization of Heider's theory. *Psychological Review*, 63:277–293.

Caulfield, M. (1983). Address to National Organization of Women. Unpublished student paper, Temple University.

Cederblom, J., and D. W. Paulsen (1982). *Critical Reasoning: Understanding and Criticizing Arguments and Theories.* Belmont, CA: Wadsworth.

Christie, R., and F. Geis, (1970). *Studies in Machiavellianism.* New York: Academic Press.

Cialdini, R. B. (1984). *Influence: How and Why People Do Things.* New York: Morrow.

Clark, T. D. (1977). An exploration of generic aspects of contemporary American Christian sermons. *Quarterly Journal of Speech*, 62:384–394.

Clarke, R. A. (1984). *Persuasive Messages.* New York: Harper and Row.

Cody, M. J., M. L. McLaughlin, and M. J. Schneider (1981). The impact of relational consequences and intimacy on the selection of interpersonal persuasion tactics: A reanalysis. *Communication Quarterly*, 29:91–106.

Cohen, A. R. (1964). *Attitude Change and Social Influence.* New York: Basic Books.

Colman, A. (1980). Flattery won't get you everywhere. *Psychology Today*, pp. 80–82.

Conway, F., and J. Siegelman (1978). *Snapping: America's Epidemic of Sudden Personality Change.* Philadelphia: Lippincott.

Copi, Irving M. (1969). *Introduction to Logic.* 3rd ed. London: Macmillan.

Coser, I. (1967). *Continuities in the Study of Social Conflict.* New York: Free Press.

Deutsch, M. (1969). Conflicts: productive and destructive. *Journal of Social Issues*, 25:7–41.

Dewey, J. (1910). *How We Think.* Boston: Heath.

Dichter, E. (1960). *The Strategy of Desire.* Garden City, NY: Doubleday.

Duncker, K. (1938). Experimental modification of children's food preference through social suggestion. *Journal of Abnormal and Social Psychology*, 33:489–507.

Eagly, A. H., and S. Himmelfarb (eds.) (1974). *Readings in Attitude Change.* New York: Wiley.

Edelman, M. (1967). *The Symbolic Uses of Politics*. Chicago: University of Illinois Press.

Ehrenberg, A. S. C. (1981). Repetitive advertising and the consumer. In M. Janowitz and P. Hirsch (eds.) *Reader in Public Opinion and Mass Communication*. 3rd ed. New York: Free Press.

Ellul, J. (1973). *Propaganda: The Formation of Men's Attitudes*. New York: Vintage. Originally published in English by Knopf, 1965.

Etzioni, A. (1972). Human beings are not so easy to change, after all. *Saturday Review*, June 3, pp. 45–47.

Festinger, L. (1957). *A Theory of Cognitive Dissonance*. Stanford, CA: Stanford University Press.

———. (Winter 1964). Behavioral support for opinion change. *Public Opinion Quarterly*, 28:404–417.

——— (ed.) (1964). *Commitment, Decision and Dissonance*. Stanford, CA: Stanford University Press.

Fish, J. M. (1973). *Placebo Therapy*. San Francisco: Jossey-Bass.

Fishbein, M., and I. Ajzen (1975). *Belief, Attitude, Intention, and Behavior*. Reading, MA: Addison-Wesley.

Fogelson, R. (1971). *Violence As Protest*. Garden City, NY: Doubleday Anchor.

Frank, J. D. (1944). Experimental studies of personal pressure and resistance. *Journal of General Psychology*, 30:23–64.

———. (1973). *Persuasion and Healing: A Comparative Study of Psychotherapy*. Baltimore: Johns Hopkins.

Freedman, J. L. (1964). Involvement, discrepancy and change. *Journal of Abnormal and Social Psychology*, 69:290–295.

Friendly, F. (1971). Television. *Harper's Magazine*, 242:30–33.

Frye, N. (1957). *Anatomy of Criticism*. Princeton, NJ: Princeton University Press.

Frost, J. H., and W. H. Wilmot (1978). *Interpersonal Conflict*. Dubuque, Iowa: Wm. C. Brown.

Gamson, W. A. (1968). *Power and Discontent*. Homewood, IL: Dorsey Press.

———. (1975). *The Strategy of Social Protest*. Homewood, IL: Dorsey Press.

Gardner, M. (1957). *Fads and Fallacies in the Name of Science*. rev. ed. New York: Dover.

Gerard, H. B., and G. Matthewson (1966). The effect of severity of initiation on liking for a group: A replication. *Journal of Experimental Social Psychology*, 2:278–287.

Gergen, K. J. (1982). *Toward Transformation in Social Knowledge*. New York: Springer-Verlag.

Gibb, J. (1961). Defensive communication. *Journal of Communication*, 11:141–148.

Gillis, J. S. (1974). The therapist as manipulator. *Psychology Today*, 8:90–95.

Goffman, E. (1959). *The Presentation of Self in Everyday Life*. Garden City, NY: Anchor.

———. (1969). *Strategic Interaction*. Philadelphia: University of Pennsylvania Press.

———. (1974). *Frame Analysis*. New York: Harper and Row.

———. (1979). *Gender Advertisements*. New York: Harper and Row.

———. (1981). *Forms of Talk*. Philadelphia: University of Pennsylvania Press.

Gornick, V. (1979). Introduction. In E. Goffman, *Gender Advertising*. New York: Harper and Row.

Gould, L. (1973). If your husband makes the bed, must you lie in it? *Ms.*, 1:92–95.

Gray, G. W. (1946). The precepts of Kagemni and Ptah-Hotep. *Quarterly Journal of Speech*, 32:446–454.

Greenwald, A. G. (1965). Behavior change following a persuasive communication. *Journal of Personality*, 33:370–391.

———. (1966). Effects of prior commitment on behavior change after a persuasive communication. *Public Opinion Quarterly*, 29:595–601.

Greenwald, H. (1964). The involvement-discrepancy controversy in persuasion research. Doctoral dissertation, Columbia University.

Gregg, R. (1984). *Symbolic Inducements and Knowing: A Study in the Foundations of Rhetoric*. Columbia: University of South Carolina Press.

Gusfield, J. (1976). The literary rhetoric of science: Comedy and pathos in drinking driver research. *American Sociological Review*, 41:16–34.

Hackett, R. A. (1984). Decline of a paradigm: Bias and objectivity in news media studies. *Critical Studies in Mass Communication*, 1:229–259.

Haiman, F. S. (1949). An experimental study of the effects of ethos in public speaking. *Speech Monographs*, 16:190–202.

Haley, J. (1976). *Problem-Solving Therapy*. San Francisco: Jossey-Bass.

Hart, R. P. (1977). *The Political Pulpit*. West Lafayette, IN: Purdue University Press.

———. (1982). A commentary on popular assumptions about political communication. *Human Communication Research*, 8:366–389.

———. (1984). *Verbal Style and the Presidency: A Computer Based Analysis*. Orlando, FL: Academic Press.

———. (1984). The functions of human communication in the maintenance of public values. In C. C. Arnold and J. W. Bowers (eds.), *Handbook of Rhetorical and Communication Theory*. Boston: Allyn and Bacon.

———. (1986). "Of genres, computers, and the Reagan Inaugural." In H. Simons and A. A. Aghazarian, (eds.) *Form, Genre, and the Study of Political Discourse*. Columbia: University of South Carolina Press.

Heider, F. (1958). *The Psychology of Interpersonal Relations*. New York: Wiley.

Herrnstein, R. J. (1982). I.Q. testing and the media. *Atlantic Monthly*, pp. 68–74.

Higbee, K. L. (1969). Fifteen years of fear arousal: Research on threat appeals. *Psychological Bulletin*, 72:426–444.

Horn, J. C. (1980). Bafflegab pays. *Psychology Today*, p. 12.

Hovland, C. I. (1959). Reconciling conflicting results derived from experimental and survey studies of attitude change. *American Psychologist*, 14:8–17.

Hovland, C. I., A. A. Lumsdaine, and F. D. Sheffield (1949). *Experiments in Mass Communication*. Princeton, NJ: Princeton University Press.

Hovland, C. I., I. L. Janis, and H. H. Kelley (1953). *Communication and Persuasion*. New Haven, CT: Yale University Press.

Hoyt, P. (1958). Civil rights. The eyes of the world are upon us. *Vital Speeches of the Day*. Southold, NY: City News Publishing Co.

Huber, R. (1955). Dwight Moody. In M. Hochmuth (ed.), *History and Criticism of American Public Address*. New York: Longmans Green.

Jamieson, K. H. (1984). *Packaging the Presidency*. New York: Oxford University Press.

———, and K. K. Campbell. (1983). *The Interplay of Influence*. Belmont, CA: Wadsworth.

Johannesen, R. L. (1971). The emerging concept of communication as dialogue. *Quarterly Journal of Speech*, 57:373–382.

Jones, E. E., K. J. Gergen, and R. G. Jones. (1963). Tactics of ingratiation among leaders and subordinates in a status hierarchy. *Psychological Monographs*, 77:566.

Jong, E. M. (1973). *Fear of Flying: A Novel*. New York: Holt, Rinehart and Winston.

Kaplan, A. (1964). *The Conduct of Inquiry*. San Francisco: Chandler.

Karlins, M., and H. Abelson. (1970). *Persuasion: How Opinions and Attitudes Are Changed*. 2nd. ed. New York: Springer.

Katz, E. (1957). The two step flow of communication: An up-to-date report on an hypothesis. *Public Opinion Quarterly*, 21:61–78.

Kelman, H. C. (1961). Processes of opinion change. *Public Opinion Quarterly*, 25:57–78.

———. (1974). Attitudes are alive and well and gainfully employed in the sphere of action. *American Psychologist*, 29:310–324.

Key, B. W. (1974). *Subliminal Seduction*. New York: Signet.

Kiesler, C. A., B. E. Collins, and N. Miller (1969). *Attitude Change: A Critical Analysis of Theoretical Approaches*. New York: Wiley.

Klapper, J. T. (1960). *The Effects of Mass Communication*. Glencoe, IL: Free Press.

Knapp, M. (1978). *Social Intercourse: From Greeting to Goodbye*. Boston: Allyn and Bacon.

Koch, S. (1964). Psychology and emerging conceptions of knowledge as unitary. In T. W. Wann (ed.), *Behaviorism and Phenomenology*. Chicago: Phoenix Books.

Kuhn, A. (1978). *Women's Pictures: Feminism and Cinema*. London: Routledge and Kegan Paul.

Kuhn, T. S. (1970). The structure of scientific revolutions. *International Encyclopedia of Unified Science*. 2nd ed. Vol. II, No. 2. Chicago: University of Chicago Press.

Kutner, B., C. Wilkins, and R. R. Yarrow (1952). Verbal attitudes and overt behavior involving prejudice. *Journal of Abnormal and Social Psychology*, 47:649–652.

Lakoff, G., and M. Johnson (1980). *Metaphors We Live By*. Chicago: University of Chicago Press.

Lambert, W. E., S. Fillenbaum, R. C. Gardner, and R. C. Hodgson (1960). Evaluational reactions to spoken languages. *Journal of Abnormal and Social Psychology*, 60:44–51.

Lapiere, R. (1934). Attitudes vs. actions. *Social Forces*, 13:230–237.

Larson, C. U. (1983). *Persuasion: Reception and Responsibility*. 3rd ed. Belmont, CA: Wadsworth.

Lazarsfeld, P. F., and H. Menzel (1963). Mass media and personal influence. In W. Schramm (ed.), *The Science of Human Communication*. New York: Basic Books.

Leathers, D. G. (1976). *Nonverbal Communication Systems*. Boston: Allyn and Bacon.

Linn, L. S. (1965). Verbal attitudes and overt behavior: A study of racial discrimination. *Social Forces*, 43:353–364.

Lofland, J. (1977). *Doomsday Cult*. New York: Irvington.

Lucas, S. (1976). *Portents of Rebellion: Rhetoric and Revolution in Philadelphia, 1765–76*. Philadelphia: Temple University Press.

Mailer, N. (1968). Miami Beach and the Siege of Chicago. *Harper's Magazine*, 237:41–130.

Mankiewicz, F., and J. Swerdlow (1978). *Remote Control*. New York: Ballantine.

McCroskey, J. C. (1969). A summary of experimental research on the effects of evidence in persuasive communication. *Quarterly Journal of Speech*, 55:169–176.

McGee, M. C. (1975). In search of "the people": A rhetorical alternative. *Quarterly Journal of Speech*, 61:235–249.

McGinniss, J. (1969). *The Selling of the President, 1968*. New York: Trident.

McGuire, W. J. (1964). Inducing resistance to persuasion: Some contemporary approaches. In L. Berkowitz (ed.), *Advances in Experimental Social Psychology*, I. New York: Academic Press.

———. (1968). Personality and susceptibility to social influence. In E. F. Borgatta and W. W. Lambert (eds.), *Handbook of Personality Theory and Research*. Chicago: Rand-McNally.

———. (1969). The nature of attitudes and attitude change. In G. E. Lindzey and E.

Aronson (eds.), *The Handbook of Social Psychology*. Vol. 3. 2nd ed. Reading, MA: Addison-Wesley.

————. (1978). Persuasion. In G. A. Miller, *Communication, Language and Meaning.* New York: Harper and Row.

Medhurst, M. J., and T. W. Benson (1984). Rhetorical studies in a media age. In M. J. Medhurst and T. W. Benson (eds.), *Rhetorical Dimensions in Media.* Dubuque, IA: Kendall-Hunt.

Mehrabian, A. (1971). *Silent Messages.* Belmont, CA: Wadsworth.

Merton, R. (1946). *Mass Persuasion.* New York: Harper.

Milgram, S. (1963). Behavioral study of obedience. *Journal of Abnormal and Social Psychology*, 67:371–378.

Mill, J. S. (1859). *On Liberty.* Reprinted as a Crofts Classic, A. Castell (ed.) New York: Meredith Corporation, 1947.

Miller, G. R. (1964). An experimental study of the relationships of fear appeals, source credibility, and attitude change. Mimeographed. Michigan State University.

————. (1980). On being persuaded: Some basic distinctions. In M. E. Roloff and G. R. Miller (eds.), *Persuasion: New Directions in Theory and Research.* Beverly Hills, CA: Sage.

————, M. Burgoon, and J. K. Burgoon (1984). The functions of human communication in changing attitudes and gaining compliance. In C. C. Arnold and J. W. Bowers (eds.), *Handbook of Rhetorical and Communication Theory.* Boston: Allyn and Bacon.

————, and H. W. Simons (1974). *Perspectives on Communication in Social Conflicts.* Englewood Cliffs, NJ: Prentice-Hall.

Miller, M. C. (1981). Massa come home. *The New Republic*, September 16, pp. 29–32.

Miner, H. (1956). Body ritual among the Nacirema. *American Anthropologist*, 58:503–507.

Minnick, C. (1957). *The Art of Persuasion.* Boston: Houghton Mifflin.

Moore, H. T. (1921). The comparative influence of majority and expert opinion. *American Journal of Psychology*, 32:16–20.

Naipaul, V. S. (1984). Among the Republicans. *New York Review*, October 25:25–31.

Newman, E. (1975). *Strictly Speaking.* New York: Warner Books.

Nichols, M. H. (1954). Lincoln's first inaugural. In W. M. Parrish and M. H. Nichols (eds.), *American Speeches.* New York: David McKay.

Nimmo, D. (1970). *The Political Persuaders: Techniques of Modern Election Campaigns.* Englewood Cliffs, NJ: Prentice-Hall.

————, and J. E. Combs (1980). *Subliminal Politics: Myths and Mythmakers in America.* Englewood Cliffs, NJ: Prentice-Hall.

Norman, R. (1976). When what is said is important: A comparison of expert and attractive sources. *Journal of Experimental Social Psychology*, 12:294–300.

O'Donnell, V., and J. Kable (1982). *Persuasion: An Interactive Dependency Approach.* New York: Random House.

Orne, M. T. (1962). On the social psychology of the psychological experiment: With particular reference to demand characteristics and their implications. *American Psychologist*, 17:776–783.

Orne, M. T., and F. J. Evans (1965). Social control in the psychological experiment. *Journal of Personality and Social Psychology*, 1:189–200.

Orr, C. J. (1980). Sustaining a counterpoised situation. *Quarterly Journal of Speech*, 66:17–32.

Osgood, C., and P. Tannenbaum (1955). The principle of congruity in the prediction of attitude change. *Psychological Review*, 62:42–55.

Paulson, S. (1954). The effects of the prestige of the speaker and acknowledgment of opposing arguments on audience retention and shift of opinion. *Speech Monographs,* 21:267–271.

Pentony, P. (1981). *Models of Influence in Psychotherapy.* New York: Free Press.

Pepitone, A., and W. Wallace (1955). Experimental studies on the dynamics of hostility. Paper read at Pennsylvania Psychological Association Meeting. Described in A. Pepitone, Attributions of causality, social attitudes, and cognitive matching processes. In R. Tagiuri and T. Petrullo (eds.), *Person Perception and Interpersonal Behavior.* Stanford, CA: Stanford University Press, 1958.

Perelman, C. (1971). The new rhetoric. In L. Bitzer and E. Black (eds.), *The Prospect of Rhetoric.* Englewood Cliffs, NJ: Prentice-Hall.

Perloff, M. (1975). Soap opera bubbles. *The New Republic,* 172:27–30.

Petty, R. E., and J. T. Cacioppo (1981). *Attitudes and Persuasion: Classic and Contemporary Approaches.* Dubuque, IA: William C. Brown.

Poincare, H. (1929). *The Foundation of Science.* New York: Science Press.

Polanyi, M. (1958). *Personal Knowledge.* Chicago: University of Chicago Press.

Regan, D. T. (1982). The Reagan revolution. *Vital Speeches of the Day,* 49(2).

Reardon, K. K. (1981). *Persuasion: Theory and Context.* Beverly Hills, CA: Sage.

Repplier, A. D. (1984). A study of verbal strategies for reducing group resistance in consultation and training. Unpublished paper.

Reston, J. (1972). McGovern's poor showing. *The New York Times Magazine,* October 4, p. 15.

Riecke, R. D., and M. O. Sillars (1975). *Argumentation and the Decision Making Process.* New York: Wiley.

Ritter, K. W. (1980). American political rhetoric and the ceremonial tradition: Presidential nomination acceptance addresses, 1960–1976. *Central States Speech Journal,* 31:153–171.

Rokeach, M. (1968). *Beliefs, Attitudes and Values.* San Francisco: Jossey-Bass.

———. (1973). *The Nature of Human Values.* New York: Free Press.

Roloff, M. E., and G. R. Miller (eds.) (1980). *Persuasion: New Directions in Theory and Research.* Berkeley: University of California Press.

Rorty, R. (1979). *Philosophy and the Mirror of Nature.* Princeton, NJ: Princeton University Press.

Rosenfield, L. W. (1968). A case study in speech criticism: The Nixon-Truman analog. *Speech Monographs,* 35:435–450.

Safire, W. (1984). Ringing rhetoric: The return of political oratory. *The New York Times Magazine,* August 19, pp. 22–25, 108–109.

Scheidel, T. M. (1967). *Persuasive Speaking.* Glenview, IL: Scott Foresman.

Schein, E. H., I. Schneier, and C. H. Barker (1961). *Coercive Persuasion: A Sociopsychological Analysis of the "Brainwashing" of American Civilian Prisoners of the Chinese Communists.* New York: Norton.

Schelling, T. C. (1960). *The Strategy of Conflict.* Cambridge, MA: Harvard University Press.

Schön, D. A. (1979). Generative metaphor: A perspective on problem-setting in social policy. In A. Ortony (ed.), *Metaphor and Thought.* New York: Cambridge University Press.

———, and C. Argyris (1978). *Organizational Learning: A Theory of Action Perspective.* Reading, MA: Addison-Wesley.

Schramm, W. (1960). *The Process and Effects of Mass Communication.* Urbana: University of Illinois Press.

Schwartzwald, J., M. Raz, and M. Zvibel (1979). The applicability of the door-in-the-face technique when established behavioral customs exist. *Journal of Applied Social Psychology*, 9:576–586.

Scott, R. (1976). On viewing rhetoric as epistemic: Ten years later. *Central States Speech Journal*, 27:258–266.

Scott, R. I., and B. Z. Brock (1972). *Methods of Rhetorical Criticism: A Twentieth Century Perspective*. New York: Harper and Row.

Seiden, H. (1976). *Advertising Pure and Simple*. New York: AMACOM.

Seligman, M. E. P. (1975). *Helplessness: On Depression, Development, and Death*. New York: W. H. Freeman and Co.

Sherif, M., C. Sherif, and R. Nebergall (1965). *Attitude and Attitude Change*. Philadelphia: Saunders.

Simons, H. W. (1966). Authoritarianism and social perceptiveness. *Journal of Social Psychology*, 68:291–297.

———. (1970). Requirements, problems and strategies: A theory of persuasion for social movements. *Quarterly Journal of Speech*, 56:1–11.

———. (1972). Persuasion in social conflicts: A critique of prevailing conceptions and a framework for future research. *Speech Monographs*, 39:227–248.

———. (1978). "Genre-alizing" about rhetoric: A scientific approach. In K. K. Campbell and K. H. Jamieson (eds.), *Form and Genre*. Annandale, VA: Speech Communication Association.

———. (1980). Are scientists rhetors in disguise? An analysis of discursive processes within scientific communities. In E. E. White (ed.), *Rhetoric in Transition: Studies in the Nature and Uses of Rhetoric*. Belmont, CA: Wadsworth.

———, and A. A. Aghazarian (eds.) (1986). *Form, Genre, and the Study of Political Discourse*. Columbia: University of South Carolina Press.

———, and E. A. Mechling (1981). The rhetoric of political movements. In D. Nimmo and K. R. Sanders (eds.), *Handbook of Political Communication*. Berkeley, CA: Sage.

———, R. J. Moyer, and N. W. Berkowitz (1970). Similarity, credibility and attitude change: A review and a theory. *Psychological Bulletin*, 73:1–16.

Skolnick, J. H. (1969). *The Politics of Protest. Violent Aspects of Protest and Confrontation. A Staff Report to the National Commission on the Causes and Prevention of Violence*. New York: Simon and Schuster.

Smith, E. E. (1961). The power of dissonance techniques to change attitudes. *Public Opinion Quarterly*, 25:626–639.

Smith, M. J. (1982). *Persuasion and Human Action*. Belmont, CA: Wadsworth.

The Smoking Controversy: A Perspective. (1978). A statement by the tobacco industry. Washington, DC: The Tobacco Institute.

Staats, A. W., and C. K. Staats (1963). *Complex Human Behavior*. New York: Holt.

Stevenson, C. L. (1945). *Ethics and Language*. New Haven, CT: Yale University Press.

Stewart, C., C. Smith, and R. E. Denton, Jr. (1984). *Persuasion and Social Movements*. Prospect Heights, IL: Waveland.

Szasz, T. S. (1970). *Ideology and Insanity: Essays on the Psychiatric Dehumanization of Man*. Garden City, NY: Anchor.

Tagiuri, R. (1969). Person perception. In G. Lindzey and E. Aronson, (eds.), *Handbook of Social Psychology*. Vol. 3. 2nd ed. Reading, MA: Addison-Wesley.

Tedeschi, J. T., B. R. Schlenker, and T. V. Bonoma (1973). *Conflict, Power and Games: The Experimental Study of Interpersonal Relations*. Chicago: Aldine.

Thompson, E. (1967). Some effects of message structure on listener's comprehension. *Speech Monographs*, 34:51–57.

Thorndike, E. L. (1935). *The Psychology of Wants, Interests and Attitudes.* New York: Appleton-Century.

Trautmann, F. (October 1970). *Political Uses of the Mass Media: A History of Rhetorical Technique.* Paper presented at Pennsylvania Speech Association Convention.

Turner, R. H., and L. M. Killian (1957). *Collective Behavior.* Englewood Cliffs, NJ: Prentice-Hall.

Vroom, V. H. (1964). *Work and Motivation.* New York: Krieger.

Waller, J. J. (1967). Identification of problem-drinkers among drunken drivers. *Journal of the American Medical Association,* 200:124–130.

Ware, B. L., and W. A. Linkugel (1973). They spoke in defense of themselves: On the general criticism of apologia. *Quarterly Journal of Speech,* 59:273–283.

Wasby, S. L. (1971). Rhetoricians and political scientists: Some lines of converging interest. *Southern Speech Journal,* 36:237–244.

Watzlawick, P. (1977). *How Real Is Real?* New York: Vintage.

Watzlawick, P., J. H. Beavin, and D. D. Jackson (1967). *Pragmatics of Human Communication: A Study of Interaction Patterns, Pathologies and Paradoxes.* New York: Norton.

Watzlawick, P., J. Weakland, and R. Fisch (1974). *Change: Principles of Problem Formation and Problem Resolution.* New York: Norton.

Weigert, A. (1970). The immoral rhetoric of scientific sociology. *American Sociologist,* 5:111–119.

White, R. W. (1959). Motivation reconsidered: The concept of competence. *Psychological Review,* 66:297–333.

Wicker, A. W. (1969). Attitudes vs. actions: The relationship of verbal and overt behavioral responses to attitude objects. *Journal of Social Issues,* 25:47–66.

Wills, G. (1972). Four more years? Learning to live with Nixon. *The New York Times Magazine,* November 5, p. 37.

———. (1974). The big week in Washington. *The New York Review of Books,* 21:17–22.

Wolin, S. (1975). Looking for "reality." *New York Review of Books,* 22:15–21.

Zimbardo, P. G. (1972). The tactics and ethics of persuasion. In B. T. King and E. McGinnies (eds.), *Attitudes, Conflict, and Social Change.* New York: Academic Press.

———, E. B. Ebbesen, and C. Maslach (1977). *Influencing Attitudes and Changing Behavior,* Rev. ed. Reading, MA: Addison-Wesley.

———, M. Weisenberg, I. Firestone, and B. Levy (1965). Communicator effectiveness in producing public conformity and private attitude change. *Journal of Personality,* 33:233–255.

AUTHOR INDEX

SUBJECT INDEX

Ad hominem, 181–182
Advertising, 9–16, 19, 21, 193
   analysis of, 9–16, 336–339
   campaigns, 336–339
   corporate image, 309–10, 317
   gender displays, 84
   Mobil ads, 309–310, 317
   of ad agencies, 9–16
   political, 330–336
   product, 336–339
   Rank's 30 second spot quiz,
     11–15
   sexism in, 84–85
Alinsky, Saul, 238
Anecdotal evidence, 191
Apologia, 284
Appeals, 11
   emotion versus reason, 194–
     195
   fear appeals, 33–35
   targeting appeal strategies,
     146–148
   unique selling propositions,
     146–147
Aristotle, 4, 26, 27
Argument, 177–199
   adapting evidence to rhetori-
     cal situations, 190–196
   implicit, explicit, 192
   tests of, 177–188
   types of, 178
Attention, 211, 213

Attitude components, 57
   beliefs and values, 22, 55–57
   theories of, 30–33, 47–75
   value weightings, 23, 56
Attitude-behavior consistency is-
     sue, 62–63, 65
   situational contexts, 63–64
Attitude modification, 23–25
Attitudes
   and intentions, 66–67
   and situations, 64–67
   as perceptual categories, 52–
     54
   conditioning of, 47–52
   theory of reasoned action, 56
   unbalancing and rebalancing
     of, 57, 152
Attribution theory, 53
Audience analysis and adapta-
     tion, 141–158
   appeal strategies, 146–147
   goals, 143–146
   learning about audiences, 154
   mixed audiences, 143
   multi-stage strategies, 147–148
   rules for different types, 153
   targeting, 143–154
   types of audiences, 153–154

Backlash effects, 71
Balance and imbalance, 319–320
Beecher, Henry Ward, 213